CLASSIC SITCOMS

CLASSIC SITCOMS

A CELEBRATION OF THE BEST PRIME-TIME COMEDY

Vince Waldron

MACMILLAN PUBLISHING COMPANY

NEW YORK

Macmillan Publishing Company
866 Third Avenue, New York, N.Y. 10022
Collier Macmillan Canada, Inc.

Library of Congress Cataloging-in-Publication Data
Waldron, Vince.
Classic sitcoms.
Includes index.
1. Comedy programs—United States.   I. Title.
PN1992.8.C66W35   1987b   791.43'09'0917   87-7871
ISBN 0-02-622770-3

Macmillan books are available at special discounts for bulk purchases
for sales promotions, premiums, fund-raising, or educational use.
For details, contact:

Special Sales Director
Macmillan Publishing Company
866 Third Avenue
New York, N.Y. 10022

10 9 8 7 6 5 4 3 2 1

Designed by Jack Meserole

Printed in the United States of America

For Buddy and Mary

Contents

Acknowledgments

This volume would have been much less interesting—and a lot thinner—without the generous cooperation of the producers, writers, directors, actors, and executives who agreed to be interviewed for this book. For sharing their insights and anecdotes, I'm indebted to Danny Arnold, Glen Charles, Les Charles, Frank Dungan, Lynne Farr, Ron Jacobs, Burt Metcalfe, Lorenzo Music, John Rich, Tony Sheehan, Jeff Stein, Alan Wagner, Ed. Weinberger, and Michael Zinberg. Thanks also to Sheldon Leonard and Carl Reiner for answering specific queries about their long and illustrious careers in television; and to Norman Lear for sharing his memories, and for letting me view rare material from his collection. I'm also obliged to Carroll O'Connor and Rob Reiner for helping me nail down the elusive creative credits for the historic pilot episodes of "All in the Family."

I'd also like to extend my heartfelt thanks to all the other writers, actors, researchers, and concerned television professionals who helped me track down specific background information on the many shows in this volume: Steve Assad of The Second City; Hal Biard and Jim Behrens at CBS; *Daily Variety*'s Tom Bierbaum; Bob Braithwaite at 20th Century–Fox Television; George Faber and Betsy Vorce, the friendly voices at Viacom International; Abby Nelson; Linda Frank at Danny Thomas Productions; Jackie Koch and Mark Pollack at Act III Communications; Jerry Leichter and the staff of *The Television Index*; Carol Navratil at Charles/Burrows/Charles; Paramount's Mike Novall; Jeff Thomas; and Tise Vahimagi, one of the British Film Institute's tireless television historians. I'm also grateful to the A. C. Nielsen Company for allowing me to print ratings figures compiled from their audience measurement services; to Howard Frank for making the marvelous photos in this book available for my use; to Vicki Siamas and Nita Boyum, Malibu's sharpest photographic team; and, of course, to all the TV columnists who responded to my original critic's choice poll.

I'm also indebted to that small group of genuine television experts who prevented me from making any serious blunders when they reviewed the finished chapters of this book for accuracy. Thanks to Brenda L. Fraunfelter, who seems to know all there is to know about "All in the Family" and "M*A*S*H"; Brenda Scott Royce, whose encyclopedic knowledge of television belies her tender age; Bill Ginch, a "Honeymooners" aficionado with a keen eye for detail; and a big thank you to Diane Albert, the able editor of *The TV Collector*, and Richard Tharp, the publisher of *Reruns: The Magazine of Television History*, who each shared invaluable material from their substantial personal archives. I also extend my deepest appreciation to the authors of other television books who so unselfishly shared their inspiration and advice: Wally Podrazik, co-author of *Watching TV*; John Javna, the writer of *Cult TV*; Cheryl L. Blythe, co-author of *The Official Cheers Scrapbook*; Coyne Steven Sanders, co-author of *The Dick Van Dyke Show: Anatomy of a Classic*; Donna McCrohan, the author of *The Honeymooners Companion*, and Bart Andrews, author of *The "I Love Lucy" Book*.

I must also express my gratitude to the helpful staff of the Margaret Herrick Library of the Academy of Motion Picture Arts and Sciences; Dan Einstein and Eleanor Tanin of the UCLA Motion Picture and Television Archives; Anne Schlosser of the American Film Institute's Louis B. Mayer Library; and Sharon Farb and Leah R. Smith of UCLA's Theater Arts Library, whose cheerful enthusiasm never wavered as they guided me through thousands and thousands of back issues of *TV Guide*. I owe a similar debt to the curators of New York's Museum of Broadcasting— Ron Simon, Jeff Fuerst, and Randy Dolnick—for the gracious hospitality they extended during my visits to their splendid stronghold of TV arcana.

My warm regards to those friends whose enthusiasm for this project kept me going throughout the uncertain days of its early genesis: Joanna Monks, Dan Castellaneta, Richard Kuhlman, Gordon Flagg, Cynthia Berry, David Meyer, Jeremiah Bosgang, and Helen MacEachron. And a special salute to Eileen Sutton, whose early confidence literally brought this book to life.

Finally, a solid round of applause to the individuals who made such major contributions to *Classic Sitcoms* that they practically deserve co-creator credit: Howard Prouty, a film and television historian whose boundless enthusiasm is matched only by his intelligence and taste; my pal Nancy Giles, whose genuine affection for the classic comedies in this book provided consistent inspiration; and my brother, Robert Waldron, who would've written this book himself—probably in half the time—if I hadn't beaten him to it. And I've reserved my last and loudest ovation for my editor, Bill Whitehead, whose wisdom guided the project safely into open waters, and his assistant, Kathy Zuckerman, who shored up all the loose ends with patience and grace.

—VINCE WALDRON

Los Angeles, California
April 29, 1987

Introduction

The better the quality of the show, the longer it will take to catch on with the general public.
—SHELDON LEONARD, TV
Producer

PRACTICALLY EVERY SHOW in this book started out—or ended up—a flop.

The pilot episodes of "All in the Family" and "Barney Miller" were initially rejected by the networks that financed them. First-season ratings for "The Dick Van Dyke Show" were so low that it was actually canceled after a single season, and its eleventh-hour revival was nothing short of miraculous; "Cheers" was one of the lowest-rated programs of the year when it started; "M*A*S*H" barely squeaked into a second season; and two different networks gave "Taxi" the heave-ho while the series was still in its prime.

Clearly, prime-time television has not been the most hospitable breeding ground for classic situation comedy. Today, all of these shows—along with "The Honeymooners," "The Bob Newhart Show," "The Mary Tyler Moore Show," and "I Love Lucy"—are revered as time-honored television classics. But each one of them owes its survival to a handful of determined visionaries who repeatedly defied the whims of a billion-dollar industry in their stubborn efforts to craft a few half hours of television that mattered.

These are their stories.

The producers most responsible for the classic TV comedies, which

1

have kept us laughing for nearly four decades, form an honor roll of television's most distinguished creators: Desi Arnaz, Danny Arnold, James Brooks, Allan Burns, James Burrows, Glen Charles and Les Charles, Stan Daniels, David Davis, Larry Gelbart, Jackie Gleason, Norman Lear, Sheldon Leonard, Lorenzo Music, Jess Oppenheimer, Carl Reiner, Gene Reynolds, John Rich, and Ed. Weinberger. Without them, prime-time comedy might still be holding out for a punch line from "Lum 'n Abner."

Of course, it's the characters, not the creators, who come to mind when we think of these classic comedies. And that's as it should be. Over the years, the inhabitants of the peculiar universe of the situation comedy have become so familiar that they've practically written their own chapter in our modern American folklore.

From Ralph Kramden to Barney Miller, they've mirrored our fondest hopes and dreams—though that never stopped them from taking merciless potshots at our silly foibles as well. From Lucy Ricardo's assault on the blandness of the Eisenhower fifties to Mary Richards's gentle struggle to stay afloat in the liberated seventies, their stories were our stories. How could we help but love them?

There's a common misconception that we welcomed each of them into our living rooms every week—but that's not exactly true. Few of us relished the thought of inviting Archie Bunker into *our* parlors; and we had better sense than to let a madman like Louie DePalma run amok among our knickknacks. But we welcomed the opportunity to accompany our favorite characters on regularly scheduled excursions into their habitats. And those journeys took us to some pretty fascinating locales.

We've gone conga dancing at the Club Babalu and stood behind bars at the Twelfth Precinct. We've suffered the stifling heat of a Korean medical compound and whiled away more hours than we care to remember hanging out with a gang of compassionate New York cabbies—without even once looking at the meter. We also spent quieter half hours in cozy parlors from Queens to Minneapolis—living rooms that we remember far more clearly than our own.

And the characters we met along the way were just as hard to forget. From the outraged Queens dockworker to the befuddled Chicago airline navigator, they all had the capacity to think and feel—and their passions rarely failed to touch us. Looking back on the friends we made—from the Cuban bandleader to that erudite barmaid in Boston—it's hard to believe we got to know them all in just a half hour a week.

*   *   *

The ten classic situation comedies that make up the present volume were chosen by a poll of American television critics, so it's not surprising that their choices reflect the wide breadth of achievement of this much-maligned art form. It's another happy coincidence that the consensus traces the history of the American situation comedy from its humble beginnings in a cold-water flat in Brooklyn to its final stronghold in an upscale Boston bar.

In the early 1950s, before "I Love Lucy" or "The Honeymooners," TV's earliest comedies—"Amos n' Andy," "The Goldbergs," "The Life of Riley"—were holdovers from radio, and their scripts usually worked just as well whether you watched the picture or not. Then, out of nowhere, an impetuous redhead barreled into prime time—with a headstrong bus driver close on her heels. Suddenly, we found it nearly impossible to take our eyes off the old Philco in the corner.

By the 1960s, Rob Petrie regularly engaged our wit as well as our imagination when "The Dick Van Dyke Show" combined the vaudeville of the fifties sitcom with an urbane charm that would become the hallmark of quality comedy in the seventies.

"The Mary Tyler Moore Show" ushered in the next decade with a whole new school of comedy, its sharp humor based on gentle observation of ordinary people who find themselves trapped in the absurd circumstances of everyday life. "The Bob Newhart Show" twisted that formula to create a view of the modern world as Lewis Carroll might have described it had he worked in Studio City instead of at Oxford.

But it was "All in the Family" that finally broke down the remaining barriers when it exposed prime time to the screaming headlines of our daily newspapers. Before anyone realized what was happening, a rowdy gang of doctors and nurses from the "M*A*S*H" 4077th took the creative license that Archie Bunker had pried loose and parlayed it into eleven seasons of deeply felt comic drama. The day's headlines also figured in the station-house humor of "Barney Miller," though the Twelfth Precinct detectives usually paid more attention to the little stories buried on page six.

Finally the decade of the seventies drew to a close, and with it, the golden age of situation comedy. "Taxi" and "Cheers"—both created by producers schooled at MTM during the studio's glory days—proved that the goal of quality television didn't completely evaporate when Mary Richards closed up shop in 1977, though few comedies would have a lasting impact in the lean period that kicked off the 1980s.

And then came Cosby.

Spurred on by the tremendous success of "The Cosby Show" in 1984, the situation comedy reclaimed its grasp on the American imagination with a boom in half-hour comedy that has already continued well past the middle of the decade. In recent years "Family Ties," "Newhart," "Kate and Allie," and "The Golden Girls" have proven their enduring popularity, while "Buffalo Bill," "Designing Women"—and an upstart from cable TV called "It's Gary Shandling's Show"—have demonstrated equally high regard for the intelligence of the TV audience, which certainly bodes well for the immediate future. Of course whether this latest sitcom renaissance will have a lasting impact as television moves into its second forty years remains to be seen.

But we'll be watching.

"I LOVE LUCY"

·

*Maybe television would be good for a
year or two . . .*
—LUCILLE BALL

THEY TOLD HER the show would never work.

The audience would never buy Lucille Ball as the wacky wife of a Cuban bandleader, the network insisted. But Lucy persevered, and her efforts resulted in a television show that has probably had a more lasting impact than any other series in the history of the medium.

Yet, ironically, "I Love Lucy" began as a last-ditch effort to save a crumbling show-biz marriage—the same marriage CBS insisted no one would believe in the first place.

Lucille Ball had come a long way from her humble start as one of the Goldwyn Girls of 1933. She'd worked her way up from contract player to starring roles in films like *Dubarry Was a Lady* and *The Big Street.* But by the late forties, she was convinced that the studio casting agents had no idea what to do with her. She'd been saddled with a succession of women's pictures and frivolous comedies, when all she really wanted was to play comic roles that were closer to herself—she wanted to develop a consistent screen personality, the way Cary Grant or Clark Gable had. "After fifteen years in motion pictures, I'd always been playing someone else," she complained. "I *wanted* to be typecast."

When she finally achieved that goal, it wasn't in a feature film at all. The actress found her first near-perfect role in radio, when she was cast as the screwball wife in "My Favorite Husband," a CBS radio sitcom that co-starred Richard Denning. It was good work, and it came along at just the right time. But then, the actress had long ago discovered that in her professional life things always seemed to fall into place.

Unfortunately, she didn't have nearly so much luck at home.

After ten stormy years with Desi Arnaz, the actress was ready to throw in the towel. The marriage had been plagued almost from the start. She'd married the Cuban bandleader shortly after they met on an RKO set in 1940. But the honeymoon ended soon after, when Desi left Hollywood to tour the country with his orchestra, while she stayed on to resume her film career. The strain of their long separations began to take its toll, and by the end of the decade, Lucy was convinced that they had but two options—they could find a way to work together professionally or they could file for divorce.

When Harry Ackerman approached Lucy with a business proposition early in 1950, the CBS program executive had no idea his offer would save her marriage. But when Ackerman told her of the network's plan to star her in a television version of "My Favorite Husband," the actress recognized a golden opportunity. She would be glad to do the series, with one stipulation—Desi Arnaz would have to play her husband.

Ackerman hadn't anticipated signing a package deal. But he was confident enough in the comedienne's talents to give the matter some thought. He had seen Lucy's rapport with live audiences, when he was the executive in charge of her radio series, and he was convinced she had a quality that could easily make the transition to television. He finally presented the case to William S. Paley, the chairman and elder statesman of the powerful network. If CBS wanted Lucy, Ackerman explained, they would have to take the Cuban as well.

Paley, who thought the idea sounded like madness, personally pleaded with his star to reconsider. But Lucy would not budge. As she remembers it, "CBS said, 'We want you to go into television, but we think your husband—well—no one would believe *he* was your husband.' And I said, 'Why not? We're married!' "

The negotiations were stalled, but Lucy and Desi refused to give up. The series would be a godsend, even if it lasted only a season or two, and the couple were determined to see it through. If the skeptical CBS executives needed proof of the pair's creative compatibility, they would get it. Lucy and Desi put together a vaudeville variety show, and in the summer of 1950 they set off on a personal-appearance tour.

The hunch paid off. They returned to Hollywood with glowing reviews, and the enthusiastic response they got from audiences all across the country proved that the public was actually quite taken by the unusual chemistry of the handsome Latin and his bubbly, clowning wife.

On the basis of that success, Harry Ackerman convinced CBS to foot the bill for a pilot film based on an entirely new series concept. The new format would be dreamed up by Lucy's radio producer, Jess Oppenheimer—who would also produce the new venture with Desi Arnaz—and scripted by Oppenheimer and Madelyn Pugh and Bob Carroll, Jr., "My Favorite Husband's" chief writers.

The classic format of the show that would become "I Love Lucy" was finally arrived at by a combination of equal parts inspiration and expedience. The idea of casting Desi as a bandleader was a natural response to the network's fears that Arnaz might not be able to handle any sterner acting demands. The writers were also careful not to stray far from the format that had worked so well on "My Favorite Husband," so they decided to cast Lucy as an ordinary housewife—with the twist that she was always trying to horn in on her husband's glamorous show-biz life.

Lucy loved the idea of playing a domestic role. As she later observed, in her entire film career "there were only three or four scenes that I cared anything about. When I put them all together, I found out they were all domestic scenes where I played a housewife."

The pilot episode that was filmed in 1951 bore little more than passing resemblance to the series that eventually premiered the following fall. The writers combined large chunks of the previous summer's vaudeville show with a story line Carroll and Pugh cribbed from one of their old "My Favorite Husband" scripts. But the results were promising enough to attract a sponsorship offer from the Phillip Morris Tobacco Company, and the series was slated to begin production.

Even so, the writers still weren't entirely satisfied with the show's format. They felt they needed more characters to enhance the story possibilities, and—turning once again to their radio show for inspiration—they introduced a second, older couple to act as friendly foils for their leading players. They had used the same basic structure to good effect on "My Favorite Husband," and Oppenheimer, like any good TV writer, was loath to abandon a workable idea just because he'd already used it. It was in this offhanded fashion that two of the most durable and well-loved characters in the entire realm of the situation comedy were born—Fred and Ethel Mertz.

When Oppenheimer and Arnaz discovered that Gale Gordon and Bea Benaderet—the actors who had played equivalent roles on the radio show—were unavailable, William Frawley and Vivian Vance were cast. There was some network opposition to Frawley, whose drinking problems had earned him an unsavory reputation in Hollywood; and Vance was another unlikely choice, with scarcely any film work to her credit. But with more than three decades' hindsight, it's impossible to imagine any other actors filling the Mertzes' well-worn shoes.

There was one element of the pilot show that everyone agreed should be retained when they shot the series—the live studio audience. Harry Ackerman remembered how audience reaction favorably affected Lucy's work on "My Favorite Husband." "Her performance without a live audience was ghastly," he recalls. "When I brought in a dress-rehearsal audience, I could see that she lifted immediately. I just knew she would be nothing without that live audience."

Oppenheimer concurred. "We talked about shooting it like a movie, and then dubbing in the laughs. But there is that quality, that response, that comes only from a live experience."

Everything was falling into place for the fall premiere. The new series had even been given a name. "I Love Lucy," the title, pleased Lucy because it gave an equal emphasis to Desi—the presumed speaker of the title phrase—while CBS was satisfied that it imparted top billing to their more well-known star.

For Lucy, it was like a dream come true. She and Desi had finally created a professional life that made it possible to build the home life she'd always wanted. She couldn't have been happier.

Until she found out that CBS wanted her and Desi to move to New York.

In those pioneering days of broadcasting—before satellites and high-quality videotape—most TV shows were telecast live from the East Coast, while the western time zones had to settle for crude kinescope films that were shot directly from TV monitors for later broadcast west of the Rockies. CBS and the sponsors had no intention of disrupting this system to suit Lucille Ball and Desi Arnaz. If they wanted to do their show in front of a live audience, they would have to do it from New York.

The Arnazes were practically in a state of shock. The whole point of doing the show initially was so that they'd be able to work close to home. When they refused to pull up stakes and move to New York, it looked as though things had reached yet another creative impasse.

The compromise that was finally reached—to film the half-hour episodes live before a Hollywood studio audience—seems a terribly obvious solution by today's standards. But in 1951, it was a revolutionary—and very risky—idea.

In the first place, no one had ever attempted to conquer the rigorous demands of shooting 35mm movie film with a noisy and distracted audience in attendance. And even if the technical problems could be ironed out, film was certainly a far costlier medium than the alternative of a live broadcast.

Desi tackled the financial complications by volunteering a salary cut for himself and his wife, in exchange for complete ownership of the show—lock, stock, and conga drum. It was a shrewd deal that only hinted at the financial acumen Desi would eventually use to build Desilu Productions into one of the wealthiest and most successful production outfits in television.

To solve the technical problems, Arnaz and Oppenheimer hired a production wizard named Al Simon, who simply adapted a system he'd used to film TV game shows—a multicamera arrangement that allowed the action to proceed onstage, almost as if the actors were performing a play. Lucy then cajoled the legendary Czech cinematographer Karl Freund into devising a system for lighting the entire stage without creating unwanted shadows—no mean feat. With minor adjustments, the method that Simon and Freund improvised for the first season of "I Love Lucy" remains the standard technique for filming live situation comedy to this day.

At long last, the show was in production. All that remained now was to see how the public responded to the series that had been labored over by so many for so long.

And that response was not slow in arriving. On Monday, October 15, 1951, we got our first glimpse of Lucy and Ricky and Fred and Ethel, and the living rooms of America haven't been the same since. For the first time ever, a sitcom showed us people we felt we really knew. And before long, we wanted to know them better.

The show had a galvanizing effect on the television audience. By May of that first season, the comedy already commanded an astonishing 11.5 million television sets each Monday evening—in the days when there were barely 15 million sets in existence! It was the dawn of a new era in broadcasting. The situation comedy had come into its own.

It's practically impossible to explain why the escapades of this kooky redhead and her family so riveted the audience of her day, or how she continues to enchant audiences today. But a close look at the 180 episodes listed here offers a clue.

Quite simply, the show was better written, performed, and photographed than anything else the audience had ever seen. Even today—more than three decades after the series ended its run—few situation comedies can match the look, pacing, and precision of the best episodes of "I Love Lucy," television's first classic sitcom.

A Critical Guide to All 180 Episodes

Lucy Ricardo	Lucille Ball
Ricky Ricardo	Desi Arnaz
Ethel Mertz	Vivian Vance
Fred Mertz	William Frawley

SUPPORTING CAST

Little Ricky	Ronald and Richard Simmons
	Joseph and Michael Meyer
	Richard Keith (Keith Thibodeaux)
Jerry, the agent	Jerry Hausner
Mrs. Mathilda Trumbull	Elizabeth Patterson
Mrs. McGillicuddy	Kathryn Card
(Lucy's mother)	
Caroline Appleby	Doris Singleton
Ralph Ramsey	Frank Nelson
Betty Ramsey	Mary Jane Croft

STOCK COMPANY

Barbara Pepper, Helen Silver, Ben Weldon, Hazel Pierce, Kenny
Morgan, Shepard Menken, Bennett Green, Richard J. Reeves,
Irving Bacon, Hazel Boynton, Allen Jenkins, Louis A. Nicoletti, Ray
Kellogg, Fred Aldrich, Peggy Rea, Helen Williams, Alberto Morin

Created by Jess Oppenheimer, Madelyn Pugh, Bob Carroll, Jr.
Music by Wilbur Hatch and the Desi Arnaz Orchestra
Theme song by Eliot Daniel, lyrics by Harold Adamson
Directors of photography were Karl Freund, Robert de Grasse, Sid
  Hickox
Principal directors were Marc Daniels, William Asher, James V. Kern

1951   THE PILOT EPISODE

Pilot   "I Love Lucy" Audition
  Writers: Jess Oppenheimer, Madelyn Pugh, Bob Carroll, Jr.
  Director: Ralph Levy
  Guest Stars: Jerry Hausner, Pepito the Clown

Determined to break into show business, Lucy schemes to replace the ailing clown in her husband's nightclub act.

This embryonic tryout episode was substantially different from the final series format. Arnaz and Ball play Larry and Lucy Lopez, and the Mertzes are nowhere to be found. The script was actually a rewrite of the Lucy/Desi vaudeville touring show, patched together with an old "My Favorite Husband" script. Kinescoped on March 2, 1951, as an audition for potential backers, the film has never been broadcast.

1951/52   THE FIRST SEASON

Year-End Rating: 50.9 (3d place)

First-season scripts explore the screwball possibilities of a Manhattan housewife's efforts to break out of her routine and share the spotlight with her husband, Ricky Ricardo, bandleader at the Tropicana Club. Lucy's comical complications are skillfully orchestrated by the show's creators, Jess Oppenheimer, Madelyn Pugh and Bob Carroll, Jr., the team that will chronicle Lucy's misadventures throughout her first five seasons.

Oppenheimer will serve as producer for the first five years, and Desi Arnaz will be executive producer for the entire run. Marc Daniels is staff director for the first season, and Al Simon is associate producer.

1   The Girls Want to Go to a Nightclub   October 15, 1951
  Writers: Jess Oppenheimer, Madelyn Pugh, Bob Carroll, Jr.
  Director: Marc Daniels

Fred and Ricky decide they'd rather attend the fights than go to a fancy nightclub on the Mertzes' anniversary.

This episode provides the cast with an early display of the show's broad farce, when the wives dress up as hicks and try to pass themselves off as their husbands' blind dates. Such stock plots were used ad nauseum in radio, but as Jess Oppenheimer told TV historian Alex C. MacKenzie, "We were the first to do them on television. Certain things were done so much in radio that no one had the guts to do them anymore. But on television, those tired bits were great."

2   Be a Pal   October 22, 1951
Writers: Jess Oppenheimer, Madelyn Pugh, Bob Carroll, Jr.
Director: Marc Daniels
Guest Stars: Richard J. Reeves, Tony Michaels

Fearing the honeymoon is over, Lucy follows the advice of a self-help text and tries to revive Ricky's interest by becoming his pal.

3   The Diet   October 29, 1951
Writers: Jess Oppenheimer, Madelyn Pugh, Bob Carroll, Jr.
Director: Marc Daniels
Guest Star: Marco Rizo

Lucy has to shed twelve pounds in two days to qualify for a part in the chorus line of Ricky's nightclub act.

4   Lucy Thinks Ricky Is Trying   November 5, 1951
to Murder Her
Writers: Jess Oppenheimer, Madelyn Pugh, Bob Carroll, Jr.
Director: Marc Daniels
Guest Star: Jerry Hausner

Her imagination spurred by a mystery novel, Lucy is convinced Ricky's plotting to poison her.

Telecast a month after the series began, this show was actually the very first episode filmed—and it shows. The lighting, pacing—even the makeup—look primitive compared with that in episodes filmed in succeeding weeks, after the cast and crew got their bearings in the pioneering three-camera system.

For this inaugural episode, the crew actually crammed a fourth back-up camera onto the crowded soundstage so they could shoot the entire script straight through—from start to finish—the method used in live television of that era. It wasn't until the second week that they realized the studio audience *would* sit patiently through the short breaks that were necessary to reposition the cameras, and the technical quality of the shows made a giant leap in subsequent episodes. Significantly, the three-camera, stop-and-start method adopted in the second week al-

lowed the writers greater flexibility to engineer the complicated prop
and costume sequences that would become Lucy's comedic trademark.

5   The Quiz Show   November 12, 1951
Writers: Jess Oppenheimer, Madelyn Pugh, Bob Carroll, Jr.
Director: Marc Daniels
Guest Stars: Frank Nelson, John Emery, Phil Ober

To qualify for a thousand-dollar prize on a radio quiz show, Lucy
must convince Ricky she was once married to another man.

The first of many guest appearances by Frank Nelson. Here he plays
Freddie Fillmore, the emcee in a parody of "Truth or Consequences,"
a popular quiz show of the day.

6   The Audition   November 19, 1951
Writers: Jess Oppenheimer, Madelyn Pugh, Bob Carroll, Jr.
Director: Marc Daniels
Guest Stars: Harry Ackerman, Jess Oppenheimer

In an all-out effort to be seen by visiting TV talent scouts, Lucy
schemes to replace an ailing clown in Ricky's big circus number.

This episode was adapted from the series' original pilot film, which
was itself based on material from Lucy and Desi's vaudeville act.
    The network honchos are played by producer Jess Oppenheimer and
Harry Ackerman, CBS vice president and longtime supporter of the
series.

7   The Séance   November 26, 1951
Writers: Jess Oppenheimer, Madelyn Pugh, Bob Carroll, Jr.
Director: Marc Daniels
Guest Star: Jay Novello

Lucy and Ethel stage a phony séance for the benefit of an eccentric producer.

8   Men Are Messy   December 3, 1951
Writers: Jess Oppenheimer, Madelyn Pugh, Bob Carroll, Jr.
Director: Marc Daniels
Guest Stars: Kenny Morgan, Harry Shannon

To teach their sloppy husbands a lesson, Lucy and Ethel turn
the Ricardo apartment into a hillbilly shanty.

9   The Fur Coat   December 10, 1951
Writers: Jess Oppenheimer, Madelyn Pugh, Bob Carroll, Jr.
Director: Marc Daniels
Guest Star: Ben Weldon

When Ricky brings home a rented mink for his act, Lucy assumes
it's a surprise gift for her.

A prime example of how Lucy's total commitment as a performer contributed immeasurably to otherwise pedestrian story lines. When the
actress squeals in abandon at the prospect of getting a fur coat, the
gesture seems remarkably genuine, and when she weeps as the fur is
taken away, her conviction renders her crocodile tears real. Through
sheer force of personality, Lucy actually engages our sympathy for a
character's pathological need to have a mink coat!

10   Lucy Is Jealous of Girl Singer   December 17, 1951
Writers: Jess Oppenheimer, Madelyn Pugh, Bob Carroll, Jr.
Director: Marc Daniels
Guest Star: Helen Silver

Lucy joins the chorus line to keep an eye on things after Ricky
hires an attractive new dancing partner.

11   Drafted   December 24, 1951
Writers: Jess Oppenheimer, Madelyn Pugh, Bob Carroll, Jr.
Director: Marc Daniels

The wives are convinced that Fred and Ricky are headed for boot
camp after they overhear the boys rehearsing a military number
for a benefit show.

12   The Adagio   December 31, 1951
Writers: Jess Oppenheimer, Madelyn Pugh, Bob Carroll, Jr.
Director: Marc Daniels
Guest Star: Shepard Menken

Lucy's desire to perform an Apache routine at the club cools
considerably after she sparks romantic desires in her French
dance coach.

13   The Benefit   January 7, 1952
   Writers: Jess Oppenheimer, Madelyn Pugh, Bob Carroll, Jr.
   Director: Marc Daniels

Lucy blackmails Ethel into letting her perform at a women's-club benefit when she promises to deliver Ricky Ricardo as headliner.

14   The Amateur Hour   January 14, 1952
   Writers: Jess Oppenheimer, Madelyn Pugh, Bob Carroll, Jr.
   Director: Marc Daniels
   Guest Stars: Gail Bonney, David Stollery, Sammy Ogg

Lucy has her hands full when she baby-sits two mischievous twins at an amateur-talent competition.

15   Lucy Plays Cupid   January 21, 1952
   Writers: Jess Oppenheimer, Madelyn Pugh, Bob Carroll, Jr.
   Director: Marc Daniels
   Guest Stars: Bea Benaderet, Edward Everett Horton

Matchmaker Lucy tries to unite the grocery man with a spinster neighbor, but succeeds in igniting the elderly clerk's passion for redheads.

16   Lucy Fakes Illness   January 28, 1952
   Writers: Jess Oppenheimer, Madelyn Pugh, Bob Carroll, Jr.
   Director: Marc Daniels
   Guest Star: Hal March

Lucy feigns a nervous breakdown after Ricky refuses to hire her for his nightclub act.

17   Lucy Writes a Play   February 4, 1952
   Writers: Jess Oppenheimer, Madelyn Pugh, Bob Carroll, Jr.
   Director: Marc Daniels
   Guest Stars: Myra Marsh, Maury Thompson

Ricky plays the lead in *A Tree Grows in Havana,* Lucy's entry in an amateur playwriting competition.

18   Breaking the Lease   February 11, 1952
Writers: Jess Oppenheimer, Madelyn Pugh, Bob Carroll, Jr.
Director: Marc Daniels
Guest Stars: Barbara Pepper, Bennett Green, Hazel Pierce

Lucy and Ricky attempt to break their lease after a disagreement with the Mertzes develops into all-out war.

In the scene where Ethel confronts Lucy the morning after their blowup, the redhead haughtily puffs a cigarette—not an uncommon occurrence in the show's early years. Not surprisingly, the show's original sponsor was the Phillip Morris Tobacco Company.

19   The Ballet   February 18, 1952
Writers: Jess Oppenheimer, Madelyn Pugh, Bob Carroll, Jr.
Director: Marc Daniels
Guest Stars: Mary Wickes, Frank Scannell

Ricky has openings for a ballet singer and a burlesque comic— and naturally, Lucy tries out for both parts.

20   The Young Fans   February 25, 1952
Writers: Jess Oppenheimer, Madelyn Pugh, Bob Carroll, Jr.
Director: William Asher
Guest Stars: Janet Waldo, Richard Crenna

Lucy comes to the rescue when a swooning bobby-soxer develops a crush on Ricky.

William Asher's debut as "I Love Lucy" director. Coincidentally, Asher had just directed guest star Richard Crenna in the TV pilot of Desilu's "Our Miss Brooks."

21   New Neighbors   March 3, 1952
Writers: Jess Oppenheimer, Madelyn Pugh, Bob Carroll, Jr.
Director: Marc Daniels
Guest Stars: K. T. Stevens, Hayden Rorke, Allen Jenkins

Lucy and Ethel jump to alarming conclusions after they spy on the new couple who've just moved into the building.

22 Fred and Ethel Fight   March 10, 1952
   Writers: Jess Oppenheimer, Madelyn Pugh, Bob Carroll, Jr.
   Director: Marc Daniels
   Guest Star: Hazel Pierce

The Ricardos attempt to reunite Fred and Ethel after a lover's
spat, only to wind up in a marital row of their own.

23 The Mustache   March 17, 1952
   Writers: Jess Oppenheimer, Madelyn Pugh, Bob Carroll, Jr.
   Director: Marc Daniels
   Guest Star: John Brown

Lucy's scheme to convince Ricky to shave off his new mustache
backfires when she finds herself unable to remove a set of false
whiskers.

24 The Gossip   March 24, 1952
   Writers: Jess Oppenheimer, Madelyn Pugh, Bob Carroll, Jr.
   Director: Marc Daniels
   Guest Stars: Richard J. Reeves, Robert Jellison

Fred and Ricky wager they can refrain from gossiping longer
than their wives.

25 Pioneer Women   March 31, 1952
   Writers: Jess Oppenheimer, Madelyn Pugh, Bob Carroll, Jr.
   Director: Marc Daniels
   Guest Stars: Florence Bates, Ruth Perrott

Fred and Ricky challenge their wives to a survival contest to see
who can survive the longest without modern conveniences.

One of the series's most memorable sight gags results when Lucy
unwittingly adds too much yeast to her bread dough, and the gargantuan
loaf practically fills the kitchen. It doesn't take a psychologist to interpret
the symbolism of a twelve-foot loaf of bread that suddenly emerges from
a hot oven to pin a housewife to the sink. Even disregarding the hilarious
Freudian connotation, the scene makes us laugh because the unexpected
sight gag meshes perfectly with the logic of the situation as it offers a
wry commentary on the contemporary domestic condition.

26   The Marriage License   April 7, 1952
   Writers: Jess Oppenheimer, Madelyn Pugh, Bob Carroll, Jr.
   Director: Marc Daniels
   Guest Stars: Elizabeth Patterson, Irving Bacon

When she finds out their marriage license is not legally binding, Lucy insists that Ricky reenact their entire courtship.

In later episodes, Elizabeth Patterson would portray Little Ricky's baby-sitter, Mrs. Trumbull.

27   The Kleptomaniac   April 14, 1952
   Writers: Jess Oppenheimer, Madelyn Pugh, Bob Carroll, Jr.
   Director: Marc Daniels
   Guest Star: Joseph Kearns

Ricky suspects Lucy is a kleptomaniac after he uncovers a stash of goods she's collected for a charity bazaar.

Veteran character actor Joseph Kearns plays Lucy's psychiatrist. Kearns made occasional guest appearances on "Lucy," but he would be better known as Mr. Wilson on "Dennis the Menace."

28   Cuban Pals   April 21, 1952
   Writers: Jess Oppenheimer, Madelyn Pugh, Bob Carroll, Jr.
   Director: Marc Daniels
   Guest Stars: Alberto Morin, Rita Convy, Lita Baron

Lucy is jealous of the gorgeous Latin dancer who was Ricky's first dancing partner in Cuba.

29   The Freezer   April 28, 1952
   Writers: Jess Oppenheimer, Madelyn Pugh, Bob Carroll, Jr.
   Director: Marc Daniels
   Guest Stars: Frank Sully, Bennett Green, Fred Aldrich

Lucy and Ethel unwittingly set themselves up in the meat business when they grossly overestimate the capacity of their new walk-in freezer.

A classic "Lucy" situation. From the moment the walk-in freezer is introduced, the audience is waiting for the impetuous redhead to get herself locked in—and naturally, they aren't disappointed.

30 Lucy Does a TV Commercial   May 5, 1952
  Writers: Jess Oppenheimer, Madelyn Pugh, Bob Carroll, Jr.
  Director: Marc Daniels
  Guest Stars: Ross Elliott, Jerry Hausner

Lucy is the TV pitchwoman for Vitameatavegamin, a cure-all tonic that packs a kick—since it's 23 percent alcohol!

The sequence where Lucy rehearses her pitch until she's absolutely bombed offers a rich example of her character's fundamental appeal—her recklessness always leads to disaster, but she's invariably the one who suffers most. And Lucy suffers brilliantly. Here she slowly, and believably, descends into a drunken stupor, no easy acting feat.

The inspiration for this comic gem may well have been Red Skelton, another movie clown who found his greatest success on CBS. In MGM's 1946 *Ziegfeld Follies*, in which Lucy also appeared, Skelton did a burlesque comedy bit where he became progressively drunk as he pitched a product called Guzzler's Gin.

31 The Publicity Agent   May 12, 1952
  Writers: Jess Oppenheimer, Madelyn Pugh, Bob Carroll, Jr.
  Director: Marc Daniels
  Guest Stars: Peter Leeds, Bennett Green, Richard J. Reeves, Gil Herman

As a publicity stunt, Lucy masquerades as a Middle Eastern princess who claims to be Ricky Ricardo's greatest fan.

32 Lucy Gets Ricky on the Radio   May 19, 1952
  Writers: Jess Oppenheimer, Madelyn Pugh, Bob Carroll, Jr.
  Director: Marc Daniels
  Guest Stars: Frank Nelson, Bobby Ellis, Roy Rowan

Ricky and Lucy are ill-prepared contestants on a radio quiz show.

Frank Nelson returns as quizmaster Freddie Fillmore, an emcee who delights in making Lucy's life miserable.

33 Lucy's Schedule   May 26, 1952
  Writers: Jess Oppenheimer, Madelyn Pugh, Bob Carroll, Jr.
  Director: Marc Daniels
  Guest Stars: Gale Gordon, Edith Meiser

Inspired by Ricky's efficient new boss, the boys impose a rigid household schedule on Ethel and Lucy.

Gale Gordon makes the first of two appearances as Alvin Littlefield, the new owner of the Club Tropicana.

34   Ricky Thinks He's Getting Bald   June 2, 1952
Writers: Jess Oppenheimer, Madelyn Pugh, Bob Carroll, Jr.
Director: Marc Daniels
Guest Star: Milton Parsons

Lucy administers a series of crackpot cures to allay Ricky's fear that he's going bald.

35   Ricky Asks for a Raise   June 9, 1952
Writers: Jess Oppenheimer, Madelyn Pugh, Bob Carroll, Jr.
Director: Marc Daniels
Guest Stars: Gale Gordon, Maurice Marsac, Edith Meiser

After Ricky's request for a raise backfires, Lucy concocts an elaborate scheme to convince the Tropicana management of her husband's immense popularity.

1952/53   THE SECOND SEASON

Year-End Rating: 67.3 (1st place)

The Ricardos and the Mertzes swing into a second year on the wave of unprecedented popularity as producer Jess Oppenheimer and writers Madelyn Pugh and Bob Carroll, Jr., seize upon their star's real-life pregnancy as inspiration for some of the series's best-remembered episodes.

William Asher assumes the show's directorial reins in the second year, and Argyle Nelson takes on the duties of production manager.

36   Job Switching   September 15, 1952
Writers: Jess Oppenheimer, Madelyn Pugh, Bob Carroll, Jr.
Director: William Asher
Guest Stars: Alvin Hurwitz, Elvia Allman, Amanda Milligan

Lucy and Ethel discover they've bitten off more than they can chew after they take assembly-line jobs at a candy factory.

The memorable sequence where Lucy and Ethel unsuccessfully cope with a relentless conveyor belt is a comic gem—reminiscent of Chaplin's bout with technology in *Modern Times*, and just as funny.

37 The Saxophone September 22, 1952
Writers: Jess Oppenheimer, Madelyn Pugh, Bob Carroll, Jr.
Director: William Asher
Guest Stars: Herb Vigran, Charles Victor

Lucy auditions for Ricky's orchestra, despite a saxophone repertoire that consists of but a single tune.

38 The Anniversary Present September 29, 1952
Writers: Jess Oppenheimer, Madelyn Pugh, Bob Carroll, Jr.
Director: Marc Daniels
Guest Stars: Gloria Blondell, Herb Vigran

Disguised as house painters, Lucy and Ethel spy on a neighbor they suspect is having an affair with Ricky.

39 The Handcuffs October 6, 1952
Writers: Jess Oppenheimer, Madelyn Pugh, Bob Carroll, Jr.
Director: Marc Daniels
Guest Stars: Paul Dubov, Will Wright

Ricky finds himself handcuffed to Lucy on the eve of his appearance on a gala television special.

40 The Operetta October 13, 1952
Writers: Jess Oppenheimer, Madelyn Pugh, Bob Carroll, Jr.
Director: Marc Daniels
Guest Star: Myra Marsh

After they're elected to stage the big musicale for their women's club, Lucy and Ethel attempt to save royalty expenses by writing their own operetta.

41 Vacation From Marriage October 27, 1952
Writers: Jess Oppenheimer, Madelyn Pugh, Bob Carroll, Jr.
Director: William Asher

In an effort to invigorate their routine married lives, the Mertzes and Ricardos embark on week-long separations.

William Asher signed on as the regular "Lucy" director with this episode, a role he would become identified with for most of the show's long run. He later produced and directed "Bewitched," the long-running sitcom that starred his wife, Elizabeth Montgomery.

42   The Courtroom   November 10, 1952
Writers: Jess Oppenheimer, Madelyn Pugh, Bob Carroll, Jr.
Director: William Asher
Guest Stars: Moroni Olsen, Harry Bartell, Robert B. Williams

Fred and Ethel take the Ricardos to court to settle a petty squabble over a broken television set.

43   Redecorating   November 24, 1952
Writers: Jess Oppenheimer, Madelyn Pugh, Bob Carroll, Jr.
Director: William Asher
Guest Star: Hans Conried

Convinced that she's won a home-furnishings contest, Lucy enlists Ethel's help in redecorating her apartment.

44   Ricky Loses His Voice   December 1, 1952
Writers: Jess Oppenheimer, Madelyn Pugh, Bob Carroll, Jr.
Director: William Asher
Guest Stars: Arthur Q. Bryan, Hazel Pierce, Barbara Pepper

Lucy and the Mertzes stage a vaudeville burlesque show at the Tropicana while Ricky's bedridden with a case of laryngitis.

45   Lucy Is Enceinte   December 8, 1952
Writers: Jess Oppenheimer, Madelyn Pugh, Bob Carroll, Jr.
Director: William Asher
Guest Stars: William R. Hamel, Richard J. Reeves

Lucy is bursting with the news that she's going to have a baby, but she finds it impossible to get Ricky alone so that she can tell him.

When Lucille Ball announced that she was pregnant at the close of the first season, the writers wisely worked her blessed event into the second-year continuity. This inspiration allowed the actress to appear on the show throughout most of her pregnancy, while it provided the writers with a raft of fresh story lines.

Today, it's hard to imagine what a stir was created by Lucy's 1952 pregnancy, but CBS and her sponsor balked loudly at the idea of depicting a pregnant mother on network television. After protracted discussions that were probably funnier than anything Carroll and Pugh could've thought up, the show's producers reached a compromise with the nervous broadcasters. They would not use the word *pregnant* in any of the episodes—and for good measure, prominent members of the clergy would be allowed to screen all the finished scripts that dealt with the stork's impending arrival.

46   Pregnant Women Are Unpredictable   December 15, 1952
   Writers: Jess Oppenheimer, Madelyn Pugh, Bob Carroll, Jr.
   Director: William Asher

Lucy begins to feel unloved and overlooked after Ricky makes a big fuss over naming the baby.

47   Lucy's Show-Biz Swan Song   December 22, 1952
   Writers: Jess Oppenheimer, Madelyn Pugh, Bob Carroll, Jr.
   Director: William Asher
   Guest Stars: Jerry Hausner, Pepito the Clown

Lucy schemes to become the fourth member of Ricky's barbershop quartet.

48   Lucy Hires an English Tutor   December 29, 1952
   Writers: Jess Oppenheimer, Madelyn Pugh, Bob Carroll, Jr.
   Director: William Asher
   Guest Star: Hans Conried

Lucy enlists the aid of a diction expert to coach the Mertzes and Ricardos in proper English usage so that they'll set a good example for the baby.

49   Ricky Has Labor Pains   January 5, 1953
   Writers: Jess Oppenheimer, Madelyn Pugh, Bob Carroll, Jr.
   Director: William Asher
   Guest Stars: Louis D. Merrill, Jerry Hausner

Lucy's afraid Ricky might be growing jealous of the baby after he begins to suffer psychosomatic morning sickness.

50   Lucy Becomes a Sculptress   January 12, 1953
   Writers: Jess Oppenheimer, Madelyn Pugh, Bob Carroll, Jr.
   Director: William Asher
   Guest Stars: Shepard Menken, Leon Belasco, Paul Harvey

In her continued efforts to bring culture into the Ricardo home, Lucy tries her hand at sculpting.

51   Lucy Goes to the Hospital   January 19, 1953
  Writers: Jess Oppenheimer, Madelyn Pugh, Bob Carroll, Jr.
  Director: William Asher
  Guest Stars: Charles Lane, Adele Longmire, Ralph
  Montgomery, Peggy Rea

Despite careful rehearsal, Fred, Ethel, and Ricky unleash chaos as they try to get Lucy to the maternity ward as the great moment arrives.

Desi Arnaz, Jr., was born on the day this show first aired, a happy coincidence that helped make this episode the highest-rated program of its day.

52   Sales Resistance   January 26, 1953
  Writers: Jess Oppenheimer, Madelyn Pugh, Bob Carroll, Jr.
  Director: William Asher
  Guest Stars: Sheldon Leonard, Verna Felton

Lucy is unable to fend off a persuasive salesman and gets stuck with an overpriced vacuum cleaner, which she then tries to palm off on a neighbor.

Sheldon Leonard was well known for playing Damon Runyonesque types in countless films and TV apearances, but he would achieve even greater success in partnership with Danny Thomas as one of the most successful sitcom producers of the fifties and sixties.

53   The Inferiority Complex   February 2, 1953
  Writers: Jess Oppenheimer, Madelyn Pugh, Bob Carroll, Jr.
  Director: William Asher
  Guest Star: Gerald Mohr

Ricky objects when a handsome psychiatrist attempts to bolster Lucy's sagging confidence with a particularly strong dose of flattery.

54   The Club Election   February 16, 1953
  Writers: Jess Oppenheimer, Madelyn Pugh, Bob Carroll, Jr.
  Director: William Asher
  Guest Stars: Lurene Tuttle, Ida Moore, Doris Singleton

It's a close race when Lucy and Ethel both vie for the presidency of their women's club.

55 The Black Eye   March 9, 1953
Writers: Jess Oppenheimer, Madelyn Pugh, Bob Carroll, Jr.
Director: William Asher
Guest Star: Bennett Green

Ricky sets off a comedy of errors when he accidentally gives Lucy a black eye.

56 Lucy Changes Her Mind   March 30, 1953
Writers: Jess Oppenheimer, Madelyn Pugh, Bob Carroll, Jr.
Director: William Asher
Guest Stars: Frank Nelson, Phil Arnold

Lucy attempts to make Ricky jealous when she pays a visit to an old boyfriend who's gone into the fur trade.

57 No Children Allowed   April 20, 1953
Writers: Jess Oppenheimer, Madelyn Pugh, Bob Carroll, Jr.
Director: William Asher
Guest Star: Elizabeth Patterson

Ethel defends the Ricardos when another tenant complains about the baby's crying—and then won't let them forget it.

The question must've occurred to the writers the moment Lucy announced her pregnancy—what would they do with the baby when Lucy Ricardo had to go off to stomp grapes or climb the side of a building somewhere? The answer would be Mrs. Trumbull, Little Ricky's all-purpose baby-sitter, introduced as an irate neighbor in this episode.

58 Lucy Hires a Maid   April 27, 1953
Writers: Jess Oppenheimer, Madelyn Pugh, Bob Carroll, Jr.
Director: William Asher
Guest Star: Verna Felton

The Ricardos regret hiring a domineering domestic after she takes charge of the entire household.

59 The Indian Show   May 4, 1953
Writers: Jess Oppenheimer, Madelyn Pugh, Bob Carroll, Jr.
Director: William Asher
Guest Stars: Carol Richards, Jerry Hausner

Lucy is determined to don a feathered headdress and join Ricky's act when he stages an Indian number at the Tropicana.

60 Lucy's Last Birthday   May 11, 1953
Writers: Jess Oppenheimer, Madelyn Pugh, Bob Carroll, Jr.
Director: William Asher
Guest Stars: Jerry Hausner, Elizabeth Patterson

Lucy is convinced she hasn't a friend in all the world after Ricky and the Mertzes apparently forget her birthday.

At Lucy's party, Ricky surprises her by singing the "I Love Lucy" theme song, with lyrics written especially for this episode by Harold Adamson.

61 The Ricardos Change Apartments   May 18, 1953
Writers: Jess Oppenheimer, Madelyn Pugh, Bob Carroll, Jr.
Director: William Asher
Guest Star: Norma Varden

Yearning for more space for the baby's nursery, the Ricardos move to a larger apartment.

62 Lucy the Matchmaker   May 25, 1953
Writers: Jess Oppenheimer, Madelyn Pugh, Bob Carroll, Jr.
Director: William Asher
Guest Stars: Hal March, Doris Singleton, Phil Arnold

Lucy tries to fix up one of her friends with a handsome lingerie salesman she meets at the Mertzes.

63 Lucy Wants New Furniture   June 1, 1953
Writers: Jess Oppenheimer, Madelyn Pugh, Bob Carroll, Jr.
Director: William Asher

Lucy buys new living-room furniture and then hides it in the kitchen until she works up the nerve to tell Ricky how much it cost.

64 The Camping Trip   June 8, 1953
Writers: Jess Oppenheimer, Madelyn Pugh, Bob Carroll, Jr.
Director: William Asher
Guest Star: Jerry Hausner

Ethel and Lucy plot to outshine their husbands when they tag along on a weekend hunting trip.

65 Ricky and Fred Are TV Fans June 22, 1953
Writers: Jess Oppenheimer, Madelyn Pugh, Bob Carroll, Jr.
Director: William Asher
Guest Stars: Larry Dobkin, Allen Jenkins, Frank Nelson

After their husbands abandon them for TV's Wednesday-night fights, Lucy and Ethel attempt to sabotage the broadcast from the rooftop antenna.

66 Never Do Business With Friends June 29, 1953
Writers: Jess Oppenheimer, Madelyn Pugh, Bob Carroll, Jr.
Director: William Asher
Guest Stars: Herb Vigran, Elizabeth Patterson

Lucy and Ricky sell their old washing machine to Fred and Ethel just before it breaks down, igniting a battle royal between the Mertzes and the Ricardos.

This dispute, like so many others, springs from Fred's incredible miserliness, one of the curmudgeon's more durable traits. Frawley invested his character with an uncanny believability, though he was certainly no Method actor. "He never knew what the story was about," Lucy confessed some years later. "He just tore out the pages he was supposed to do! But he was a funny, irascible, wonderful man that the writers wrote for perfectly."

1953/54 THE THIRD SEASON

Year-End Rating: 58.8 (1st place)

Producer Jess Oppenheimer heads a creative staff that remains largely unchanged as the series moves into a third season of uninterrupted critical and popular success.

67 Ricky's Life Story October 5, 1953
Writers: Jess Oppenheimer, Madelyn Pugh, Bob Carroll, Jr.
Director: William Asher
Guest Star: Louis Nicoletti

Life magazine does a big story on Ricky, but leaves Lucy out of the picture.

68 The Girls Go Into Business   October 12, 1953
Writers: Jess Oppenheimer, Madelyn Pugh, Bob Carroll, Jr.
Director: William Asher
Guest Stars: Mabel Paige, Emory Parnell

Lucy and Ethel figure to make a killing when they buy a dress shop, but revise their optimistic projections when they sell only five outfits—to each other.

69 Lucy and Ethel Buy the Same Dress   October 19, 1953
Writers: Jess Oppenheimer, Madelyn Pugh, Bob Carroll, Jr.
Director: William Asher
Guest Stars: Shirley Mitchell, Doris Singleton

Lucy and Ethel are horrified to discover they both plan to wear the same outfit on a TV talent show.

70 Equal Rights   October 26, 1953
Writers: Jess Oppenheimer, Madelyn Pugh, Bob Carroll, Jr.
Director: William Asher
Guest Stars: Lawrence Dobkin, Fred Aldrich, Louis A. Nicoletti

Lucy and Ethel demand equal rights, but their protest backfires when Fred and Ricky stick them with an equal portion of the dinner check at a restaurant.

71 Baby Pictures   November 2, 1953
Writers: Jess Oppenheimer, Madelyn Pugh, Bob Carroll, Jr.
Director: William Asher
Guest Stars: Doris Singleton, Hy Averback

Caroline and Charlie Appleby arouse Lucy's competitive instincts when they brag endlessly about their son, Stevie, who was born the same day as Little Ricky.

The Applebys seem well suited to provide the writers with fresh plot springboards: They have a boy the same age as Little Ricky; Charlie runs a local TV station; and Caroline is involved with the wives in the women's club. Oddly, Charlie Appleby rarely figures in future stories, and the character is soon dropped. But his wife, Caroline, would prove a frequent and worthy foil for Lucy and Ethel during this and ensuing seasons.

72 Lucy Tells the Truth   November 9, 1953
   Writers: Jess Oppenheimer, Madelyn Pugh, Bob Carroll, Jr.
   Director: William Asher
   Guest Stars: Doris Singleton, Shirley Mitchell, Charles Lane, Mario Siletti

Lucy alienates practically everyone she knows when she attempts to go twenty-four hours without telling a single lie.

73 The French Revue   November 16, 1953
   Writers: Jess Oppenheimer, Madelyn Pugh, Bob Carroll, Jr.
   Director: William Asher
   Guest Stars: Alberto Morin, Louis A. Nicoletti

Lucy hires a French waiter to teach her the language after Ricky announces his plans to stage a French revue at the club.

74 Redecorating the Mertzes' Apartment   November 23, 1953
   Writers: Jess Oppenheimer, Madelyn Pugh, Bob Carroll, Jr.
   Director: William Asher

Lucy wreaks her usual quotient of disaster when she organizes a painting party to redecorate the Mertzes' apartment.

75 Too Many Crooks   November 30, 1953
   Writers: Jess Oppenheimer, Madelyn Pugh, Bob Carroll, Jr.
   Director: William Asher
   Guest Stars: Elizabeth Patterson, Allen Jenkins, Alice Wills

Lucy and Ethel mistake each other for Madame X, the neighborhood cat burglar.

No matter how ludicrous the situation, according to head writer Jess Oppenheimer, logic remained the key to the comedy of "I Love Lucy." "I insisted on starting every show with a very basic, utterly believable premise," the producer explained to broadcast historian Alex C. Mackenzie. "If you motivate your audience in a series of small steps, you can go to absolute heights."

76   Changing the Boys' Wardrobe   December 7, 1953
   Writers: Jess Oppenheimer, Madelyn Pugh, Bob Carroll, Jr.
   Director: William Asher
   Guest Stars: Oliver Blake, Alberto Calderone, Jerry Hausner,
   Lee Millar

Indignant over their husbands' utter disregard for fashion, Lucy
and Ethel donate the boys' cherished old clothes to a second-
hand store.

77   Lucy Has Her Eyes Examined   December 14, 1953
   Writers: Jess Oppenheimer, Madelyn Pugh, Bob Carroll, Jr.
   Director: William Asher
   Guest Stars: Arthur Walsh, Dayton Lummis, Shepard Menken

Lucy valiantly auditions for the part of a jitterbugging coed, even
though eye drops have left her temporarily blind.

78   Ricky's Old Girlfriend   December 21, 1953
   Writers: Jess Oppenheimer, Madelyn Pugh, Bob Carroll, Jr.
   Director: William Asher
   Guest Stars: Rosa Turich, Lillian Molieri, Jerry Hausner

Ricky is more surprised than anyone when the old flame he
invented to make Lucy jealous suddenly arrives in New York.

79   The Million-Dollar Idea   January 11, 1954
   Writers: Jess Oppenheimer, Madelyn Pugh, Bob Carroll, Jr.
   Director: William Asher
   Guest Star: Frank Nelson

Lucy and Ethel are convinced they've finally struck it rich when
they're deluged with orders for homemade salad dressing.

80   Ricky Minds the Baby   January 18, 1954
   Writers: Jess Oppenheimer, Madelyn Pugh, Bob Carroll, Jr.
   Director: William Asher

Concerned that Ricky isn't spending enough time with his son,
Lucy leaves the new father to baby-sit Little Ricky.

81 The Charm School   January 25, 1954
Writers: Jess Oppenheimer, Madelyn Pugh, Bob Carroll, Jr.
Director: William Asher
Guest Stars: Tyler McVey, Vivi Janiss, Natalie Schafer, Maury Hill

Lucy and Ethel enroll in charm school after an attractive young bombshell overwhelms their husbands.

Natalie Schafer later found considerable recognition when she was stranded with six other castaways on "Gilligan's Island" in the 1960s.

82 Sentimental Anniversary   February 1, 1954
Writers: Jess Oppenheimer, Madelyn Pugh, Bob Carroll, Jr.
Director: William Asher
Guest Stars: Barbara Pepper, Bennett Green, Hazel Pierce

Lucy and Ricky plan to commemorate their anniversary with a romantic, candlelight supper, but the Mertzes have other ideas.

83 Fan Magazine Interview   February 8, 1954
Writers: Jess Oppenheimer, Madelyn Pugh, Bob Carroll, Jr.
Director: William Asher
Guest Stars: Joan Banks, Jerry Hausner, Kathryn Card

The Ricardos and Mertzes put on airs for the benefit of a reporter who arrives to do a magazine piece on a day in the life of Ricky Ricardo.

84 Oil Wells   February 15, 1954
Writers: Jess Oppenheimer, Madelyn Pugh, Bob Carroll, Jr.
Director: William Asher
Guest Stars: Harry Cheshire, Ken Christy, Sandra Gould

The Ricardos and Mertzes buy shares in an oil well but have second thoughts when they suspect they've been swindled.

85 Ricky Loses His Temper   February 22, 1954
Writers: Jess Oppenheimer, Madelyn Pugh, Bob Carroll, Jr.
Director: William Asher
Guest Stars: Madge Blake, Byron Kane, Max Terhune

To win a fifty-dollar bet, Lucy has to force Ricky to blow his top within twenty-four hours.

86   Home Movies   March 1, 1954
Writers: Jess Oppenheimer, Madelyn Pugh, Bob Carroll, Jr.
Director: William Asher
Guest Star: Stanley Farrar

Lucy and the Mertzes create an unintentional comedy when they splice scenes from their home movies into the workprint of Ricky's new TV pilot.

87   Bonus Bucks   March 8, 1954
Writers: Jess Oppenheimer, Madelyn Pugh, Bob Carroll, Jr.
Director: William Asher
Guest Stars: Tony Michaels, Don Garner, Frank Jacquet

Lucy loses a lucky buck that's worth three hundred dollars in a newspaper contest and then sets off on a mad chase as she tracks the bill across the city.

88   Ricky's Hawaiian Vacation   March 22, 1954
Writers: Jess Oppenheimer, Madelyn Pugh, Bob Carroll, Jr.
Director: William Asher
Guest Star: Frank Nelson

Lucy once again suffers abuse from radio quizmaster Freddie Fillmore when she attempts to qualify for an all-expenses-paid trip to Hawaii.

89   Lucy Is Envious   March 29, 1954
Writers: Jess Oppenheimer, Madelyn Pugh, Bob Carroll, Jr.
Director: William Asher
Guest Stars: Mary Jane Croft, Herb Vigran, Dick Elliott, Kay Wiley

Lucy tries to earn five hundred dollars to cover an impossibly large charity pledge by performing a dangerous publicity stunt atop the Empire State Building.

Mary Jane Croft appears as Lucy's society friend, Cynthia Harcourt— a role she would reprise when she played Lucy's sidekick, under various names, on later variations of the star's sitcoms over the next two decades.

90 Lucy Writes a Novel   April 5, 1954
Writers: Jess Oppenheimer, Madelyn Pugh, Bob Carroll, Jr.
Director: William Asher
Guest Stars: Pierre Watkin, Dayton Lummis

Ricky, Fred, and Ethel are less than flattered to find themselves depicted in Lucy's novel—a *roman à clef* about life around the Ricardo household.

91 Lucy's Club Dance   April 12, 1954
Writers: Jess Oppenheimer, Madelyn Pugh, Bob Carroll, Jr.
Director: William Asher
Guest Stars: Shirley Mitchell, Doris Singleton

Ricky is drafted into service to conduct the would-be musicians in Lucy's all-girl band.

92 The Black Wig   April 19, 1954
Writers: Jess Oppenheimer, Madelyn Pugh, Bob Carroll, Jr.
Director: William Asher
Guest Stars: Eva McVeagh, Douglas Evans

Ethel and Lucy test their husbands' fidelity by disguising themselves as a pair of exotic foreigners.

Another sturdy plot line enters the lexicon of situation comedy when Lucy discovers the invigorating effect a different-colored coiffure can have on a jaded marriage. The tactic would be used by countless sitcom wives, from "Dick Van Dyke's" Laura Petrie to Gloria Stivic, who donned a black wig of her own on "All in the Family" some twenty years later.

93 The Diner   April 26, 1954
Writers: Jess Oppenheimer, Madelyn Pugh, Bob Carroll, Jr.
Director: William Asher
Guest Stars: James Burke, Fred Sherman, Don Garner

The Mertzes and Ricardos pool their finances to buy a diner, but soon find themselves competing with each other for a single customer.

94   Tennessee Ernie Visits   May 3, 1954
Writers: Jess Oppenheimer, Madelyn Pugh, Bob Carroll, Jr.
Director: William Asher
Guest Star: Tennessee Ernie Ford

The Ricardos play reluctant hosts to Cousin Ernest Ford, a back-woods rube with a powerful yen for big-city life.

95   Tennessee Ernie Hangs On   May 10, 1954
Writers: Jess Oppenheimer, Madelyn Pugh, Bob Carroll, Jr.
Director: William Asher
Guest Star: Tennessee Ernie Ford

The Ricardos' schemes to rid themselves of their unwanted hous-eguest backfire, and they end up performing with Cousin Ernie on a hayseed amateur hour.

This two-parter, featuring the popular hillbilly performer Tennessee Ernie Ford, scored ratings that were far above average, a fact that was not lost on the network or the producers. From that moment on, special guest stars became an integral part of the Lucy formula.

96   The Golf Game   May 17, 1954
Writers: Jess Oppenheimer, Madelyn Pugh, Bob Carroll, Jr.
Director: William Asher
Guest Stars: Jimmy Demaret, George Pirrone

To discourage Lucy and Ethel from tagging along to the golf course, Fred and Ricky conspire to make their wives' day on the green as difficult as possible.

97   The Sublease   May 24, 1954
Writers: Jess Oppenheimer, Madelyn Pugh, Bob Carroll, Jr.
Director: William Asher
Guest Stars: Virginia Brissac, Jay Novello

Skinflint Fred foils Ricky's efforts to sublease the Ricardo apart-ment for the summer after he discovers his tenants will make a small profit.

1954/55   THE FOURTH SEASON

Year-End Rating: 49.3 (1st place)

It's westward ho, Ricardo, when Ricky lands a movie role and moves to California with Lucy and the Mertzes—a slant that provides fresh inspiration for producer Jess Oppenheimer and writers Madelyn Pugh and Bob Carroll, Jr., as they embark on their fourth consecutitve year as Lucy's preeminent scripters. William Asher once again directs every episode in the season.

98   The Business Manager   October 4, 1954
Writers: Jess Oppenheimer, Madelyn Pugh, Bob Carroll, Jr.
Director: William Asher
Guest Stars: Charles Lane, Elizabeth Patterson

Lucy invigorates her sagging household finances with a novel cash-flow system: She buys the neighbors' groceries on credit and keeps the cash.

Charles Lane plays Ricky's accountant in one of his frequent TV guest spots. His stint as Homer Bedloe, the villain of Paul Henning's "Petticoat Junction," would assure the actor's lasting fame—for better or worse.

99   Mertz and Kurtz   October 11, 1954
Writers: Jess Oppenheimer, Madelyn Pugh, Bob Carroll, Jr.
Director: William Asher
Guest Stars: Charles Winninger, Stephen Wootton

After trying to impress an old vaudeville chum with his prosperity, Fred discovers his former partner is no better off than he and Ethel.

100   Lucy Cries Wolf   October 18, 1954
Writers: Jess Oppenheimer, Madelyn Pugh, Bob Carroll, Jr.
Director: William Asher
Guest Stars: Beppy DeVries, Fred Aldrich, Louis A. Nicoletti

Lucy tests Ricky's devotion by calling him home from the club for a series of phony emergencies.

101   The Matchmaker   October 25, 1954
Writers: Jess Oppenheimer, Madelyn Pugh, Bob Carroll, Jr.
Director: William Asher
Guest Stars: Sarah Selby, Milton Frome

Lucy hopes to inspire an engaged couple to finally tie the knot when she invites them to share an evening of domestic bliss at the Ricardos.

102   Ricky's Movie Offer   November 8, 1954
Writers: Jess Oppenheimer, Madelyn Pugh, Bob Carroll, Jr.
Director: William Asher
Guest Stars: Frank Nelson, James Dobson, Elizabeth Patterson

The entire neighborhood shows up to audition after word leaks out that a Hollywood talent scout plans to pay a call on Ricky.

103   Ricky's Screen Test   November 15, 1954
Writers: Jess Oppenheimer, Madelyn Pugh, Bob Carroll, Jr.
Director: William Asher
Guest Stars: Clinton Sundberg, Ray Kellogg

Lucy is assigned a bit role in Ricky's Hollywood screen test—but there's no such thing as a small part for this actress, and she sets out to prove it.

104   Lucy's Mother-in-law   November 22, 1954
Writers: Jess Oppenheimer, Madelyn Pugh, Bob Carroll, Jr.
Director: William Asher
Guest Stars: Mary Emery, Fortunio Bonanova

The arrival of Ricky's mother spells trouble in two languages when Lucy tries to make her Cuban mother-in-law at home in New York City.

Lucy so earnestly wants to impress Mother Ricardo with her command of Spanish that she plants a bilingual translator in the kitchen to coach her by secret microphone. Of course the ruse backfires, but—as was often the case—Lucy's touching emotional investment in the hare-brained scheme makes us laugh even harder at her pathetic attempt to fake her way through the conversation.

105 Ethel's Birthday   November 29, 1954
   Writers: Jess Oppenheimer, Madelyn Pugh, Bob Carroll, Jr.
   Director: William Asher

Fred and Ricky plan to take the girls out for Ethel's birthday, even though the pair aren't speaking to each other.

106 Ricky's Contract   December 6, 1954
   Writers: Jess Oppenheimer, Madelyn Pugh, Bob Carroll, Jr.
   Director: William Asher

After weeks of waiting by the phone, Ricky finally gets the fateful summons to Hollywood, and the great trip begins.

107 Getting Ready   December 13, 1954
   Writers: Jess Oppenheimer, Madelyn Pugh, Bob Carroll, Jr.
   Director: William Asher

Ricky invites the Mertzes to join them on the drive to Hollywood, and then makes the mistake of letting Fred pick out the car.

108 Lucy Learns to Drive   January 3, 1955
   Writers: Jess Oppenheimer, Madelyn Pugh, Bob Carroll, Jr.
   Director: William Asher

Lucy has barely learned the rules of the road when she decides to teach Ethel to drive—behind the wheel of Ricky's brand-new convertible!

109 California, Here We Come!   January 10, 1955
   Writers: Jess Oppenheimer, Madelyn Pugh, Bob Carroll, Jr.
   Director: William Asher
   Guest Stars: Kathryn Card, Elizabeth Patterson

When the departing travelers encounter a flurry of last-minute complications, Ricky begins to wonder if they'll ever make it out of their parking space.

Kathryn Card joins the cast as Lucy's mother, Mrs. McGillicuddy, in this finely structured sitcom episode. Like most of the best "Lucy" scripts, a perfectly ordinary situation—packing the family car—soon blossoms, in small, logical steps, to heights of absurdity. And as always, the complications are ironed out by the end of the half hour as the foursome drive off singing "California, Here I Come" in the euphoric finale.

110 First Stop   January 17, 1955
Writers: Jess Oppenheimer, Madelyn Pugh, Bob Carroll, Jr.
Director: William Asher
Guest Star: Olin Howlin

At the end of their first day, the intrepid travelers are bilked by a canny roadside innkeeper.

111 Tennessee Bound   January 24, 1955
Writers: Jess Oppenheimer, Madelyn Pugh, Bob Carroll, Jr.
Director: William Asher
Guest Stars: Tennessee Ernie Ford, Will Wright, Rosalyn and Marilyn Borden

The tourists are glad to see their old friend Cousin Ernie after a backwoods sheriff snags them in a speed trap.

112 Ethel's Hometown   January 31, 1955
Writers: Jess Oppenheimer, Madelyn Pugh, Bob Carroll, Jr.
Director: William Asher
Guest Stars: Irving Bacon, Chick Chandler

Arriving in Ethel's hometown, the gang is surprised to discover that all of Albuquerque thinks of little Ethel Mae Potter as a Hollywood-bound celebrity.

Ethel is the comic foil when Fred, Lucy, and Ricky decide to upstage the darling of Albuquerque as she performs her big comeback number, "Short'nin' Bread."

113 L.A. at Last   February 7, 1955
Writers: Jess Oppenheimer, Madelyn Pugh, Bob Carroll, Jr.
Director: William Asher
Guest Stars: William Holden, Eve Arden, Robert Jellison

Lucy makes a mess of things when she spies actor William Holden at the Brown Derby.

Eve Arden, Lucy's old cohort at RKO, takes a break from filming her own Desilu series, "Our Miss Brooks," to make a cameo appearance.

Movie stars like Holden generally appeared on the show for minimum pay in exchange for the chance to plug their latest film before "Lucy's" vast television audience, which explains why the guest stars invariably announce their latest release in none-too-subtle tones somewhere in each episode's script. The big studios still kept an arm's distance from television as late as the mid-1950s, but that didn't prevent them from climbing into bed with TV's most popular couple when the opportunity arose.

114   Don Juan and the Starlets   February 14, 1955
   Writers: Jess Oppenheimer, Madelyn Pugh, Bob Carroll, Jr.
   Director: William Asher
   Guest Stars: Ross Elliot, Dolores Donlon, Beverly Thompson, Shirlee Tigge

Lucy is jealous when Ricky's studio publicist insists that he escort a bevy of beautiful starlets to a Hollywood premiere.

115   Lucy Gets Into Pictures   February 21, 1955
   Writers: Jess Oppenheimer, Madelyn Pugh, Bob Carroll, Jr.
   Director: William Asher
   Guest Stars: Lou Krugman, Onna Conners, Robert Jellison

Lucy makes another director's life miserable when she lands a small part as a showgirl in an MGM musical.

Lucy's burning desire to prove her talents takes on even greater urgency when Fred and Ethel—and even the hotel bellboy—all land movie roles. Of course, she milks her moment in the spotlight for all it's worth as she totters down a long staircase with an immense feathered headdress balanced atop her head.

116   The Fashion Show   February 28, 1955
   Writers: Jess Oppenheimer, Madelyn Pugh, Bob Carroll, Jr.
   Director: William Asher
   Guest Stars: Don Loper, Amzie Strickland

Lucy decides to get a California tan—and quickly—after she finagles her way into a celebrity wives' fashion show.

The wives of Alan Ladd, Forrest Tucker, Dean Martin, William Holden, Van Heflin, Gordon MacRae, and Richard Carlson make cameo appearances here.

117   The Hedda Hopper Story   March 14, 1955
Writers: Jess Oppenheimer, Madelyn Pugh, Bob Carroll, Jr.
Director: William Asher
Guest Stars: Hedda Hopper, Hy Averback, Kathryn Card

A studio press agent convinces Lucy and Ricky to pull a poolside rescue stunt, hoping Ricky's mock heroics will earn a mention in Hedda Hopper's gossip column.

118   Don Juan Is Shelved   March 21, 1955
Writers: Jess Oppenheimer, Madelyn Pugh, Bob Carroll, Jr.
Director: William Asher
Guest Stars: Kathryn Card, Robert Jellison, Phil Ober

When MGM cancels Ricky's picture, Lucy schemes to trick studio head Dore Schary into renewing her husband's contract.

Dore Schary actually was the head of production at MGM, though Vivian Vance's husband, Phil Ober, was called in to play him after the executive begged off at the last minute.

119   Bullfight Dance   March 28, 1955
Writers: Jess Oppenheimer, Madelyn Pugh, Bob Carroll, Jr.
Director: William Asher
Guest Stars: Ross Elliot, Ray Kellogg

Lucy threatens to feed an exposé of Ricky Ricardo to the fan press unless he promises her a role in his TV special.

120   Hollywood Anniversary   April 4, 1955
Writers: Jess Oppenheimer, Madelyn Pugh, Bob Carroll, Jr.
Director: William Asher
Guest Stars: Ross Elliot, Robert Jellison, Kathryn Card

Ricky surprises Lucy with a gala anniversary party at a fancy Hollywood nightclub.

121   Mr. and Mrs. TV Show   April 11, 1955
Writers: Jess Oppenheimer, Madelyn Pugh, Bob Carroll, Jr.
Director: William Asher
Guest Stars: John Litel, Lee Millar

Ricky is excited when he's offered the chance to host a TV talk show, until he discovers that the producers expect his wife to act as co-host.

122 The Star Upstairs   April 18, 1955
    Writers: Jess Oppenheimer, Madelyn Pugh, Bob Carroll, Jr.
    Director: William Asher
    Guest Stars: Cornel Wilde, Robert Jellison

Cornel Wilde is the latest object of Lucy's star-struck enthusiasm when she discovers he's staying in the suite directly above theirs.

123 In Palm Springs   April 25, 1955
    Writers: Jess Oppenheimer, Madelyn Pugh, Bob Carroll, Jr.
    Director: William Asher
    Guest Stars: Rock Hudson, Kathryn Card

Lucy and Ethel meet Rock Hudson during a Palm Springs getaway vacation.

Hudson's guest shot here marked the first time Universal Studios allowed one of their contract players to appear in a filmed teleplay. Their resistance to such guest shots is ironic—in a few short years, their willingness to exploit the hungry market for television films would make Universal one of the strongest studios in Hollywood.

124 The Dancing Star   May 2, 1955
    Writers: Jess Oppenheimer, Madelyn Pugh, Bob Carroll, Jr.
    Director: William Asher
    Guest Stars: Van Johnson, Doris Singleton

Caroline Appleby unexpectedly arrives in California to call Lucy's bluff after the redhead brags about her friendship with film star Van Johnson.

125 Harpo Marx   May 9, 1955
    Writers: Jess Oppenheimer, Madelyn Pugh, Bob Carroll, Jr.
    Director: William Asher
    Guest Stars: Harpo Marx, Doris Singleton

Lucy's ruse to convince Caroline that the Ricardos' suite is the hub of Hollywood's social scene is further complicated by the unexpected arrival of Harpo Marx.

The justly lauded mirror scene, where Lucy mimes Harpo's actions perfectly through a doorway, is an homage to a similar scene Harpo performed in the early Marx Brothers feature *Duck Soup*.

126   Ricky Needs an Agent   May 16, 1955
   Writers: Jess Oppenheimer, Madelyn Pugh, Bob Carroll, Jr.
   Director: William Asher
   Guest Stars: Parley Baer, Helen Kleeb

Lucy masquerades as Ricky's agent, and in no time at all she negotiates him right out of a job.

127   The Tour   May 30, 1955
   Writers: Jess Oppenheimer, Madelyn Pugh, Bob Carroll, Jr.
   Director: William Asher
   Guest Stars: Richard Widmark, Juney Ellis, Benny Rubin

Lucy is determined to snatch a souvenir grapefruit from a tree in Richard Widmark's backyard.

1955/56   THE FIFTH SEASON

Year-End Rating: 46.1 (2d place)

The Mertzes and Ricardos travel to Europe in fifth-year episodes written once again by producer Jess Oppenheimer, Madelyn Pugh, and Bob Carroll, Jr., who welcome newcomers Bob Schiller and Bob Weiskopf to their overworked writing staff at the top of the season. And James V. Kern replaces William Asher as the show's regular director.

128   Lucy Visits Grauman's   October 3, 1955
   Writers: Jess Oppenheimer, Madelyn Pugh, Bob Carroll, Jr.,
   Bob Schiller, Bob Weiskopf
   Director: James V. Kern
   Guest Stars: Gege Pearson, Hal Gerard

Lucy cons Ethel into helping her remove a chunk of the historic sidewalk in front of Grauman's Chinese Theatre as the ultimate Hollywood souvenir.

Writers Schiller and Weiskopf had acquired a respectable résumé of sitcom assignments when they began a long association with Lucy, which would last well into the mid-1960s. The writing team eventually bridged two generations of situation comedy when they applied the skills they'd honed on "I Love Lucy" to a long run of memorable scripts for Norman Lear's "Maude" and "All in the Family" in the mid-1970s.

129 Lucy and John Wayne   October 10, 1955
 Writers: Jess Oppenheimer, Madelyn Pugh, Bob Carroll, Jr.,
 Bob Schiller, Bob Weiskopf
 Director: James V. Kern
 Guest Stars: John Wayne, Ralph Volkie

Lucy finds out how difficult it is to refill John Wayne's boots
after she destroys the star's concrete slab from Grauman's Chinese
Theatre.

130 Lucy and the Dummy   October 17, 1955
 Writers: Jess Oppenheimer, Madelyn Pugh, Bob Carroll, Jr.,
 Bob Schiller, Bob Weiskopf
 Director: James V. Kern
 Guest Star: Lee Millar

Ricky declines an invitation to perform at a studio party, but Lucy
volunteers her services—along with those of a stuffed "Ricky."

Lucy's inspired dance with a determined mannequin provides ample
evidence of the broad physical business that writers Schiller and
Weiskopf favored in their story contributions during the show's final
seasons.

131 Ricky Sells the Car   October 24, 1955
 Writers: Jess Oppenheimer, Madelyn Pugh, Bob Carroll, Jr.,
 Bob Schiller, Bob Weiskopf
 Director: James V. Kern
 Guest Stars: Donald Brodie, Bennett Green

Ricky books return passage home by rail, but the Mertzes feel
abandoned when he forgets to buy their tickets as well.

132 The Great Train Robbery   October 31, 1955
 Writers: Jess Oppenheimer, Madelyn Pugh, Bob Carroll, Jr.,
 Bob Schiller, Bob Weiskopf
 Director: James V. Kern
 Guest Stars: Frank Nelson, Lou Krugman, Joseph Crehan

Lucy's quotient for confusion on the train ride home involves a
flustered conductor, two jewel thieves, and one slightly abused
emergency brake.

The train ride provides yet another opportunity for the systematic pandemonium that Schiller and Weiskopf reintroduced to the series.

133 Homecoming   November 7, 1955
Writers: Jess Oppenheimer, Madelyn Pugh, Bob Carroll, Jr.,
Bob Schiller, Bob Weiskopf
Director: James V. Kern
Guest Stars: Elvia Allman, Elizabeth Patterson

Lucy is jealous of all the attention lavished on Ricky, until finally even she starts to believe her husband's press.

134 The Ricardos Are Interviewed   November 14, 1955
Writers: Jess Oppenheimer, Madelyn Pugh, Bob Carroll, Jr.,
Bob Schiller, Bob Weiskopf
Director: James V. Kern
Guest Stars: John Gallaudet, Elliot Reid

Fred and Ethel are offended when Ricky's agent suggests he find an apartment more befitting his celebrity status.

Latter-day viewers of "Lucy" reruns are unlikely to recognize the live interview show that hosts the tearful reconciliation of the Ricardos and the Mertzes as a parody of Edward R. Murrow's ground-breaking "Person-to-Person."

135 Lucy Goes to a Rodeo   November 28, 1955
Writers: Jess Oppenheimer, Madelyn Pugh, Bob Carroll, Jr.,
Bob Schiller, Bob Weiskopf
Director: James V. Kern
Guest Stars: Dub Taylor, John Gallaudet, Doyle O'Dell

Ricky gets roped into performing in a rodeo show with Lucy and the Mertzes.

136 Nursery School   December 5, 1955
Writers: Jess Oppenheimer, Madelyn Pugh, Bob Carroll, Jr.,
Bob Schiller, Bob Weiskopf
Director: James V. Kern
Guest Stars: Olan E. Soule, Howard Hoffman, Iva Shepard

The Ricardos argue over modern childrearing methods when Lucy refuses to let Little Ricky attend nursery school.

137 Ricky's European Booking December 12, 1955
Writers: Jess Oppenheimer, Madelyn Pugh, Bob Carroll, Jr.,
Bob Schiller, Bob Weiskopf
Director: James V. Kern
Guest Stars: Harry Antrim, Barney Phillips, Dorothea Wolbert

After Ricky offers Fred a job on his band's European tour, Ethel
and Lucy stage an illegal charity raffle to raise money for their
own passage.

138 The Passports December 19, 1955
Writers: Jess Oppenheimer, Madelyn Pugh, Bob Carroll, Jr.,
Bob Schiller, Bob Weiskopf
Director: James V. Kern
Guest Stars: Sheila Bromley, Robert Forrest, Sam Hearn

When her passport application gets bogged down in red tape,
Lucy decides to stow away in a steamer trunk all the way to
Europe.

139 Staten Island Ferry January 2, 1956
Writers: Jess Oppenheimer, Madelyn Pugh, Bob Carroll, Jr.,
Bob Schiller, Bob Weiskopf
Director: James V. Kern
Guest Stars: Charles Lane, Stanley Farrar

Lucy tries to cure Fred of his chronic seasickness by spending
the day with him on the Staten Island Ferry.

140 Bon Voyage January 16, 1956
Writers: Jess Oppenheimer, Madelyn Pugh, Bob Carroll, Jr.,
Bob Schiller, Bob Weiskopf
Director: James V. Kern
Guest Stars: Kathryn Card, Elizabeth Patterson, Tyler McVey,
Jack Albertson

Ricky and the Mertzes are ready to set sail, when Lucy misses
the boat.

Jack Albertson plays the helicopter dispatcher who gets Lucy to her
ship on time. The veteran supporting player became an unlikely sitcom

star when he was cast opposite comic Freddie Prinze in the 1974 NBC series "Chico and the Man."

141 Second Honeymoon   January 23, 1956
   Writers: Jess Oppenheimer, Madelyn Pugh, Bob Carroll, Jr.,
   Bob Schiller, Bob Weiskopf
   Director: James V. Kern
   Guest Stars: Tyler McVey, Harvey Grant, Virginia Barbour,
   Louis A. Nicoletti

Neptune plays Cupid when the sea air rekindles a romantic spark in the Mertzes, and Lucy's jealous of their ardour.

The Mertzes cooing like lovebirds was a rare sight indeed. Frawley's offscreen dislike for his TV wife was long a well-kept secret, but in *The "I Love Lucy" Book*, Bart Andrews reveals that the two actors couldn't stand each other. Frawley referred to his co-star as an "old sack of doorknobs," and Vivian Vance was convinced the sixty-four-year-old actor would've been more appropriately cast as her father than her husband. The offscreen animosity certainly never harmed their performances—in fact, it may have accounted for their utter believability as a couple who've been married for twenty-five years.

142 Lucy Meets the Queen   January 30, 1956
   Writers: Jess Oppenheimer, Madelyn Pugh, Bob Carroll, Jr.,
   Bob Schiller, Bob Weiskopf
   Director: James V. Kern
   Guest Stars: Sam Edwards, Robert Shafter, Nancy Kulp

Lucy works her way into Ricky's routine at the London Palladium in order to gain an audience with the queen.

143 The Fox Hunt   February 6, 1956
   Writers: Jess Oppenheimer, Madelyn Pugh, Bob Carroll, Jr.,
   Bob Schiller, Bob Weiskopf
   Director: James V. Kern
   Guest Stars: Walter Kingsford, Hilary Brooke, Trevor Ward

Lucy's plans for a pleasant weekend in the country are dashed when she becomes a reluctant participant in a fox hunt.

144 Lucy Goes to Scotland   February 20, 1956
Writers: Jess Oppenheimer, Madelyn Pugh, Bob Carroll, Jr.,
Bob Schiller, Bob Weiskopf
Director: James V. Kern
Guest Stars: Larry Orenstein, John Gustafson, Norma Zimmer

Ricky, Fred, and Ethel each assume mythic roles when Lucy dreams
of visiting her ancestral stamping grounds in Scotland.

145 Paris at Last   February 27, 1956
Writers: Jess Oppenheimer, Madelyn Pugh, Bob Carroll, Jr.,
Bob Schiller, Bob Weiskopf
Director: James V. Kern
Guest Stars: Lawrence Dobkin, Shepard Menken, Fritz Feld,
Maurice Marsac

Lucy inflicts more havoc on the streets of Paris than Marie An-
toinette, and almost meets the same fate when she makes an
unscheduled stop at the Bastille.

146 Lucy Meets Charles Boyer   March 5, 1956
Writers: Jess Oppenheimer, Madelyn Pugh, Bob Carroll, Jr.,
Bob Schiller, Bob Weiskopf
Director: James V. Kern
Guest Stars: Charles Boyer, Jack Chefe

Lucy and Ethel spot Charles Boyer at a sidewalk café, and before
long he finds himself mixed up in the usual shenanigans.

147 Lucy Gets a Paris Gown   March 19, 1956
Writers: Jess Oppenheimer, Madelyn Pugh, Bob Carroll, Jr.,
Bob Schiller, Bob Weiskopf
Director: James V. Kern
Guest Star: John Bliefer

Lucy and Ethel threaten a hunger strike to extort Paris designer
gowns from their practical husbands.

148   Lucy in the Swiss Alps   March 26, 1956
   Writers: Jess Oppenheimer, Madelyn Pugh, Bob Carroll, Jr.,
   Bob Schiller, Bob Weiskopf
   Director: James V. Kern
   Guest Star: Torben Meyer

Lucy, the Alps, avalanche.

An irresistible exchange occurs when the foursome, facing almost
certain death in an avalanche, confess their darkest secrets: Fred has
been quietly bilking the Ricardos on their monthly rent, while Ethel
admits she's been secretly returning it each month. When it's Ricky's
turn to bare his soul, he defers, insisting, "I'm no fool . . . we might be
saved!"

149   Lucy Gets Homesick in Italy   April 9, 1956
   Writers: Jess Oppenheimer, Madelyn Pugh, Bob Carroll, Jr.,
   Bob Schiller, Bob Weiskopf
   Director: James V. Kern
   Guest Stars: Vincent Padula, Bart Bradley, Kathryn Card

Lucy, homesick for Little Ricky, throws the toddler a long-distance
birthday party with an Italian shoeshine boy as his stand-in.

Perhaps nowhere in the Lucy chronicles is her patented crying jag
used to better effect than here, when she repeatedly breaks down at the
mere thought of her baby so many miles away on his birthday.
   Crocodile tears were an effective tool in Lucy's bag of tricks, though
she probably didn't realize she was creating a monster—the blubbering
sitcom wife became a self-perpetuating TV convention that stubbornly
hung on for decades to come. The bit was used to good effect by Mary
Tyler Moore on "The Dick Van Dyke Show" and "That Girl's" Marlo
Thomas in the 1960s, and also—with less effective results—by Sally
Struthers on "All in the Family."

150   Lucy's Italian Movie   April 16, 1956
   Writers: Jess Oppenheimer, Madelyn Pugh, Bob Carroll, Jr.,
   Bob Schiller, Bob Weiskopf
   Director: James V. Kern
   Guest Stars: Franco Corsaro, Saverio Lo Medico, Ernesto
   Molinari, Teresa Tirelli

When Lucy is unexpectedly cast in an Italian epic, her character research leads her to the grape-stomping vat of an old-fashioned vineyard.

A memorable later episode that demonstrates how Lucy could transform the broad slapstick of a fight in a giant vat of grapes into a hilarious bit of comic choreography.

151   Lucy's Bicycle Trip   April 23, 1956
Writers: Jess Oppenheimer, Madelyn Pugh, Bob Carroll, Jr.,
Bob Schiller, Bob Weiskopf
Director: James V. Kern
Guest Stars: Mario Siletti, Francis Ravel

The Ricardos and Mertzes bicycle all the way to the French border before Lucy realizes she's misplaced her passport.

152   Lucy Goes to Monte Carlo   May 7, 1956
Writers: Jess Oppenheimer, Madelyn Pugh, Bob Carroll, Jr.,
Bob Schiller, Bob Weiskopf
Director: James V. Kern
Guest Stars: John Mylong, Gordon Clark, Jacques Villon

Lucy inadvertently wins a small fortune at Monte Carlo, even though Ricky has forbidden her to enter the gaming casino.

153   Return Home From Europe   May 14, 1956
Writers: Jess Oppenheimer, Madelyn Pugh, Bob Carroll, Jr.,
Bob Schiller, Bob Weiskopf
Director: James V. Kern
Guest Stars: Mary Jane Croft, Mildred Law, Frank Nelson, Ray Kellogg

Bound for home at last, Lucy attempts to smuggle a twenty-five-pound hunk of Italian cheese aboard the plane to avoid excess baggage fees.

This would be the last episode written and produced by Jess Oppenheimer, who left the series at the end of the fifth year for an executive post at NBC. In his long tenure as "Lucy's" head writer, producer, and co-creator, Oppenheimer's contribution had been enormous—a factor that would become obvious as the show moved into a final uneven season without the unifying vision of the man who had steered the Ricardos' fate for the past five years.

1956/57   THE SIXTH SEASON
Year-End Rating: 43.7 (1st place)

The show ends its phenomenally successful run as a half-hour sitcom at the close of the sixth year, as the Ricardos and the Mertzes settle down to a new life in Connecticut during the final thirteen installments. New cast members include Keith Thibodeaux as the five-year-old Little Ricky; and Frank Nelson and Mary Jane Croft, who play neighbors Ralph and Betty Ramsey in the Connecticut episodes.

Desi Arnaz is the producer of the show's final year, and writers Madelyn Pugh Martin, Bob Carroll, Jr., Bob Schiller, and Bob Weiskopf continue to pen all of the scripts. William Asher replaces James V. Kern as staff director for the final thirteen episodes.

154   Lucy and Bob Hope   October 1, 1956
   Writers: Madelyn Pugh Martin, Bob Carroll, Jr., Bob Schiller, Bob Weiskopf
   Director: James V. Kern
   Guest Stars: Bob Hope, Lou Krugman, Peter Leeds, Dick Elliott, Maxine Semon

Lucy tries to talk Bob Hope into appearing as the opening-night act at Ricky's new nightclub.

Bob Hope was an old friend of the Arnazes. Desi had been his orchestra leader in radio, and Lucy co-starred with him in *Sorrowful Jones* and *Fancy Pants*.

155   Little Ricky Learns to Play the Drums   October 8, 1956
   Writers: Madelyn Pugh Martin, Bob Carroll, Jr., Bob Schiller, Bob Weiskopf
   Director: James V. Kern
   Guest Stars: Elizabeth Patterson, Keith Thibodeaux

Ricky decides to give his son a head start in show business when he buys the five-year-old a snare drum.

Keith Thibodeaux, officially the world's tiniest professional drummer—and a dead ringer for the senior Arnaz—was brought in to play the five-year-old Little Ricky in the sixth season.

156 Lucy Meets Orson Welles   October 15, 1956
Writers: Madelyn Pugh Martin, Bob Carroll, Jr., Bob Schiller, Bob Weiskopf
Director: James V. Kern
Guest Stars: Orson Welles, Ellen Corby, Lou Krugman

When Orson Welles invites Lucy to take part in his act, she starts brushing up on her Shakespeare—only to discover the director has other plans for her.

Welles uses Lucy in his magic act, much as he called on the service of two other redheads—Marlene Dietrich and Rita Hayworth—to fill the role when he performed the novelty act for USO troupes during World War II.

Clearly demonstrating how the ambitions of Desilu had grown beyond "I Love Lucy," in 1956, Arnaz engaged Welles to direct a proposed series of classic short-story adaptations for television. The director fashioned a Peabody Award–winning adaptation of John Collier's "Fountain of Youth" as a pilot film, but the series never sold.

157 Little Ricky Gets Stage Fright   October 22, 1956
Writers: Madelyn Pugh Martin, Bob Carroll, Jr., Bob Schiller, Bob Weiskopf
Director: James V. Kern
Guest Stars: Howard McNear, Marjorie Bennett

Little Ricky gets cold feet on the eve of his first music-school recital.

Ricky's drum teacher is played by Howard McNear, the lovable character actor who later portrayed "The Andy Griffith Show's" Floyd the barber.

158 Visitor from Italy   October 29, 1956
Writers: Madelyn Pugh Martin, Bob Carroll, Jr., Bob Schiller, Bob Weiskopf
Director: James V. Kern
Guest Stars: Jay Novello, Eduardo Ciannelli, Aldo Formica

The Ricardos offer a helping hand to a visiting gondolier they met during their tour of Venice.

159   Off to Florida   November 12, 1956
    Writers: Madelyn Pugh Martin, Bob Carroll, Jr., Bob Schiller,
    Bob Weiskopf
    Director: James V. Kern
    Guest Stars: Elsa Lanchester, Strother Martin

When Lucy loses the train tickets for her trip to Florida, she and
Ethel are forced to share a ride with an eccentric old woman.

160   Deep-Sea Fishing   November 19, 1956
    Writers: Madelyn Pugh Martin, Bob Carroll, Jr., Bob Schiller,
    Bob Weiskopf
    Director: James V. Kern
    Guest Stars: James Hayward, Billy McLean

Ricky and Fred stage a fishing competition with the wives to see
who can hook the largest catch on a deep-sea-fishing expedition.

Jay Sandrich, the son of RKO director Mark Sandrich, signed on as
assistant director with this episode. After a stint as director of "He and
She" in the late sixties, Sandrich distinguished himself as the Emmy-
winning director of "The Mary Tyler Moore Show" in the seventies and
of "The Cosby Show" in the eighties, making him one of the few directors whose career has spanned three generations of superior TV comedy.

161   Desert Island   November 26, 1956
    Writers: Madelyn Pugh Martin, Bob Carroll, Jr., Bob Schiller,
    Bob Weiskopf
    Director: James V. Kern
    Guest Stars: Claude Akins, Jil Jarmyn, Joi Lansing

The wives go to extreme measures to prevent their husbands
from participating as judges in a Miami Beach beauty pageant.

162   The Ricardos Visit Cuba   December 3, 1956
    Writers: Madelyn Pugh Martin, Bob Carroll, Jr., Bob Schiller,
    Bob Weiskopf
    Director: James V. Kern
    Guest Stars: George Trevino, Nacho Galindo, Mary Emery

Lucy is a nervous wreck at the prospect of meeting Ricky's Uncle
Alberto at the Ricardos' family reunion in Cuba.

163 Little Ricky's School Pageant December 17, 1956
Writers: Madelyn Pugh Martin, Bob Carroll, Jr., Bob Schiller,
Bob Weiskopf
Director: James V. Kern
Guest Star: Candy Rogers Schoenberger

The Mertzes and Ricardos are the improbable supporting players
in Little Ricky's kindergarten production of *The Enchanted Forest*.

164 "I Love Lucy" Christmas Show December 24, 1956
Writers: Madelyn Pugh Martin, Bob Carroll, Jr., Bob Schiller,
Bob Weiskopf
Director: James V. Kern
Guest Star: Cameron Grant

As the Ricardos and Mertzes trim the tree on Christmas Eve, they
reminisce how much their lives have changed since the arrival
of Little Ricky.

Here's one for video archaeologists. Because of its seasonal theme
and an uncharacteristic reliance on flashbacks, this show was left out of
the bundle when the series was later packaged for syndication, making
it the only episode of "I Love Lucy" that has never been rerun!

165 Lucy and the Loving Cup January 7, 1957
Writers: Madelyn Pugh Martin, Bob Carroll, Jr., Bob Schiller,
Bob Weiskopf
Director: James V. Kern
Guest Stars: Robert Foulk, Johnny and Hazel Longden, Jesslyn
Fax

Lucy gets lost on the New York subway system with a loving-
cup trophy stuck on her head.

166 Lucy and Superman January 14, 1957
Writers: Madelyn Pugh Martin, Bob Carroll, Jr., Bob Schiller,
Bob Weiskopf
Director: James V. Kern
Guest Stars: George Reeves, Doris Singleton, George
O'Hanlon, Steven Kay

Lucy impersonates Superman at Little Ricky's birthday party when she's unable to arrange an appearance by the real man of steel.

167 Little Ricky Gets a Dog   January 21, 1957
Writers: Madelyn Pugh Martin, Bob Carroll, Jr., Bob Schiller, Bob Weiskopf
Director: James V. Kern
Guest Star: John Emery

Lucy schemes to let Little Ricky keep a puppy, despite the no-pets clause in their lease agreement with Fred and Ethel.

June Foray, the voice of Rocky the flying squirrel, provided the yelps of Little Ricky's dog, Fred. Unlike most sitcom pups, who vanish unaccountably from subsequent episodes, Fred did manage another appearance in the final episode of the series.

168 Lucy Wants to Move to the Country   January 28, 1957
Writers: Madelyn Pugh Martin, Bob Carroll, Jr., Bob Schiller, Bob Weiskopf
Director: William Asher
Guest Stars: Frank Wilcox, Eleanor Audley

The Ricardos make plans to forsake Manhattan's grit and grime for a new home in suburban Connecticut.

The decision to remove the Ricardos from the familiar surroundings of their New York apartment house seems almost sacrilegious, but after five and a half years, and close to 170 scripts, the writers had finally run out of movie stars for Lucy to pester, and they'd long since exhausted her repertoire of material for Ricky's nightclub.

Of course, the Mertzes and Ricardos weren't alone in their urban flight. By the late 1950s, the colorful melting pot of Ralph Kramden's Bensonhurst, Amos n' Andy's Harlem, and Molly Goldberg's Bronx would give way to a half dozen bucolic and geographically undefined towns with names such as Mayfield, Hilldale, and Springfield. By the mid-1960s, TV's prime-time atlas read like the Farmer's Almanac, with the most popular sitcoms set in exotic rural communities such as Mayberry, Pixley, and Hooterville—all far from the harsh urban reality that had typified the shows of Lucy's era.

169 Lucy Hates to Leave   February 4, 1957
Writers: Madelyn Pugh Martin, Bob Carroll, Jr., Bob Schiller,
Bob Weiskopf
Director: William Asher
Guest Stars: Gene Reynolds, Mary Ellen Kaye

Lucy and Ricky double up and cram in with the Mertzes until
their new home in Connecticut is ready.

Guest star Gene Reynolds, a former child actor, discovered far greener
pastures as a producer of such acclaimed series as "Room 222,"
"M*A*S*H," and "Lou Grant."

170 Lucy Misses the Mertzes   February 11, 1957
Writers: Madelyn Pugh Martin, Bob Carroll, Jr., Bob Schiller,
Bob Weiskopf
Director: William Asher
Guest Stars: Tristam Coffin, Jesse Kirkpatrick, Robert Brice

After less than eight hours in their new home, Lucy and Ricky
find life almost unbearable without the Mertzes.

171 Lucy Gets Chummy With the Neighbors   February 18, 1957
Writers: Madelyn Pugh Martin, Bob Carroll, Jr., Bob Schiller,
Bob Weiskopf
Director: William Asher
Guest Stars: Frank Nelson, Mary Jane Croft

The Ricardos decide to redecorate with the help of their new
neighbors, Ralph and Betty Ramsey.

172 Lucy Raises Chickens   March 4, 1957
Writers: Madelyn Pugh Martin, Bob Carroll, Jr., Bob Schiller,
Bob Weiskopf
Director: William Asher
Guest Stars: Tyler McVey, Mary Alan Hokenson, Mary Jane
Croft

Fred and Ethel join the Ricardos in their newest venture as Connecticut chicken ranchers.

173 Lucy Does the Tango   March 11, 1957
Writers: Madelyn Pugh Martin, Bob Carroll, Jr., Bob Schiller,
Bob Weiskopf
Director: William Asher
Guest Star: Ray Ferrell

When the Mertzes and Ricardos invest in two hundred laying
hens, Lucy ends up with egg on her face—and everywhere else.

174 Ragtime Band   March 18, 1957
Writers: Madelyn Pugh Martin, Bob Carroll, Jr., Bob Schiller,
Bob Weiskopf
Director: William Asher

Ricky is enlisted as reluctant bandleader when Lucy and the
Mertzes combine their meager musical talents to form a band
to play at a charity bazaar.

175 Lucy's Night in Town   March 26, 1957
Writers: Madelyn Pugh Martin, Bob Carroll, Jr., Bob Schiller,
Bob Weiskopf
Director: William Asher
Guest Stars: Joseph Kearns, Gladys Hurlbut, Doris Packer, John
Eldredge

The Mertzes and Ricardos plan to see the latest Broadway hit,
until Lucy realizes she bought the wrong tickets.

176 Housewarming   April 1, 1957
Writers: Madelyn Pugh Martin, Bob Carroll, Jr., Bob Schiller,
Bob Weiskopf
Director: William Asher
Guest Stars: Ray Ferrell, Mary Jane Croft

Ethel is jealous of Lucy's burgeoning friendship with her new
neighbor Betty Ramsey.

177 Building a Barbecue   April 8, 1957
Writers: Madelyn Pugh Martin, Bob Carroll, Jr., Bob Schiller,
Bob Weiskopf
Director: William Asher

Lucy is convinced that she's lost her wedding ring in the wet
cement of their freshly constructed backyard barbecue.

The episode provided Lucy and Ethel with one of their last comic set pieces—a huge brick barbecue that they stay up all night to dismantle and then rebuild, brick by brick.

178   Country Club Dance   April 22, 1957
   Writers: Madelyn Pugh Martin, Bob Carroll, Jr., Bob Schiller, Bob Weiskopf
   Director: William Asher
   Guest Stars: Frank Nelson, Mary Jane Croft, Barbara Eden, Tristam Coffin, Ruth Brady

Lucy and Ethel decide to give a local glamour girl some mature competition.

179   Lucy Raises Tulips   April 29, 1957
   Writers: Madelyn Pugh Martin, Bob Carroll, Jr., Bob Schiller, Bob Weiskopf
   Director: William Asher
   Guest Stars: Peter Brocco, Eleanor Audley

Lucy tries her hand at gardening when she competes with Betty Ramsey to win a tulip-judging competition.

180   The Ricardos Dedicate a Statue   May 6, 1957
   Writers: Madelyn Pugh Martin, Bob Carroll, Jr., Bob Schiller, Bob Weiskopf
   Director: William Asher

Lucy accidentally destroys a statue that Ricky is supposed to dedicate during Westport's Yankee Doodle Days.

The Mertzes and Ricardos would return in a series of thirteen hour-long specials over the next few years, but no episodes of "I Love Lucy" would be made after the show left the air on May 6, 1957, while still the highest-rated show on television.

Of course, "I Love Lucy" didn't really end there.

In 1957, Desi Arnaz sold the rerun rights to CBS, and the series began what is probably the most successful afterlife in TV history. To this day it remains one of the most durable half-hour sitcoms in syndication, appearing almost perpetually in every major market in the country.

Finally, in 1986, the most innovative comedy of the 1950s was ushered into the new video age, when "I Love Lucy" became one of the first TV series to be made widely available on home videocassette. It's not hard to imagine historians from some far-distant age stumbling across one of these odd little videotapes as they explore the remains of the third planet from the sun. If that happens, and assuming they're able to dig up a videoplayer—VHS format—it's almost certain that those explorers from that faraway era will find the antics of this twentieth-century Earthling as worthy of repeated viewing as we did.

And before long, it's a sure bet, they'll love Lucy, too.

EMMY AWARDS

The following is a complete listing of the Emmy Awards bestowed on "I Love Lucy" by the National Academy of Television Arts and Sciences.

1952　　Best Situation Comedy
　　　　　Best Comedienne: Lucille Ball

1953　　Best Situation Comedy
　　　　　Best Series Supporting Actress: Vivian Vance

1955　　Best Actress, Continuing Performance: Lucille Ball

"THE HONEYMOONERS"

People like the show because we are
them.
—JACKIE GLEASON

THE INSPIRATION for the longest honeymoon in television history was very simple—a couple of writers wanted to come up with a sketch that would round out an hour of live TV.

Joe Bigelow and Harry Crane, staff writers for "Cavalcade of Stars"—the flagship variety show of the tiny Dumont network—listened as the up-and-coming comic who'd been brought in to host the show a few weeks earlier described his latest brainstorm. Jackie Gleason had an idea for the week's final comedy sketch. He wanted to play an ordinary guy, an everyday working stiff who lived with his wife in Brooklyn. "This dame is very wise and very tired. She knows this guy inside out, see, and he's always got a gripe. They got a little flat in Brooklyn. Flatbush Avenue, maybe."

The writers had to admit the idea sounded like a keeper.

In his first few weeks as host of the Dumont network variety show, the rotund comedian had already developed a popular cast of comic alter egos—Joe the Bartender, The Poor Soul, and the expansive Reginald Van Gleason III, among others. Each one was just a little bit bigger than life, but the star and his writers agreed there was no reason why they couldn't mine just as many laughs from the less-exotic routine of an ordinary guy living an ordinary life.

Bigelow and Crane worked up a sketch that described a domestic squabble between Ralph and Alice Kramden of Brooklyn, USA. The scene was short—the Kramdens had barely enough time to finish the round—but in less than twelve minutes, Jackie Gleason's immortality was assured.

Of course, in 1950, no one guessed the eventual impact that short sketch would have on American television. Even Jackie Gleason ventured no more than a smile when he told his writers, "You know, maybe we got something here."

The honeymoon had begun.

"Make it real," Gleason told his writers. "Make it the way people live. If it isn't credible, nobody's going to laugh." And if anyone was qualified to act as technical adviser on the everyday reality of working-class Brooklyn, it was Jackie Gleason. He'd grown up in the same neighborhood as Ralph Kramden and then quit school to hustle pool before he finally worked his way into show business via nightclubs and bit parts in World War II programmers at Warner Brothers.

He first hit television in 1949, when he allowed himself to be miscast as the lead in the first TV version of "The Life of Riley." The disastrous experience convinced him of one thing—if he was going to make it in television, he would have to trust his own instincts. Gleason resolved that on his next television series—if there was one—*he* would be the one to call the shots.

And call the shots he did. As host of the fledgling "Cavalcade of Stars," Gleason lavished loving attention on each of his growing cast of characters, but he was particularly fond of the recurring sketch about his battling couple from Brooklyn, Ralph and Alice Kramden. Gleason and his writers flirted with the notion of giving Ralph a job as a cop, but they finally put him to work behind the wheel of a bus, since, as the star remembers it, "Bus drivers get aggravated, and I was delighted with anything that would aggravate Ralph."

But it was Kramden's tender side that most appealed to the actor. When the writers proposed calling the segment "The Beast," Gleason nixed the idea. He had a better title—"The Honeymooners." In his mind, the story of the Kramdens was basically an old-fashioned romance. "The guy really loves this broad," he maintained. "They fight, sure. But they always end in a clinch."

That "clinch"—the embrace that ended so many episodes—was the demonstrative flourish of a healthy physical attraction, something that was rare on fifties television. As played by Audrey Meadows, Alice's smoldering allure wasn't hard to see through Ralph's eyes. And, as

Gleason hinted in a recent interview, the attraction was certainly more erotic than anyone acknowledged in the Eisenhower era. "You never got to see the bedroom," recalled the star. "I felt it was best to leave that to the imagination. But at the end of each show, when they'd kiss—you could imagine that they must get along pretty good."

Even stronger than the Kramdens' conjugal ties—and perhaps even more crucial, finally, to the show's delicate chemistry—was the strange, spiritual bond shared by lodge brothers Ralph Kramden and Ed Norton. Wiry, even-tempered, and reasonably satisfied with his life—Art Carney's Norton was everything Ralph wasn't. And yet, the hapless sewer worker sympathized with his neighbor's absurd obsessions as Alice never could. In Norton's childlike devotion, Kramden found strength.

Jackie Gleason once remarked that Art Carney was responsible for 90 percent of "The Honeymooners' " success. Even allowing for the star's characteristic exaggeration, it *is* very difficult to overestimate Carney's contribution to the series. Like Gleason, he was a gifted physical actor. In his hands, the simplest physical shtick—chalking a pool cue, sleepwalking, even signing his name!—became a graceful comic choreography. The chemistry of his pairing with Gleason was instant, and unmistakable. "The first time I worked with him I saw that this guy knew what the hell he was doing," Gleason remembers. "Every move he made was the right move."

It's entirely possible that Carney's comic influence on television may prove even greater than Gleason's. Stretching far beyond "The Honeymooners," Ed Norton's comic legacy continues to inspire television's most sophisticated situation comedy even today. It's difficult to watch such latter-day loons as "Bob Newhart's" Howard Borden, "Taxi's" Jim Ignatowski, or "Cheers's" Coach Ernie Pantusso without acknowledging the inspired clowning of their distant cousin, a guy who worked beneath the streets of Brooklyn.

The popular "Honeymooners" sketches continued as a staple of Gleason's variety show throughout the early 1950s, even after he moved his comic caravan to CBS in 1952. By the time the Buick Motor Company approached Gleason with an offer to sponsor the sketch as a freestanding sitcom in 1955, it had been running, in one form or another, since 1950. It's not surprising that "The Honeymooners" emerged as one of TV's all-time classics in the space of a single season—they'd already been rehearsing for over four years!

The Buick deal was the largest sponsorship commitment in television's brief history. The motor company paid over six million dollars for the privilege of bringing us two years of half-hour "Honeymooners," with an option for a third season of thirty-nine more shows after that. Gleason also arranged for the episodes to be shot live on film, mainly so that his company could reap a few extra bucks when the programs were rerun while he took the summer off. It was a crucial detail in what turned out to be the most fortunate marriage of commerce and art in the history of the situation comedy.

It was also one of the shortest. After only thirty-nine weeks, Gleason called the whole deal off.

But, what a thirty-nine weeks they were!

The eleven hundred people who crowded into New York's Adelphi Theatre for the twice-weekly filming of live "Honeymooners" episodes probably never guessed they were watching television history in the making—most of them were too busy laughing. Just as audiences have continued laughing at those same thirty-nine timeless half-hour films for well over three decades.

The show has a timeless appeal that's as mysterious as it is unarguable. It's practically impossible to watch an episode without getting drawn in—once again—to the relentless comic drama of the indefatigable bus driver who always kept his head in the clouds, even while the rest of him was sinking fast.

Whether he's trying to foist off a warehouse full of useless can openers on late-night TV or causing Alice heartache by withholding a five-dollar rent increase, his foolhardy shortcuts to self-fulfillment invariably end in some poetically appropriate disaster. And yet, no matter how brutal his fate, we're comforted by the knowledge that Ralph will always bounce back to attempt one of the thirty-eight other schemes in his perpetual bag of tricks.

By all accounts, events behind the scenes of "The Honeymooners" were often as chaotic as anything that happened to the Kramdens and Nortons onstage. Gleason maintained that too much rehearsal—which, for him, was anything beyond a cursory run-through—destroyed the show's spontaneity. As a result, the actors often found themselves relying on prayer and their raw instincts to get them through live performances where almost anything could happen.

And despite his near-photographic memory, Gleason himself got lost more frequently than most people guessed. According to legend, when the star did blank out, he would pace back and forth and pat his stomach—the prearranged distress signal that told the other actors to start winging it. Of course, some performers adjusted to the star's unorthodox rehearsal procedures more quickly than others.

"I came close to walking out on Jackie Gleason before the show even got off the ground," Audrey Meadows told *TV Guide* many years later. "I felt totally unprepared and desperate. Standing in the wings, ready to go on, I'd tell him, 'You are a simply dreadful man.' "

But like everyone else on the series, Meadows adapted, and soon developed a great trust for her fellow actors' unerring instincts, particularly Gleason's. "I've always maintained that there's no way you could play a scene wrong with Jackie," she told a recent interviewer. "He is so good, and so real."

That sense of reality permeated every fiber of the series, from Norton's dusty felt hat—a relic that Carney had carried with him since high-school days—to the Kramdens' ill-furnished apartment—itself an only slightly exaggerated model of the flat where Gleason grew up. The burden of re-creating the Kramdens' little universe each week fell to a staff of six dedicated writers—Marvin Marx and Walter Stone, Andy Russell and Herbert Finn, and Leonard Stern and Sydney Zelinka—all unsung heroes of "The Honeymooners" classic episodes.

Since the shows were cranked out and filmed—two each week—until all thirty-nine were shot, the pressure to supply the insatiable demand for top-grade material could be grueling. "We'd be there twelve to fourteen hours each day, Monday through Friday," Leonard Stern told "Honeymooners" historian Donna McCrohan. "No social life. No escape. It probably was more painful than I remember."

And yet, in the entire season, there was barely a clinker in the bunch. Given the show's breakneck pace, it's not surprising that the scribes kept their catalog of stock situations close at hand. But the characters were so genuine—and the scripts so inventive—that the plays transcended the occasional shopworn premise to create a fully developed world that remains convincing—and alluring—to this day.

But Gleason wasn't so sure at the time.

Convinced that "the excellence of the material could not be maintained," the quixotic comedian pulled the plug after a single season. "We had done every script you could think of," the star later complained. The show's ratings might have been another persuasive factor. Despite the audience's obvious affection for the series, "The Honeymooners" barely broke into the year's top twenty. Whatever his reasons, Gleason irrevocably returned to his more successful variety-show format, and the Kramdens and Nortons were relegated to supporting status once again.

But the honeymoon didn't end there.

The series began a second, far more profitable life as a TV rerun when Gleason sold the syndication rights to those thirty-nine half hours in 1957. And since that time, a day hasn't passed when the Kramdens and the Nortons haven't invoked bellows of laughter in some corner of the United States. Perhaps the only real secret of "The Honeymooners' " durability is that it remains just as funny, if not funnier, on the third, fourth—or tenth—viewing, as it was on the first.

Like a fine symphony that reveals new depth and coloration with each performance, "The Honeymooners" has proved impervious to age. The show's classic status grows stronger each year, as new generations are charmed by the simple comic premise that began life as a throwaway sketch on an obscure variety show and climaxed in the most enduring—and endearing—season of situation comedy ever made.

A Critical Guide to the Classic 39 Episodes

THE 1955/56 SEASON

Year-End Rating: 20th place

Jack Philbin was executive producer for "The Honeymooners' " single, bountiful season as a half-hour situation comedy, and all thirty-nine were produced by Jack Hurdle. Three of Gleason's veteran writing teams traded off scripting chores throughout the season—Marvin Marx and Walter Stone, A. J. Russell and Herbert Finn, and Leonard Stern and Sydney Zelinka. Frank Satenstein was the director, and the entire production was supervised by Jackie Gleason.

1   TV or Not TV   October 1, 1955
Writers: Marvin Marx, Walter Stone
Director: Frank Satenstein

The wonders of television disrupt life in the Kramden household when Ed and Ralph share custody of a brand-new TV set.

Marvin Marx and Walter Stone scripted more classic "Honeymooners" dialogue than any other two men on earth. They first teamed up in the writers' pool on Gleason's "Cavalcade of Stars" and soon found themselves resident scribes of the chronicles of Kramden and Norton— a task to which they were ideally suited, according to the series's executive producer. "Marx and Walter Stone were Ralph and Ed's counterparts," observed Jack Philbin, "Marx thought like Ralph, Stone thought like Norton."

2   Funny Money   October 8, 1955
Writers: Marvin Marx, Walter Stone
Director: Frank Satenstein
Guest Stars: Boris Aplon, Frank Marth, Eddie Hanley, Ethel Owen, Vic Rendina, Jack Davis

There's no extravagance too grand for the Kramdens after Ralph discovers a satchel filled with fifty thousand dollars—all of it counterfeit.

3   The Golfer   October 15, 1955
Writers: A. J. Russell, Herbert Finn
Director: Frank Satenstein
Guest Stars: Frank Marth, John Griggs, John Gibson, George Petrie, Jack Davis

To curry favor with his boss, Ralph brags about his skill on the green—a boast the nongolfer lives to regret when Mr. Harper invites him to play that weekend.

4   A Woman's Work Is Never Done   October 22, 1955
Writers: Marvin Marx, Walter Stone
Director: Frank Satenstein
Guest Stars: Betty Garde, Frank Marth

Tired of Ralph's endless domestic complaints, Alice takes a job and leaves a maid to take care of the housework.

5 A Matter of Life and Death   October 29, 1955
Writers: Marvin Marx, Walter Stone
Director: Frank Satenstein
Guest Stars: George Petrie, Les Damon

Convinced that he's got only six months to live, Ralph sells his deathbed story to a weekly magazine.

Ralph is worried when he contracts the fictitious malady arterial monochromia, but he'd already survived *cerebral* monochromia in an early "Honeymooners" sketch that provided the inspiration for this script. As authors Donna McCrohan and Peter Crescenti reveal in *The Honeymooners Lost Episodes*, Gleason's writers thought nothing of filching whole sequences—and sometimes entire plots—from scenes they'd written in the early fifties. At least two other episodes from the classic 1955/56 season, "The Loudspeaker" and " 'Twas the Night Before Christmas," were virtual remakes of earlier sketches that eventually reappeared when many of the "lost episodes" resurfaced—to the delight of "Honeymooners" fans everywhere—in early 1985.

6 The Sleepwalker   November 5, 1955
Writers: A. J. Russell, Herbert Finn
Director: Frank Satenstein
Guest Star: George Petrie

Norton's sleepwalking wreaks havoc with Ralph's well-ordered routine when Trixie appoints him caretaker for her husband's somnambulant strolls.

7 Better Living Through TV   November 12, 1955
Writers: Marvin Marx, Walter Stone
Director: Frank Satenstein
Guest Star: Eddie Hanley

Ralph is the tongue-tied "chef-of-the-future" in an ill-fated late-night TV commercial that he and Norton concoct to sell two thousand Happy Housewife Helpers.

One of the funniest episodes in a very funny season. Norton and Kramden's chefs of the past and future create even greater pandemonium than Lucy's classic Vitameatavegamin pitch when they topple an entire TV studio in their efforts to demonstrate the superior way to "core an apple."

8   Pal O'Mine   November 19, 1955
Writers: Leonard Stern, Sydney Zelinka
Director: Frank Satenstein
Guest Stars: John Seymour, Abbie Lewis, Ned Glass

Ralph's feelings are bruised when Ed buys a friendship ring for one of his pals on the sewer crew.

Veteran comedy scribes Stern and Zelinka wrote their first "Honeymooners" sketch for "The Jackie Gleason Show" in 1954. Leonard Stern continued to create classic television comedy as a writer for "The Phil Silvers Show" and later as creator of the influential 1967 sitcom "He and She."

9   Brother Ralph   November 26, 1955
Writers: Marvin Marx, Walter Stone
Director: Frank Satenstein

Ralph's insecurity gets the better of him after Alice lands a job with a handsome employer, who thinks she's a single girl.

The tempest is short-lived, and by the fade-out, Ralph once again intones, "Baby, you're the greatest," and envelops Alice in the embrace that could elevate broad slapstick into divine romantic comedy. "That kiss was very important," Gleason told interviewer Bill Zehme. "Without it, people would have hated 'The Honeymooners.' They would have thought, 'Jesus, it's just arguing all the time.' "

10   Hello, Mom   December 3, 1955
Writers: Marvin Marx, Walter Stone
Director: Frank Satenstein

Ralph seeks sanctuary with the Nortons when he and Alice have a major row over an impending visit from her mother.

11   The Deciding Vote   December 10, 1955
Writers: A. J. Russell, Herbert Finn
Director: Frank Satenstein
Guest Stars: George Petrie, John Gibson

Ralph regrets his most recent outburst at Norton when his pal suddenly holds the deciding vote in an important election at the Raccoon Lodge.

12   Something Fishy   December 17, 1955
  Writers: Leonard Stern, Sydney Zelinka
  Director: Frank Satenstein
  Guest Stars: Dick Bernie, Joseph Ruskin, Sammy Birch, Eddie Hanley, John Gibson

Ralph and Ed persuade the lodge brothers to ban their wives from the Raccoons' annual fishing trip but have a little more trouble convincing Trixie and Alice.

13   'Twas the Night Before Christmas   December 24, 1955
  Writers: Marvin Marx, Walter Stone
  Director: Frank Satenstein
  Guest Star: Anne Seymour

Ralph trades in his bowling ball to buy Alice's Christmas gift in this modern revamp of O. Henry's "Gift of the Magi."

The episode ends with a priceless moment that preserves forever the spontaneity of the show's theatrical origins, when Gleason—obviously buoyed by holiday cheer—stops the final curtain to introduce the cast in an impromptu curtain call.

14   The Man From Space   December 31, 1955
  Writers: A. J. Russell, Herbert Finn
  Director: Frank Satenstein
  Guest Stars: Eddie Hanley, Vic Rendina

Hoping to win a fifty-dollar prize, Ralph attends the annual Raccoon Lodge costume ball dressed as a man from space.

15   A Matter of Record   January 7, 1956
  Writers: A. J. Russell, Herbert Finn
  Director: Frank Satenstein
  Guest Stars: Ralph Robertson, Ethel Owen

Ralph is at loose ends when Alice moves in with her mother after his latest outburst, until Norton convinces him to transcribe his apology onto a record.

16   Oh, My Aching Back   January 14, 1956
   Writers: Leonard Stern, Sydney Zelinka
   Director: Frank Satenstein
   Guest Stars: George Petrie, Frank Marth

Ralph goes bowling on the eve of his company physical—against Alice's warning—and returns home with a sore sacroiliac.

17   The Baby-sitter   January 21, 1956
   Writers: Leonard Stern, Sydney Zelinka
   Director: Frank Satenstein
   Guest Stars: Vic Rendina, Frank Marth, Sid Raymond

When Alice takes on baby-sitting jobs to pay for the phone she's secretly installed, Ralph suspects she's having an affair.

Telephones and children were both taboo in the Kramdens' coldwater walk-up. The gross misunderstandings that fueled many "Honeymooners" plots would too easily have been cleared up with a simple phone call, and who wanted that? And Gleason and his writers left the Kramdens childless largely because of the show's stringent production demands. "Kids can't time jokes or lines or dialogue," Gleason explained. "To do a live show with them, you'd be dead. So I decreed it—no kids."

18   The $99,000 Answer   January 28, 1956
   Writers: Leonard Stern, Sydney Zelinka
   Director: Frank Satenstein
   Guest Stars: Jay Jackson, Rita Colton, Ethel Owen, Bill Zuckert, Zamah Cunningham, Jack Davis

Ralph is a man obsessed when he lands a chance to break the bank on a big-money quiz show.

19   Ralph Kramden, Inc.   February 4, 1956
   Writers: A. J. Russell, Herbert Finn
   Director: Frank Satenstein
   Guest Star: John Seymour

Con-man Ralph sells Ed a percentage of his entire future earnings, but has second thoughts after an eccentric old woman bequeaths him a fortune in her will.

20   Young at Heart   February 11, 1956
   Writers: Marvin Marx, Walter Stone
   Director: Frank Satenstein
   Guest Star: Ronnie Burns

Inspired by a pair of teenagers, the Kramdens and Nortons decide to recapture their lost youth at a skating rink.

The writers rarely passed an opportunity to exact a sight gag from Gleason's graceful girth, whether it meant dressing him up as a man from space for a costume ball or, as in this episode, setting him loose at a skating rink to make a spectacle of himself on wheels.
   Ronnie Burns, George and Gracie's son, took a break from "The Burns and Allen Show" to make a guest appearance in this episode.

21   A Dog's Life   February 18, 1956
   Writers: Leonard Stern, Sydney Zelinka
   Director: Frank Satenstein
   Guest Stars: George Petrie, John Griggs, Eddie Hanley, Frank Marth, Les Damon

Only after Ralph convinces his boss to invest in his new snack-food sensation does he discover that KramMar's Delicious Mystery Appetizer is dog food.

22   Here Comes the Bride   February 25, 1956
   Writers: Marvin Marx, Walter Stone
   Director: Frank Satenstein
   Guest Stars: John Gibson, Treva Frazee

Ralph ruins his sister-in-law's wedding night when he convinces her mild-mannered groom to assume his rightful place as lord of the manor.

23   Momma Loves a Mambo   March 3, 1956
   Writers: Marvin Marx, Walter Stone
   Director: Frank Satenstein
   Guest Stars: Charles Korvin, Louis Sorin, Zamah Cuningham

The husbands are jealous when a Latin lover moves into the building and sweeps the wives off their feet with suave manners and free mambo lessons.

24   Please Leave the Premises   March 10, 1956
     Writers: Marvin Marx, Walter Stone
     Director: Frank Satenstein
     Guest Star: Luis Van Rooten

The Kramdens are evicted after Ralph stubbornly refuses to pay a five-dollar rent increase.

25   Pardon My Glove   March 17, 1956
     Writers: A. J. Russell, Herbert Finn
     Director: Frank Satenstein
     Guest Star: Alexander Clark

Ralph suspects hanky-panky when Alice postpones his surprise birthday party to arrange a clandestine meeting with a genteel interior decorator.

26   Young Man With a Horn   March 24, 1956
     Writers: A. J. Russell, Herbert Finn
     Director: Frank Satenstein
     Guest Stars: Charles Eggleston, Nel Harrison

A chance meeting with a self-made millionaire inspires Ralph to embark on a rigorous self-improvement program.

27   Head of the House   March 31, 1956
     Writers: Leonard Stern, Sydney Zelinka
     Director: Frank Satenstein
     Guest Stars: Frank Marth, Dick Bernie

Ralph thinks he's king of his castle, but it's Alice who lays down the law when the local paper prints his inflammatory views on a woman's place in the home.

28   The Worry Wart   April 7, 1956
     Writers: Marvin Marx, Walter Stone
     Director: Frank Satenstein
     Guest Star: Warren Parker

A summons from the IRS has Ralph imagining the worst.

29 Trapped   April 14, 1956
Writers: Leonard Stern, Sydney Zelinka
Director: Frank Satenstein
Guest Stars: Frank Marth, Larry Barton, Ken Lynch, Ralph
Robertson, Sammy Birch, George Petrie, Eddie Hanley

A pair of thugs holds Ed and the Kramdens hostage after Ralph
witnesses a robbery outside Harry's pool hall.

30 The Loudspeaker   April 21, 1956
Writers: Marvin Marx, Walter Stone
Director: Frank Satenstein
Guest Star: Jock MacGregor

Ralph is so sure he's about to be named Raccoon of the Year
that he drives Alice mad rehearsing his acceptance speech.

31 Onstage   April 28, 1956
Writers: Leonard Stern, Sydney Zelinka
Director: Frank Satenstein
Guest Stars: George Neise, Alexander Clark, George Petrie

Ralph is delighted to be cast as the lead in the Lodge's annual
fund-raiser, until he finds out Norton is slated to appear as his
co-star.

32 Opportunity Knocks, But   May 5, 1956
Writers: Leonard Stern, Sydney Zelinka
Director: Frank Satenstein
Guest Stars: John Griggs, George Petrie

Ralph attempts to schmooze his boss over a game of pool, but
it's Norton who scores all the points.

33 Unconventional Behavior   May 12, 1956
Writers: Marvin Marx, Walter Stone
Director: Frank Satenstein
Guest Star: Humphrey Davis

A long train ride gets even longer after Norton accidentally handcuffs himself to Ralph during their trip to the Raccoon convention in Minneapolis.

The episode is fondly remembered for the classic handcuff routine, but in *The Official Honeymooners Treasury*, authors Peter Crescenti and Bob Columbe revealed that the entire bit was a last-minute improvisation devised to fill time after another gag was cut at dress rehearsal. "Jackie and Art played this incredible routine of trying to sleep in the upper and lower berths with their hands locked together in these handcuffs," reports actor Humphrey Davis. "And five minutes was used up just like that, with absolutely incredible comic invention."

34   The Safety Award   May 19, 1956
  Writers: Leonard Stern, Sydney Zelinka
  Director: Frank Satenstein
  Guest Stars: Eddie Hanley, Frank Marth, George Petrie, Les Damon

Ralph has his first traffic accident—on the way to accept an award for being the safest bus driver in the city.

35   Mind Your Own Business   May 26, 1956
  Writers: Leonard Stern, Sydney Zelinka
  Director: Frank Satenstein

Norton follows Ralph's advice to gain a promotion at work, and soon finds himself selling irons door-to-door.

36   Alice and the Blonde   June 2, 1956
  Writers: Leonard Stern, Sydney Zelinka
  Director: Frank Satenstein
  Guest Stars: Freda Larsen, Frank Behrens

Alice and Trixie are abandoned by their husbands at a dinner party while Ed and Ralph heap lavish attention on a vapid blonde.

37   Bensonhurst Bomber   September 8, 1956
  Writers: Marvin Marx, Walter Stone
  Director: Frank Satenstein
  Guest Stars: Leslie Barrett, George Mathews

After Ralph is challenged to a boxing match by a local tough, he and Ed devise a scheme to force his flinty opponent to back down.

38 Dial J for Janitor   September 15, 1956
Writers: A. J. Russell, Herbert Finn
Director: Frank Satenstein
Guest Stars: Luis Van Rooten, Zamah Cunningham

With dreams of free rent, a salary—and tips!—Ralph signs on
as building superintendent at 328 Chauncey Street.

39 A Man's Pride   September 22, 1956
Writers: Leonard Stern, Sydney Zelinka
Director: Frank Satenstein
Guest Stars: Dick Bernie, Vic Rendina

Ralph brags about his success to one of Alice's old suitors and
then has to make good on his boast when the man unexpectedly
arrives at the garage.

The series came to an abrupt end with this episode.

After Gleason voluntarily retired the half-hour "Honeymooners" at
the end of the 1955/56 season, the Kramdens and Nortons continued to
make occasional appearances on his variety show until it, too, was finally
canceled in 1970—an incidental casualty in the CBS housecleaning that
cleared the way for the network's bold new comedies, including a new
show called "All in the Family."

Within a few months, Ralph's traditional Saturday-night spot would
be occupied by another bellicose, blue-collar Everyman. He was a little
older than Ralph, but they shared similar tastes in interior decoration.
Like the diligent bus driver, Archie Bunker worked hard at his job—
though he was quick to spot any scheme that might net him a quick
profit. And like Ralph, he was utterly dependent on the patience and
wisdom of his long-suffering wife—though he never understood just
how much.

They created quite a stir, this new family on the block. They were
often loud, usually abrasive, and really very much in love. We were
certain we'd never met anyone quite like Archie and Edith Bunker.

And yet, in so many ways, we'd known them all along.

EMMY AWARDS

The following is a complete listing of the Emmy Awards bestowed
on "The Honeymooners" by the National Academy of Television Arts
and Sciences.

1955   Best Actor in a Supporting Role: Art Carney

(Carney and Audrey Meadows were also honored for their work on "The Honeymooners" while it was part of "The Jackie Gleason Show." Carney received the Best Supporting Actor Award in 1953 and 1954, and Meadows walked off with the Best Supporting Actress Award in 1954.)

"THE DICK VAN DYKE SHOW"

*It was like a lovely party you never
wanted to end.*
—MOREY AMSTERDAM

IN THE SUMMER OF 1959, Carl Reiner packed his typewriter for the trip
to Fire Island but left the suntan lotion behind. It would be nice to spend
a few weeks in the cool ocean breeze of the Long Island community,
far from the stifling inferno of summertime Manhattan—but he knew
he would scarcely see the beach. While his neighbors tanned, the writer
would spend his holiday polishing off a baker's dozen of the most innovative comedy scripts ever written.

And yet, just a few months earlier, Carl Reiner never dreamed he'd
spend his summer vacation writing his own sitcom. When the performer
told his agent he was anxious to give situation comedy a try—after nine
seasons in the cast of "Your Show of Shows" and Sid Caesar's subsequent variety shows—he envisioned starring in one, not writing it.

But the inspiration to build a better sitcom came from his wife, Estelle,
after she'd leafed through a pile of lackluster sitcom scripts his agent
sent over. "She told me, 'You can write better than this!' " explains
Reiner. "Of course, I'd never written a sitcom. But when your wife
thinks you can—you can."

With little more preparation than that, he set out for Fire Island,
determined to stay until he'd finished a series of scripts that would
reflect his unique view of the world, and no one else's. He started by

asking himself, "On what piece of ground do I stand that no one else occupies?"

The answer was quite simple. The New York comedy writer would simply write about a New York comedy writer. The idea was a natural. After all, explained Reiner, "I had a nine-year backlog of material from 'Your Show of Shows.'"

He had little trouble examining his own life through the comic prism of a situation comedy. "I wrote a script every four days," he remembers. And in a remarkable burst of creative energy, he didn't stop until he had finished a full thirteen episodes of "Head of the Family," as he would call his new series.

The writer bundled the scripts together and presented them to his agent, Harry Kalcheim, who immediately recognized their enormous potential. He showed the scripts to film star and TV producer Peter Lawford, who was then married to Patricia Kennedy, of the powerful Boston political clan.

According to Reiner, Lawford submitted one of the scripts to his father-in-law, Joseph P. Kennedy, who insisted on approval of any venture that involved the family money. Finally, with the blessing of the father of the next president of the United States, the pilot for "Head of the Family" was filmed with Carl Reiner in the starring role. It was like a dream come true.

But the writer would wake up soon enough. With Barbara Britton as his co-star, Reiner shot the first—and, as it would turn out, only—episode of "Head of the Family." Then he waited for the offers to come pouring in.

But nobody was buying.

Westerns were in that year—family sitcoms were out. Reiner finally saw "Head of the Family" air as an unsold pilot during the summer of 1960, after which he resolved to forget the whole painful affair.

But Harry Kalcheim wouldn't let him. The agent was so convinced of the quality of Reiner's unsold scripts that he sought a second opinion from another of his clients, Sheldon Leonard—a veteran actor who had found considerable success as a TV producer and director. The former movie gangster read the thirteen scripts Reiner had written during his summer on Fire Island and was mightily impressed.

"I thought that basketful of scripts was the best body of material it had been my good luck to find," enthused Leonard, "and I had worked on some pretty good shows."

The director of "The Danny Thomas Show" and producer of "Andy Griffith" and "The Real McCoys," Leonard was one of the most powerful creators in television. So, naturally, Carl Reiner was intrigued when the producer offered to help revamp the concept of "Head of the Family" into an all-new series that he thought he could sell to CBS. But, the producer hastened to add, he did have one strong suggestion—one that might not be popular with the show's creator.

In Leonard's opinion, they would have to recast the lead—Carl Reiner was completely wrong for the part of Rob Petrie.

"I wondered how to break the news," Leonard explained. "How do you tell an actor he's just not the type to play himself?" But when he finally suggested that Reiner would be better off behind the cameras than in front of them, the writer appeared almost relieved. "I'll always be grateful to Sheldon Leonard," Reiner later exclaimed, "for telling me I was a producer, when I thought I was an actor."

Leonard offered his services as executive producer, despite the advice of well-meaning friends who warned him not to get involved with a series that was so clearly destined for failure. Leonard chose to follow his instincts and eventually convinced his business partner, Danny Thomas, to finance a new pilot.

And so Carl Reiner and his new executive producer began the delicate process of casting the reborn series. For the crucial role of Rob Petrie, Leonard suggested Reiner look at an actor who was already making a name for himself on Broadway—a lanky comedian named Dick Van Dyke.

Long before he made it to the Great White Way, Van Dyke paid his rent with the usual assortment of show-biz jobs—he'd been a record pantomimist and radio talk-show host before he signed with CBS-TV in the mid-1950s, where he spent most of television's Golden Age in a succession of thankless assignments ranging from game-show emcee to host of the "CBS Cartoon Theater." His break finally came when he landed a part in *The Girls Against the Boys*, a revue that starred Bert Lahr and Nancy Walker.

Van Dyke's performance in that revue left an indelible impression on Sheldon Leonard, who considered offering the actor a supporting part on "The Danny Thomas Show." Finally, Pat Harrington got that role, while Van Dyke went on to even greater acclaim in *Bye Bye Birdie*, on Broadway. But there was never any doubt in the producer's mind that Dick Van Dyke would be dynamite on television.

And when Reiner finally saw the actor in *Bye Bye Birdie*, he was quick to agree.

The only other serious contender for the role of Rob Petrie had been Johnny Carson, but finally, the producers decided that Van Dyke was unmistakably right for the part. "We wanted a guy who was shy—like a writer," Reiner insists, "but who was also a naturally funny performer. And Dick Van Dyke had those qualities."

The producers then hired Rose Marie and Morey Amsterdam in supporting roles and discovered—to their delight—that the veteran character actors invested their roles with such depth that distinctions between star players and secondary roles soon vanished. The serendipity continued when the producers signed Richard Deacon and Larry Mathews; and finally, Ann Morgan Guilbert and Jerry Paris would round out one of the most inspired ensembles ever to grace a half-hour comedy.

But that ensemble maintained a conspicuous gap as the deadline to begin shooting loomed, and Reiner and Leonard still hadn't found their Laura Petrie. The producers had seen scores of actresses but couldn't envision any of them in the pivotal role of Rob's wife. They finally came close to signing Eileen Brennan—by far the best of the actresses they'd looked at—but decided against her, because, Reiner admits, "We knew she would be too strong for Dick."

With time running short, they consulted Leonard's partner, Danny Thomas, who had fronted the money for the new pilot. Thomas recalled an actress he'd recently auditioned for the part of his older daughter on "The Danny Thomas Show." She didn't get that role, but Thomas thought she would make a perfect Laura Petrie. The only problem was neither he nor Sheldon Leonard could remember her name.

At the tender age of twenty-two, lack of recognition seemed to be Mary Tyler Moore's professional curse. In her most memorable role to date—as Sam, the leggy secretary on "Richard Diamond, Private Detective"—the camera never even showed her face! It was not the most promising start for an ambitious young actress, and by the time Sheldon Leonard finally tracked her down, her professional enthusiasm was clearly on the wane.

But when she walked though Carl Reiner's door for the first time, Mary Tyler Moore had no way of knowing that her career was about thirty seconds away from being turned completely inside out.

"I had her read three lines," Reiner remembers, and "Hello, Rob" was one of them. "That was all it took. I grabbed her by the top of her head and dragged her over to Sheldon. 'This is her!' I told him. 'She said *hello* like a real person!' "

By January 1961, with all the pieces finally in place, Leonard directed Reiner's "The Sick Boy and the Sitter" script as the pilot episode of the newly christened "Dick Van Dyke Show." On the basis of that outstanding opener, Procter and Gamble offered to sponsor the show as a weekly series on CBS.

But even with the sponsorship commitment, the producers allowed themselves only guarded optimism. Before the show found a spot on the network's fall schedule, they would have to counter an ominous resistance from a most unlikely source—the president of CBS himself.

Jim Aubrey was not an affable man. His coldhearted demeanor had earned him the nickname "The Smiling Cobra," and the show's producers learned early on that he had no particular affection for "The Dick Van Dyke Show." According to Leonard, at one point the executive even suggested they change Rob Petrie's job from that of a writer to an insurance agent.

But in the early 1960s, powerful sponsors like Procter and Gamble still exerted a considerable influence over which programs did—or did not—make it to the network schedules. And in 1961, the soap manufacturer wanted "The Dick Van Dyke Show" on the air.

Carl Reiner recalls vividly the exact moment when he realized the show was actually going to make it, when he happened to notice a high-ranking executive from Procter and Gamble sitting across from him on a commuter train from Manhattan. "He sat across the aisle from me and didn't say a word. Then I noticed that he made a little 'okay' sign with his hand. That was when I knew we were going to be all right."

Procter and Gamble's demands formed an edict that even a network president couldn't ignore, and finally Aubrey slated "The Dick Van Dyke Show" to premiere in early October. But despite his acquiescence, Sheldon Leonard maintains that the executive saddled their show with one of the worst time slots available—Tuesday nights at eight o'clock, far too early to reach the sophisticated adult audience they were counting on.

And there it languished, proving Sheldon Leonard's axiom that "the higher the quality of a show, the longer it will take to catch on with the general public." By that standard, "The Dick Van Dyke Show" must have been of very high quality indeed. The first year's ratings were so low that the series was actually canceled at the end of the season.

And yet, even as the cast and crew staged their farewell party, Sheldon Leonard refused to abandon hope.

He insisted that "The Dick Van Dyke Show" was on the brink of finding its audience and that—if given time—it would succeed. But the only ones who could buy that time were the executives at Procter and Gamble, and they had already withdrawn their sponsorship for the second season. The executive producer resolved to change their minds—even if he had to fly to the soap company's doorstep in Cincinnati, Ohio.

Which is exactly what he did.

Bleary-eyed after the all-night flight to Ohio, Sheldon Leonard made his eleventh-hour pitch in the office of a slightly astonished Procter and Gamble executive early one morning. He reached into his actor's bag of tricks and poured on the charm, drawing on the charisma that had made his countless portrayals of self-assured con men so lovably persuasive. In his own words, "I went back east, got down on one knee, and sang 'Mammy.' "

And it worked.

Procter and Gamble put up half the cash for a second season of "The Dick Van Dyke Show," and Leonard repeated his performance for executives of the Lorillard Tobacco Company, who agreed to sign on as co-sponsors. And, sure enough, by the end of the second year, the series *had* caught on—beyond anyone's wildest dreams.

By the time "The Dick Van Dyke Show" left the air in 1966, it would be widely hailed as a masterpiece in the admittedly thin annals of television art. The show's unique combination of warmth, intelligence, and believability finally forced television comedy to grow out of a painful adolescence, setting a standard of excellence that would remain a dominant influence on quality television comedy for decades to come.

A Critical Guide to All 158 Episodes

Rob Petrie	Dick Van Dyke
Laura Petrie	Mary Tyler Moore
Sally Rogers	Rose Marie
Buddy Sorrell	Morey Amsterdam
Mel Cooley	Richard Deacon
Jerry Helper	Jerry Paris
Millie Helper	Ann Morgan Guilbert
Ritchie Petrie	Larry Mathews
Alan Brady	Carl Reiner

SUPPORTING CAST

Fiona "Pickles" Sorrell	Barbara Perry
	Joan Shawlee
Sam Pomeroy (a.k.a. Pomerantz)	Allan Melvin
Sol Pomeroy	Marty Ingels
Freddie Helper	Peter Oliphant
	David Fresco
Herman Glimscher	Bill Idelson
Sam Petrie (Rob's father)	Tom Tully
	J. Pat O'Malley
Edward Petrie (Rob's father)	Will Wright
Clara Petrie (Rob's mother)	Isabel Randolph
	Carol Veasie
Mr. Meehan (Laura's father)	Carl Benton Reid
Mrs. Meehan (Laura's mother)	Geraldine Wall
Stacey Petrie (Rob's brother)	Jerry Van Dyke

STOCK PLAYERS

Allan Melvin, Frank Adamo, Jamie Farr, Isabel Randolph, Herbie Faye, Jerry Hausner, Johnny Silver, Doris Singleton, Amzie Strickland

Created by Carl Reiner
Music and theme song by Earle Hagen
Director of photography was Robert de Grasse
Principal directors were John Rich, Jerry Paris

1960   THE PILOT EPISODE

Pilot   Head of the Family   July 19, 1960
  Writer: Carl Reiner
  Director: Don Weis
  Guest Stars: Carl Reiner, Barbara Britton, Gary Morgan, Sylvia
  Miles, Morty Gunty, Jack Wakefield, Milt Kamen, Nancy
  Kenyon

Comedy writer Rob Petrie tries to convince his skeptical son that
writing for TV is as exciting as the jobs held by any of the other
kids' dads.

A better-than-average one-camera sitcom, Carl Reiner's prototype for
"The Dick Van Dyke Show" was no more than a rough blueprint for
the series that followed, so direct comparisons are unfair—if irresistible.
Reiner's aggressive interpretation of Rob Petrie as a slightly confused,
but well-intentioned dad is not without its charm, though there's far
less warmth in the office scenes than we would later come to expect.
And the romantic sparks that would soon ignite Rob and Laura's do-
mestic interplay are almost entirely lacking in this embryonic version.
   The episode, which aired on CBS's "Comedy Spot" anthology series,
also starred Barbara Britton as Laura, and Gary Morgan as a surprisingly
winning Ritchie Petrie; Morty Gunty and Sylvia Miles played Buddy and
Sally; and Jack Wakefield essayed the positively demonic Alan Sturdy.
   Stuart Rosenberg and Martin Poll were the credited producers, and
Bernard Green composed the musical score.

1961/62   THE FIRST SEASON

Year-End Rating: 16.1 (80th place)

The triumphs and struggles of TV writer Rob Petrie and his wife,
Laura, are chronicled in a first season of exceptional scripts written or

supervised by Carl Reiner, who will shepherd the series through its first three seasons as head writer, story consultant, and producer.

Sheldon Leonard serves as executive producer throughout each of the show's five seasons, and Ron Jacobs is associate producer for the entire run. John Rich signs on as regular director, and he will continue to direct most episodes through the show's first two seasons. Jay Sandrich is assistant director in the first year.

1   The Sick Boy and the Sitter   October 3, 1961
Writer: Carl Reiner
Director: Sheldon Leonard
Guest Stars: Mary Lee Dearing, Barbara Eiler, Stacy Keach, Sr.

Rob talks Laura into going to a party at Alan Brady's apartment, even though she'd rather stay home and look after their ailing five-year-old.

Rob and Laura Petrie emerge as believable human beings from the very first episode, as we watch them argue, cook liver, and fret about leaving their boy with the baby-sitter—just like real people. They also share a physical attraction that was remarkably frank for television, a direct result of Carl Reiner's refusal to let the couple telegraph their devotion in words. In five years, the pair rarely uttered "I love you" on-screen—because they never had to.

2   My Blonde-Haired Brunette   October 10, 1961
Writer: Carl Reiner
Director: John Rich
Guest Star: Benny Rubin

Laura dyes her hair blonde to rekindle Rob's interest after she's convinced the romance has gone out of their marriage.

Confronted with a disastrous dye job and a thoroughly confused husband, Laura finally breaks down and sobs her exasperation in a string of barely coherent phrases that communicate her poignant needs in a seemingly indecipherable code. Finally, at her wit's end, she collapses in Rob's arms—and somehow, he gets the message loud and clear. And so do we.

This script was actually the ninth episode filmed, but the producers scheduled it to run in the second week to spotlight the quickly emerging talents of Mary Tyler Moore. As Reiner told a reporter for *TV Guide,* "It was obvious from the first that we had accidentally stumbled on a kid of 23 who could do comedy."

3   Sally and the Lab Technician   October 17, 1961
Writer: Carl Reiner
Director: John Rich
Guest Stars: Eddie Firestone, Jamie Farr

Laura plays matchmaker for Sally—with disastrous results—when she pairs the talkative comedy writer with her shy cousin.

The first episode filmed by John Rich, the series's regular director through the start of the third season. A veteran director of "Our Miss Brooks" and scores of TV westerns in the 1950s, he had a knack for getting involved with classic comedies; a decade later he would direct four years of "All in the Family," and he was also a key figure in the genesis of "Barney Miller."

4   Washington Versus the Bunny   October 24, 1961
Writer: Carl Reiner
Director: John Rich
Guest Stars: Jesse White, Jamie Farr

Rob is plagued by fatherly guilt when he's forced to take a business trip on the night of Ritchie's debut in the school play.

5   Oh, How We Met the Night   October 31, 1961
  That We Danced
Writer: Carl Reiner
Director: Robert Butler
Guest Stars: Marty Ingels, Glenn Turnbull, Jennifer Gillespie, Chickie James

Rob recalls his frustrated attempts to date Laura when she was a USO showgirl and he was an overeager sergeant in the Special Services.

The saga of the Petries takes on an epic quality in the first of many flashback episodes that describe significant moments in Rob and Laura's life.

6   Harrison B. Harding   November 6, 1961
   of Camp Crowder, Mo.
Writer: Carl Reiner
Director: John Rich
Guest Stars: Allan Melvin, Peter Leeds, June Dayton

Rob is too embarrassed to admit he doesn't remember the mysterious stranger who arrives claiming to be an old army pal from Camp Crowder.

Ironically, Allan Melvin actually did play Rob's best army pal in numerous later episodes. The well-known character actor also held down regular roles on "The Phil Silvers Show," "Gomer Pyle," and "All in the Family," among others.

7   Jealousy!   November 7, 1961
Writer: Carl Reiner
Director: Sheldon Leonard
Guest Star: Joan Staley

Laura's jealousy gets the better of her when Rob begins working overtime with Alan Brady's gorgeous guest star.

8   To Tell or Not to Tell   November 14, 1961
Writer: David Adler
Director: John Rich
Guest Star: Jamie Farr

When Mel offers Laura an opportunity to dance on "The Alan Brady Show," Rob worries that she might be tempted back into show business full-time.

David Adler, the first writer other than Carl Reiner to contribute scripts to the series, was actually a pseudonym for Frank Tarloff, a Hollywood screenwriter blacklisted as a Communist sympathizer in the fifties. A decade later, his son, Erik, would be a regular contributor to "All in the Family."

9   The Unwelcome Houseguest   November 21, 1961
Writer: Carl Reiner
Director: Robert Butler

The Petries' plans for a weekend in the country are spoiled after

Buddy suckers Rob into looking after his family pet—Larry, a giant German shepherd.

10   The Meershatz Pipe   November 28, 1961
Writer: Carl Reiner
Director: Sheldon Leonard
Guest Star: Jon Silo

Rob worries about his job security when Buddy and Sally polish off an entire script while he's out sick.

11   Forty-four Tickets   December 5, 1961
Writer: Carl Reiner
Director: John Rich
Guest Stars: Eleanor Audley, Opal Euard, Joe Devlin, Paul Bryar

Rob turns to scalpers as a last resort after he forgets to reserve forty-four tickets to "The Alan Brady Show" for his local PTA.

12   Empress Carlotta's Necklace   December 12, 1961
Writer: Carl Reiner
Director: James Komack
Guest Stars: Gavin MacLeod, Carol Veasie, Will Wright

Rob surprises Laura with an unexpected gift—a thoroughly tasteless necklace that she's far too embarrassed to wear.

Gavin MacLeod plays Maxwell, the jewelry salesman, in a role that predates his memorable stint as "Mary Tyler Moore's" Murray Slaughter by almost a decade.

13   Sally Is a Girl   December 19, 1961
Writer: David Adler
Director: John Rich
Guest Stars: Jamie Farr, Paul Tripp, Barbara Perry

Buddy and Mel jump to conclusions when Rob decides to start treating Sally like a lady.

14   Buddy, Can You Spare a Job?   December 26, 1961
Writer: Walter Kempley
Director: James Komack
Guest Star: Len Weinrib

When Buddy's plan to leave for greener pastures backfires, Rob and Sally face the difficult task of convincing Mel to let him return.

Director James Komack became a successful TV producer in the 1970s, with a string of hits that included "The Courtship of Eddie's Father," "Welcome Back, Kotter," and "Chico and the Man."

15   Where Did I Come From?   January 3, 1962
   Writer: Carl Reiner
   Director: John Rich
   Guest Stars: Herbie Faye, Jerry Hausner, Tiny Brauer

Rob recalls the final frantic days of Laura's pregnancy, which culminated in her arrival at the maternity ward in a laundry truck.

16   The Curious Thing About Women   January 10, 1962
   Writer: David Adler
   Director: John Rich
   Guest Star: Frank Adamo

Unable to control her curiosity, Laura can't resist opening a mysterious package that contains a large, self-inflating life raft.

17   Punch Thy Neighbor   January 17, 1962
   Writer: Carl Reiner
   Director: John Rich
   Guest Stars: Frank Adamo, Peter Oliphant, Jerry Hausner, Peter Leeds

Rob gets fighting mad after Jerry thoughtlessly broadcasts his low opinion of "The Alan Brady Show" throughout the neighborhood.

18   Who Owes Who What?   January 24, 1962
   Writer: Carl Reiner
   Director: John Rich

Buddy remains oblivious to Rob's efforts to collect an old debt.

19	The Talented Neighborhood	January 31, 1962
Writer: Carl Reiner
Director: John Rich
Guest Stars: Doris Singleton, Ken Lynch, Michael Davis, Jack Davis, Barry Livingston, Anne Marie Hediger, Ilana Dowding, Kathleen Green, Christian Van Dyke, Barry Van Dyke, Cornell Chulay

When Alan Brady announces a juvenile talent competition, Rob is besieged by pushy stage mothers and their would-be child stars.

20	A Word a Day	February 7, 1962
Writer: Jack Raymond
Director: John Rich
Guest Stars: William Schallert, Lia Waggner

Rob and Laura are disturbed when Ritchie's vocabulary expands to include a small glossary of four-letter words.

21	The Boarder Incident	February 14, 1962
Writers: Norm Liebmann, Ed Haas
Director: John Rich

Rob invites Buddy to spend a few days at his house while Pickles is out of town.

22	Father of the Week	February 21, 1962
Writers: Arnold and Lois Peyser
Director: John Rich
Guest Stars: Isabel Randolph, Allan Fielder, Patrick Thompson

Rob is crushed when he's not invited to speak on career day at Ritchie's school because his son is embarrassed about how he makes his living.

A rewrite of Carl Reiner's pilot script for "Head of the Family." In the original, Reiner's Rob Petrie redeemed himself with a clever poem composed for Ritchie's class, but in this version—adapted to emphasize the unique talents of Dick Van Dyke—Rob wins the kids over with an impromptu demonstration of physical clowning.

23 The Twizzle   February 28, 1962
Writer: Carl Reiner
Director: John Rich
Guest Stars: Jerry Lanning, Jack Albertson, Tony Stag, Freddie Blassie

Sally drags Mel and the writing staff to a bowling alley to audition her latest discovery—a reluctant pop singer who's invented a new dance craze.

Jerry Lanning sings "The Twizzle," written by pop tunesmiths Mack David and Jerry Livingston.

24 One Angry Man   March 7, 1962
Writers: Leo Solomon, Ben Gershman
Director: John Rich
Guest Stars: Sue Ann Langdon, Dabbs Greer, Lee Bergere, Doodles Weaver, Herb Vigran, Herbie Faye, Patsy Kelly, Howard Wendell

Laura is convinced that a pretty face has tipped the scales of justice when Rob—on jury duty—sides with the attractive defendant.

25 Where You Been, Fassbinder?   March 14, 1962
Writer: John Whedon
Director: John Rich
Guest Stars: George Neise, Barbara Perry

Sally pins her romantic dreams on Leo Fassbinder, an old acquaintance she hopes will arrive to brighten a lonely birthday celebration.

26 I Am My Brother's Keeper   March 21, 1962
Writer: Carl Reiner
Director: John Rich
Guest Star: Jerry Van Dyke

Rob knows something's wrong when his brother arrives telling jokes and singing songs—shy, retiring Stacey Petrie acts that way only when he's sleepwalking.

Jerry Van Dyke's two-part appearance led to a checkered TV career for the star's younger brother that included starring parts in two sitcoms—"My Mother the Car" and "Accidental Family"—and a supporting role on "The Judy Garland Show" the following season.

27   The Sleeping Brother   March 28, 1962
  Writer: Carl Reiner
  Director: John Rich
  Guest Star: Jerry Van Dyke

Rob's somnambulant brother lands a guest spot on "The Alan Brady Show" and then wonders how he'll get through the show if he happens to be awake.

Whenever Rob and the gang break into song at a party—which they did quite often, particularly in the early seasons—the show reveals its strong ties to "The Danny Thomas Show," which, like "I Love Lucy," regularly incorporated music and dancing into its show-biz format. It was a happy coincidence that Reiner ended up filming his show at Danny Thomas Productions, since the creator identified Thomas's program as one of two sitcoms—along with "Leave It to Beaver"—that provided inspiration when he created his own series.

28   The Bad Old Days   April 4, 1962
  Writers: Norm Liebmann, Ed Haas
  Director: John Rich

Rob rebels against Laura's domestic tyranny after Buddy convinces him that he's become hopelessly henpecked.

29   Sol and the Sponsor   April 11, 1962
  Writer: Walter Kempley
  Director: John Rich
  Guest Stars: Marty Ingels, Patty Regan, Roy Roberts, Isabel Randolph

Rob can't bring himself to tell a boisterous old army buddy he's not invited to stay for the fancy dinner the Petries are hosting for an important sponsor.

Marty Ingels left the occasional role of Sol Pomeroy to star in "I'm Dickens, He's Fenster" in 1962. Allan Melvin assumed the role of Rob's army pal in later episodes.

30 The Return of Happy Spangler   April 18, 1962
  Writer: Carl Reiner
  Director: John Rich
  Guest Star: Jay C. Flippen

Rob runs into the old-timer who gave him his first break in show business and makes the mistake of trying to return the favor.

1962/63   THE SECOND SEASON

Year-End Rating: 27.1 (9th place)

Carl Reiner continues as producer and head writer in the show's second year, once again contributing most of the season's scripts, with a welcome assist from Sheldon Keller and Howard Merrill, who would continue to write for the show through the fourth season. John Rich returns as staff director, and John C. Chulay signs on as assistant director—a position he maintains for the remainder of the show's run.

31 Never Name a Duck   September 26, 1962
  Writer: Carl Reiner
  Director: John Rich
  Guest Stars: Jerry Hausner, Jane Dulo, Geraldine Wall, Frank Adamo

Ritchie is grief-stricken by the death of his pet duck.

32 The Two Faces of Rob   October 3, 1962
  Writers: Sheldon Keller, Howard Merrill
  Director: John Rich
  Guest Star: Herbie Faye

Posing as a mysterious stranger, Rob calls Laura and asks for a date—a prank that backfires when she accepts his invitation.

33 The Attempted Marriage   October 10, 1962
  Writer: Carl Reiner
  Director: John Rich
  Guest Stars: Sandy Kenyon, Ray Kellogg, Dabbs Greer

Rob recalls the disastrous circumstances that led to his beleaguered arrival at his own wedding—battered, bruised, and three hours late.

Carl Reiner fondly recalls the sequence where Rob shudders as he summons the courage to propose to Laura in an open jeep. "That was my proposal! When I asked my wife to marry me, I got chills just like that." The producer took pride that most of the stories on the show sprang from events that had actually happened to him, or someone on the staff. "I would always ask writers," he explained, "what happened to you today? And not, what have you seen lately—and how can we change it around for a story?"

Writer Bill Persky found that the search for story lines could become a comical obsession. In *Look* magazine, he recalled getting a flat tire on a deserted Mexican roadway. "I was scared to death, but I was thinking, how can I put this in the show?"

34   Bank Book 6565696   October 17, 1962
Writers: Ray Allen Saffian, Harvey Bullock
Director: John Rich

Rob's imagination runs rampant when he discovers a sizable sum of cash stowed away in Laura's secret bank account.

35   Hustling the Hustler   October 24, 1962
Writer: Carl Reiner
Director: John Rich
Guest Star: Phil Leeds

Buddy worries that his incorrigible brother plans to fleece Rob when the reformed gambler challenges the head writer to a friendly game of pool.

36   My Husband Is Not a Drunk   October 31, 1962
Writer: Carl Reiner
Director: Al Rafkin
Guest Stars: Charles Aidman, Roy Roberts

Rob suffers from a posthypnotic suggestion that forces him to act hopelessly inebriated every time he hears a bell ring.

37   What's in a Middle Name?   November 7, 1962
Writer: Carl Reiner
Director: John Rich
Guest Stars: Carl Benton Reid, Geraldine Wall, Cyril Delevanti, J. Pat O'Malley, Isabel Randolph

Rob tells Ritchie how he was given the middle name Rosebud in order to settle a feud that raged among his grandparents before he was born.

38 Like a Sister   November 14, 1962
  Writer: Carl Reiner
  Director: Hal Cooper
  Guest Star: Vic Damone

Rob is concerned that Sally may be developing romantic illusions about Ric Vallone, the handsome singer who's been flirting with her all week.

39 The Night the Roof Fell In   November 21, 1962
  Writer: John Whedon
  Director: Hal Cooper
  Guest Star: Peter Oliphant

Rob and Laura recount vastly different versions of a spat that sent Rob storming out of the house.

40 The Secret Life of Buddy and Sally   November 28, 1962
  Writer: Lee Erwin
  Director: Coby Ruskin
  Guest Star: Phil Arnold

Rob suspects foul play when Buddy and Sally mysteriously disappear together every weekend.

41 A Bird in the Head Hurts   December 5, 1962
  Writer: Carl Reiner
  Director: John Rich
  Guest Star: Cliff Norton

Rob and Laura worry that Ritchie may be suffering from an overactive imagination when he complains that he's been attacked by a giant woodpecker.

42 Gesundheit, Darling   December 12, 1962
  Writer: Carl Reiner
  Director: John Rich
  Guest Star: Sandy Kenyon

A sudden fit of uncontrollable sneezing has Rob worried that he's developed an allergic reaction to Laura.

43   A Man's Teeth Are Not His Own   December 19, 1962
Writer: Carl Reiner
Director: John Rich

Rob is afraid Jerry will never forgive him after he lets another
dentist perform emergency work on his teeth.

44   Somebody Has to Play Cleopatra   December 26, 1962
Writer: Martin A. Ragaway
Director: John Rich
Guest Stars: Valerie Yerke, Eleanor Audley, Bob Crane, Shirley
Mitchell

Rob has his hands full directing the latest neighborhood variety
show; none of the husbands are too keen on letting *their* wife
play Cleopatra.

Guest star Bob Crane would move on to a regular spot on "The
Donna Reed Show" before he assumed the lead role in CBS's long-
running wartime sitcom "Hogan's Heroes."

45   The Cat Burglar   January 2, 1963
Writer: Carl Reiner
Director: John Rich
Guest Stars: Barney Phillips, Johnny Silver

Rob and Laura are unable to unravel the mystery of how a cat
burglar stole their living-room set without leaving any clues.

46   The Foul-Weather Girl   January 9, 1963
Writer: Carl Reiner
Director: John Rich
Guest Star: Joan O'Brien

The TV weather girl from Rob's hometown asks him to help her
land a role on "The Alan Brady Show"—a proposition that Laura
eyes with suspicion.

Rob responds to Laura's jealousy by accusing her of sounding "exactly like one of those wives in a situation comedy." That such a com-
ment could be delivered without self-consciousness offers a clue to the
show's growing sophistication. The world of the Petries had become so
real that we could easily envision Rob and Laura sitting through annoying half-hour comedies, just as we did.

47 Will You Two Be My Wife? January 16, 1963
Writer: Carl Reiner
Director: John Rich
Guest Stars: Barbara Bain, Ray Kellogg, Allan Melvin

Rob faces the fury of a woman scorned in a flashback that recounts how he lowered the boom on his hometown sweetheart after his engagement to Laura.

48 Ray Murdock's X ray January 23, 1963
Writer: Carl Reiner
Director: Jerry Paris
Guest Stars: Gene Lyons, Jerry Hausner

Laura feels betrayed when Rob tells a TV interviewer how she inspired most of the outlandish domestic situations featured on "The Alan Brady Show."

Jerry Paris began his long tenure as the primary director of "The Dick Van Dyke Show" with this episode. John Rich recalls how he came to appoint the actor as his successor when he left the series to direct feature films. "Carl and Sheldon were worried about what would happen to the show," he remembers. "But it was already firmly on the tracks. The cast and the writing were so solid, I told them, that *anyone* could direct the show—I looked around, and Jerry happened to be standing there—even *him*. Actually, Jerry turned out to be a fine director. He did an excellent job."

The show's creator recalls a different account of how the talented director found his calling. According to Carl Reiner, Paris had been anxious to direct from the very start. "But he was such a fidgety guy, no one thought he'd be very good as a director. After John left, we finally gave Jerry a chance, and he did better than anyone dreamed. He finally surprised us all."

49 I Was a Teenage Head Writer January 30, 1963
Writers: Sheldon Keller, Howard Merrill
Director: Jerry Paris

When Buddy and Sally refuse to join Rob in an impulsive walkout, he recalls his tempestuous early days as a writer on "The Alan Brady Show."

50   It May Look Like a Walnut!   February 6, 1963
   Writer: Carl Reiner
   Director: Jerry Paris
   Guest Star: Danny Thomas

A late-show thriller gives Rob a nightmare about a world-domination plot cooked up by an alien who looks exactly like Danny Thomas.

51   My Husband Is a Check-Grabber   February 13, 1963
   Writer: Carl Reiner
   Director: Al Rafkin
   Guest Stars: Phil Arnold, Bill Idelson, Joan Shawlee

The Petries' latest skirmish springs from Rob's annoying habit of always picking up the check when they're out with friends.

Laura gives Rob the silent treatment on the ride home from the restaurant as he tries to figure out just what he did that got her so riled. "Well," she finally volunteers, "I think it's pretty terrible not to be able to send our son to college." And from that marvelous leap in logic, the quarrel escalates in a funny, dizzying spiral, and we laugh as we recognize how in comedy—as well as in marriage—what *isn't* said often reveals more than what is.

52   Don't Trip Over That Mountain   February 20, 1963
   Writer: Carl Reiner
   Director: Coby Ruskin
   Guest Stars: Jean Allison, Ray Kellogg

Fearing disaster, Laura warns Rob not to go on a weekend ski trip and then blames herself for the inevitable accident.

53   Give Me Your Walls!   February 27, 1963
   Writer: Carl Reiner
   Director: Jerry Paris
   Guest Star: Vito Scotti

Laura hires a flamboyant artist to paint the living-room walls but has second thoughts when the ingratiating con man takes over the entire household.

54 The Sam Pomerantz Scandals   March 6, 1963
   Writer: Carl Reiner
   Director: Claudio Guzman
   Guest Stars: Henry Calvin, Len Weinrib, Joan Shawlee

Rob convinces Laura and the gang to stage a variety show at an old pal's Catskills resort.

Rob and his old army pal revive their Laurel and Hardy routine in what amounts to Van Dyke's homage to the movie comedy team. Dick Van Dyke frequently acknowledged Stan Laurel's influence on his work, especially the screen comedian's talent for "taking one simple prop and doing fifteen minutes with it"—a gift that would also prove to be Van Dyke's forte in the many extended solo bits that would appear in later episodes.

55 The Square Triangle   March 20, 1963
   Writer: Bill Idelson
   Director: Jerry Paris
   Guest Star: Jacques Bergerac

Buddy and Sally are puzzled when Rob vanishes every time the show's handsome French guest star walks in.

Writer Bill Idelson also portrayed Sally's forlorn boyfriend, Herman Glimscher. He continued to forge a distinguished career as a comedy writer and eventually produced much of the first year of MTM's "The Bob Newhart Show."

56 I'm No Henry Walden!   March 27, 1963
   Writer: Carl Reiner
   Director: Jerry Paris
   Guest Stars: Everett Sloane, Doris Packer, Roxanne Berard,
   Betty Lou Gerson, Frank Adamo, Howard Wendell, Carl Reiner

Rob feels self-conscious when he discovers he's the only comedy writer at a literary gathering.

Carl Reiner does a lively bit as Yale Sampson, an English philosopher prone to double-talk. The canny producer supplied himself with ample opportunities to chew scenery, even after he assumed the role of Alan Brady on camera in the third year.

57   Racy Tracy Rattigan   April 3, 1963
   Writers: Ronald Alexander, Carl Reiner
   Director: Sheldon Leonard
   Guest Star: Richard Dawson

Alan Brady's summer replacement is Tracy Rattigan, a lecherous flirt who tests Rob's patience when he zeroes in on Laura.

Richard Dawson later discovered enormous popularity as a game-show host, and in scores of sitcom appearances—including regular roles on "Hogan's Heroes," and the final incarnation of "The New Dick Van Dyke Show" in the early seventies.

58   Divorce   April 10, 1963
   Writer: Carl Reiner
   Director: Jerry Paris
   Guest Stars: Joan Shawlee, Charles Cantor, Marian Collier

Rob plays amateur marriage counselor when Buddy threatens to divorce Pickles over a silly misunderstanding.

59   It's a Shame She Married Me   April 17, 1963
   Writers: Sheldon Keller, Howard Merrill
   Director: James Niver
   Guest Star: Robert Vaughn

Rob makes a fool of himself by attempting to outdo Laura's old boyfriend, a suave and wealthy industrialist.

60   A Surprise Surprise Is a Surprise   April 24, 1963
   Writer: Carl Reiner
   Director: Jerry Paris

Rob tries to second-guess Laura's plan to surprise him on his birthday.

61   Jilting the Jilter   May 1, 1963
   Writer: Ronald Alexander
   Director: Jerry Paris
   Guest Star: Guy Marks

Sally's latest heartthrob is a stand-up comic who's badly in need of a new writer, which is exactly what Rob and Buddy suspect he's after.

62 When a Bowling Pin Talks, Listen   May 8, 1963
   Writer: Martin A. Ragaway
   Director: Jerry Paris
   Guest Stars: Jon Silo, Herbie Faye, Carl Reiner

Ritchie helps his dad overcome a bout with writer's block when he inadvertently causes Rob to plagiarize a sketch idea from a TV kid's show.

1963/64   THE THIRD SEASON

Year-End Rating: 33.3 (3d place)

The creative team expands with the permanent addition of Bill Persky and Sam Denoff, who—along with Jerry Belson and Garry Marshall—make their first significant story contributions in the third year. The new writers work under the close supervision of Carl Reiner, who continues as producer, story consultant, and head writer in the third season.

Jerry Paris succeeds John Rich as the series's regular director, a position he will maintain for the final three seasons.

63 That's My Boy??   September 25, 1963
   Writers: Bill Persky, Sam Denoff
   Director: John Rich
   Guest Stars: Greg Morris, Mimi Dillard, Amzie Strickland

Rob recalls Ritchie's birth and a series of mix-ups that had him convinced he'd brought the wrong baby home from the hospital.

Of course, as Rob discovers when he finally meets them, it's unlikely that Mr. and Mrs. Peters could've confused the Petries' baby for their own, since they're black. Strange as it seems now, this relatively innocuous topper caused great controversy in 1963. After being rejected by both CBS and the sponsor, the script was only filmed after executive producer Sheldon Leonard offered to reshoot the ending if it didn't play to the live studio audience. The producers were vindicated when the gag received the longest ovation in the show's history.

Writers Persky and Denoff began their long tenure on the show with this script, after a false start the previous year. In *The Dick Van Dyke Show: Anatomy of a Classic,* authors Ginny Weissman and Coyne Steven Sanders recount how Carl Reiner rejected the team's first submission outright. When they returned a few months later with "That's My Boy??"

the producer was so impressed that he offered them permanent jobs. "If I hadn't found Persky and Denoff in the third year," Reiner observed, only half joking, "I think I would have had a heart attack."

64   The Masterpiece   October 2, 1963
   Writers: Sam Denoff, Bill Persky
   Director: John Rich
   Guest Stars: Howard Morris, Alan Reed, Amzie Strickland, Ray Kellogg

The Petries become instant art collectors when Rob accidentally places the high bid at an art auction.

Guest star Howard Morris—an old crony from Carl Reiner's days with Sid Caesar in the 1950s—also directed a handful of episodes in the show's third and fourth seasons.

65   Laura's Little Lie   October 9, 1963
   Writers: Carl Reiner, Howard Merrill
   Director: John Rich
   Guest Star: Charles Aidman

The Petries discover that their marriage may not be legally binding after Laura confesses that she lied about her age on their marriage license.

66   Very Old Shoes, Very Old Rice   October 16, 1963
   Writer: Carl Reiner
   Director: John Rich
   Guest Stars: Burt Mustin, Madge Blake, Russell Collins

Rob and Laura renew their vows in a hastily arranged ceremony, even though neither is speaking to the other.

This was the farewell episode directed by John Rich, who left the series to direct feature films.

67   All About Eavesdropping   October 23, 1963
   Writers: Sheldon Keller, Howard Merrill
   Director: Stanley Cherry

The Petries get an earful when they accidentally listen in on Millie and Jerry over Ritchie's toy intercom.

68 Too Many Stars   October 30, 1963
   Writers: Sheldon Keller, Howard Merrill
   Director: Jerry Paris
   Guest Stars: Sylvia Lewis, Eleanor Audley, Jerry Hausner, Eddie Ryder

Rob has to choose between Laura and a beautiful new neighbor for the lead role when he directs the annual PTA revue.

69 Who and Where Was Antonio   November 6, 1963
       Stradivarius?
   Writer: Carl Reiner
   Director: Jerry Paris
   Guest Stars: Sallie Janes, Betty Lou Gerson, Hal Peary, Amzie Strickland, Chet Stratton

Rob finds himself the life of the party in Red Hook, New Jersey, during a temporary bout with amnesia, while Laura waits up nervously in New Rochelle.

70 Uncle George   November 13, 1963
   Writer: Bill Idelson
   Director: Jerry Paris
   Guest Stars: Denver Pyle, Bill Idelson, Elvia Allman

Rob's exuberant Uncle George comes to New York to find a wife and sets his sights on Sally.

71 Big Max Calvada   November 20, 1963
   Writers: Bill Persky, Sam Denoff
   Director: Jerry Paris
   Guest Stars: Sheldon Leonard, Art Batanides, Jack Larson, Sue Casey, Tiny Brauer, Johnny Silver

Rob, Buddy, and Sally's latest assignment finds them under the gun—perhaps literally—when a mobster asks them to pen a comedy routine for his nephew.

Executive producer Sheldon Leonard was a natural for the role of Big Max, having played scores of Runyonesque tough guys in his career as an actor in films and TV. The character's name was also an in-joke— Calvada Productions was the company that owned "The Dick Van Dyke Show."

72   The Ballad of the Betty Lou   November 27, 1963
     Writer: Martin A. Ragaway
     Director: Howard Morris
     Guest Star: Danny Scholl

Landlubbers Rob and Jerry buy a sailboat, but run aground due to their petty squabbles on deck.

73   Turtles, Ties, and Toreadors   December 4, 1963
     Writer: John Whedon
     Director: Jerry Paris
     Guest Stars: Miriam Colon, Tiny Brauer, Alan Dexter

Rob hires a maid to help out around the house, but the incompetent domestic who arrives only makes Laura's life more complicated.

Maria offers the Petries an unusual gift—a box turtle with the family's caricature painted on its shell. The actual cartoon was sketched by Van Dyke himself, an enthusiastic doodler.

74   The Sound of the Trumpets   December 11, 1963
     of Conscience Falls Deafly
     on a Brain That Holds Its Ears
     Writers: Bill Persky, Sam Denoff
     Director: Jerry Paris
     Guest Stars: Ken Lynch, Bernie Hamilton, Edward Holmes

Rob can't decide whether to testify when he discovers he's the only witness to a jewelry store holdup.

75   The Alan Brady Show Presents   December 18, 1963
     Writers: Bill Persky, Sam Denoff
     Director: Jerry Paris
     Guest Stars: Carl Reiner, Cornell Chulay, Brendan Freeman

Alan Brady revamps his Christmas show into a yuletide extravaganza starring Rob, Laura, and the rest of his show's talented writing staff.

Carl Reiner makes his first full on-screen appearance as Alan Brady, after hiding in the shadows for his occasional appearances during the first two seasons. The producer resisted casting an actor in the role because he didn't think a bit player would be convincing enough playing a star of Alan Brady's magnitude. "I wanted the audience to think of Milton Berle or Danny Thomas," Reiner said, "not some guy I hired for six hundred dollars."

76 The Third One From the Left   January 1, 1964
Writer: John Whedon
Director: Jerry Paris
Guest Stars: Cheryl Holdridge, Jimmy Murphy

Rob seeks Laura's advice when he finds himself the reluctant object of an enthusiastic young dancer's affections.

77 My Husband Is the Best One   January 8, 1964
Writer: Martin A. Ragaway
Director: Jerry Paris
Guest Stars: Valerie Yerke, Carl Reiner, Frank Adamo

Rob faces a frigid reception from his co-workers after Laura convinces a journalist that her husband is the brains behind "The Alan Brady Show."

78 The Lady and the Tiger and the Lawyer   January 15, 1964
Writers: Garry Marshall, Jerry Belson
Director: Jerry Paris
Guest Stars: Anthony Eisley, Lyla Graham

The Petries stage a matchmaking competition to see whether a new bachelor in the neighborhood prefers Sally to Laura's cousin, Donna.

An early script from Garry Marshall and Jerry Belson, the talented pair who later turned Neil Simon's *Odd Couple* into a hit series. Garry Marshall would eventually forge one of the most formidable dynasties in sitcom history with "Happy Days" and its family of spin-offs in the 1970s.

79 The Life and Love of Joe Coogan   January 22, 1964
Writer: Carl Reiner
Director: Jerry Paris
Guest Stars: Michael Forrest, Johnny Silver

Rob is overcome with jealousy when he meets one of Laura's old beaus at the golf club and then discovers she saved a box of his old love poems.

80   A Nice Friendly Game of Cards   January 29, 1964
   Writer: Ernest Chambers
   Director: Howard Morris
   Guest Stars: Edward C. Platt, Shirley Mitchell

Rob is a big winner in poker, though it nearly costs him his friends after they discover he's been dealing from a marked deck.

81   Happy Birthday and Too Many More   February 5, 1964
   Writers: Bill Persky, Sam Denoff
   Director: Jerry Paris
   Guest Stars: Michael Chulay, Cornell Chulay, Brendan Freeman, Tony Paris, Johnny Silver

After Rob scotches Laura's elaborate plans for Ritchie's birthday party, he faces the challenge of entertaining sixty-three screaming kids in the Petrie living room.

82   The Brave and the Backache   February 12, 1964
   Writers: Sheldon Keller, Howard Merrill
   Director: Jerry Paris
   Guest Stars: Ken Berry, Ross Elliott

Laura is convinced that Rob's recurring backache is a subconscious sign that he really doesn't want to spend the weekend alone with her.

83   The Pen Is Mightier Than the Mouth   February 19, 1964
   Writers: Bill Persky, Sam Denoff
   Director: Jerry Paris
   Guest Stars: Dick Patterson, Herb Vigran, Johnny Silver

Sally considers leaving her job on "The Alan Brady Show" after she makes a big splash on a late-night talk show.

84   My Part-Time Wife   February 26, 1964
   Writers: Bill Persky, Sam Denoff
   Director: Jerry Paris
   Guest Star: Jackie Joseph

Rob reluctantly hires Laura as interim secretary during Sally's absence.

Buddy and Rob's inability to cope with Sally's temporary absence underscores the creative symbiosis the trio enjoyed under normal circumstances. Not surprisingly, Carl Reiner's fictional staff had real-life counterparts in the writers' room of "Your Show of Shows." "Alan Brady was Sid Caesar," the creator admits. "Sally was a combination of Lucille Kallen and Selma Diamond, and Buddy was Mel Brooks."

85 Honeymoons Are for the Lucky   March 4, 1964
Writer: Carl Reiner
Director: Jerry Paris
Guest Stars: Johnny Silver, Kathleen Freeman, Allan Melvin, Peter Hobbs

Rob recalls how he and Laura spent their honeymoon in a dilapidated wedding suite when he went AWOL from Camp Crowder.

86 How to Spank a Star   March 11, 1964
Writers: Nathaniel Curtis, Bill Idelson
Director: Jerry Paris
Guest Star: Lola Albright

Laura is jealous when Rob is appointed producer of "The Alan Brady Show" merely to please the show's beautiful, but spoiled, guest star.

This episode offers a vivid comic portrait of marital discord in the painfully funny sequence where Laura chews her pot roast and potatoes alone while Rob feebly explains how he dined on chicken fricassee with the flirtatious starlet. Laura's fuming anger suggests a more complex motivation than petty jealousy: She also resents that Rob gets to travel through a world of movie stars and romantic temptation while she's stuck at home with a faulty garbage disposal. Mary Tyler Moore once observed, "Laura Petrie was nothing more than an extension of her husband and child, but she didn't question it." But if Laura never questioned her role, she was certainly no stranger to the frustrations of its limitations.

The actress presumably had no such complaints about the character she played in her own series a few years later. And yet, it's doubtful that Mary Richards would ever have considered trying to make it on her own if the seeds of her independence hadn't been planted so many years earlier by a headstrong young housewife in Capri pants.

87   The Plots Thicken   March 18, 1964
Writers: Carl Reiner, Bill Persky, Sam Denoff
Director: Jerry Paris
Guest Stars: J. Pat O'Malley, Isabel Randolph, Geraldine Wall,
Carl Benton Reid

The Petries are caught in a raging debate as their in-laws fight
to determine where Rob and Laura will make their final resting-
place.

88   Scratch My Car and Die   March 25, 1964
Writer: John Whedon
Director: Howard Morris

Rob is obsessed with his new sports car, which doesn't make it
any easier for Laura to confess when she brings it home with a
brand-new scratch.

Dick Van Dyke had a similar weakness for fancy sports cars. When
the episode was written, he had recently indulged himself with the
purchase of a Jaguar XKE.

89   The Return of Edwin Carp   April 1, 1964
Writer: Carl Reiner
Director: Howard Morris
Guest Stars: Richard Haydn, Arlene Harris, Bert Gordon

Rob attempts to coax a legendary radio star out of retirement
for a guest spot on a TV special.

90   October Eve   April 8, 1964
Writers: Bill Persky, Sam Denoff
Director: Jerry Paris
Guest Stars: Carl Reiner, Howard Wendell, Genevieve Griffin

Laura encounters a long-forgotten skeleton from her closet when
a nude oil portrait bearing her face surfaces at a prominent
gallery.

A classic episode that features Carl Reiner in one of his best guest
roles, as the newly respectable bohemian artist Serge Carpetna.

91 Dear Mrs. Petrie, Your Husband Is in Jail   April 15, 1964
   Writers: Jerry Belson, Garry Marshall
   Director: Jerry Paris
   Guest Stars: Herkie Styles, Barbara Stuart, Jackie Joseph,
   Johnny Silver, Art Batanides, Henry Scott

   Rob ventures into a steamy honky-tonk to catch an old buddy's
   nightclub act and winds up in jail on vice charges.

92 My Neighbor's Husband's Other Life   April 22, 1964
   Writers: Carl Reiner, Bill Persky, Sam Denoff
   Director: Jerry Paris
   Guest Star: Johnny Silver

   Laura and Rob suspect the worst after they spot Jerry having
   dinner at a fancy restaurant with a beautiful blonde.

93 I'd Rather Be Bald Than Have No Head at All   April 29, 1964
   Writers: Bill Persky, Sam Denoff
   Director: Jerry Paris
   Guest Star: Ned Glass

   Worried that he might be going prematurely bald, Rob consults
   a quack, who administers a bizarre vinegar-and-oil treatment.

94 Teacher's Petrie   May 13, 1964
   Writers: Jerry Belson, Garry Marshall
   Director: Jerry Paris
   Guest Stars: Bernard Fox, Cheerio Meredith

   Rob is unable to share Laura's enthusiasm for a creative-writing
   course when he begins to suspect her attentive instructor's motives.

1964/65   THE FOURTH SEASON

Year-End Rating: 27.1 (7th place)

Carl Reiner continues as producer of the series's fourth season of
popular and critical acclaim. Story consultants Bill Persky and Sam Den-

off write a majority of the season's scripts, with notable contributions from Reiner, Garry Marshall, Jerry Belson, and Joseph C. Cavella, among others.

95 My Mother Can Beat Up My Father   September 23, 1964
   Writers: Bill Persky, Sam Denoff
   Director: Jerry Paris
   Guest Stars: Paul Gilbert, Ken Berry, Tom Avera, Imelda de Martin, Lou Cutell

Laura flattens an obnoxious drunk after he slugs Rob, but only succeeds in wounding her husband's delicate pride.

96 The Ghost of A. Chantz   September 30, 1964
   Writers: Bill Persky, Sam Denoff
   Director: Jerry Paris
   Guest Stars: Maurice Brenner, Milton Parsons

Rob and Laura share an unsettling night with Buddy and Sally in a haunted cabin.

97 The Lady and the Baby-sitter   October 7, 1964
   Writers: Bill Persky, Sam Denoff
   Director: Jerry Paris
   Guest Star: Eddie Hodges

The Petries' teenage baby-sitter develops an adolescent crush on Laura.

98 A Vigilante Ripped My Sports Coat   October 14, 1964
   Writer: Carl Reiner
   Director: Peter Baldwin

Rob and Jerry lock horns when Rob refuses to join the vigilante group Jerry formed to police the neighborhood lawns.

Carl Reiner, himself a former resident of the sleepy suburb of New Rochelle, concocts a sly satire of suburban life in his dark tale of how one man's unruly crabgrass very nearly incites the neighborhood to mob action.

99 The Man From Emperor October 21, 1964
   Writers: Bill Persky, Sam Denoff, Carl Reiner
   Director: Jerry Paris
   Guest Stars: Lee Philips, Gloria Neil, Nadia Sanders, Sally
   Carter, Tracy Butler

Rob is tempted by an offer to join the editorial staff of a glossy
men's magazine, though Laura has other ideas.

100 Romance, Roses, and Rye Bread October 28, 1964
   Writers: Garry Marshall, Jerry Belson
   Director: Jerry Paris
   Guest Stars: Sid Melton, Jeri Lou James, Frank Adamo

Sally discovers an unlikely admirer when the local deli man delivers a single red rose along with her chicken salad.

101 4½ November 4, 1964
   Writers: Bill Persky, Sam Denoff
   Director: Jerry Paris
   Guest Star: Don Rickles

Rob recalls the story of Lyle Delp—a hapless stickup man who
had the misfortune to rob the Petries in a stalled elevator.

The holdup man is played by Don Rickles, who had known Bill
Persky and Sam Denoff since the days when they wrote material for his
nightclub act.

102 "The Alan Brady Show" Goes to Jail November 11, 1964
   Writers: Bill Persky, Sam Denoff
   Director: Jerry Paris
   Guest Stars: Don Rickles, Robert Strauss, Arthur Batanides,
   Ken Lynch, Allan Melvin, Vincent Barbi

The gang's all set to perform a show inside prison gates when
Rob is mistaken for one of the inmates.

103 Three Letters From One Wife November 18, 1964
   Writers: Bill Persky, Sam Denoff
   Director: Jerry Paris
   Guest Stars: Carl Reiner, Valerie Yerke

Millie and Laura wage an ill-fated write-in campaign to praise Alan Brady for appearing in a cultural TV documentary at Rob's insistence.

104 Pink Pills and Purple Parents   November 25, 1964
Writers: Garry Marshall, Jerry Belson
Director: Alan Rafkin
Guest Stars: Isabel Randolph, Tom Tully

Rob recalls Laura's first disastrous encounter with his parents, after she'd taken a few too many of Millie's little pink pills to relax her nerves.

Director Alan Rafkin went on to become one of TV's most prolific comedy directors; his later credits include early episodes of "The Andy Griffith Show," "One Day at a Time," and MTM's "The Bob Newhart Show," among many others.

105 It Wouldn't Hurt Them   December 2, 1964
          to Give Us a Raise
Writers: Jay Burton, Ernest Chambers
Director: Peter Baldwin
Guest Star: Roger C. Carmel

Rob enters the labyrinth of corporate finance when he tries to squeeze a raise for Buddy and Sally from Alan Brady's tightfisted accountant.

106 The Death of the Party   December 9, 1964
Writers: Bill Persky, Sam Denoff
Director: Alan Rafkin
Guest Stars: Willard Waterman, Jane Dulo, Patty Regan, Pitt Herbert

Despite chills and a raging fever, Rob is determined to get through Laura's family reunion without anyone guessing that he's deathly ill.

107 My Two Show-offs and Me   December 16, 1964
Writers: Sheldon Keller, Howard Merrill
Director: Jerry Paris
Guest Star: Doris Singleton

The attentions of a visiting reporter transform Alan Brady's writing staff into a trio of bickering grandstanders.

108   Stretch Petrie Versus Kid Schenk   December 30, 1964
   Writers: Garry Marshall, Jerry Belson
   Director: Jerry Paris
   Guest Stars: Jack Carter, Peter Hobbs, Lynn Borden, Albert
   Carrier, Judy Taylor, Sally Carter

Rob finds it impossible to stand up to Neil Schenk, an oppor-
tunistic old friend who comes fishing for a job in return for an
ancient favor.

109   Brother, Can You Spare $2,500?   January 6, 1965
   Writers: Garry Marshall, Jerry Belson
   Director: Jerry Paris
   Guest Stars: Gene Baylos, Herbie Faye, Jimmy Cross, Tiny
   Brauer, Larry Blake, Brian Nash, Sheila Rogers

A lost "Alan Brady Show" script is recovered by a vagrant, who
demands that Rob pay $2,500 in exchange for its safe return.

110   The Impractical Joke   January 13, 1965
   Writers: Bill Persky, Sam Denoff
   Director: Jerry Paris
   Guest Stars: Lennie Reinrib, Alvy Moore, Johnny Silver

Wary of being taken in by a practical joke, Buddy refuses to heed
a visit from an agent of the Internal Revenue Service.

111   Stacey Petrie—Part I   January 20, 1965
   Writer: Carl Reiner
   Director: Jerry Paris
   Guest Stars: Jerry Van Dyke, Howard Wendell, Bill Idelson

Rob talks Sally into coaching his withdrawn brother, Stacey,
through a practice date at her apartment.

112   Stacey Petrie—Part II   January 27, 1965
   Writers: Carl Reiner, Bill Persky, Sam Denoff
   Director: Jerry Paris
   Guest Stars: Jerry Van Dyke, Jane Wald, Kendrick Huxham,
   Herbie Faye, Carl Reiner

Rob and Laura help Stacey recover from a cold rejection by the
woman of his dreams.

113   Boy Number 1 Versus Boy Number 2   February 3, 1965
    Writer: Martin A. Ragaway
    Director: Jerry Paris
    Guest Stars: Peter Oliphant, Colin Male

Millie and Laura become overnight stage mothers when Ritchie
and Freddie are chosen to play small parts on "The Alan Brady
Show."

114   The Redcoats Are Coming   February 10, 1965
    Writers: Bill Persky, Sam Denoff
    Director: Jerry Paris
    Guest Stars: Chad Stuart, Jeremy Clyde, Mollie Howerton, Bill
    Beckley, Wendy Wilson, Ellie Sommers, Trudi Ames

The Petrie home becomes a potential mob scene when Rob and
Laura offer secret asylum to the Redcoats, a pair of teen idols
from England.

The Redcoats were played by the British folk-rock duo, Chad and
Jeremy, who would repeat their performance in similar roles on ABC's
"Patty Duke Show" a few weeks later.

115   The Case of the Pillow   February 17, 1964
    Writers: Bill Persky, Sam Denoff
    Director: Howard Morris
    Guest Stars: Ed Begley, Alvy Moore, Joel Fluellen, Amzie
    Strickland

Rob fancies himself a crusading lawyer when he takes an unscrupulous pillow salesman to small claims court.

116   Young Man With a Shoehorn   February 24, 1965
    Writers: Garry Marshall, Jerry Belson
    Director: Jerry Paris
    Guest Stars: Lou Jacobi, Milton Frome, LaRue Farlow, Amzie
    Strickland, Jane Dulo

Rob and Buddy sign on as silent partners in a discount shoe
store, but before long, they're pushing pumps on the sales
floor.

117   Girls Will Be Boys   March 3, 1965
   Writers: Garry Marshall, Jerry Belson
   Director: Jerry Paris
   Guest Stars: Bernard Fox, Tracy Stratford, Doris Singleton

Ritchie runs into girl trouble when he comes home with bruises inflicted by a bully named Priscilla.

118   Bupkiss   March 10, 1965
   Writers: Bill Persky, Sam Denoff
   Director: Lee Philips
   Guest Stars: Robert Ball, Greg Morris, Patty Regan, Tim Herbert, Charles Dugdale

Rob is surprised when a novelty song he penned with an old army buddy pops up on the radio, but is dismayed to find out his partner took all the credit.

Writers Persky and Denoff wrote "Bupkiss," which was recorded for the show by pop singers Dick and Dee Dee.

119   Your Home Sweet Home Is My Home   March 17, 1965
   Writers: Howard Ostroff, Joan Darling
   Director: Lee Philips
   Guest Stars: Stanley Adams, Eddie Ryder

Rob recalls the day he and Laura decided to buy their dream house, even after they discovered a massive rock in the basement.

120   Anthony Stone   March 24, 1965
   Writer: Joseph C. Cavella
   Director: Jerry Paris
   Guest Stars: Richard Angarola, Bob Hoffman

Rob and Buddy make the startling discovery that Sally's mysterious new boyfriend is a mortician—and a married one, at that.

121   Never Bathe on Saturday   March 31, 1965
   Writer: Carl Reiner
   Director: Jerry Paris
   Guest Stars: Bernard Fox, Bill Idelson, Kathleen Freeman, Arthur Malet, Johnny Silver

Laura finds herself in an embarrassing fix when she gets her toe stuck in the water spout of a fancy hotel bathtub—with the door locked from the inside.

122   A Show of Hands   April 14, 1965
Writer: Joseph C. Cavella
Director: Theodore J. Flicker
Guest Stars: Joel Fluellen, Henry Scott, Herkie Styles

Rob and Laura attend a prestigious awards banquet wearing gloves after they accidentally dye their hands an indelible shade of black.

123   Baby Fat   April 21, 1965
Writers: Garry Marshall, Jerry Belson
Director: Jerry Paris
Guest Stars: Strother Martin, Carl Reiner, Sandy Kenyon, Richard Erdman

Rob agrees to doctor the script for Alan Brady's Broadway debut, then has second thoughts about performing the thankless task without recognition.

124   100 Terrible Hours   May 5, 1965
Writers: Bill Persky, Sam Denoff
Director: Theodore J. Flicker
Guest Stars: Carl Reiner, Fred Clark, Howard Wendell, Dabbs Greer, Harry Stanton.

Rob recalls the time he broadcast a radio show for one hundred hours straight before he stumbled in to meet Alan Brady for the first time.

Rob's early career as a disc jockey was another facet of his character borrowed from real life. The actor hosted popular radio talk shows in Atlanta and New Orleans before he moved into television in the mid-1950s.

125   Br-room, Br-room   May 12, 1965
Writers: Dale McRaven, Carl Kleinschmitt
Director: Jerry Paris
Guest Stars: Sandy Kenyon, Jimmy Murphy, Johnny Silver, Bob Random, Carl Reindel, Linda Marshall

Rob takes his new motorcycle out for a spin and unwittingly falls in with a gang of teenage bikers.

126 There's No Sale Like Wholesale   May 26, 1965
Writers: Garry Marshall, Jerry Belson
Director: Jerry Paris
Guest Stars: Lou Krugman, Jane Dulo, Peter Brocco, A. G. Vitanza

Rob decides to save a few bucks on Laura's new fur coat by letting Buddy order it wholesale—a decision he lives to regret.

1965/66   THE FIFTH SEASON

Year-End Rating: 23.6 (16th place)

After the show's creators announce their intention to quit while they're ahead of the game, the series ends its celebrated run at the close of the fifth year. Carl Reiner trades off producer's chores with story consultants Bill Persky and Sam Denoff, who maintain the show's high standards in a final season that includes some of the show's most fondly remembered episodes.

Fifth-year scripts are contributed by a wide array of writers, including notable efforts from Garry Marshall and Jerry Belson, Carl Kleinschmitt and Dale McRaven, John Whedon, and, as usual, Bill Persky and Sam Denoff.

127 Coast-to-Coast Big Mouth   September 15, 1965
Writers: Bill Persky, Sam Denoff
Director: Jerry Paris
Guest Stars: Carl Reiner, Dick Curtis

Laura faces Alan Brady's wrath after a fast-talking game-show host goads her into admitting the star wears a toupee.

128 A Farewell to Writing   September 22, 1965
Writers: Fred Freeman, Lawrence J. Cohen
Director: Jerry Paris
Guest Star: Guy Raymond

Rob hopes a few days of seclusion in a mountain cabin will motivate him to complete his novel, but it nearly drives him stir-crazy instead.

Rob expends most of his efforts on avoiding writing, as he perfects his paddle-ball swing and horses around with a pair of cowboy six-shooters he finds in the cabin. The producers knew Van Dyke well enough to know they couldn't go wrong by leaving Rob Petrie alone in a room filled with funny props.

129   Uhny Uftz   September 29, 1965
Writers: Carl Kleinschmitt, Dale McRaven
Director: Jerry Paris
Guest Stars: Karl Lukas, Ross Elliott, Madge Blake, John Mylong

No one seems to believe Rob's claim that he's seen a flying saucer hovering outside the office window.

130   The Ugliest Dog in the World   October 6, 1965
Writers: Bill Persky, Sam Denoff
Director: Lee Philips
Guest Stars: Billy De Wolfe, George Tyne, Michael Conrad, Florence Halop, Barbara Dodd

A homely mongrel becomes the temporary ward of the Petries after his abbreviated appearance on "The Alan Brady Show."

131   No Rice at My Wedding   October 13, 1965
Writers: Bill Persky, Sam Denoff
Director: Lee Philips
Guest Stars: Van Williams, Bert Remsen, Johnny Silver, Allan Melvin

Rob recalls his only serious competition for Laura's hand, a charming army corporal who won a date with her in a USO charity auction.

132   Draw Me a Pear   October 20, 1965
Writers: Art Baer, Ben Joelson
Director: Jerry Paris
Guest Stars: Ina Balin, Jackie Joseph, Frank Adamo, Jody Gilbert, Dorothy Neumann

Laura suspects that Rob's comely drawing instructor may be interested in something other than her husband's artistic abilities.

133 The Great Petrie Fortune   October 27, 1965
Writers: Ernest Chambers, Jay Burton
Director: Jerry Paris
Guest Stars: Dan Tobin, Herb Vigran, Forrest Lewis, Elvia
Allman, Amzie Strickland, Howard Wendell, Tiny Brauer

Rob discovers he's the heir to a mysterious fortune that's hidden
somewhere in his Uncle Hezekiah's rolltop desk.

134 Odd but True   November 3, 1965
Writers: Garry Marshall, Jerry Belson
Director: Jerry Paris
Guest Stars: James Millhollin, Hope Summers, Peter Oliphant,
David Fresco, Bert May, Ray Kellogg

Rob becomes a reluctant candidate for the "Odd but True"
newspaper column when Ritchie connects the freckles on his
back and discovers the Liberty Bell.

Bill Persky and Sam Denoff begin their stint as producers with this
episode, after Carl Reiner takes a temporary leave to appear in *The
Russians Are Coming, The Russians Are Coming.*

135 Viva Petrie   November 10, 1965
Writer: John Whedon
Director: Jerry Paris
Guest Stars: Joby Baker, Jack Bernardi

Rob and Laura attempt to find work for a newly landed immigrant
whose only occupational skill is professional bullfighting.

136 Go Tell the Birds and Bees   November 17, 1965
Writer: Rick Mittleman
Director: Jerry Paris
Guest Stars: Alberta Nelson, Peter Hobbs

After Ritchie regales his schoolmates with tall tales about where
babies come from, Rob sits him down and tells him the real story.

137 Body and Sol   November 24, 1965
Writers: Carl Kleinschmitt, Dale McRaven
Director: Jerry Paris
Guest Stars: Allan Melvin, Ed Peck, Michael Conrad, Garry
Marshall, Barbara Dodd, Paul Stader, Burt Taylor

Rob recalls his short-lived career as Pitter Patter Petrie—middleweight champ of the U.S. Army special services.

Writer Garry Marshall has a cameo as the referee of Rob's boxing match.

138   See Rob Write, Write Rob, Write   December 8, 1965
Writers: Lawrence J. Cohen, Fred Freeman
Director: Jerry Paris
Guest Star: John McGiver

The Petries find themselves locked in literary competition after Rob volunteers his help on a children's book that Laura's writing.

139   You're Under Arrest   December 15, 1965
Writer: Joseph C. Cavella
Director: Jerry Paris
Guest Stars: Phillip Pine, Lee Krieger, Sandy Kenyon, Ed McCready, Bella Bruck, Tiny Brauer, Johnny Silver

Rob has difficulty coming up with a plausible alibi when the police accuse him of taking part in a barroom brawl.

140   Fifty-two Forty-five or Work   December 29, 1965
Writer: Rick Mittleman
Director: Jerry Paris
Guest Stars: Reta Shaw, Dabbs Greer, Al Ward, John Chulay, Jerry Hausner, James Frawley

Rob recalls the financial strain that forced him to take a job writing copy for an electronics catalog during his first hiatus from "The Alan Brady Show."

141   Who Stole My Watch?   January 5, 1966
Writer: Joseph Bonaduce
Director: Jerry Paris
Guest Star: Milton Frome

Rob plays amateur sleuth when his new watch turns up missing during his birthday party and he's convinced it was stolen by one of his friends.

142 I Do Not Choose to Run January 19, 1965
Writers: Dale McRaven, Carl Kleinschmitt
Director: Jerry Paris
Guest Stars: Arte Johnson, Philip Ober, George Tyne, Peter Brocco, Howard Wendell, Helen Spring

Rob's stirring speech at a citizen's meeting brings him an unexpected nomination for a seat on the New Rochelle City Council.

Arte Johnson, later a star of NBC's "Laugh-In," has a role as the high-powered media coordinator of Rob's political campaign.

143 The Making of a Councilman January 26, 1966
Writers: Carl Kleinschmitt, Dale McRaven
Director: Jerry Paris
Guest Stars: Wally Cox, George Tyne, Margaret Muse, Lia Waggner, Arthur Adams, Remo Pisani, James Henaghan, Jr., Kay Stewart, Holly Harris, Marilyn Hare, Lorna Thayer

Rob has second thoughts about running for city council after he meets his emminently more qualified opponent.

Wally Cox, TV's "Mr. Peepers" in the early 1950s, plays Rob's well-versed competitor, Lincoln Goodheart.

144 The Curse of the Petrie People February 2, 1966
Writers: Dale McRaven, Carl Kleinschmitt
Director: Jerry Paris
Guest Stars: Tom Tully, Isabel Randolph, Leon Belasco

Laura single-handedly destroys generations of Petrie family tradition when she accidentally crunches a garish heirloom brooch in the garbage disposal.

145 The Bottom of Mel Cooley's Heart February 9, 1966
Writer: John Whedon
Director: Jerry Paris
Guest Star: Carl Reiner

Mel loses his job after Rob convinces him to stand up to Alan Brady's bullying.

146   Remember the Alimony   February 16, 1966
   Writers: Dale McRaven, Carl Kleinschmitt
   Director: Jerry Paris
   Guest Stars: Lee Krieger, Allan Melvin, Don Diamond, Bernie
   Kopell, Shelah Hackett, Jose Nieto, Guillermo DeAnda

Rob and Laura recall a hectic trip to Mexico that almost spelled
the end of their new marriage.

147   Dear Sally Rogers   February 23, 1966
   Writer: Ronald Axe
   Director: Richard Erdman
   Guest Stars: Richard Schaal, Bill Idelson, Bert Remsen

Sally's televised plea for a husband on a late-night talk show
yields unexpected results—including a letter from Mr. Right.

This episode suggests one possible conclusion to the bittersweet saga
of Sally's oft-stalled love life when her secret admirer is revealed to be
Herman Glimscher.
   Dick Schaal plays talk-show host Stevie Parsons. The talented character actor would hit his stride a few years later as a recurring player
on "The Mary Tyler Moore Show" and its offspring.

148   Buddy Sorrell—Man and Boy   March 2, 1966
   Writers: Ben Joelson, Art Baer
   Director: Richard Erdman
   Guest Stars: Pippa Scott, Ed Peck, Arthur Ross Jones, Sheldon
   Golomb, Maria Sokolov

Buddy's strange behavior has Rob and Sally completely puzzled
until they discover he's been nervously preparing for his belated
bar mitzvah.

149   Bad Reception in Albany   March 9, 1966
   Writers: Garry Marshall, Jerry Belson
   Director: Jerry Paris
   Guest Stars: Bert Remsen, Tom D'Andrea, Joseph Mell, Johnny
   Haymer, Robert Nichols, Chanin Hale, Bella Bruck, Lorraine
   Bendix, Joyce Wellington, Tiny Brauer

Rob encounters endless difficulties at a hotel in Albany when
he tries to find a functioning TV set during the annual convention
of the Seals Lodge.

150 Talk to the Snail   March 23, 1966
   Writers: Jerry Belson, Garry Marshall
   Director: Jerry Paris
   Guest Stars: Paul Winchell, Henry Gibson, Carl Reiner

Fearing that network budget cuts might cost him his job, Rob interviews for a position as staff writer for a talking snail.

As Sally's date, Henry Gibson recites "Keep A-goin'," the poem that would be his trademark on NBC's "Laugh-In." Jellybean the Snail is brought to life by ventriloquist Paul Winchell.

151 A Day in the Life of Alan Brady   April 6, 1966
   Writer: Joseph Bonaduce
   Director: Jerry Paris
   Guest Stars: Carl Reiner, Kim Ford, Lou Wills, John Chulay, Joyce Jameson

Pandemonium results when Alan Brady arrives at Millie and Jerry's anniversary party with a documentary-film crew recording his every move.

Assistant director John C. Chulay has a cameo as the director of the documentary crew.

152 Obnoxious, Offensive, Egomaniac, Etc.   April 13, 1966
   Writers: Carl Kleinschmitt, Dale McRaven
   Director: Jerry Paris
   Guest Stars: Forrest Lewis, Carl Reiner

Rob, Buddy, and Sally try to retrieve a script that contains less-than-flattering descriptions of their arrogant boss before he has a chance to see it.

153 The Man From My Uncle   April 20, 1966
   Writers: Garry Marshall, Jerry Belson
   Director: Jerry Paris
   Guest Stars: Godfrey Cambridge, Biff Elliott, Steve Geray

The Petries' dull weekend is enlivened by the arrival of an unlikely secret agent, who wants to conduct a stakeout from Ritchie's bedroom.

154   You Ought to Be in Pictures   April 27, 1966
  Writer: Jack Winter
  Director: Jerry Paris
  Guest Stars: Michael Constantine, Jayne Massey, Frank Adamo

When Rob is cast opposite a voluptuous Italian in an underground film, Laura keeps a close watch on the star chemistry.

Jack Winter won a Writer's Guild Award for this script, which features Rob at his most endearing as a would-be actor who can barely stammer out a line and fumbles even worse when he's called on to kiss the beautiful starlet. Ever the dutiful husband, he first asks his wife, "May I?"

155   Love Thy Other Neighbor   May 4, 1966
  Writers: Dale McRaven, Carl Kleinschmitt
  Director: Jerry Paris
  Guest Stars: Joby Baker, Sue Taylor

Jerry and Millie fly into a jealous fit when Rob and Laura begin spending time with a new couple on the block.

Joby Baker, a favorite of writers Persky and Denoff, made his second appearance of the season in this episode. In 1967, the writers would co-star the actor in "Good Morning World," a series that bore distinct echoes of "Dick Van Dyke"—including a set design that afforded an unsettling glimpse of what the Petries' living room might have looked like in full color.

156   Long Night's Journey Into Day   May 11, 1966
  Writers: Jerry Belson, Garry Marshall
  Director: Jerry Paris
  Guest Star: Ogden Talbot

Laura and Millie spend a terrifying night with only a mynah bird to keep them company after Rob and Jerry go off for a weekend fishing trip.

157   The Gunslinger   May 25, 1966
  Writers: Bill Persky, Sam Denoff
  Director: Jerry Paris
  Guest Stars: Carl Reiner, Allan Melvin

Under Jerry's anesthetic, Rob dreams that he's a sheriff in the Old West, the only man who can save the town from the threat of Big Bad Brady.

For the last episode of the series filmed, the cast and crew allowed themselves the final indulgence of this irreverent parody of the Old West—a well-earned release of all the silly gags and priceless puns they managed to restrain during five seasons of the most deceptively disciplined comedy on television.

158 The Last Chapter June 1, 1966
Writers: Carl Reiner, Bill Persky, Sam Denoff
Directors: Jerry Paris, John Rich
Guest Stars: Carl Reiner, Dabbs Greer, Herbie Faye, Frank Adamo, Tiny Brauer, Greg Morris, Mimi Dillard

Laura excitedly reads the completed manuscript of Rob's autobiography, a comical look at the life and times of a TV comedy writer and his loving wife.

High points in the colorful saga of Rob and Laura Petrie are recounted in flashbacks of Rob's stuttering marriage proposal, his faltering stumble down the aisle, and Laura's eventful trip to the maternity ward. The show finally ends where it began, as Carl Reiner's Alan Brady announces his plan to produce and star in a TV show based on the real-life story of a TV comedy writer.

When "The Dick Van Dyke Show" voluntarily left the air in 1966, it had already distinguished itself as the most honored show of its time, and its demise would be lamented by viewers in living rooms all across the country. With intelligence and keen wit, the show proved that a sitcom for grown-ups could not only survive, it could thrive.

Thankfully, the lesson wasn't lost on the next generation of TV creators. When Mary Richards, Archie Bunker, and Barney Miller arrived to burst the floodgates of intelligent, meaningful TV comedy in the 1970s, all they had to do was fling open the door that Rob Petrie had so thoughtfully left ajar in 1966.

EMMY AWARDS

The following is a complete listing of the Emmy Awards bestowed on "The Dick Van Dyke Show" by the National Academy of Television Arts and Sciences.

1961/62 Outstanding Writing Achievement in Comedy

1962/63 Outstanding Program Achievement in the Field of Humor
Outstanding Writing Achievement in Comedy: Carl Reiner
Outstanding Directorial Achievement in Comedy: John Rich

1963/64 Outstanding Program Achievement in the Field of Comedy
Outstanding Continued Performance by an Actor in a Series (Lead): Dick Van Dyke
Outstanding Continued Performance by an Actress in a Series (Lead): Mary Tyler Moore
Outstanding Writing Achievement in Comedy or Variety: Carl Reiner, Sam Denoff, Bill Persky
Outstanding Directorial Achievement in Comedy: Jerry Paris

1964/65 Outstanding Program Achievement in Entertainment
Outstanding Individual Achievement in Entertainment (Actors and Performers): Dick Van Dyke

1965/66 Outstanding Comedy Series
Outstanding Continued Performance by an Actor in a Leading Role in a Comedy Series: Dick Van Dyke
Outstanding Continued Performance by an Actress in a Leading Role in a Comedy Series: Mary Tyler Moore
Outstanding Writing Achievement in Comedy: Bill Persky, Sam Denoff, "Coast-to-Coast Big Mouth"

"THE MARY TYLER MOORE SHOW"

Perhaps perkiness will save the world.
—JOHN LEONARD, TV critic

THANK GOD for *Thoroughly Modern Millie.*

If it hadn't been for that thoroughly forgettable 1967 Julie Andrews movie, America's most popular and critically acclaimed situation comedy might never have made it to our twelve-inch diagonally measured screens. The film is notable mainly because it featured the big-screen debut of Mary Tyler Moore, fresh from a successful five-year stint on the popular early sixties TV series "The Dick Van Dyke Show." Her beguiling characterization of the perky and impulsive Laura Petrie—she was just like Jackie Kennedy, except that *she* wasn't afraid to wear capri pants around the house—had earned her a matched set of Emmys while it established her as one of the most popular performers on television. By the time the series voluntarily left the air, Mary Tyler Moore was perched at the very top of the television industry.

But in 1966, none of that mattered to her. You see, what she *really* wanted was to be a musical-comedy star—a modern-day Ginger Rogers. The young actress didn't realize that the road to Forty-second Street, like the pathway to hell, was paved with good intentions.

Her first setback came when she starred in a Broadway musical version of Truman Capote's *Breakfast at Tiffany's.* Luckily, no one remembers it because it closed before lunch. Undaunted, the star was certain *Thor-*

oughly Modern Millie would be different. Hadn't Universal Pictures already begun its campaign to groom her for movie stardom? Weren't they starting her out as second lead in this big-budget musical spoof of the Roaring Twenties, starring Julie Andrews? How could it fail? Surely, she would never again face the daily grind of a weekly television series!

Unfortunately, what no one counted on was the public's widespread lack of interest in big-budget musical spoofs of the Roaring Twenties in 1967. The film didn't exactly catch fire; it just sort of fumed. And Mary's fantasy of becoming a latter-day Ginger Rogers was fading very, very quickly.

Meanwhile, the CBS-TV network was having troubles of its own. By the late 1960s, the network had developed a highly successful prime-time schedule that relied heavily on corn-pone silliness like "Petticoat Junction," "Green Acres," and "Gomer Pyle." Though they all delivered consistently high ratings, it was clear to the advertisers of that era that CBS's hayseed comedies weren't being watched by the audience that the ad men most wanted to reach—the urban men and women who annually spend much more money on the sponsor's products than do their country cousins. In order to keep Madison Avenue happy, CBS desperately needed to upgrade their programming image by replacing the scent of hush puppies and haywagons with the more profitable fragrance of urbane, sophisticated, adult entertainment.

Enter Mary Tyler Moore.

In 1969, her screen career having steadfastly refused to move out of first gear, she agreed to return to CBS for a musical-comedy special that reunited her with her old friend and mentor, Dick Van Dyke. The special was very well received. Quicker than you can say "I Love Lucy," CBS realized all over again that Mary Tyler Moore was a potential gold mine. Here was a star who could attract the bright, upscale audience they so desperately wanted to reach.

Suddenly, the network was willing to forgive her string of unmemorable movies—even the one in which she played a nun in love with Elvis Presley—if only she would return to CBS in a brand-new sitcom. They offered her the moon atop the Hollywood Hills, gambling that lightning would strike twice and the network would end up with another "Dick Van Dyke Show."

Mary wasn't so sure. She knew as well as anyone that the success of the original Dick Van Dyke series resulted from a rare confluence of talent that would be very difficult to duplicate. Where would she find a tightly knit ensemble of veteran actors and writers capable of creating a sophisticated and witty adult situation comedy in an era when "The

Beverly Hillbillies" regularly rode shotgun over the weekly Nielsen ratings?

But still, the specter of *Thoroughly Modern Millie* hovered over the star's perky and impulsive brow.

She consulted her husband, Grant Tinker, a successful executive at Twentieth Century–Fox. Together, they came up with a solution. She would return to CBS in a new sitcom, but only on the condition that she and Tinker maintain total responsibility for creating, casting, and producing the series. Only in an atmosphere free of network interference could they reasonably expect to create a truly original series for prime-time television. CBS happily agreed, and in any event, they were in no position to argue. And so, "The Mary Tyler Moore Show" was announced on the CBS lineup for fall 1970.

Tinker and Moore wasted no time inaugurating MTM Productions, a production house where the new series would grow and flourish in a creative environment that was unique in television. To create the new show's format and produce the series, Tinker hired two young writers, James L. Brooks and Allan Burns. Brooks, a former CBS newswriter, had created "Room 222" for ABC the year before, a warm classroom comedy set in a somewhat idealized inner-city high school. Burns had a varied background in Hollywood. After a rocky start writing Bullwinkle cartoons, he'd written scripts for "Get Smart" and CBS's landmark sitcom "He and She." Ironically, he was also co-creator of "My Mother the Car," a series that is probably as reviled as "Mary Tyler Moore" is revered.

It's impossible to say whether Tinker knew then that this most unlikely pair would create one of television's all-time classics, but there's no doubt he had confidence in the team from the very start. When CBS program executives objected to his offbeat choice of producers and suggested he hire a more reliable creative team, Tinker refused to waver—an early indication of the strong executive leadership that Tinker himself feels was his single most important contribution to the eventual success of the fledgling production company.

For the format of "The Mary Tyler Moore Show," the producers created a pastiche that contained echoes of practically every great sitcom ever aired. Like "The Dick Van Dyke Show," the new series would feature a dual emphasis on the leading character's home and work environments—with a strong family of ensemble players in both settings. Like "The Honeymooners," Mary's new show would be filmed on very few sets before a live audience—a luxury that allowed the performers to develop an ensemble that more closely resembled a theatrical rep-

ertory troupe than a TV factory. Like any truly original work, "The Mary
Tyler Moore Show" was a hybrid of great ideas that had come before,
infused with freshness and inspiration enough to allow it to forge ahead
into unknown territory.

Next, Tinker, Brooks, and Burns cast an inspired—and largely unknown—group of character actors to fill the roles Brooks and Burns had
created. Valerie Harper, Ed Asner, Gavin MacLeod, Cloris Leachman,
and Ted Knight formed the nucleus of this actors' ensemble—and each
of them would probably agree they did some of the best work of their
careers on the show.

Finally, and perhaps most significantly, Tinker and his producers
hired a roster of young and talented writers—many of them women—
all of whom were familiar enough with authentic human behavior to
portray the characters as real, believable people. In Mary's Minneapolis,
it was decided, they would banish the sitcom zombies that ran rampant
through the towns and cities of practically every other comedy on television.

And so, MTM Productions was born. By bringing together such a
formidable group of talented writers, performers, and directors—and
then building a framework that made it easy for each one of them to
contribute their very best work—Tinker and Moore had secured a running start toward creative success long before the first episode was even
filmed.

When the show finally premiered on Saturday, September 19, 1970,
there was little doubt in anyone's mind that "The Mary Tyler Moore
Show" was not just another sitcom. Clearly, this show heralded a new
commitment to television entertainment that took as a given the intelligence and experience of an adult audience—an audience that had been
largely ignored by network programmers during the previous decade.

The first few bars of the opening theme song set the tone for the
series and gave a clue that this show would indeed be different. For the
first time ever, television was going to show us a beautiful young woman
who was single—not by chance, but by choice.

> How will you make it on your own?
> This world is awfully big,
> and, girl, this time you're all alone . . .

Ironically, the creators of the show had originally planned to make
Mary Richards a recently divorced woman who strikes out on her own.
But, in one of the few instances where the network did manage to exert
influence on the series, CBS insisted that Mary Richards be an unmarried

single girl. Apparently they felt the American audience wasn't yet ready to laugh at a sitcom based on the comic possibilities in the life of a divorced woman. And besides, they reasoned, wouldn't people remember Mary as Laura Petrie and think she had really just divorced Dick Van Dyke?

Whatever the reason for the adjustment, changing Mary to a single woman who freely chooses her independence made for a much more interesting and contemporary character. This is borne out in a marvelous scene from the premiere episode where the boyfriend who has jilted Mary arrives in Minneapolis to talk her out of her foolhardy plan to move into the city to start a new life on her own. It's clear that Mary still has her doubts about the move, and at least a part of her hopes her old boyfriend will provide the easy answer of a marriage proposal.

But when the manipulative Lothario proves unable even to speak the words "I love you," Mary realizes his only interest in getting her back is to salvage his own ego. In that moment of painful recognition, she finds the strength finally to end the affair. "Take care of yourself," he blurts out, as she ushers him into the hallway. "I think I just did" is her parting shot as she closes the door on her past, ready to begin a new life without ever looking back.

The scene is a masterpiece of comic surprise and invention. Mary's confrontation with the man from her past is unexpected. And even when we eventually see where the scene is inexorably headed, we are so wrapped up in the drama of the situation that we remain engrossed until Mary's final, pivotal line. We are surprised, amused, and touched— all at the same time. Suddenly we feel a kinship with this confused, vulnerable, and ultimately wise young woman. In an instant, we can see that there's a little bit of Mary Richards in all of us.

The eloquence of that one short scene is typical of the skill and subtlety that the writers, performers, and directors unfailingly brought to the show. The scene also serves to demonstrate what must have been the unwritten dictum of everyone connected with the series: When in doubt, have the character act like a real person.

From the very start, the characters on "The Mary Tyler Moore Show" always behaved like real people, and the situations they found themselves in, no matter how absurd, were always plausible. And that's what made the world of Mary's Minneapolis such a compelling and completely believable place. It was a world that often looked a lot like the one we live in, with all the confusion, embarrassments—and yes, the unexpected joys—intact.

All of which goes a long way toward explaining the almost universal acclaim that was lavished on "The Mary Tyler Moore Show" throughout its long run—and, thanks to syndication, continues even today.

Remarkably, the writing, directing, and performances on the show never diminished over the entire seven years the series was on the air. On the contrary, as the critical episode guide that follows demonstrates in great detail, the series never stopped developing and maturing. Eventually, the show reached a peak of sophistication in theme, performance, and subject matter that had never been attempted in television comedy before. Indeed, to this day, "The Mary Tyler Moore Show" remains the benchmark for judging quality television entertainment programming of any kind.

A Critical Guide to All 168 Episodes

REGULAR CAST

Mary Richards	Mary Tyler Moore
Lou Grant	Ed Asner
Rhoda Morgenstern	Valerie Harper
Murray Slaughter	Gavin MacLeod
Ted Baxter	Ted Knight
Phyllis Lindstrom	Cloris Leachman
Georgette Franklin Baxter	Georgia Engel
Sue Ann Nivens	Betty White

SUPPORTING CAST

Ida Morgenstern (Rhoda's mother)	Nancy Walker
Martin Morgenstern (Rhoda's father)	Harold Gould
Marie Slaughter	Joyce Bulifant
Bess Lindstrom	Lisa Gerritsen
Edie Grant (Lou's wife)	Priscilla Morrill
Gordy the Weatherman	John Amos
Dottie Richards (Mary's mother)	Nanette Fabray
Walter Richards (Mary's father)	Bill Quinn
Flo Meredith (Mary's aunt)	Eileen Heckart
David Baxter (Ted's son)	Robbie Rist

Created by James L. Brooks, Allan Burns
Music by Pat Williams
Theme song ("Love Is All Around") written and sung by Sonny Curtis
Directors of photography were Paul Uhl, William T. Cline
Principal director was Jay Sandrich

1970/71   THE FIRST SEASON

Year-End Rating: 20.3 (22d place)

Mary's first season on CBS finds her settling into Minneapolis and the WJM newsroom, with an equal emphasis on the trials and tribulations she and Rhoda face as contemporary single women in their thirties. Many of these episodes are written with the knowing eye of Treva Silverman, who, along with James L. Brooks and Allan Burns, David Davis and Lorenzo Music, and Steve Pritzker, wrote most of the scripts aired during the first season.

Jay Sandrich becomes firmly established as the series's most prominent director, a role he will hold for the next seven years. David Davis is producer for the first two seasons, assisted by his partner, Lorenzo Music. The show's creators, James L. Brooks and Allan Burns, serve as executive producers for the run of the series.

1   Love Is All Around   September 19, 1970
Writers: James L. Brooks, Allan Burns
Director: Jay Sandrich
Guest Stars: Angus Duncan, Dave Morick

Mary Richards gets a fresh start in Minneapolis when she moves into a new apartment and takes a job as associate producer of the city's bottom-rated TV news show.

The show had been in preproduction for nine months by the time this episode aired. Producer Allan Burns recently recalled that this gestation period, so rare in television, contributed immeasurably to the overall quality of the series because it allowed the producers time to refine and adjust the backlog of scripts to reflect new developments as the series evolved.

This premiere episode offers ample evidence of just how sharp the series was from the very start. Already, the characters are well rounded enough to carry a number of classic scenes, not the least of which depicts Mary's WJM job interview. Here Mary first experiences Lou Grant's peculiar worldview when he tells her she's got spunk . . . and he *hates* spunk.

2   Today I Am a Ma'am   September 26, 1970
Writer: Treva Silverman
Director: Jay Sandrich
Guest Stars: Richard Schaal, Jack DeMave, Sheila Wells

When a man in his twenties addresses Mary as "ma'am," she panics at the prospect of being an old maid; finally she and Rhoda invite two unlikely bachelors over for dinner, one of whom brings his wife!

This episode features Richard Schaal's first guest appearance. Schaal, then Valerie Harper's real-life husband, got his start at Chicago's Second City improvisational theater in the 1960s and later worked with his wife in *Paul Sills' Story Theatre*. He would appear semiregularly on "Mary Tyler Moore" throughout the first few seasons, invariably playing one of Mary's, uh, "less sensitive" suitors.

This was also the first episode written by Treva Silverman, one of the many women who would script for the show and also one of the most prolific writers for the series. Though Silverman contributed many uniformly strong scripts essential to the development of the series and its characters, she is best remembered as the author of the many early episodes that explored and defined the friendship of Mary and Rhoda.

There always seemed to be a sting of truth in those early scripts that centered on the pair's struggles to find success and gain independence as two thirtyish single women. Silverman invested her observations of these often painful situations with an authenticity that had rarely been seen on sitcoms—and has been seen far too infrequently since.

This humorous approach to looking at the ways we cope with all the painful indignities of everyday life became the comic philosophy of "The Mary Tyler Moore Show" and was eventually adopted as the house style for all MTM Productions.

3   Bess, You Is My Daughter Now   October 3, 1970
Writer: John D. F. Black
Director: Jay Sandrich

When Mary is asked to baby-sit for Phyllis, she soon finds herself losing a friend and gaining a daughter.

4   Divorce Isn't Everything   October 10, 1970
Writer: Treva Silverman
Director: Alan Rafkin
Guest Stars: Shelley Berman, Jane Connell, Pat Finley, Dave Ketchum, Gino Conforti, Vernon Weddle

Rhoda and Mary deceptively join a group of divorced singles to qualify for a cut-rate trip to Europe.

Another painfully funny Treva Silverman script. This time Silverman takes the desperation shared by members of a support group for divorced people and milks it for every laugh. The fact that Mary and Rhoda seem willing to exploit these people just so that they can save money on a vacation only makes the situation even more painful—and that much funnier. The dark humor of the mildly maladjusted therapy group is territory that was to be mined more fully on MTM's "The Bob Newhart Show."

5   Keep Your Guard Up   October 17, 1970
Writer: Steve Pritzker
Director: Alan Rafkin
Guest Stars: John Schuck, Tim Brown

A sensitive but incompetent ex-football player wants a job as WJM's sportscaster and won't leave Mary alone until he gets it.

6   Support Your Local Mother   October 24, 1970
Writers: James L. Brooks, Allan Burns
Director: Alan Rafkin
Guest Star: Nancy Walker

Rhoda's mother pays a visit but ends up spending all her time with Mary when her daughter refuses to see her.

Incredibly, CBS initially refused to allow this script to be shot, insisting that a story about a daughter who turns her back on her mother was not suitable for a comedy. "Their hair turned white," Allan Burns told journalist Paul Weingarten. "They said 'This is not funny. You can't shoot this show. You can't.' " The writers finally appealed to Grant Tinker, who calmly okayed the script, despite the network veto. Later, this classic episode—one of the funniest of all the early scripts—went on to earn an Emmy Award for writers Brooks and Burns.

7   Toulouse-Lautrec Is One of My   October 31, 1970
       Favorite Artists
Writers: Lloyd Turner, Gordon Mitchell
Director: Jay Sandrich
Guest Star: Hamilton Camp

Mary's fledgling romance with a professional writer hits a snag when she discovers she's at least a foot taller than he is.

8   The Snow Must Go On   November 7, 1970
Writers: David Davis, Lorenzo Music
Director: Jay Sandrich
Guest Stars: Richard Schaal, Ivor Francis, Robert Rothwell

The WJM newsroom is snowbound, and Mary faces the challenge of producing an up-to-the-minute election broadcast without any incoming results.

9   Bob and Rhoda and Teddy and Mary   November 14, 1970
Writer: Bob Rodgers
Director: Peter Baldwin
Guest Stars: Greg Mullavey, Henry Corden

It's professional glory but personal strife for Mary when she's nominated for a Teddy Award at the same time that Rhoda's new boyfriend seems more attracted to her than to Rhoda.

The first of many shows to revolve around the durable premise of a local Minneapolis broadcast award, the Teddy. Here the comic potential of the Ted Baxter character is in full swing as he is once again left at the starting gate in the Teddy derby.

Guest star Greg Mullavey would later appear as Mary Hartman's husband in Norman Lear's soap opera spoof, "Mary Hartman, Mary Hartman."

10   Assistant Wanted, Female   November 21, 1970
Writer: Treva Silverman
Director: Peter Baldwin
Guest Star: John Amos

Mary unwisely hires Phyllis as her new assistant.

John Amos debuts as Gordy the Weatherman in the first of many appearances. The show's creators thought it would be funny to have a black weatherman at a time when most blacks in broadcasting were still relegated to the sports booth. Amos later achieved far greater fame as the star of Norman Lear's "Good Times," as well as in the immensely popular miniseries "Roots."

11   1040 or Fight   November 28, 1970
   Writers: David Davis, Lorenzo Music
   Director: Jay Sandrich
   Guest Star: Paul Sand

Mary's tax return is audited by a romantically inclined IRS man.

The auditor is played by Paul Sand, though the part was originally tailored for the talents of Bob Newhart. Writers Music and Davis were undaunted when the nightclub comic passed on the role—they would get a second chance two years later when they created and produced "The Bob Newhart Show" for MTM.

And Paul Sand was certainly a worthy substitute. Yet another talented comic actor who—like Valerie Harper and Ed Asner—got his start with improvisational theater director Paul Sills in Chicago. In 1974, Sand also landed his own MTM series, when Jim Brooks and Allan Burns created the highly regarded, but short-lived "Paul Sand in Friends and Lovers."

12   Anchorman Overboard   December 5, 1970
   Writer: Lorenzo Music
   Director: Jay Sandrich
   Guest Star: Bill Fiore

Mary tries to bolster Ted's sagging confidence after he bombs at a women's-club speaking engagement.

Mary's role as den mother to the WJM staff is by now firmly established in this first of many episodes to explore her paradoxical, but characteristically protective attitude toward the newsroom's terror, Ted Baxter.

13   He's All Yours   December 12, 1970
   Writer: Bob Rodgers
   Director: Jay Sandrich
   Guest Star: Wes Stern

A young cameraman is so enchanted with Mary that he invents tall tales of their romantic involvement.

14   Christmas and the Hard-Luck Kid   December 19, 1970
   Writers: James L. Brooks, Allan Burns
   Director: Jay Sandrich
   Guest Star: Ned Wertimer

Depressed because she has to work on Christmas Day, Mary tries to create some yuletide spirit in the WJM newsroom.

15 Howard's Girl   January 2, 1971
  Writer: Treva Silverman
  Director: Jay Sandrich
  Guest Stars: Richard Schaal, Henry Jones, Mary Jackson

Mary dates her former boyfriend's brother, much to the consternation of his parents.

16 Party Is Such Sweet Sorrow   January 9, 1971
  Writer: Martin Cohan
  Director: Jay Sandrich
  Guest Star: Dick Clair

Mary faces the prospect of leaving WJM when she's offered a promotion by a rival station.

17 Just a Lunch   January 16, 1971
  Writers: James L. Brooks, Allan Burns
  Director: Bruce Bilson
  Guest Stars: Monte Markham, Joyce Bulifant

Mary becomes involved with a charming newsman—the only problem is, he's married.

Joyce Bulifant makes her first appearance in the semiregular role of Marie Slaughter, Murray's faithful and understanding wife. The faithful and understanding wife is the most thankless role in television, but Bulifant held her own throughout all six remaining seasons. Before signing on with MTM, she had been a regular on Bill Cosby's first NBC sitcom, "The Bill Cosby Show."

18 Second-Story Story   January 23, 1971
  Writer: Steve Pritzker
  Director: Jay Sandrich
  Guest Stars: Bob Dishy, Burt Mustin, Vic Tayback

Mary is the victim of a rare Minneapolis crime spree when her apartment is burglarized twice in as many days.

19 We Closed in Minneapolis   January 30, 1971
Writers: Kenny Solms, Gail Parent
Director: Jay Sandrich
Guest Star: Elliot Street

Murray is given good news, and bad—his play about life in a newsroom is finally going to be produced, but Ted Baxter will play a featured role.

20 Hi!   February 6, 1971
Writer: Treva Silverman
Director: Jay Sandrich
Guest Stars: Pat Carroll, Bruce Kirby, Robert Casper

When Mary is hospitalized for a minor operation, she finds that even *her* sunny disposition can't dispel the clouds that hang over her curmudgeonly roommate.

Veteran actress Pat Carroll, late of "The Danny Thomas Show," portrays the disagreeable patient.

21 The Boss Isn't Coming to Dinner   February 13, 1971
Writers: David Davis, Lorenzo Music
Director: Jay Sandrich
Guest Star: Paul Micale

Mary is shocked to learn that Lou and his wife, Edie, are separating.

Though the series didn't really tackle Lou's divorce for another two years, the seeds of compassion that Mary will feel for Mr. Grant are very clearly planted in this episode. The writers probably didn't realize it then, but they were setting the stage for what was to become one of the most graceful love affairs in popular fiction—the unconsummated romance of Mary Richards and Lou Grant.

22 A Friend in Deed   February 20, 1971
Writer: Susan Silver
Director: Jay Sandrich
Guest Star: Pat Finley

Mary's long-forgotten childhood friend arrives and begins ingratiating herself with each of Mary's newsroom friends.

Pat Finley would later play Bob's sister, Ellen, on "The Bob Newhart Show."

23 Smokey the Bear Wants You   February 27, 1971
Writer: Steve Pritzker
Director: Jay Sandrich
Guest Star: Michael Callan

Rhoda falls in love with a successful businessman who plans to drop out of society and sign up as a forest ranger.

24 The Forty-five-Year-Old Man   March 6, 1971
Writer: George Kirgo
Director: Herbert Kenwith
Guest Stars: Slim Pickens, Richard Libertini, Richard Roat

Lou Grant is the scapegoat when the show's ratings falter, but Mary tries to convince WJM's eccentric station owner to give him his job back.

Western character actor Slim Pickens plays the cowboy station owner with such reckless abandon, it's a pity his character was used only as a one shot in this single episode.

1971/72   THE SECOND SEASON

Year-End Rating: 23.7 (10th place)

As the series enters its second season, plots that offer insight into the personalities of the regular characters set the stage for the strong ensemble company that will be in full flower by the middle of the following year.

David Davis continues as producer, and Jay Sandrich shares directing chores with Peter Baldwin and Jerry Paris. Primary writers for the season are David Davis, Lorenzo Music, Treva Silverman, Susan Silver, and Steve Pritzker.

25 The Birds . . . And . . . Um . . . Bees   September 18, 1971
Writer: Treva Silverman
Director: Jay Sandrich
Guest Star: Lisa Gerritsen

Phyllis decides that Mary is the person best suited to tell her daughter, Bess, the facts of life.

26   I Am Curious Cooper   September 25, 1971
Writers: David Davis, Lorenzo Music
Director: Jay Sandrich
Guest Stars: Michael Constantine, Shizuko Iwamatsu

Lou plays Cupid when he tries to orchestrate a romance between Mary and one of his middle-aged friends.

27   He's No Heavy, He's My Brother   October 2, 1971
Writer: Allan Burns
Director: Jerry Paris
Guest Star: Frank Ramirez

When Mary and Rhoda decide to take a midwinter vacation in Mexico, they get involved in a mysterious plot involving the owner of a Mexican restaurant.

This episode represented a creative family reunion of sorts. Director Jerry Paris played the next-door neighbor and directed many classic episodes of "The Dick Van Dyke Show." He would later sign on as director of "Happy Days," Garry Marshall's long-running hit.

28   Room 223   October 9, 1971
Writer: Susan Silver
Director: Jay Sandrich
Guest Stars: Michael Tolan, Florida Friebus, Val Bisoglio

Mary dates her professor in a night-school class.

Handsome Dan Whitfield, played by Michael Tolan, was one of Mary's more persistent suitors. He would return, still carrying a torch, as late as the sixth season.

29   A Girl's Best Mother Is Not Her Friend   October 16, 1971
Writers: David Davis, Lorenzo Music
Director: Jay Sandrich
Guest Star: Nancy Walker

Rhoda's mother returns, and this time she's determined to be friends with her daughter.

Writers David Davis and Lorenzo Music continue to expand the comic possibilities of Rhoda's character. The groundwork they lay here will serve them well in 1974 when they produce the successful spin-off series "Rhoda."

30 Cover Boy October 23, 1971
Writer: Treva Silverman
Director: Jay Sandrich
Guest Star: Jack Cassidy

Ted tries to impress his visiting brother, Hal, by pretending Mary is his sweetheart.

In his portrayal of Ted's brother, Jack Cassidy draws heavily on Oscar North, the arrogant actor he played in the highly regarded CBS series "He and She." In fact, there are enough echoes of Oscar North in the character of Ted Baxter himself to suggest that the creators of MTM drew at least a passing inspiration from that short-lived 1967 series. Of course, it's not exactly an airtight case of creative larceny, since most of "Mary Tyler Moore's" creative staff also labored on "He and She," including director Jay Sandrich, writers David Davis and Allan Burns, as well as the writer of this particular episode, Treva Silverman.

31 Didn't You Used to Be . . . Wait . . . October 30, 1971
Don't Tell Me!
Writer: Allan Burns
Director: Jay Sandrich
Guest Stars: Richard Schaal, Jack Riley, Kermit Murdock, Ron Masak, Pippa Scott

Mary learns you can never go home again when she attends her high school reunion and runs into her old boyfriend Howard Arnell.

Jack Riley is featured in his first MTM guest slot. His excellent timing and delivery were particularly well suited to the MTM style, and he was later used to good advantage in the role of Elliot Carlin on MTM's "The Bob Newhart Show."

32 Thoroughly Unmilitant Mary November 6, 1971
Writer: Martin Cohan
Director: Jay Sandrich
Guest Stars: Dick Balduzzi, Larry Gelman, Paul Micale

The WJM newsroom goes on strike, leaving Mary and Lou to produce the entire show by themselves.

33 And Now, Sitting in for Ted Baxter   November 13, 1971
Writer: Steve Pritzker
Director: Jerry Paris
Guest Stars: Jed Allen, Bill Woodson

Ted is worried about his job security when he sees the more competent anchorman who is brought in as his vacation replacement.

34 Don't Break the Chain   November 20, 1971
Writers: David Davis, Lorenzo Music
Director: Jerry Paris
Guest Stars: Jack DeMave, Gino Conforti

Mary must decide whether to answer a chain letter sent to her by Lou.

35 The Six-and-a-Half-Year Itch   November 27, 1971
Writer: Treva Silverman
Director: Jay Sandrich
Guest Stars: Lawrence Pressman, Elizabeth Berger

Lou suspects his son-in-law of philandering when he spots him at a movie with a strange woman.

36 . . . Is a Friend in Need   December 4, 1971
Writer: Susan Silver
Director: Jay Sandrich
Guest Star: Beverly Sanders

When Rhoda loses her job as a department-store window dresser, Mary tries to help her land another one.

37 The Square-Shaped Room   December 11, 1971
Writer: Susan Silver
Director: Jay Sandrich

Mary talks Lou into letting Rhoda redecorate his house, though he soon lives to regret it.

38   Ted Over Heels   December 18, 1971
Writers: David Davis, Lorenzo Music
Director: Peter Baldwin
Guest Star: Arlene Golonka

Ted develops a crush on the daughter of Chuckles the Clown.

Guest star Arlene Golonka has appeared in scores of sitcom episodes since the late 1960s, when she had a featured role on "The Andy Griffith Show."

39   The Five-Minute Dress   January 1, 1972
Writers: Pat Nardo, Gloria Banta
Director: Jay Sandrich

Mary's new boyfriend is a politician who can't seem to find time in his schedule to see her.

40   Feeb   January 8, 1972
Writers: Dick Clair, Jenna McMahon
Director: Peter Baldwin
Guest Star: Barbara Sharma

Mary feels guilty when she causes an incompetent waitress to be fired, so she hires the girl to work in the newsroom.

Director Peter Baldwin had previously worked with Mary Tyler Moore when both starting out on "The Dick Van Dyke Show" in the early 1960s.

41   The Slaughter Affair   January 15, 1972
Writer: Rick Mittleman
Director: Peter Baldwin
Guest Star: Joyce Bulifant

When Murray takes a second job to buy his wife, Marie, an anniversary present, she suspects he's having an affair with Mary.

42   Baby Sitcom   January 22, 1972
Writer: Treva Silverman
Director: Jay Sandrich
Guest Stars: Joshua Bryant, Leslie Graves

Mary has to back out of an agreement to baby-sit Bess, she talks Lou into pinch-hitting for her.

43 More Than Neighbors   January 29, 1972
Writer: Steve Pritzker
Director: Jay Sandrich
Guest Star: Jack Bender

Mary and Rhoda try to talk Ted out of becoming their neighbor when he decides to move into their building.

44 The Care and Feeding of Parents   February 5, 1972
Writers: Dick Clair, Jenna McMahon
Director: Jay Sandrich
Guest Stars: Jon Locke, Brad Trumbull

Mary finds herself playing literary agent for an eleven-year-old after Phyllis hears her glowing over Bess's school composition.

45 Where There's Smoke, There's Rhoda   February 12, 1972
Writer: Martin Cohan
Director: Peter Baldwin

After Rhoda's apartment is destroyed by a fire, Mary offers to put her up for a few days—a favor that nearly ruins their friendship.

46 You Certainly Are a Big Boy   February 19, 1972
Writer: Martin Cohan
Director: Jay Sandrich
Guest Stars: Bradford Dillman, John Rubinstein, Beverly Saunders

Mary is unnerved to discover that the handsome architect she's been dating has a son who's practically her age.

47 Some of My Best Friends Are Rhoda   February 26, 1972
Writer: Steve Pritzker
Director: Peter Baldwin
Guest Star: Mary Frann

Mary forms a fast kinship with a woman she meets in a minor traffic accident, but the friendship sours when Mary discovers the woman is prejudiced.

An atypical foray into the Norman Lear social-consciousness arena, this episode delves into Mary's staunch liberalism—and Rhoda's Jewishness—two themes that weren't often confronted in such a head-on fashion. A comparison between MTM's humanist approach to politics and the more didactic approach adopted by Norman Lear for his contemporary sitcoms would make an interesting study indeed.

A decade later, Mary Frann would play Bob Newhart's second TV wife on "Newhart."

48 His Two Right Arms   March 4, 1972
Writers: Jim Parker, Arnold Margolin
Director: Jay Sandrich
Guest Stars: Bill Daily, Carol Androsky, Janet MacLachlan, Wally Taylor, Isabel Sanford, Patrick Campbell

Mary schedules an ignorant politician on a WJM talk show and then tries to groom him so that he doesn't make a complete fool of himself.

This episode was designed as a pilot for a proposed spin-off series that was to star Bill Daily as befuddled politician Pete Peterson. When that series failed to sell, MTM producers wisely tapped the talented actor for the role of Howard Borden, the equally befuddled navigator on "The Bob Newhart Show."

1972/73   THE THIRD SEASON

Year-End Rating: 23.6 (7th place)

The characters are by now so familiar that the writers are able to base many episodes on previously unknown facets of their personalities—Murray's occasional feelings of inadequacy; Rhoda's newly blossomed beauty; and, of course, Mary's slowly maturing relationships with the men in her life. Even Ted Baxter is taken more seriously when he gets involved with Georgette, a new addition to the regular cast during the third season.

Ed. Weinberger signs on to produce in a season that features scripts from the widest variety of writers yet, including primary contributions from Weinberger, Dick Clair and Jenna McMahon, Martin Cohan, as well as the occasional gem from regulars Steve Pritzker and Treva Silverman, who also serves as story editor.

49   The Good-Time News   September 16, 1972
    Writers: James L. Brooks, Allan Burns
    Director: Hal Cooper
    Guest Stars: Robert Hogan, John Amos

Lou cringes when Mary is assigned to develop a new happy-talk format for "The Six O'Clock News."

50   What Is Mary Richards Really Like?   September 23, 1972
    Writer: Susan Silver
    Director: Jerry Belson
    Guest Star: Peter Haskell

Mary dates a muckraking columnist who happens to be doing a story on her.

Director Jerry Belson was one of the staff writers of "The Dick Van Dyke Show," and a co-creator, with Garry Marshall, of TV's "Odd Couple."

51   Who's in Charge Here?   September 30, 1972
    Writer: Martin Cohan
    Director: Jay Sandrich

Confusion ensues when Lou is promoted to program director and Murray is put in charge of the newsroom.

52   Enter Rhoda's Parents   October 7, 1972
    Writer: Martin Cohan
    Director: Jay Sandrich
    Guest Stars: Nancy Walker, Harold Gould, Leanna Roberts

Rhoda's parents come for a visit and end up tackling their marital difficulties.

Harold Gould and Nancy Walker continued to play Rhoda's parents on Valerie Harper's spin-off series, "Rhoda," in 1974.

53   It's Whether You Win or Lose   October 14, 1972
    Writer: Martin Donovan
    Director: Jay Sandrich
    Guest Star: Patrick Campbell

Mary arranges a friendly poker game for the newsroom staff, only to discover that Murray has a compulsive gambling streak.

54 Rhoda the Beautiful   October 21, 1972
Writer: Treva Silverman
Director: Jay Sandrich

Rhoda, still lacking confidence in her looks even after she's lost twenty pounds, is chosen to compete in a store-sponsored beauty contest.

Treva Silverman confronts Rhoda's metamorphosis from a pudgy duckling to an attractive single woman with a script that is so sensitive to the character's emotional plight that it is both funny and surprisingly touching at the same time.

55 Just Around the Corner   October 28, 1972
Writer: Steve Pritzker
Director: Jay Sandrich
Guest Stars: Nanette Fabray, Bill Quinn

Mary is apprehensive when her parents move to Minneapolis to be near her.

Nanette Fabray and Bill Quinn were brought in as semiregulars to play Mary's parents, but judging by how few episodes the writers were able to work them into, it must have been clear early on that they had no real need for the characters. They were never seen after the third season.

56 But Seriously, Folks   November 4, 1972
Writer: Phil Mishkin
Director: Peter Baldwin
Guest Stars: Jerry Van Dyke, John Fox

Mary tries to help a frustrated comedian who has higher aspirations than writing material for Chuckles the Clown.

Van Dyke appeared with Mary Tyler Moore a decade earlier as an occasional guest star on his brother's series "The Dick Van Dyke Show."

57 Farmer Ted and the News   November 11, 1972
Writer: Martin Donovan
Director: Jay Sandrich
Guest Star: Lurene Tuttle

Ted becomes a pitchman on local TV commercials, to the chagrin of Lou and the rest of the newsroom staff.

58   Have I Found a Guy for You   November 18, 1972
Writer: Charlotte Brown
Director: Hal Cooper
Guest Stars: Bert Convy, Beth Howland

Mary is faced with an awkward situation when two married friends split up and she finds out the husband is interested in her.

59   You've Got a Friend   November 25, 1972
Writer: Steve Pritzker
Director: Jerry Belson
Guest Stars: Nanette Fabray, Bill Quinn

When Mary's father retires, she decides he should form a new friendship—with Lou.

60   It Was Fascination, I Know   December 2, 1972
Writer: Ed. Weinberger
Director: Jay Sandrich
Guest Stars: Gerald Michenaud, Lisa Gerritsen

Mary unwittingly gets involved in an odd triangle with Phyllis's daughter, Bess.

An early "Mary" script by Ed. Weinberger, who—with partner Stan Daniels—would write and produce many of the finest episodes of the series. Weinberger joined MTM after writing and producing Bill Cosby's first NBC sitcom, the softspoken and intelligent "Bill Cosby Show." In 1978, Weinberger and Daniels would team up with Jim Brooks and Dave Davis to create "Taxi" for ABC.

61   Operation: Lou   December 9, 1972
Writers: Elias Davis, David Pollack
Director: Jay Sandrich
Guest Stars: Florida Friebus, Michael McGinnis

Lou undergoes minor surgery and reluctantly leaves the newsroom in Mary's tentative care.

62   Rhoda Morgenstern: Minneapolis   December 16, 1972
         to New York
Writer: Treva Silverman
Director: Jay Sandrich
Guest Stars: Jack Riley, Robert Casper

Rhoda decides to move back to New York City but has second thoughts when all her friends arrive for a farewell party.

This episode introduces the character of Georgette Franklin, played by Georgia Engel. Though Rhoda's exit from the show didn't actually occur for another two seasons, the producers were aware they'd have to build a second generation of supporting players if they were to keep the series strong over the long haul. The introduction of Georgette as a love interest for Ted Baxter indicated yet another radical shift: The show's creators were finally going to build Ted into something more than pure comic relief.

63 The Courtship of Mary's December 23, 1972
 Father's Daughter
Writers: Elias Davis, David Pollack
Director: Jay Sandrich
Guest Stars: Michael Tolan, Barra Grant, Steve Franken, Bill Quinn, Gordon Jump, Arthur Abelson

When Mary attends the engagement party of an old boyfriend, she ends up on the receiving end of his awkward proposal.

64 Lou's Place January 6, 1973
Writer: Ed. Weinberger
Director: Jay Sandrich
Guest Stars: Dick Balduzzi, Jack Spritt, Arthur Abelson, Lew Horn

Lou goes into partnership with Ted to buy their own bar, but it fails miserably.

65 My Brother's Keeper January 13, 1973
Writers: Dick Clair, Jenna McMahon
Director: Jay Sandrich
Guest Star: Robert Moore

Phyllis is surprised when her visiting brother seems more interested in Rhoda than Mary, though it never occurs to her that he's gay.

Gay rights groups applauded the show for presenting a nonstereotypical gay characterization, but producer James Brooks confesses that it was largely unintentional, since Phyllis's brother wasn't even gay in the original script! The twist was added at a last-minute rewrite session after a previous ending fell flat during rehearsal.

66 The Georgette Story January 20, 1973
Writer: Ed. Weinberger
Director: Peter Baldwin

Ted and Georgette's blossoming romance gets off to a rocky start when Georgette starts to think Ted is taking advantage of her.

67 Romeo and Mary January 27, 1973
Writers: Jim Mulholland, Mike Barrie
Director: Peter Baldwin
Guest Stars: Stuart Margolin, Joe Warfield, Bo Kaprall

Rhoda fixes Mary up with a zany obsessive who insists on marrying her.

68 What Do You Do When the Boss Says, February 3, 1973
"I Love You"?
Writers: David Pollack, Elias Davis
Director: Jay Sandrich
Guest Stars: Lois Nettleton, Dick Balduzzi

Lou panics when the attractive new station manager appears to have designs on him.

69 Murray Faces Life February 10, 1973
Writer: Martin Cohan
Director: Jay Sandrich

Murray becomes depressed when he begins to fear that he hasn't accomplished anything important in his life.

70 Remembrance of Things Past February 17, 1973
Writers: Dick Clair, Jenna McMahon
Director: Jay Sandrich
Guest Star: Joseph Campanella

An old boyfriend of Mary's pays a visit, but she's afraid to rekindle the flame of a painful romance.

Joseph Campanella plays the ingratiating former lover, a role that he was to repeat in the semiregular part of Ann Romano's former husband on Norman Lear's long-running sitcom "One Day at a Time."

71 Put on a Happy Face   February 24, 1973
Writers: Marilyn Suzanne Miller, Monica Magowan
Director: Jay Sandrich
Guest Stars: Steve Franken, Art Gilmore, Herbie Faye

Mary is nominated for a Teddy Award, but her personal life seems jinxed when everything she does turns out wrong.

72 Mary Richards and the Incredible Plant Lady   March 3, 1973
Writer: Martin Cohan
Director: John C. Chulay
Guest Stars: Louise Lasser, Robert Karvelas, Henry Corgen

Rhoda decides to open a plant store—with Mary's savings as seed money.

1973/74   THE FOURTH SEASON

Year-End Rating: 23.1 (9th place)

The fourth season sees the characters and situations developed to a level of depth and sophistication that few people thought was possible on a network sitcom. Lou Grant's separation and eventual divorce were a recurring plot springboard that demonstrated the show's remarkable ability to deal with sobering issues of real life in a funny, but not frivolous, way.

Other developments during this peak middle period of the show's development include the addition of Sue Ann Nivens to the regular cast. The verbally assaultive and sexually voracious character is a potent source of fresh plot ideas, and she will be used to very good advantage over the three remaining years of the series.

Ed. Weinberger continues to serve as producer, while Jay Sandrich once again directs most of the episodes; and Treva Silverman is executive story consultant in the fourth year.

73 The Lars Affair   September 15, 1973
Writer: Ed. Weinberger
Director: Jay Sandrich
Guest Star: Betty White

Phyllis discovers that her husband, Lars, is having an affair with WJM's "Happy Homemaker," Sue Ann Nivens.

This episode marks the introduction of Betty White as Sue Ann Nivens, host of "The Happy Homemaker Show." Legend has it that the show's creators wanted to add a bitchy, bright, and sexually omnivorous female character to the series and thought it would be a funny twist to cast against type and use a clean-living, all-American "Betty White type" in the role. On a lark, they sent her the script, she loved the idea, and no male in the WJM newsroom has been safe since.

Cloris Leachman, whose star had risen meteorically since the series began, was busy pursuing other avenues of her career, and so was seen less frequently on the show by this time. However, she did make occasional guest appearances, such as her performance here—for which she was awarded an Emmy.

74   Angels in the Snow   September 22, 1973
Writers: Marilyn Suzanne Miller, Monica Magowan Johnson
Director: Jay Sandrich
Guest Stars: Peter Strauss, Elayne Heilveil

Mary's new boyfriend is in his twenties, which suddenly makes her feel very old.

75   Rhoda's Sister Gets Married   September 29, 1973
Writer: Karyl Geld
Director: Jerry Belson
Guest Stars: Liberty Williams, Nancy Walker, Harold Gould

Mary and Rhoda fly to New York for the marriage of Rhoda's sister, Debbie.

This prototype version of Rhoda's sister was not the same one used in the spin-off series "Rhoda." It must've been some honeymoon: Poor Debbie vanished and was never heard from again.

76   The Lou and Edie Story   October 6, 1973
Writer: Treva Silverman
Director: Jay Sandrich
Guest Stars: Priscilla Morrill, Darrel Zwerling

Lou and his wife, Edie, separate after raising a family, leaving Lou heartbroken.

A compassionate development in the life of one of the show's most interesting, and real, characters. The relationship of Mary and Lou continues to develop in subtle and complex ways that mirror the way two real people might grow close—by building a fond attachment, without ever really admitting they're in love. The script for this episode won a well-deserved Emmy, surely a sign that the television industry was keenly aware of the level of sophistication the series had attained.

77   Hi There, Sports Fans   October 13, 1973
     Writer: Jerry Mayer
     Director: Jay Sandrich
     Guest Stars: Dick Gautier, Gordon Jump, John Gabriel

Mary wants more responsibility, so Lou awards her the task of firing the WJM sportscaster.

78   Father's Day   October 20, 1973
     Writers: Ed. Weinberger, Stan Daniels
     Director: Jay Sandrich
     Guest Stars: Liam Dunn, John Holland

Ted is nervous at the prospect of a reunion with his long-lost father.

79   Son of "But Seriously, Folks"   October 27, 1973
     Writer: Phil Mishkin
     Director: Jay Sandrich
     Guest Star: Jerry Van Dyke

When Mary's old comedy-writer boyfriend joins the newsroom staff, he concentrates more on Mary than his work.

80   Lou's First Date   November 3, 1973
     Writers: Ed. Weinberger, Stan Daniels
     Director: Jay Sandrich
     Guest Stars: Florence Lake, Priscilla Morrill, Jeff Thompson

Lou, now a bachelor, asks Mary to drum him up a date for an awards banquet.

81   Love Blooms at Hempel's   November 10, 1973
Writers: Sybil Adelman, Barbara Gallagher
Director: Jay Sandrich
Guest Stars: William Burns, Barbara Barrett, Meg Wyllie, Roy West

Rhoda falls head over heels for the manager of the department store where she works.

82   The Dinner Party   November 17, 1973
Writer: Ed. Weinberger
Director: Jay Sandrich
Guest Stars: Irene Tedrow, Henry Winkler

Mary is surprised when a congresswoman accepts her rhetorical invitation to a dinner party.

Henry Winkler plays one of the dinner guests, in a role that predates his imminent fame as a star of "Happy Days."

83   Just Friends   November 24, 1973
Writer: William Wood
Director: Nancy Walker
Guest Star: Priscilla Morrill

When Lou becomes Mary's perennial dinner guest, she decides to reunite him with Edie.

Directed by Nancy Walker, the actress we usually thought of as Rhoda's mother.

84   We Want Baxter   December 1, 1973
Writer: David Lloyd
Director: Jay Sandrich
Guest Star: John Amos

Phyllis convinces Ted to forgo his news career and run for city council.

This is the first "Mary Tyler Moore" episode written by David Lloyd, who had once written jokes for both Jack Paar and Merv Griffin. Lloyd's daughter, a fan of "The Mary Tyler Moore Show," suggested he submit a script—which he did, without ever watching the show! Working from character descriptions his daughter gave him, Lloyd constructed a sample script that was good enough to land him a regular spot on the writers' roster. A gifted comedy writer, Lloyd would contribute many of the show's most memorable later episodes.

85 I Gave at the Office   December 8, 1973
Writers: Don Reo, Allan Katz
Director: Jay Sandrich
Guest Stars: Tammi Bula, Bruce Boxleitner

Mary hires Murray's daughter, Bonnie, to work in the newsroom.

86 Almost a Nun's Story   December 15, 1973
Writers: Ed. Weinberger, Stan Daniels
Director: Jay Sandrich
Guest Star: Gail Strickland

Georgette is prepared to join a convent after she spies Ted with another woman in his dressing room.

87 Happy Birthday, Lou   December 22, 1973
Writer: David Lloyd
Director: George Tyne
Guest Star: Priscilla Morrill

Mary plans an unwanted surprise party for Lou's birthday.

The decision to separate Lou from his wife has become a bonanza for new plots involving Lou and Mary. Actor Ed Asner rises to the challenge by developing the irascible old newshawk into a compelling portrait of a man facing middle age, suddenly alone.

88 WJM Tries Harder   January 5, 1974
Writer: Karyl Geld
Director: Jay Sandrich
Guest Stars: Anthony Eisley, Ned Wertimer, Regis Cordic

Mary begins to have doubts about the integrity of her own show after she dates the anchorman at a competing station.

89 Cottage for Sale   January 12, 1974
Writer: George Atkins
Director: Jay Sandrich
Guest Star: Michele Nichols

Phyllis tries to convince Lou to let her sell his house, despite his sentimental attachment to it.

90   The Co-producers   January 19, 1974
Writers: David Pollack, Elias Davis
Director: Jay Sandrich

Mary and Rhoda become producers of a show that features the unlikely team of Ted and Sue Ann.

91   Best of Enemies   January 26, 1974
Writers: Marilyn Suzanne Miller, Monica Magowan Johnson
Director: Jay Sandrich

Mary and Rhoda have a blowup that threatens to devastate their friendship.

92   Better Late . . . That's a Pun . . .   February 2, 1974
     Than Never
Writer: Treva Silverman
Director: John C. Chulay
Guest Star: Jennifer Leak

Mary writes a joke obituary that Ted reads on the air, forcing Lou to punish her with a suspension.

93   Ted Baxter Meets Walter Cronkite   February 9, 1974
Writer: Ed. Weinberger
Director: Jay Sandrich
Guest Stars: Walter Cronkite, John Gabriel, John Pringle

Ted develops delusions of network stardom when Walter Cronkite drops by the newsroom.

94   Lou's Second Date   February 16, 1974
Writer: Ed. Weinberger
Director: Jerry London

Lou dates Rhoda, causing all sorts of speculation in the newsroom.

Valerie Harper left the cast after this episode to star in "Rhoda," which would begin the following fall.

95　Two Wrongs Don't Make a Writer　　　February 23, 1974
Writer: David Lloyd
Director: Nancy Walker
Guest Star: Shirley O'Hara

Ted horns in on a creative-writing course that Mary's attending and then has the nerve to paraphrase and plagiarize her touching personal reminiscence.

Writer David Lloyd seemed to possess a unique understanding of the character of Ted Baxter that few of the show's other writers could match. The episodes that he wrote with Ted as a central character are among the funniest ever aired, as this particular show aptly demonstrates. Lloyd exploits Ted's boyish malevolence in a chilling fashion in the scene where Ted claims Mary's assignment as his own and then reinterprets it aloud in class, leaving her to stammer out a new composition on the spot. A comic masterpiece that is one of actor Ted Knight's finest moments.

96　I Was a Single for WJM　　　　　　March 2, 1974
Writer: Treva Silverman
Director: Mel Ferber
Guest Stars: Richard Schaal, Penny Marshall, Arlene Golonka, Robert Riesel

Mary goes on location for an in-depth report on the singles scene.

The scene where Mary and Lou must improvise an entire half-hour show on location from the suddenly deserted singles bar is another hilarious example of a staple MTM situation—as well-intentioned Lou and Mary find themselves having to endure a magnificently embarrassing situation while trying not to reveal the slightest discomfort.

Penny Marshall, who plays one of the singles, would soon achieve lasting notoriety as one-half of "Laverne and Shirley."

1974/75　THE FIFTH SEASON

Year-End Rating: 24.0 (11th place)

The show practically glides into a fifth season, buoyed aloft by critical and popular acclaim, as well as a cast and creative team that are among the finest ever assembled for the production of a weekly situation comedy.

Major developments in the continuing story include the engagement of Ted and Georgette and the final appearance of Phyllis, who will move to San Francisco and her own series the following fall.

The show continues to benefit from the contributions of many talented scripters, with stalwart David Lloyd acting as executive story editor. The prolific writing team of Ed. Weinberger and Stan Daniels also acts as producers for the show, a position they will hold for the remainder of the series. Jay Sandrich continues to head the roster of directors, though Mary herself directs an episode this season—her single venture behind the camera.

97   Will Mary Richards Go to Jail?   September 14, 1974
  Writers: Ed. Weinberger, Stan Daniels
  Director: Jay Sandrich
  Guest Stars: Barbara Colby, James Randolph

Mary spends the night in jail after she refuses to reveal a news source.

98   Not Just Another Pretty Face   September 21, 1974
  Writers: Ed. Weinberger, Stan Daniels
  Director: Jay Sandrich
  Guest Star: Robert Wolders

Mary dates a man because of his striking looks, even though she knows they have nothing in common.

An episode that takes the risk of exploring what seems a more shallow side of Mary's nature, her ability to date a rather dull man because he's very good-looking. In fact, her actions demonstrate her newfound maturity, as she makes the refreshingly adult realization that she *is* capable of dating a great-looking man for purely physical reasons—and why, she wonders, shouldn't she? This sophisticated treatment of an essentially feminist issue wouldn't have been possible in an earlier phase of the series's development, when Mary was still constrained by the rules of what good girls did, and didn't do, on sitcoms.

99 You Sometimes Hurt   September 28, 1974
    the One You Hate
    Writer: David Lloyd
    Director: Jackie Cooper

After he tosses Ted from the newsroom in an angry fit, Lou takes stock of his temper and begins to treat Ted with kid gloves.

100 Lou and That Woman   October 5, 1974
    Writer: David Lloyd
    Director: Jay Sandrich
    Guest Stars: Sheree North, Fred Festinger

Lou gets involved with a lounge singer of dubious reputation.

101 The Outsider   October 12, 1974
    Writer: Jack Winter
    Director: Peter Bonerz
    Guest Star: Richard Masur

When a consultant tries to bolster the ratings of "The Six O'Clock News," he succeeds only in enraging the newsroom staff.

102 I Love a Piano   October 19, 1974
    Writer: Treva Silverman
    Director: Jay Sandrich
    Guest Star: Barbara Barrie

Murray comes very close to having an affair with an attractive woman.

Barbara Barrie would play "Barney Miller's" wife, Liz, when the station-house comedy premiered in 1975.

103 A New Sue Ann   October 26, 1974
    Writer: David Lloyd
    Director: Jay Sandrich
    Guest Stars: Linda Kelsey, Ron Rifkin

Sue Ann meets her match when a manipulative young woman tries to take over "The Happy Homemaker Show."

Linda Kelsey guests as the unscrupulous girl—a far cry from Billie Newman, the earthy reporter she would play on "Lou Grant."

104   Ménage à Phyllis   November 2, 1974
Writer: Treva Silverman
Director: Jay Sandrich
Guest Star: John Saxon

Phyllis dates a man for purely intellectual stimulation but is alarmed when he begins dating Mary for a different kind of exhilaration.

105   Not a Christmas Story   November 9, 1974
Writers: Ed. Weinberger, Stan Daniels
Director: John C. Chulay

Sue Ann attempts to introduce a little yuletide cheer, a month and a half too early, when the staff gets snowbound at work in early November.

106   What Are Friends For?   November 16, 1974
Writer: David Lloyd
Director: Allan Rafkin
Guest Stars: Noble Willingham, David Huddleston, Dan Barrows, Robert Karvelas

Sue Ann tries to nudge Mary into the fast lane when they attend a broadcasters' convention together in Chicago.

107   A Boy's Best Friend   November 23, 1974
Writer: David Lloyd
Director: Mary Tyler Moore
Guest Star: Nolan Leary

Ted is shocked when his mother announces that she intends to move in with her boyfriend.

108   A Son for Murray   November 30, 1974
Writers: Ed. Weinberger, Stan Daniels
Director: Jay Sandrich
Guest Stars: Michael Higa, John Gabriel

Murray desperately wants a son but can't convince Marie to have another child after she's already had three girls.

109 Neighbors   December 7, 1974
   Writer: Ziggy Steinberg
   Directors: James Burrows, John C. Chulay
   Guest Star: Clifford Davis

When Lou decides to move out of his house and into Rhoda's old apartment, Mary is afraid she'll lose all sense of privacy.

One of director James Burrows's apprentice assignments. His long association with "Taxi" and "Cheers" would establish his credentials as one of the brightest young directors in the business.

110 A Girl Like Mary   December 14, 1974
   Writers: Ann Gibbs, Joel Kimmel
   Director: Jay Sandrich
   Guest Star: Rosalind Cash

When Lou decides to add a female newscaster to the show, he's faced with two unlikely candidates—Sue Ann and Mary.

111 An Affair to Forget   December 21, 1974
   Writers: Ed. Weinberger, Stan Daniels
   Director: Jay Sandrich

Ted convinces the newsroom that he and Mary are having a torrid love affair.

A perfect example of the kind of character comedy that was to become the trademark of the early MTM sitcoms. The absurd situation arises organically from the personalities of the characters; it was inevitable that Ted would try this stunt sooner or later. And it was equally inevitable that Mary would be unable to rationally cope with the galling repercussions of Ted's innuendo.

Because we're so familiar with Mary's and Ted's personalities, we can see instantly that both are merely victims of their own character. We are able to sympathize with Ted's desperate plight just as much as we identify with Mary's utter mortification. The entire embarrassing situation is made funny largely because we are convinced it could conceivably happen to any one of us.

112   Mary Richards: Producer   January 4, 1975
   Writer: David Lloyd
   Director: Norman Campbell
   Guest Stars: Anthony Holland, Phillip R. Allen

Mary feels dissatisfied with the scope of her job and asks for the chance to produce "The Six O'Clock News."

113   The System   January 11, 1975
   Writers: Ed. Weinberger, Stan Daniels
   Director: Jay Sandrich

Ted invents a seemingly foolproof scheme for betting on the football pools, luring Lou into partnership with him.

114   Phyllis Whips Inflation   January 18, 1975
   Writers: Ed. Weinberger, Stan Daniels
   Director: Jay Sandrich
   Guest Star: Doris Roberts

When Lars takes away her credit cards, Phyllis is dismayed at the prospect of actually having to look for a job.

Cloris Leachman won an Emmy for her role in this episode, her last regular appearance on the series. She began her own spin-off, "Phyllis," the following season.

115   The Shame of the Cities   January 25, 1975
   Writers: Michael Elias, Arnie Kogen
   Director: Jay Sandrich
   Guest Stars: Sheree North, Robert Emhardt, Chuck Bergansky, James Jeter

Lou rashly mounts a tough exposé of a Minneapolis civic leader, who turns out to have a spotless reputation.

116   Marriage: Minneapolis-Style   February 1, 1975
   Writer: Pamela Russell
   Director: Jay Sandrich
   Guest Star: Eileen McDonough

Ted proposes to Georgette in the middle of his "Six O'Clock News" broadcast.

117 You Try to Be a Nice Guy February 8, 1975
   Writer: Michael Leeson
   Director: Jay Sandrich
   Guest Star: Barbara Colby

Mary agrees to lend a hand when the woman she met in jail is finally released.

Barbara Colby reprises her role as Sherry, the inmate Mary first met when she was jailed for contempt of court in an earlier episode.

118 You Can't Lose Them All February 15, 1975
   Writer: David Lloyd
   Director: Marjorie Mullen

Lou is indignant when he is honored with an award that is usually bestowed on broadcasters who have outlived their usefulness.

Director Marjorie Mullen regularly acted as script supervisor on the series, a job she also performed during five seasons of "The Dick Van Dyke Show" a decade before.

119 Ted Baxter's Famous Broadcasters School February 22, 1975
   Writer: Michael Zinberg
   Director: Jay Sandrich
   Guest Stars: Bernie Kopell, Leonard Frey, Norman Bartold

Ted is conned into endorsing a shady broadcasting school that turns out to have a total student enrollment of one.

Another classic episode. The strange fabric of the newsroom staff's paternal relationship with Ted Baxter is demonstrated when they all endure undeniable embarrassment in order to bail Ted out of a jam. The scene where Lou, Murray, and Mary take turns lecturing to the lone student is an absolute gem.

120 Anyone Who Hates Kids and Dogs March 8, 1975
   Writer: Jerry Mayer
   Director: Jay Sandrich
   Guest Stars: Laurence Luckinbill, Lee H. Montgomery, Mabel Albertson, Ian Wolfe

Mary must face the difficult fact that she can't stand her new boyfriend's young son.

1975/76   THE SIXTH SEASON

Year-End Rating: 21.9 (19th place)

With both Phyllis and Rhoda gone from the series, the dual focus on Mary's home- and work-life environments is diminished, allowing a greater emphasis on situations involving the characters in the newsroom. This shift has the benefit of creating an even tighter ensemble, where each character can interact with the others in practically every episode, with Mary still at the center.

On the creative end, Ed. Weinberger and Stan Daniels return as sixth-year producers and Bob Ellison signs on as executive story editor, replacing David Lloyd, who takes on the position of creative consultant for the final two seasons of the series.

121   Edie Gets Married   September 13, 1975
   Writer: Bob Ellison
   Director: Jay Sandrich
   Guest Stars: Priscilla Morrill, Nora Heflin

Lou can't bring himself to attend the ceremony when Edie gets remarried.

122   Mary Moves Out   September 20, 1975
   Writer: David Lloyd
   Director: Jay Sandrich
   Guest Star: John Lehne

Convinced that her life is stuck in a rut, Mary moves into a new apartment.

The scene where Mary demonstrates her tedium by accurately predicting every word the newsroom staff will utter is even more compelling when one realizes that the creators of the show must've found themselves in a very similar rut. How could they keep the series fresh when they were going into a sixth season with characters and situations that by now must've seemed completely familiar to every man, woman, and child in the country?

One way they faced the challenge was to move Mary out of her old apartment. Since it was clear that Rhoda and Phyllis would not be replaced, it made sense to finally close the book on that part of her life.

There is a touching moment in this episode when Mary seems to acknowledge the evolution her character has undergone. She is trying to hang the big letter *M* that she brought over from the old apartment, but she can't get it to hang the same way in the newer, more sterile high rise. She finally puts down her hammer and nails and whirls around in frustration. Suddenly, she realizes how much she misses her old life, her old friends, and her old apartment—and how much she hates the new place.

Finally, she walks from the room, struck by the irony of her new independence. Mary Richards no longer wonders how she will make it on her own—she already has. Now she just wonders if the struggle was worth it.

123   Mary's Father   September 27, 1975
Writer: Earl Pomerantz
Director: Jay Sandrich
Guest Star: Ed Flanders

Mary fears a dynamic Catholic priest may leave the church because he's fallen in love with her.

An episode that explores a rarely exposed area of Mary's character. When the priest reveals that his infatuation with Mary existed largely in her mind, her ego takes a slight trouncing. "I'm not unattractive," she exclaims, and we get a rare glimpse at the insecurity and vanity that lurk deep in the heart of every former prom queen. The show's creators took a risk depicting Mary in this unfavorable light—but it was a gamble that paid off in added dividends. By the end of this half hour, we better understood her and liked her all the more for revealing a very human side of her character.

The scene where Lou tries to warn the priest of the moral danger of his actions is a masterpiece of comic misunderstanding, offering Asner one of his best monologues of the series. When he starts to launch into a story that begins when he was twelve years old, the impatient priest interrupts him: "Lou, give me a hint. How old are you at the *end* of the story?"

124   Murray in Love   October 4, 1975
Writer: David Lloyd
Director: Jay Sandrich
Guest Stars: Penny Marshall, Mary Kay Place, Peter Hobbs

Murray confides to Mary that he's fallen deeply in love with her.

A probing and surprisingly touching episode. When Mary reveals the nature of her love toward Murray—"I don't know what tomorrow morning may bring, but the last five years have been the most important of my life"—the actress and her character become one. The scene where Murray, the idealist, realizes he must learn to accept himself—and not his dreams—is a powerful moment of recognition that suddenly makes worthy the five-year journey of this most sophisticated of "supporting" characters.

125   Ted's Moment of Glory   October 11, 1975
   Writers: Charles Lee, Gig Henry
   Director: Jay Sandrich
   Guest Stars: Richard Balin, Marilyn Roberts

Ted plans to move to New York to accept an offer to host a game show, until Lou and Mary convince him to stay at WJM.

A character exploration of Ted Baxter that doesn't quite add up. There is nothing in Ted's personality that allows him the integrity to forgo an extra one thousand dollars a week in salary just to stay in Minneapolis. The scene where Mary and Lou decide they want to keep Ted at WJM seems a little forced, as well. At least the writers *were* smart enough to keep Murray out of the picture when Mary and Lou decide to convince Ted not to take the other offer.

126   Mary's Aunt   October 18, 1975
   Writer: David Lloyd
   Director: Jay Sandrich
   Guest Star: Eileen Heckart

Mary's Aunt Flo—a world-class foreign correspondent—drops in for a visit and begins a friendly rivalry with Lou.

Mary's Aunt Flo, played by Oscar-winner Eileen Heckart, was the only character from "The Mary Tyler Moore Show" ever to make a crossover, however brief, to the more serious "Lou Grant" series of the late 1970s.

127   Chuckles Bites the Dust   October 25, 1975
   Writer: David Lloyd

Director: Joan Darling
Guest Stars: John Harkins, Helen Kleeb

The death of Chuckles the Clown under the most ridiculous of circumstances prompts a nervous rash of gallows humor in the newsroom.

Director Joan Darling and writer David Lloyd both earned Emmy Awards for this outstanding episode that questions our culture's sanctimonious attitude toward death and dying, with irresistible irreverence—all within the realm of a half-hour sitcom. The plot bears echoes of a scene in an old Second City revue where a family is similarly convulsed by the absurd death of their father—which only shows how much "The Mary Tyler Moore Show," like "Saturday Night Live" in the 1970s, drew from the same comic vein as the improvisational comedians of the 1960s.

128 Mary's Delinquent   November 1, 1975
     Writers: Mary Kay Place, Valerie Curtin
     Director: Jay Sandrich
     Guest Stars: Mackenzie Phillips, Tamu, Phillip R. Allen

Mary and Sue Ann become big sisters to two wayward girls.

Writer Valerie Curtin would be one of the creators of the short-lived but critically acclaimed series "Square Pegs."

129 Ted's Wedding   November 8, 1975
     Writer: David Lloyd
     Director: Jay Sandrich
     Guest Star: John Ritter

Ted and Georgette are wed in an impulsive ceremony improvised in Mary's apartment.

There was really no chance of a June marriage for Ted and Georgette—sitcom weddings are invariably held in mid-November to boost viewership while the networks compete in their ratings sweeps.

130   Lou Douses an Old Flame   November 15, 1975
   Writer: David Lloyd
   Director: Jay Sandrich
   Guest Star: Beverly Garland

Lou has a rare opportunity to even the score with the woman who jilted him during the war.

131   Mary Richards Falls in Love   November 22, 1975
   Writers: Ed. Weinberger, Stan Daniels
   Director: Jay Sandrich
   Guest Stars: Ted Bessell, Valerie Harper, David Groh, Beth Howland, Michael Perrotta

Mary thinks she may have finally found a man she'd like to settle down with but begins to have second thoughts when he seems reluctant to make a commitment.

Mary could've saved about five years of looking for Mr. Right by watching reruns of "That Girl." Long before he rode a white horse into Mary Richards's life as Joe Warner, Ted Bessell played the boyfriend on that late-sixties sitcom—a show that preceded "The Mary Tyler Moore Show" in theme, if not precisely in flavor. Bessell also shared billing with a chimpanzee in another sitcom—but that's a whole other story.

132   Ted's Tax Refund   November 29, 1975
   Writer: Bob Ellison
   Director: Marjorie Mullen
   Guest Star: Paul Lichtman

Ted is pleased when he gets an unusually large income tax refund, until he finds out he's scheduled to be audited by the IRS.

133   The Happy Homemaker Takes Lou   December 6, 1975
       Home
   Writer: David Lloyd
   Director: James Burrows
   Guest Stars: Wynn Irwin, Titos Vandis

Lou is tricked into spending the evening in Sue Ann's desperate clutches.

134 One Boyfriend Too Many   December 13, 1975
     Writer: David Lloyd
     Director: Jay Sandrich
     Guest Stars: Michael Tolan, Ted Bessell

Mary is forced to choose between her current heartthrob and an old boyfriend who suddenly reenters her life.

135 What Do You Want to Do   December 20, 1975
     When You Produce?
     Writers: Shelley Nelbert, Craig Allen Hafner
     Director: Jay Sandrich
     Guest Star: Joyce Bulifant

Murray's life is transformed into a nightmare when he volunteers to become producer of domineering Sue Ann's "Happy Homemaker Show."

136 Not With My Wife, I Don't   January 3, 1976
     Writer: Bob Ellison
     Director: Jay Sandrich
     Guest Star: Allan Manson

Georgette decides to seek professional marital counseling when she feels Ted no longer loves her.

137 The Seminar   January 10, 1976
     Writers: James MacDonald, Robert Gerlach
     Director: Stuart Margolin
     Guest Stars: Betty Ford, Dabney Coleman

Mary refuses to believe that Lou is on a first-name basis with Capitol Hill luminaries, until he's paid a surprise visit by First Lady Betty Ford.

138 Once I Had a Secret Love   January 17, 1976
     Writers: Pat Nardo, Gloria Banta
     Director: Jay Sandrich

Lou's faith in Mary is tested when he confides to her that he once spent the night with Sue Ann.

139   Ménage à Lou   January 24, 1976
   Writer: Bob Ellison
   Director: Jay Sandrich
   Guest Stars: Janis Paige, Penny Marshall, Jeff Conaway

Lou is distraught when one of his old girlfriends arrives at Mary's
party with her new beau.

140   Murray Takes a Stand   January 31, 1976
   Writer: David Lloyd
   Director: Jay Sandrich
   Guest Star: Joyce Bulifant

Murray dares to speak out against the mercurial new station
owner, but he soon finds himself out of a job.

141   Mary's Aunt Returns   February 7, 1976
   Writer: David Lloyd
   Director: Jay Sandrich
   Guest Star: Eileen Heckart

Lou once again locks horns with Mary's Aunt Flo. This time they
squabble over the journalistic integrity of a documentary they're
co-producing.

142   A Reliable Source   February 21, 1976
   Writer: Richard M. Powell
   Director: Jay Sandrich
   Guest Star: Edward Winter

A conflict of ideals erupts when Lou decides to do an exposé
on a politician who is also a good friend of Mary's.

143   Sue Ann Falls in Love   February 28, 1976
   Writer: Bob Ellison
   Director: Doug Rogers
   Guest Stars: James Luisi, Pat Gaynor, Larry Wilde

Sue Ann falls in love, *and* is finally nominated for a Teddy Award,
both in the same week.

144   Ted and the Kid   March 6, 1976
   Writer: Bob Ellison
   Director: Marjorie Mullen
   Guest Star: Robbie Rist

After Ted finds out he's unable to father a child, he and Georgette adopt a precocious young boy.

This episode demonstrates one of the more difficult attempts to expand and deepen a regular character on the series—the childlike anchorman Ted Baxter. When the role was created six years earlier, he was designed to offer the sort of broad comic relief that was a necessary and successful component of the show. A combination of good writing, as well as a perfect marriage of actor and role, soon made Ted one of the most popular characters on the show. But when the time came to humanize and expand his role, the show's creative staff ran into trouble. How could they humanize a character whose comic purpose was based on his lack of any believable human integrity? Essentially, they solved the problem by creating a new, more sympathetic character who still possessed the unsympathetic characteristics that made Ted so funny. It was an uneasy combination at best, and, as this episode indicates, a not entirely successful solution.

1976/77   THE SEVENTH SEASON

Year-End Rating: 19.2 (39th place)

Acknowledging the pressures involved in maintaining the high standards of a series's like "The Mary Tyler Moore Show," the series's creators decide to bow out gracefully by announcing that the seventh season will be the last, ending the long run of one of the most popular and critically acclaimed series in television history.

Ed. Weinberger and Stan Daniels return as producer for the final season. Bob Ellison serves as executive story editor, and David Lloyd acts as creative consultant.

145   Mary Midwife   September 25, 1976
   Writer: David Lloyd
   Director: Jay Sandrich
   Guest Star: Ford Rainey

Georgette unexpectedly has her baby in Mary's apartment.

146 Mary the Writer   October 2, 1976
  Writer: Burt Prelutsky
  Director: James Burrows

Mary fulfills her desire to become a creative writer, despite Lou's harsh criticism of her abilities.

147 Sue Ann's Sister   October 9, 1976
  Writer: David Lloyd
  Director: Jay Sandrich
  Guest Star: Pat Priest

Sue Ann's sister is hired as the hostess of a rival station's home-maker show.

148 What's Wrong With Swimming?   October 16, 1976
  Writer: David Lloyd
  Director: Marjorie Mullen
  Guest Star: Caren Kaye

Mary hires an Olympic swimmer as WJM's new sportscaster—against Lou's better judgment.

149 Ted's Change of Heart   October 23, 1976
  Writer: Earl Pomerantz
  Director: Jay Sandrich
  Guest Stars: Harvey Vernon, Jerry Fogel

After a brush with death, Ted decides to explore the joys of life—and he convinces the rest of the newsroom to join him.

150 One Producer Too Many   October 30, 1976
  Writer: Bob Ellison
  Director: Jay Sandrich
  Guest Stars: Richard Self, Murray Korda

Lou appoints Murray co-producer of "The Six O'Clock News," which causes an unhealthy rivalry between Murray and Mary.

151 My Son, the Genius   November 6, 1976
  Writer: Bob Ellison
  Director: Jay Sandrich
  Guest Stars: Robbie Rist, William Bogart, Ned Glass

Ted and Georgette discover that their adopted son has the IQ of a genius.

152 Mary Gets a Lawyer November 13, 1976
Writer: Burt Prelutsky
Director: Jay Sandrich
Guest Star: John McMartin

Mary finally faces a judge for her contempt charges, but her defense lawyer seems more intent on winning *her* than defeating the case.

153 Lou Proposes November 20, 1976
Writer: David Lloyd
Director: Jay Sandrich
Guest Stars: Eileen Heckart, T. J. Castronova

Lou finally musters the courage to propose to Mary's Aunt Flo.

154 Murray Can't Lose November 27, 1976
Writer: David Lloyd
Director: Jay Sandrich
Guest Stars: Joyce Bulifant, Larry Wilde

Murray is convinced he'll never be awarded a Teddy statuette, until Lou builds his confidence with the implication that this year, he's a shoo-in.

155 Mary's Insomnia December 4, 1976
Writer: David Lloyd
Director: James Burrows
Guest Star: Sherry Hursey

Mary develops a dependence on sleeping pills, and Lou tries to force her off the habit.

An extraordinary look at an obsessive side of Mary's character that we never knew existed—and a revealing portrait of the true interdependency of Lou and Mary. This is a rare example of a sitcom episode that approaches successful human drama, largely due to the depth and believability the characters have developed during the later seasons.

156   Ted's Temptation   December 11, 1976
    Writer: Bob Ellison
    Director: Harry Mastrogeorge
    Guest Star: Trisha Noble

While in Hollywood for a newsmen's convention, Ted is almost seduced by a beautiful young reporter who's hoping for an in-depth interview.

157   Look at Us, We're Walking   December 25, 1976
    Writer: Bob Ellison
    Director: Jay Sandrich
    Guest Star: David Ogden Stiers

Lou and Mary decide to quit their jobs in order to bluff the new station manager into meeting their salary demands.

David Ogden Stiers played station manager Mel Price in only a few seventh-season episodes, but they would lead to the actor's far more lasting assignment as Major Charles Winchester of the 4077th, after "M*A*S*H" producer Burt Metcalfe spotted him on the show.

158   The Critic   January 8, 1977
    Writer: David Lloyd
    Director: Martin Cohan
    Guest Stars: Eric Braedon, David Ogden Stiers

In order to boost the ratings, WJM's new station manager hires a controversial critic for "The Six O'Clock News."

159   Lou's Army Reunion   January 15, 1977
    Writer: Bob Ellison
    Director: Jay Sandrich
    Guest Star: Alex Rocco

An old army buddy of Lou's comes to town and decides to collect a favor—he wants a date with Mary.

160   The Ted and Georgette Show   January 22, 1977
    Writer: David Lloyd
    Director: Jay Sandrich
    Guest Stars: David Ogden Stiers, Alex Henteloff

Ted and Georgette host a successful variety show on WJM, until Georgette discovers she can't stand the pressure.

161 Sue Ann Gets the Ax   January 29, 1977
Writer: Bob Ellison
Director: Jay Sandrich
Guest Star: Louis Guss

When Sue Ann's cooking show is canceled, she takes over as host of the afternoon kid's show.

162 Hail the Conquering Gordy   February 5, 1977
Writer: Earl Pomerantz
Director: Jay Sandrich
Guest Star: John Amos

Weatherman Gordy—now a well-known talk-show host—returns to WJM, only to face Ted, who volunteers his services as talk-show second banana.

163 Mary and the Sexagenarian   February 12, 1977
Writers: Les Charles, Glen Charles
Director: Jay Sandrich
Guest Stars: Lew Ayres, Jon Lormer

Mary goes out on a date with Murray's father, despite the ribbing she receives from the newsroom staff.

An early script from Glen Charles and Les Charles, two brothers who would one day create the popular and critically acclaimed NBC sitcom "Cheers."

164 Murray Ghosts for Ted   February 19, 1977
Writer: David Lloyd
Director: Jay Sandrich

Ted plans to take full credit—and make a large cash profit— when an article Murray has ghosted for him is picked up by a major magazine.

165 Mary's Three Husbands   February 26, 1977
Writer: Bob Ellison
Director: Jay Sandrich
Guest Star: Bill Darth

In dream sequences, we see what life would have been like had Mary become the wife of Lou, Ted, or Murray.

166   Mary's Big Party   March 5, 1977
    Writer: Bob Ellison
    Director: Jay Sandrich
    Guest Stars: Johnny Carson, Irene Tedrow

To ensure that at least one of her parties will be a success, Mary
invites Johnny Carson as guest of honor.

There are two sure signs that a sitcom is headed for the end of a
long run on network TV. The first is when there's an entire episode
devoted to flashbacks from earlier episodes, and the second is when a
single show revolves around the surprise appearance of a special guest
star. It's a credit to the ambition of the creative staff of "The Mary Tyler
Moore Show" that they dared to dust off *both* those old sitcom chestnuts
in a single audacious episode.

167   Lou Dates Mary   March 12, 1977
    Writer: David Lloyd
    Director: Jan Sandrich
    Guest Stars: John Reilly, Kenny Waller

Lou and Mary finally have their first, and only, date.

Around the time this episode first aired, Ed Asner half jokingly described the way he thought this episode should end. Lou and Mary
would be alone at the crest of the evening—in the dark, esconced in a
newly discovered bliss. As the credits began to roll, there would be a
long silence. Finally, the silence would be punctuated by Mary's familiar
exclamation, "Oh, Mr. Grant!" Fade out . . . cut to commercial.

As tempting as that scenario must've seemed to Asner, it's not surprising that the show's creators opted for a more realistic ending to the
big date, with Mary and Lou barely exchanging a goodnight kiss. The
show's writers must've known all along that Lou and Mary were able
to enjoy the most passionate love affair in TV history largely because it
was unconsummated. Not sullied by carnal pleasure, they were free to
exchange the passion of two thinking, feeling adults traveling together
through seven years of highs and lows—through giddy pleasures and
painful truths, through old divorces and new beginnings. Lou and Mary
shared a respect for each other that was not unlike the respect that
existed between the show's audience and its many creators—which
gives some clue to the immense popularity of the series during its seven-
year run.

Just as Mary grew to depend on Lou in her strange, ineffable way, so did we grow to expect the very best from this most unusual TV series. And right up to the very end, neither we, nor Mary, were ever disappointed.

168 The Last Show March 19, 1977
Writers: Allan Burns, James L. Brooks, Ed. Weinberger, Stan Daniels, David Lloyd, Bob Ellison
Director: Jay Sandrich
Guest Stars: Robbie Rist, Vincent Gardenia, Cloris Leachman, Valerie Harper

WJM's new station owner decides to revamp "The Six O'Clock News," so he fires everyone—except Ted Baxter.

It's a lucky thing the show's creators decided to stage a final episode to end the series. The audience needed a proper occasion to say farewell to all those Saturday nights spent at home, often intentionally, with Mary Tyler Moore and the crew. The overall mood of this episode was that of a big, teary-eyed good-bye kiss, and there was a built-in poignancy to this last hurrah that was rarely equaled in series television.

Many viewers may still find it hard to stifle that lump in their throat when this episode is rerun on local TV at two or three in the morning. Although now that the show's in syndication, it must be a sobering consolation to know that Mary Richards will be back in Minneapolis the very next day, still tossing that silly hat in the air and finding out that Lou Grant thinks she's got spunk—and he *hates* spunk.

Fade out . . . cut to commercial.

EMMY AWARDS

The following is a complete listing of the Emmy Awards bestowed on "The Mary Tyler Moore Show" by the National Academy of Television Arts and Sciences.

1970/71　Outstanding Performance by an Actor in a Supporting
　　　　　Role in Comedy: Edward Asner
　　　　Outstanding Performance by an Actress in a Supporting
　　　　　Role in Comedy: Valerie Harper
　　　　Outstanding Directorial Achievement in Comedy (Series):
　　　　　Jay Sandrich, "Toulouse-Lautrec Is One of My Favorite
　　　　　Artists"

Outstanding Writing Achievement in Comedy: James L. Brooks, Allan Burns, "Support Your Local Mother"

1971/72 Outstanding Performance by an Actor in a Supporting Role in Comedy: Edward Asner

Outstanding Performance by an Actress in a Supporting Role in a Comedy: Valerie Harper (tied with Sally Struthers)

1972/73 Outstanding Continued Performance by an Actress in a Leading Role in a Comedy Series: Mary Tyler Moore

Outstanding Performance by an Actor in a Supporting Role in Comedy: Ted Knight

Outstanding Performance by an Actress in a Supporting Role in Comedy: Valerie Harper

Outstanding Directorial Achievement in Comedy: Jay Sandrich, "It's Whether You Win or Lose"

1973/74 Best Lead Actress in a Comedy Series: Mary Tyler Moore

Actress of the Year, Series: Mary Tyler Moore

Best Supporting Actress in Comedy: Cloris Leachman, "The Lars Affair"

Best Writing in Comedy: Treva Silverman, "The Lou and Edie Story"

Writer of the Year, Series: Treva Silverman

1974/75 Outstanding Comedy Series

Outstanding Continuing Performance by a Supporting Actor in a Comedy Series: Edward Asner

Outstanding Continuing Performance by a Supporting Actress in a Comedy Series: Betty White

Outstanding Single Performance by a Supporting Actress in a Comedy or Drama Series: Cloris Leachman, "Phyllis Whips Inflation"

Outstanding Writing in a Comedy Series: Ed. Weinberger, Stan Daniels, "Mary Richards Goes to Jail"

1975/76 Outstanding Comedy Series

Outstanding Lead Actress in a Comedy Series: Mary Tyler Moore

Outstanding Continuing Performance by a Supporting Actor in a Comedy Series: Ted Knight

Outstanding Continuing Performance by a Supporting Actress in a Comedy Series: Betty White

Outstanding Writing in a Comedy Series: David Lloyd, "Chuckles Bites the Dust"

1976/77 Outstanding Comedy Series
Outstanding Writing in a Comedy Series: Allan Burns, James L. Brooks, Ed. Weinberger, Stan Daniels, David Lloyd, Bob Ellison, "The Final Show" (a.k.a. "The Last Show")

"ALL IN THE FAMILY"

·

*It was kind of like breaking
peanut brittle with a ballpeen
hammer.*
—ROBERT WOOD, former
president of CBS

STANDING in the dark, Norman Lear had an inspiration.

The balding, middle-aged movie producer had been cooped up in a New York editing room for the last few months of 1967, trying to make sense out of the disastrous first cut of *The Night They Raided Minsky's*. Standing in the shadows of the moviola for what seemed like an eternity, he fondly recalled the manic pace he'd kept in the days of live television. As a scriptwriter for Dean Martin and Jerry Lewis in the early fifties, he could write a sketch on Wednesday morning and see it performed on "The Colgate Comedy Hour" the following Sunday night.

As he sweated out the endless months of postproduction on his fourth film in five years, he decided that his next project would be fast, cheap, and topical—everything a feature film wasn't. He resolved to return to television, where it was still possible to pick a story out of the headlines and put it up on the screen within weeks—not years.

It didn't matter to Norman Lear that, in the mid-1960s, prime-time TV ventured no closer to current events than the international intrigue of the latest world takeover bid on "The Man From U.N.C.L.E." And it didn't faze the writer that the satirical venom he perfected in his screenplay for *Divorce American Style*—a scathing send-up of marriage rituals and family life—had no precedent on network television. He'd already found his inspiration, in a TV program that no one in this country had even seen—himself included.

"Til Death Do Us Part" had been a hit in England for two years by 1966, when Norman Lear first heard about it. According to the small item in *TV Guide*, the BBC domestic comedy offered an uncensored look at British working-class life through the eyes of Alf Garnett, a bigoted dockworker who constantly locked horns with his nagging wife, vapid daughter, and deadbeat son-in-law. "My God," Lear thought, "if I could only get this kind of thing on American television."

Lear and Bud Yorkin, partners in Tandem Productions since the late fifties, quickly optioned the rights to do a U.S. adaptation of "Til Death Do Us Part." As Lear continued to edit *Minsky's* throughout 1968, he spent every spare minute brainstorming "Those Were the Days," as he named his version of the BBC comedy.

The Garnetts of England eventually landed in the states as the Bunkers of Queens, New York—although the writer's tempestuous clan had more in common with the Lears of Connecticut than the British originals. When he finally got to see a tape of Johnny Speight's "Til Death Do Us Part," Lear discovered that the characters were too abrasive for his taste. For inspiration, he looked instead to his own family. Many of the heated exchanges between Archie Bunker and his meathead son-in-law had been played out much earlier by Norman Lear and his own father. "I'd accuse him of making racial slurs," Lear confessed, "and we'd get into real Mike-and-Archie shouting matches. And we were a nice *Jewish* family."

The unretouched family portrait that Lear painted in "Those Were the Days" offered a startling departure from the bucolic view of domestic life that still prevailed on most sitcoms—there was certainly no white picket fence at 704 Hauser Street in Queens. The head of the family was Archie Bunker, described by the writer as "basically a horse's ass"; he was a seething mass of prejudice, half-truths, and malapropisms. In this family, father *never* knew best.

Playing a hunch that the third-place network had nothing to lose by taking a chance on his groundbreaker, Lear convinced ABC to finance a pilot episode. With a shooting date set for January 1969, Lear and Bud Yorkin scouted around for an actor to play Archie Justice—renamed Bunker after the original pilot was shot—a character who had to be both outrageous and likable.

Mickey Rooney was briefly considered, but Norman Lear recalls that the former child star didn't think much of his concept when he pitched the show to Rooney during a transcontinental phone call in 1968. "It was one of those calls you never forget," chuckled Lear. "I told Mickey I wanted him to play a bigot, and he stopped me and said, 'Norman, if you go on the air with that, they're gonna kill you dead in the streets!' "

Apparently, Rooney had a different format in mind for his next television series. Remembers Lear, "He told me, 'You wanna do a show with the Mick? I'll give you the idea—Vietnam vet. Detective. Short. Blind. Big dog.' "

The pair never met.

Instead, Lear chose an accomplished character actor he first saw perform on a jet—during an inflight screening of *What Did You Do in the War, Daddy?* Carroll O'Connor loved Lear's script, but like Rooney he didn't think the show had a chance. "I honestly thought it would be a big bomb," O'Connor later confessed. Jean Stapleton was the inspired choice to play Edith Bunker; the stage-trained actress invested Archie's dingbat wife with a comic depth that surprised even the writer. Together, O'Connor and Stapleton sparked an instantaneous chemistry, and the producers were delighted to discover the incongruous pair made an absolutely convincing married couple.

As portrayed by Carroll O'Connor, Archie Bunker was a comic figure of epic proportions, a colorful—if somewhat pathetic—folk hero. Lear would describe him as "the bigger-than-life epitome of something that's in all of us, like it or not." And yet, there was no doubt that Archie was a bigot, pure and simple. In the very first episode of the show, originally written as the pilot script, Archie rails against Spics, spades, Chinks, hebes—and everyone else he holds responsible for the chaotic state of the Union, particularly his liberal son-in-law, the "pinko Polack atheist."

But beneath all the blustery polemics of the startling pilot script, the Bunkers quickly emerge as an ordinary, loving family who just display their affection a little more loudly than most. When Gloria protests Archie's abuse by threatening to move out, Edith blurts out her deepest fears with logic only a mother could fathom, "If she leaves here, she'll be dead inside a year."

The comic desperation of Stapleton's delivery underscores the central irony of the show. Despite the apparent rancor, the Bunker living room still offers the last sanctuary from the cruel uncertainties of the outside world. As Archie assures his wife in sarcastic understatement, "You don't have to worry, they ain't going nowhere."

Over the course of a single half hour, Lear and his cast launched a full-blown assault on the delicate sensibilities of a television audience that had grown soft on a steady diet of flying nuns and wisecracking secret agents. The network executives who financed the original pilot wanted no part of it. "ABC didn't quite have the guts to put the show on," Lear recalled, "so they decided we had to shoot a second pilot, claiming they weren't happy with the kids."

The same script was shot again, four months later, with two different actors in the roles that would eventually be played by Sally Struthers and Rob Reiner. But no one was surprised when ABC quietly dropped their option on the series.

Norman Lear put the setback out of his mind and boarded a plane for Iowa, to begin shooting his fifth feature film, *Cold Turkey*. He was editing it a few months later when his agent called with good news. CBS had been in touch, and they were suddenly *very* interested in "Those Were the Days."

"Don't let that tape leave the building," Fred Silverman warned. He'd just left the CBS screening room after watching Lear's ABC pilot and was on his way to fetch Bob Wood, the network president. Silverman, the recently installed head of CBS programming, was unaware that the network had tried to option "Til Death Do Us Part" themselves two years earlier—ironically, as a potential Jackie Gleason vehicle. But in 1970, Silverman had very different reasons to be enthusiastic about this most unusual program.

He knew that Bob Wood was personally engineering a badly needed face-lift for the aging network. After a decade of hayseed hits like "The Beverly Hillbillies," "Petticoat Junction," and "Mayberry RFD," CBS was in danger of losing the young, urban audience—those affluent viewers most prized by the advertisers. To lure this desirable demographic group back to the fold, the network needed a show so innovative that even the most sophisticated viewers would sit up and take notice. As he watched Lear's pilot, the CBS president laughed out loud. Not just because it was funny, but because it was exactly what he was looking for.

"It was very provocative if you consider what television was like in 1971 . . . kind of like breaking peanut brittle with a ballpeen hammer," Wood recalled. "I thought it might take some of the wrinkles out of the aging face of television. I knew it was a gamble, but I took a run at it."

The first person Wood had to convince was also his toughest audience. In 1970, William Paley, the sixty-nine-year-old monarch of CBS, still had the last word on what did—or did not—get on the air. He watched Lear's pilot impassively, as Bob Wood patiently explained how he thought prime time was finally ready to grow up and that CBS was in a unique position to lead the pack. Paley leaned back in his chair and sniffed, "You may be right."

That was all the encouragement Wood needed. He ordered thirteen episodes of the new series to be ready by January for midseason replacement. At the same time, he offered Lear a list of changes that the network standards and practices department demanded before the show could go on the air. The producer reviewed the censor's suggestions and rejected every single one of them on the spot.

Lear refused to soften the show's impact by even one epithet. "I felt we had to get the network wet completely," was his negotiating stance. "Once you're completely wet, you can't get any wetter." And the producer clearly had the upper hand: If the CBS deal fell through, he could always return to his successful career as a screenwriter and director. Norman Lear stood firm; the show would be done his way, or not at all.

Bob Wood intervened and finally convinced the producer to make two small changes in the first episode. Lear excised a suggestive bit of business that showed Mike zipping his fly as he came downstairs from the bedroom; and the expletive "goddamn it" was deleted from Archie's dialogue. Lear incorporated one other change before the show premiered. CBS thought "Those Were the Days" sounded old-fashioned and suggested a new title, which Lear quickly adopted.

And so, on Tuesday, January 12, 1971, "All in the Family" was born.

The programming executives, understandably nervous on that fateful night, braced themselves for a deluge of irate phone calls, but were surprised when the network switchboard operators reported business as usual. "My God, I think we got twenty-three phone calls," remarked Bob Wood, puzzled at the public's massive indifference.

The mystery was solved when the first Nielsen returns came in. The reason so few people complained about "All in the Family" was that so few of them chose to watch.

Norman Lear was outwardly undaunted by the dismal ratings. "I knew we were going to be talked about," he predicted, confident that positive word of mouth would build an audience, eventually. But less optimistic observers conceded what the producer refused to acknowledge: The new show, buried—without advance publicity—at 9:30 on Tuesday night, would need a miracle to survive its first thirteen weeks.

The miracle arrived in May.

That's when the cast performed a sketch on the highly visible Emmy Awards broadcast and then walked off with three of the coveted statuettes. The sudden exposure to millions of new viewers transformed the show's small cult following into a mass phenomenon. By the fall of 1971, there was scarcely a man, woman, or child anywhere in the country who didn't have an opinion, pro or con, on America's most vocal citizen—Archie Bunker.

"All in the Family" became a cause célèbre, simultaneously praised and vilified in editorial columns all across the country. *Ebony* accused the show of giving new currency to arcane racial slurs, and the Teamsters International lodged a protest against Archie's unflattering portrayal of the American working man as a bigoted slob. "Liberals were our first and loudest detractors," Carroll O'Connor observed, but "conservatives howled aplenty."

Norman Lear remained detached from the controversy. "The public is wise enough to take care of itself," he ventured. "If the bigots of America want to make Archie Bunker their hero—I think they deserve him."

"If Norman had continued to depend on the topical, he would not have succeeded," Fred Silverman observed. And of course, Lear and his talented staff of writers made sure that life with Archie, Edith, Mike, and Gloria wasn't all Sturm und Drang. The Bunkers confronted taboos such as racial prejudice, rape, and homosexuality head-on—but they also found time for the less dramatic though no less compelling activities that occupy any ordinary family. In between bouts with impotence and unemployment, they played Monopoly, fended off aluminum-siding salesmen, and came down with the flu.

Ironically, the family was at its very best during their most mundane moments. Today, long after the screaming headlines that fueled the Bunkers' fiercest battles look as dated as the yellowing newspapers they were printed on, what remains fresh is the show's affectionate portrait of a family whose members ate and slept, worked and played, fought and made love—just like the rest of us.

When "All in the Family" frightened prime time out of its lingering postadolescence in 1971, it heralded a bold new era of sophistication, intelligence, and sensitivity. By breaking down every established notion of how TV comedy should be written, performed, edited, and scored, the series revolutionized the creative community's attitude toward the medium. By changing the way television looked, "All in the Family" changed forever the way we look at television.

A Critical Guide to All 202 Episodes

Archie Bunker	Carroll O'Connor
Edith Bunker	Jean Stapleton
Gloria Bunker Stivic	Sally Struthers
Michael Stivic	Rob Reiner
Lionel Jefferson	Mike Evans
Louise Jefferson	Isabel Sanford
Stephanie Mills	Danielle Brisebois
Joey Stivic	Jason Draeger, Cory Miller

SUPPORTING CAST

Henry Jefferson	Mel Stewart
George Jefferson	Sherman Hemsley
Irene Lorenzo	Betty Garrett
Frank Lorenzo	Vincent Gardenia
Bert Munson	Billy Halop
Tommy Kelcy	Brendon Dillon, Bob Hastings
Barney Hefner	Allan Melvin
Harry the Bartender	Jason Wingreen
Hank Pivnik	Danny Dayton
Teresa Betancourt	Liz Torres
Justin Quigley	Burt Mustin
Jo Nelson	Ruth McDevitt

Created by Norman Lear
Based on "Til Death Do Us Part," created by Johnny Speight
Theme song ("Those Were the Days") by Lee Adams, Charles Strouse
Closing theme ("Remembering You") by Roger Kellaway, lyrics by Carroll O'Connor
Principal directors were John Rich, Bob LaHendro, H. Wesley Kenney, Paul Bogart

1968/69   THE PILOT EPISODES

Pilot 1   Those Were the Days
   Writer: Norman Lear
   Director: Norman Lear
   Guest Stars: Carroll O'Connor, Jean Stapleton, Tim McIntire,
   Kelly Jean Peters

Archie and Edith Justice celebrate their twenty-second anniversary at an impromptu party thrown by their daughter, Gloria, and her husband, Richard.

Pilot 2   Those Were the Days
   Writer: Norman Lear
   Directors: Bud Yorkin, Norman Lear
   Guest Stars: Carroll O'Connor, Jean Stapleton, Chip Oliver,
   Candy Azzara, D'Urville Martin

Generations clash in the Justice household when Richard and Gloria throw a surprise party for Archie and Edith.

Both ABC pilots were drawn from the exact same script that was eventually used, with minor revisions, for the show's broadcast premiere on CBS in 1971. The key differences were in casting—Kelly Jean Peters and Candy Azzara played Gloria before Sally Struthers finally landed the role, and Tim McIntire and Chip Oliver played Archie's son-in-law, then named Richard. Interestingly, no reference was made to the son-in-law's ethnic heritage until Rob Reiner adopted the role in the third and final version for CBS, when he was renamed Michael Stivic, and his Polish background was introduced as a further source of friction for the beleaguered family.

The original pilot was taped in October 1968 at the Dick Cavett Theater in New York City, and the second was shot a few months later, on February 16, 1969, at ABC's Hollywood studios, where it was produced by Edward Stephenson. The theme song, performed by Stapleton and O'Connor in both pilots, was written by Broadway composers Lee Adams and Charles Strouse, who decided on the spare arrangement after Lear informed them that he had only eight hundred dollars left in his budget to record the title song.

1970/71   THE FIRST SEASON

Year-End Rating: 18.9 (34th place)

America meets its newest—and noisiest—neighbors, the Bunkers of Queens, New York, in thirteen trailblazing comic dramas that provide a Tuesday-night forum for the outspoken Archie Bunker. Producer Norman Lear presides over the raucous proceedings as head writer, aided and abetted in the first year by story editor Don Nicholl and writers Bryan Joseph and Jerry Mayer, among others.

Director John Rich is the dominant force behind the camera for the first four seasons, and Jane Thompson is the associate producer for the initial thirteen shows.

1   Meet the Bunkers   January 12, 1971
Writer: Norman Lear
Director: John Rich

A surprise anniversary party is the setting for the latest high-decibel debate between Archie Bunker and his son-in-law, Michael Stivic.

"I used the excuse of the Bunkers' wedding anniversary to go potshotting around—just to establish the people and the mood," Norman Lear told *TV Guide*, grossly understating the effect of a show that slew an entire herd of television's most sacred cows in its very first half hour. The language and controversy got all the press, but it was the less controversial—though no less radical—novelty of seeing a recognizably real family on television that brought the audience back week after week.

2   Writing the President   January 19, 1971
Writers: Paul Harrison, Lennie Weinrib, Norman Lear
Story: Les Erwin, Fred Freiberger
Director: John Rich
Guest Star: Helen Page Camp

Mike writes a letter to the White House protesting the sorry state of the Union, prompting Archie to take pen in hand for his own rebuttal.

3 Archie's Aching Back January 26, 1971
Writer: Stanley Ralph Ross
Director: John Rich
Guest Stars: George Furth, Salem Ludwig, Richard Stahl

Archie is convinced he'll collect a larger settlement from a petty traffic accident if a Jewish lawyer handles the case.

The stylistic minimalism of the Bunker's sparsely furnished set is on full display in this early episode. According to director John Rich, who grew up not far from Archie's neighborhood, the spartan decor of the Bunker's living room was a painstakingly assembled effect. The director remembers personally supervising the cracking of windows and repainting of walls to give the place a run-down, lived-in look. "I told the set designers to take all the color out of it," remembers Rich. "Norman and I wanted to do the show in black and white, but CBS nearly went into a coma. So we decided to do the next best thing and shoot the entire show in muted sepia tones."

4 Archie Gives Blood February 2, 1971
Writer: Norman Lear
Director: John Rich
Guest Star: Jeannie Linero

Archie refuses to donate blood because he's afraid his vital fluids might get mixed in with those of a different race.

5 Judging Books by Covers February 9, 1971
Writers: Burt Styler, Norman Lear
Director: John Rich
Guest Stars: Philip Carey, Tony Geary, Billy Halop, Linn Patrick

Archie scorns one of Mike's effeminate friends, unaware that one of his toughest beer-drinking buddies is himself a well-adjusted gay.

Guest star Tony Geary became well known to daytime TV viewers as Luke Spencer on "General Hospital."

6   Gloria Is Pregnant   February 16, 1971
Writer: Jerry Mayer
Director: John Rich
Guest Stars: Holly Near, Jon Silo

Archie's dreams of becoming a grandfather are dashed when Gloria suffers a sudden miscarriage.

This landmark episode established Norman Lear's willingness to go beyond the boundaries of situation comedy in subject matter as well as language. And as he soon discovered, controversy attracted viewers. Before long, millions tuned in each week just to see what outrageous taboo might bite the dust this week.

7   Now That You Know the Way,   February 23, 1971
     Let's Be Strangers
Writers: Philip Mishkin, Rob Reiner, Don Nicholl, Bryan Joseph
Story: Philip Mishkin, Rob Reiner
Director: John Rich
Guest Stars: Jack Bender, Corey Fischer, Jenny Sullivan

Mike invites one of his hippie friends to spend the night in the Bunkers' living room, despite Archie's strenuous objections.

8   Lionel Moves Into the Neighborhood   March 2, 1971
Writers: Don Nicholl, Bryan Joseph
Director: John Rich
Guest Stars: Vincent Gardenia, Isabel Sanford

Archie does his best to keep a black family from buying the house next door, only to discover that the prospective buyers are Lionel's parents.

Louise Jefferson makes her first appearance, though husband George will remain an offscreen character for another two seasons. Their son, Lionel, had been a regular visitor to the Bunkers since the pilot episode, when the writers discovered how effective the street-smart black youth was at gently letting the air out of Archie's sails.

9 Edith Has Jury Duty   March 9, 1971
Writers: Susan Harris, Don Nicholl, Bryan Joseph
Story: Susan Harris
Director: John Rich
Guest Stars: Holly Irving, Doris Singleton

Edith abandons the kitchen for the courtroom when she is chosen for jury duty, leaving Archie to fend for himself.

Susan Harris marks her writing debut by spotlighting Edith Bunker's innate intelligence and unflagging humanity in a script that casts the housewife as a juror with the integrity of Henry Fonda in *Twelve Angry Men*. Harris's knack for scripting interesting and intelligent roles for women flourished when she masterminded "Soap" for ABC in 1977 and NBC's "The Golden Girls" in 1985.

10 Archie Is Worried About His Job   March 16, 1971
Writers: Norman Lear, Don Nicholl, Bryan Joseph
Story: William Bickley, Jr.
Director: John Rich
Guest Stars: Holly Irving, Burt Mustin, Jack Perkins, Sandy Kenyon.

No one in the family gets any sleep when Archie spends the night worrying that he might lose his job.

Holly Irving has a cameo as Clara Weidermeyer, the empty-headed next-door neighbor who stumbled into the Bunkers' living room to provide comic relief exactly two times before she was forever banished to sitcom limbo.

11 Gloria Discovers Women's Lib   March 23, 1971
Writers: Norman Lear, Sandy Stern
Director: John Rich

Gloria leaves the house in a rage when Mike refuses to recognize her as an equal partner in their marriage.

12 Success Story   March 30, 1971
Writer: Burt Styler
Director: John Rich
Guest Stars: Len Lesser, Herbie Faye, George Savalas, Frank Ford, William Windom

Archie reevaluates his definition of success after he meets an old army buddy who's become wealthy in the used-car trade.

13   The First and Last Supper   April 6, 1971
   Writer: Jerry Mayer
   Director: John Rich
   Guest Stars: Mel Stewart, Billy Benedict

The Jeffersons arrive for dinner at the Bunkers'—minus husband George, who refuses to socialize with his white neighbors.

Mel Stewart would play George's brother, Henry, until Sherman Hemsley finally graced the Bunkers' living room with his presence in the fourth season.

1971/72   THE SECOND SEASON

Year-End Rating: 34.0 (1st place)

Archie's confounding opinions help anchor the series at the top of the ratings in the show's second year, but the family emerges as the star of the show in second-season episodes that paint a bizarre, but believable portrait of one man's family, 1970s-style.

Joining producer Norman Lear as script supervisors are Michael Ross and Bernie West, who, along with Don Nicholl, contribute most of the show's very best early scripts. Writers Phil Mishkin and Lee Kalcheim also make significant contributions in the second year.

14   The Saga of Cousin Oscar   September 18, 1971
   Writers: Burt Styler, Norman Lear
   Story: Burt Styler
   Director: John Rich
   Guest Stars: Jack Grimes, Will B. Able, Peggy Rea, Connie Sawyer, Billy Benedict

Archie is incensed when his sponging cousin Oscar has the nerve to drop dead in the upstairs bedroom.

15   Gloria Poses in the Nude   September 25, 1971
   Writers: Michael Ross, Bernie West, Norman Lear
   Director: John Rich
   Guest Star: David Soul

Mike has second thoughts after he agrees to let Gloria pose as a nude model for one of his artist friends.

16   Archie in the Lock-up   October 2, 1971
   Writers: Paul Wayne, Michael Ross, Bernie West
   Story: Paul Wayne
   Director: John Rich
   Guest Stars: Allan Melvin, Ken Lynch, Kelly Houser, Corey
   Fischer

Archie suffers the ultimate indignity when he's arrested along
with a group of radicals at a protest rally.

17   Edith Writes a Song   October 9, 1971
   Writer: Lee Kalcheim
   Director: John Rich
   Guest Stars: Cleavon Little, Demond Wilson

A pair of burglars holds the family at bay with Archie's own pistol.

The homebreakers are Tony Award winner Cleavon Little and Demond Wilson, who would join Redd Foxx as co-star of "Sanford and
Son," NBC's midseason smash.

18   Flashback: Mike Meets Archie   October 16, 1971
   Writers: Philip Mishkin, Rob Reiner
   Director: John Rich

On the Stivics' first wedding anniversary, the family recalls the
day Archie and Michael met.

Ironically, by the time Archie launches into a chorus of "God Bless
America" to defy his unwanted dinner guest, the script has already
established that the pair's differences have little to do with their conflicting ideologies. Actually, Archie dislikes Mike far more for being the
interloper who's come to take away his little girl. As Norman Lear observed, "It doesn't really matter what the men say—the audience is
watching a father and his son-in-law. The behavior is what's important."
   By the second season, Archie has emerged in a more sympathetic
light. An insecure man facing middle age in a world that's changing
much too quickly, he's terrified of the new society that his son-in-law
envisions, afraid there won't be any place in it for him. In defense, he
clings stubbornly to the prejudices of a bygone era that suddenly looks
very rosy. It's an attitude that makes the short verse he sings at the start
of every episode ring with plaintive irony: "Guys like us, we had it
made. . . . those were the days."

19   The Election Story   October 30, 1971
Writers: Michael Ross, Bernie West
Director: John Rich
Guest Stars: Barbara Cason, Frank Whiteman, Ida McKenzie, Robert Gibbons

Mike and Gloria campaign for the liberal candidate in a local election, while Archie places himself in the opposing camp.

20   Edith's Accident   November 6, 1971
Writers: Michael Ross, Bernie West
Story: Tom and Helen August
Director: John Rich
Guest Star: Barnard Hughes

A priest pays a call to reward Edith's honesty for leaving a note on his car after she accidentally dents it with a large can of cling peaches.

21   The Blockbuster   November 13, 1971
Writers: Austin and Irma Kalish, Michael Ross, Bernie West
Story: Austin and Irma Kalish
Director: John Rich
Guest Stars: Jack Crowder, Peggy Rea

An unscrupulous black real estate salesman tempts Archie to sell his house to a black family at an inflated profit.

22   Mike's Problem   November 20, 1971
Writers: Alan J. Levitt, Philip Mishkin
Story: Alan J. Levitt
Director: John Rich
Guest Stars: Brendon Dillon, Mel Stewart

Gloria is upset when Mike's nervousness over his grades causes him to become temporarily impotent.

This story met with greater network resistance than any script since the original pilot. "CBS didn't want that show done at all," Norman Lear told interviewers Horace Newcomb and Robert Alley in their book *The Producer's Medium*. "It was the first time that I said, 'If you know what America wants and what America will fall apart over—then YOU produce the show.' At the last moment they allowed us to make the show. Nothing happened, the network didn't fall apart. States did not secede from the union. America even liked it."

23   The Insurance Is Canceled   November 27, 1971
   Writers: Lee Kalcheim, Michael Ross, Bernie West
   Story: Lee Kalcheim
   Director: John Rich
   Guest Stars: Philip Proctor, Rafael Campos

Archie lays off a Puerto Rican worker during a cutback at the dock; and his homeowner's policy is canceled when his neighborhood is redlined as a bad risk.

24   The Man in the Street   December 4, 1971
   Writers: Lennie Weinrib, Paul Harrison, Don Nicholl
   Story: Lennie Weinrib, Paul Harrison
   Director: John Rich
   Guest Stars: Jack Griffin, Neil J. Schwartz, Bob Hastings

Archie Bunker becomes the voice of the American working man when his man-on-the-street interview is scheduled to appear on Walter Cronkite's "Evening News."

Bob Hastings, the sniveling Lieutenant Carpenter from "McHale's Navy," would appear as Tommy Kelcy, the proprietor of Archie's favorite watering hole, until it changed hands in the eighth year.

25   Cousin Maude's Visit   December 11, 1971
   Writers: Philip Mishkin, Michael Ross, Bernie West
   Story: Philip Mishkin
   Director: John Rich
   Guest Star: Bea Arthur

Edith's feisty cousin, Maude, drops in for a visit during a flu epidemic at the Bunker House

Like many "All in the Family" guest stars, Bea Arthur was a successful New York actress whom Norman Lear recruited to play a particularly juicy role—Edith's twice-divorced and fearlessly outspoken cousin, Maude, the first woman to fight Archie Bunker to a standoff. The sparks that erupted during their confrontation weren't lost on CBS program chief Fred Silverman, who convinced the producers they'd stumbled onto something. "Maude" premiered the following fall, the first spin-off in what would become Norman Lear's prime-time dynasty.

26   Christmas Day at the Bunkers   December 18, 1971
Writer: Don Nicholl
Director: John Rich
Guest Stars: Peggy Doyle, Noam Pitlik, Mel Stewart, Isabel Sanford

Archie casts a pall on the family's yuletide spirits when he complains that he was passed over for this year's Christmas bonus.

27   The Elevator Story   January 1, 1972
Writer: Alan J. Levitt
Director: John Rich
Guest Stars: Roscoe Lee Browne, Eileen Brennan, Hector Elizondo, Edith Diaz

Archie gets caught in an elevator, along with a pregnant Puerto Rican and her husband, an aging hippie, and an erudite black businessman.

Naturally, the expectant mother gives birth while stranded in the elevator. But instead of the unbearable slapstick TV has taught us to expect from such stock situations, we're treated to a privileged moment. As each of the passengers succumbs to the charm of the newborn infant, even Archie Bunker drops his defenses long enough to join the spontaneous celebration of a new life, and we see the birth through his eyes.

According to Carroll O'Connor, that sublime moment wasn't even written into the original script. "The situation was thought to be a real howl," the actor wrote in *TV Guide*. "I was sure the way it was written, crudely and incredibly, would evoke audience revulsion." The solution came only after the actor stormed off the set, the pages of his script scattered on the floor. Producer Norman Lear intervened and finally convinced him to join the other actors in improvising a new ending, coached by Lear and director John Rich. Their revisions were incorporated into the final episode, and as O'Connor recalls, "We found a way to save the childbirth and make it a touching sequence."

28   Edith's Problem   January 8, 1972
Writer: Burt Styler
Story: Burt Styler, Steve Zacharias
Director: John Rich
Guest Star: Jeannie Linero

Edith is suddenly moody and irritable with the approach of menopause.

A welcome stretch for Emmy winner Jean Stapleton. The actress had such a firm grasp on Edith's personality that even the severe mood swings brought on by her hot flashes seem absolutely in character. By the second year, the writers played catch-up to keep pace with Stapleton's portrayal, which had evolved to a depth that was barely suggested in the early scripts.

29 Archie and the FBI   January 15, 1972
  Writers: Michael Ross, Bernie West, Susan Harris
  Director: John Rich
  Guest Stars: Graham Jarvis, Larry Grundy, John Korkes

Archie's paranoia during a mysterious government investigation drives him to betray a long-standing friendship.

What separates "All in the Family" from so many later, vastly inferior imitations—a few of them produced at Norman Lear's factory—was that the writers rarely felt compelled to tack on a tidy or simple resolution. This allegory of the McCarthy era witch-hunts is no exception. Once Archie and his neighbor betray each other over what amounts to a routine investigation, it's already too late to shake hands and make up. So they don't. Instead, Archie sits alone and contemplates his tragic folly with the halfhearted rationalization "All that best buddy stuff . . . that's all for kids anyhow."

30 Mike's Mysterious Son   January 22, 1972
  Writer: Warren Murray
  Director: John Rich
  Guest Stars: Marcia Rodd, Stephen Manley

An old girlfriend of Mike's suddenly arrives at the Bunkers' with a four-year-old boy that she claims is his son.

31 Archie Sees a Mugging   January 29, 1972
  Writers: Philip Mishkin, Don Nicholl
  Story: Henry Garson
  Director: John Rich
  Guest Stars: Jack Somack, Val Bisoglio, Frank Campanella, Bill Macy

Archie refuses to get involved with police, even though he's the only witness to a neighborhood mugging.

32   Archie and Edith Alone   February 5, 1972
Writers: Lee Kalcheim, Michael Ross, Bernie West
Story: Tina and Les Pine
Director: John Rich
Guest Star: Connie Sawyer

The Bunkers are on their own for eight days after Mike and Gloria go off to spend a week at a commune.

The series's most accomplished comic drama to date, a twenty-three-minute sketch that offers a touching look at the rich fabric of a marriage that's still going strong after a quarter of a century. After Mike and Gloria go off to find their utopian dream of a week's stay at a mountain commune, the camera lingers behind on Archie and Edith as they settle down to face the more commonplace realities of their own life together. In the aftermath of a tense quarrel, they quietly share the litany of lost dreams and failed promises they've both endured over the years as they come to realize what a gift their durable union has been. By the time Mike and Gloria come trudging home, disillusioned by their tour of Shangri-La, Archie and Edith are swaying to the strains of "The Moonlight Serenade" on Edith's phonograph. They haven't found utopia either, but they've come close.

33   Edith Gets a Mink   February 12, 1972
Writers: Elias Davis, Dave Pollack, Don Nicholl
Story: David Pollack, Elias Davis
Director: John Rich
Guest Stars: Rae Allen, Richard Dysart

Archie is too proud to let Edith accept a mink stole from her cousin Amelia, until he sees a chance to make a three-hundred-dollar profit.

34   Sammy's Visit   February 19, 1972
Writer: Bill Dana
Director: John Rich
Guest Stars: Sammy Davis, Jr., Billy Halop, Fay De Witt, Keri Shutleton

Sammy Davis, Jr., encounters Archie Bunker in all his glory when the star ventures out to Queens to retrieve a briefcase he left in Munson's taxicab.

When the producers discovered that Sammy was a big fan of the series, they couldn't resist having the unlikely pair meet on camera. According to director John Rich, Archie's part-time job as a cab driver was introduced in an earlier episode largely to set up a plausible excuse for the famous nightclub performer to enter the Bunkers' Queens living room in this episode.

35   Edith the Judge   February 26, 1972
   Writer: Lee Kalcheim
   Director: John Rich
   Guest Star: Jack Weston

Edith arbitrates a dispute between Archie and the irate proprietor of a Laundromat.

36   Archie Is Jealous   March 4, 1972
   Writer: Rod Parker
   Director: John Rich
   Guest Star: Brendon Dillon

Archie is disturbed to discover Edith once spent an entire weekend with an old beau.

37   Maude   March 11, 1972
   Writer: Rod Parker
   Director: John Rich
   Guest Stars: Beatrice Arthur, Bill Macy, Marcia Rodd, Bob Dishy, Bernie West

The Bunkers attend the wedding of cousin Maude's daughter, Carol.

This episode was the pilot for "Maude." In the series, Maude's daughter would be played by Adrienne Barbeau.

1972/73   THE THIRD SEASON

Year-End Rating: 33.3 (1st place)

By the third year, the creators trust the material enough to downplay the earsplitting polemics in favor of scripts that chronicle the more mundane, though no less interesting, everyday hopes and frustrations of life at 704 Hauser Street.

Norman Lear assumes the role of executive producer when director John Rich takes over the show's production reins as well. Story editors Michael Ross and Bernie West continue to write most of the season's scripts, along with story consultant Don Nicholl.

38 Archie and the Editorial   September 16, 1972
   Writers: George Bloom, Don Nicholl
   Story: George Bloom
   Director: Norman Campbell
   Guest Stars: Sorrell Booke, Val Bisoglio, Brendan Dillon, Diane Sommerfield, Lynnette Mettey

After he rails against gun control in a TV editorial, Archie meets his two biggest supporters—a pair of stickup artists who rob him at gunpoint.

John Rich takes a break from directing to get his bearings as the show's new producer. The veteran sitcom director never planned to stay with the show past the first episode. "When Norman and Bud Yorkin asked me to direct the pilot, I said I'd sign on for just two episodes," Rich recalled. But one season led to another, until by the third and fourth years, Rich found himself producing the show and directing the actors while associate director Bob LaHendro directed the cameras from the booth.

39 Archie's Fraud   September 23, 1972
   Writers: Michael Ross, Bernie West
   Director: Norman Campbell
   Guest Stars: Billy Halop, James McEachin

Archie is audited by the IRS after he fails to report income he made driving Munson's taxicab.

40 The Threat   September 30, 1972
   Writers: Michael Elias, Lila Garrett
   Story: Bill Manhoff, Michael Elias, Lila Garrett
   Director: John Rich
   Guest Star: Gloria LeRoy

Archie can barely contain himself when the attractive young wife of an old army buddy spends an eventful night in the Bunker household.

41 Gloria and the Riddle   October 7, 1972
Writer: Don Nicholl
Director: Bob Livingston
Guest Stars: Patricia Stich, Brendon Dillon, Billy Sands, Allan Melvin

Gloria tests Mike and Archie's male chauvinism with a riddle that stumps the men but is easily answered by Edith.

42 Lionel Steps Out   October 14, 1972
Writers: Michael Ross, Bernie West
Story: Terry Ryan, Michael Ross, Bernie West
Director: Michael Kidd
Guest Stars: Mike Evans, Diane Hull, Mel Stewart

Archie is aghast to find out that his visiting niece plans to go out dancing with Lionel Jefferson.

43 Edith Flips Her Wig   October 21, 1972
Writers: Sam Locke, Olga Vallance, Don Nicholl
Director: Hal Cooper
Guest Stars: Barnard Hughes, James Gregory

Edith is worried she may be a kleptomaniac after she absent-mindedly takes a wig from a department store.

O'Connor and Stapleton get stiff competition from scene stealers Barnard Hughes and James Gregory in this episode. Both actors soon landed regular roles on a pair of other classic sitcoms: Gregory appeared as "Barney Miller's" Inspector Luger; and Hughes was Bob's father on "The Bob Newhart Show" before MTM starred him as Doc in his own CBS series in 1975.

44 The Bunkers and the Swingers   October 28, 1972
Writers: Lee Kalcheim, Michael Ross, Bernie West
Story: Norman Lear
Directors: John Rich, Bob LaHendro
Guest Stars: Vincent Gardenia, Rue McClanahan

Edith unwittingly invites a pair of wife-swapping swingers to dinner when she responds to a newspaper ad for pen pals.

This wasn't the last we'd see of the swingers. Vincent Gardenia would return the following season as the Bunkers' neighbor Frank Lorenzo; and Rue McClanahan was Bea Arthur's best friend on "Maude," a role she'd continue for six seasons before the pair renewed their friendship in 1985 as two of "The Golden Girls" on NBC.

45 Mike Comes Into Money   November 4, 1972
   Writers: Michael Ross, Bernie West
   Directors: John Rich, Bob LaHendro

Mike sparks the latest family feud when he donates two hundred dollars to George McGovern's presidential campaign instead of paying Archie for room and board.

46 Flashback: Mike and Gloria's Wedding   November 11, 1972
   (Part 1)
   Writers: Rob Reiner, Philip Mishkin, Don Nicholl
   Directors: John Rich, Bob LaHendro
   Guest Star: Michael Conrad

On the Stivics' second anniversary, the family recalls the comedy of errors that transpired on their wedding day.

In the tradition of "The Dick Van Dyke Show," the script illuminates the characters in an extended flashback that gives the writers an opportunity to take a revisionist look at events long past. The episode suggests that Archie has actually mellowed somewhat under Mike's influence—he was even more narrow-minded and stubborn in the flashback.

47 Flashback: Mike and Gloria's Wedding   November 18, 1972
   (Part 2)
   Writers: Rob Reiner, Philip Mishkin
   Directors: John Rich, Bob LaHendro
   Guest Stars: Michael Conrad, Peter Hobbs

The Stivics' wedding is jeopardized when Michael's uncle insists, over Archie's virulent objections, that the marriage be performed by a Catholic priest.

The Meathead's Uncle Cas is the late Michael Conrad, best remembered as Sergeant Esterhaus of "Hill Street Blues."

48 Mike's Appendix   December 2, 1972
Writers: Michael Ross, Bernie West
Directors: John Rich, Bob LaHendro
Guest Stars: John Zaremba, Ann Summers

Gloria is outraged when Mike insists that a male doctor perform his appendix operation.

49 Edith's Winning Ticket   December 9, 1972
Writer: Don Nicholl
Directors: John Rich, Bob LaHendro
Guest Star: Mel Stewart

Archie schemes to bilk the Jeffersons out of their winnings from a lottery ticket that Edith bought for Louise.

50 Archie and the Bowling Team   December 16, 1972
Writers: Allan Katz, Don Reo
Story: Don Nicholl
Directors: John Rich, Bob LaHendro
Guest Stars: Brad Logan, Allan Melvin

Archie loses his spot on a top bowling team to a black player.

51 The Locket   December 23, 1972
Writers: Robert Fisher, Arthur Marx
Director: Hal Cooper
Guest Stars: Liam Dunn, John Randolph, Louis Guss, Mario Roccuzzo

Archie tries to cheat the insurance company out of three hundred dollars after Edith misplaces her family-heirloom locket.

52 Archie in the Hospital   January 6, 1973
Writer: Don Nicholl
Story: Stanley Ralph Ross, Martin Cohan
Directors: John Rich, Bob LaHendro
Guest Stars: Roscoe Lee Browne, Priscilla Morrill, John Heffernan

Archie befriends the other patient in his semiprivate hospital room, unaware that he's black.

The comic shenanigans over Archie's black bunkmate merely underscore what we already know: Poor Archie gets along fine with his fellow man—until he sees the color of his skin. The producers let us in on the gag at the outset, placing the audience in a superior position to the folly of Archie's bigotry. But the results would have been more interesting had the show challenged our own prejudice by concealing the neighbor's color from the audience, as well as Archie, until the very end.

53 Oh Say Can You See January 20, 1973
Writers: Michael Ross, Bernie West
Story: Joe Kerr
Directors: John Rich, Bob LaHendro
Guest Stars: Larry Storch, Arlene Golonka

An old school chum tries to convince Archie that his fears of growing old are all in his mind.

54 Archie Goes Too Far January 27, 1973
Writers: Austin and Irma Kalish
Directors: John Rich, Bob LaHendro
Guest Stars: Pamela Murphy, Mary Kay Place, Patty Weaver

Edith and Gloria end the latest family brawl when they storm out of the house to spend the night on their own.

The wives hide out at a sorority slumber party to await their husbands' overdue apologies, setting the scene for one of Edith's classic flights of fancy. After she and Gloria conjure romantic visions of their spouses returning the way Cary Grant always came back to Irene Dunne, or Bette Davis to Humphrey Bogart, Edith cautiously intones, "You were never sure about Bette Davis. Sometimes she'd come back . . . and sometimes she'd just die."

55 Class Reunion February 10, 1973
Writer: Don Nicholl
Story: Stanley Ralph Ross, Don Nicholl
Directors: John Rich, Bob LaHendro
Guest Stars: Harvey Lembeck, Rae Allen, Priscilla Morrill

Archie refuses to tag along to Edith's thirtieth high school reunion—until he finds out that one of her old beaus will be attending.

56 Hot Watch   February 17, 1973
Writers: Sam Locke, Olga Vallance
Directors: John Rich, Bob LaHendro
Guest Star: Jack Tesler

Archie buys an expensive watch of dubious pedigree and has to find a jeweler who'll fix it with no questions asked.

As Archie schemes to profit from his blunder, he reveals his ancestral ties to Ralph Kramden, another blustery New Yorker who was similarly undone by his own greed.

57 Archie Is Branded   February 24, 1973
Writer: Vincent Bogert
Directors: John Rich, Bob LaHendro
Guest Stars: Gregory Sierra, Billy Halop, Michael Gregory, John Putch, Patrick Campbell

Archie wakes up to find a swastika painted on his front door.

A classic episode that forces Archie to question the basic tenets of his political extremism when he discovers how much he has in common with the radical terrorist that arrives to defend them. In one of the series's most unsettling finales, the family's would-be protector is murdered outside their window as the family looks on in stunned horror.

58 Everybody Tells the Truth   March 3, 1973
Writer: Don Nicholl
Directors: John Rich, Bob LaHendro
Guest Stars: Ron Glass, Ken Lynch, Maurice Marsac

It's *Rashomon* Bunker-style when the family recounts vastly different versions of the same disastrous encounter with a pair of handymen in the Bunker kitchen.

59 Archie Learns His Lesson   March 10, 1973
Writers: Michael Ross, Bernie West
Story: John Christopher Strong III, Michael R. Stein
Directors: John Rich, Bob LaHendro

Archie attends night-school classes to qualify for a high school diploma.

Mike and Archie discuss their differing perspectives on manifest destiny in a sharp scene that mines humor from Archie's desperate attempts to guard his stubborn ignorance in the face of his growing enlightenment.

60   Gloria, the Victim   March 17, 1973
   Writers: Austin and Irma Kalish, Don Nicholl
   Directors: John Rich, Bob LaHendro
   Guest Stars: Charles Durning, Mel Stewart

After an attempted sexual assault, Gloria turns to the family for guidance as she suffers through the legal aftermath of reporting the crime.

61   The Battle of the Month   March 24, 1973
   Writers: Michael Ross, Bernie West
   Directors: John Rich, Bob LaHendro

In a foul mood, Gloria lambasts Edith for her constant acquiescence to Archie's whims.

The writers clearly established that Gloria's irritation stemmed from premenstrual stress—a character motivation that brought more outraged mail than any other episode in the show's history. Writer Michael Ross defended his script when he told interviewer John Brady, "We didn't do the menstrual episode for shock value. We needed Gloria irritated to the point where she would blow up at Edith. In fact, we got the idea from Sally Struthers herself."

1973/74   THE FOURTH SEASON

Year-End Rating: 31.2 (1st place)

Archie is matched with two worthy new opponents in his fourth season of contentious controversy—Irene Lorenzo, a staunch believer in women's rights; and George Jefferson, an opinionated bigot with even less patience than Archie.

Once again, story consultant Don Nicholl and story editors Michael Ross and Bernie West are responsible for more than half the season's scripts. John Rappaport and Austin and Irma Kalish also make outstanding contributions in the fourth year.

62 We've Having a Heat Wave   September 15, 1973
Writer: Don Nicholl
Directors: John Rich, Bob LaHendro
Guest Stars: Betty Garrett, Vincent Gardenia, Victor Argo

Henry Jefferson joins Archie in trying to prevent a Hispanic family from moving into the neighborhood.

Betty Garrett and Vincent Gardenia signed on as neighbors Irene and Frank Lorenzo during the show's most tempestuous period offscreen. "All in the Family" had become the most astonishing success story in CBS's history, and Carroll O'Connor thought he deserved a bigger share of the stupendous profits the show was pulling in—which he got—as well as greater creative control, which Norman Lear and his producers staunchly refused to yield.

It was in the midst of this turbulence that the series gained—and lost—the services of Sada Thompson, the award-winning Broadway actress who later brought her gifts to the role of Kate Lawrence on ABC's "Family." She'd been the producers' original choice to play the Bunkers' feisty neighbor, Irene, but O'Connor didn't share their enthusiasm. After less than a week on the tense set, she tired of O'Connor's cold shoulder and returned to New York. The part went to Betty Garrett, a musical-comedy star from MGM's heyday and a friend of O'Connor's who posed no threat to the testy star.

Vincent Gardenia, another New York transplant, also left the show after only a handful of appearances. He made his frustrations known at an infamous testimonial dinner for Norman Lear, where more than one actor voiced his opinion. As the producer stood at the podium, the actor heckled from his seat, shouting, "I love ya, Norman. I don't know what I'm doing in the show, but I love ya!" Not surprisingly, Gardenia left the series shortly thereafter.

63 We're Still Having a Heat Wave   September 22, 1973
Writers: Michael Ross, Bernie West
Directors: John Rich, Bob LaHendro

As the Lorenzos settle in, Archie grows jealous of Edith's friendship with Irene.

Betty Garrett's Irene gave Archie his first new female contender since Bea Arthur left to carve out her own prime-time grubstake. Less strident than Maude, Irene's even-tempered logic was her strongest weapon in the war against Archie. But his greatest fear was realized when, under

Irene's influence, Edith began to lash out against his petty household tyranny. To Archie's dismay, he discovered he'd lost a dingbat and gained a partner in marriage.

64   Edith Finds an Old Man   September 29, 1973
   Writers: Michael Ross, Bernie West
   Story: Susan Harris
   Directors: John Rich, Bob LaHendro
   Guest Stars: Burt Mustin, Ruth McDevitt

Edith befriends a lonely old man, though Archie is less than thrilled to have a constant reminder of his own advancing years hanging around the house.

Burt Mustin had cornered the market on affable grandfather types from his very first appearance as Gus the fireman on "Leave It to Beaver." He and Ruth McDevitt continued to make occasional visits throughout the fifth and sixth seasons.

65   Archie and the Kiss   October 6, 1973
   Writer: John Rappaport
   Directors: John Rich, Bob LaHendro

Gloria brings home a Rodin replica for the living room, but the erotic sculpture makes Archie cringe.

A half-hour meditation on art and romance that begins with Edith's hilarious paean to Henry Mancini's "Moon River"—positive proof that beauty lies in the eye of the beholder.

66   Archie the Gambler   October 13, 1973
   Writers: Michael Ross, Bernie West
   Story: Steve Zacharias, Michael Leeson
   Directors: John Rich, Bob LaHendro

Edith is deeply disturbed to find out Archie's been playing the horses after he promised never to gamble again.

67   Henry's Farewell   October 20, 1973
   Writer: Don Nicholl
   Directors: John Rich, Bob LaHendro
   Guest Stars: Mel Stewart, Sherman Hemsley

Archie finally meets George Jefferson at Henry's going-away party.

Sherman Hemsley inherited the part of Henry Jefferson's brother,

George, after Mel Stewart opted out of the series to star in "Roll Out!" a short-lived "M*A*S*H"-style military sitcom.

68 Archie and the Computer   October 27, 1973
   Writers: Lloyd Turner, Gordon Mitchell, Don Nicholl
   Directors: John Rich, Bob LaHendro
   Guest Star: Jack Grimes

Edith receives a small fortune in quarters as a result of a computer error, while another computer informs Archie that he's been officially declared dead.

69 The Games Bunkers Play   November 3, 1973
   Writers: Michael Ross, Bernie West
   Story: Susan Perkis Haven, Dan Klein, Michael Ross, Bernie West
   Directors: John Rich, Bob LaHendro

Mike childishly refuses to accept criticism during an informal group-therapy game.

"We're always looking for important subjects," writer Michael Ross once told a reporter, "but we've also found that a simple topic—like the family sitting around playing a little game of group therapy—often makes as funny and exciting a show as the big topic, if we do it right."

70 Edith's Conversion   November 10, 1973
   Writers: Ray Taylor, Don Nicholl
   Directors: John Rich, Bob LaHendro
   Guest Stars: Barnard Hughes, Phyllis Avery

Archie thinks Irene Lorenzo is trying to convert Edith to Catholicism.

71 Archie in the Cellar   November 17, 1973
   Writer: Don Nicholl
   Directors: John Rich, Bob LaHendro
   Guest Star: Juan DeCarlos

Locked in his cellar with a bottle of vodka, Archie spends a long night contemplating his life through the haze of a drunken stupor.

72   Black Is the Color of My True Love's   November 24, 1973
         Wig
Writer: Michael Morris
Directors: John Rich, Bob LaHendro

Gloria is insulted when Michael's ardor is renewed after she
dons a cheap dime-store wig.

73   Second Honeymoon   December 1, 1973
Writers: Warren S. Murray, Michael Ross, Bernie West
Story: Warren S. Murray
Directors: John Rich, Bob LaHendro
Guest Star: Mel Bryant

Archie and Edith rekindle their romance during a second honeymoon in Atlantic City.

74   The Taxi Caper   December 8, 1973
Writer: Dennis Klein
Directors: John Rich, Bob LaHendro
Guest Stars: Michael Pataki, Al Stellone, Robert Mandan

An influential politician attempts to dissuade Archie from press-
ing charges against his son after the boy robs Archie in Munson's
cab.

75   Archie Is Cursed   December 15, 1973
Writers: John Rappaport, Michael Ross, Bernie West
Directors: John Rich, Bob LaHendro
Guest Stars: Bob Hastings, Sherman Hemsley

Irene challenges Archie to a pool match, but he begs off, complaining of a sore back.

76   Edith's Christmas Story   December 22, 1973
Writers: Austin and Irma Kalish, Don Nicholl
Story: Austin and Irma Kalish
Director: John Rich

During the Christmas holidays, Edith tries to hide the fact that
she may have breast cancer.

The yuletide season was invariably a dramatic time around the Bunker
household. Archie spent the series's first holiday show grousing that

he was broke, and this year Edith nervously awaits the results of her cancer test. In a later Christmas episode, Edith's faith is shaken when she loses a dear friend to a gang of muggers; and in the series's final year, the Bunkers awake on Christmas morning only to discover that Mike and Gloria have separated. Makes you wonder why they didn't just leave town during the holidays.

77 Mike and Gloria Mix It Up   January 5, 1974
   Writers: Michael Ross, Bernie West
   Directors: John Rich, Bob LaHendro

The Stivics' love life reaches another impasse when Michael is put off by Gloria's romantic aggressiveness.

78 Archie Feels Left Out   January 12, 1974
   Writers: Paul Lichtman, Howard Storm, Don Nicholl
   Directors: John Rich, Bob LaHendro
   Guest Stars: Burt Mustin, Ruth McDevitt

Archie refuses to attend his own birthday party.

79 Et Tu, Archie   January 26, 1974
   Writers: Mickey Rose, Lila Garrett
   Directors: John Rich, Bob LaHendro
   Guest Stars: Vic Tayback, David Doyle

Archie sabotages an old friend's efforts to land a job at the loading dock because he's afraid the man might be in line for his position.

80 Gloria's Boyfriend   February 2, 1974
   Writers: Bud Wiser, Don Nicholl
   Director: John Rich
   Guest Stars: Richard Masur, Joseph Mascolo

Archie's misconceptions run amok when Gloria befriends the retarded box boy from the local market.

81 Lionel's Engagement February 9, 1974
Writers: Michael Ross, Bernie West
Director: John Rich
Guest Stars: Charles Aidman, Lynn Moody, Kim Hamilton,
Samuel Olden, Jess Bolero, Eddie Carroll, Zara Cully

Archie squares off with George Jefferson's mother when he and
Edith attend Lionel's engagement party.

George Jefferson is as dismayed as Archie that Lionel's fiancé hails
from an interracial marriage. The basic situation would be retained when
the Jeffersons began their own series the following year, but most of
the roles would be recast—with the notable exception of Zara Cully as
George's acid-tongued mother.

82 Archie Eats and Runs February 16, 1974
Writers: Paul Wayne, George Burditt
Director: John Rich
Guest Stars: Richard Stahl, Jane Dulo, Joseph George

The Bunkers are in a panic after Archie eats a stew made from
mushrooms that might have been contaminated.

83 Gloria Sings the Blues March 2, 1974
Writers: Michael Ross, Bernie West
Director: John Rich

Gloria is bewildered after she falls temporarily out of love with
Michael, until she discovers her mother went through the same
thing with Archie.

A gentle episode that defied the series's popular conception as a
show where communication took place only above seventy-five decibels.
"You only have twenty-two minutes and thirty seconds to touch your
audience," Lear once explained. "You have to hit them hard." And yet,
many of the show's finest moments take place in an atmosphere of quiet
introspection, as in this moving episode that contains nothing more
strident than a mother and daughter comparing notes at their kitchen
table.

84 Pay the Twenty Dollars   March 9, 1974
Writers: Robert L. Goodwin, Woody Kling
Director: John Rich

Archie unwittingly passes George Jefferson a counterfeit twenty-dollar bill and sets off a string of hilarious exchanges as the family attempts to rectify the error.

85 Mike's Graduation   March 16, 1974
Writer: Don Nicholl
Director: John Rich

Archie's spirits soar on Mike's graduation day, until he discovers that his meathead son-in-law has accepted a fellowship and won't be moving out for another year.

1974/75   THE FIFTH SEASON

Year-End Rating: 30.2 (1st place)

As the series closes in on the midway point of its nine-year run, the creative staff explores new territory when Mike and Gloria decide to move into their own apartment at the end of the season.

After four years as director, John Rich is succeeded by H. Wesley Kenney, who will direct all fifth-year episodes. Michael Ross and Bernie West take over as producers, Bill Davenport and Lou Derman sign on as story editors, and Don Nicholl is appointed executive producer.

86 The Bunkers and Inflation   September 14, 1974
Writers: Don Nicholl, Michael Ross, Bernie West
Director: H. Wesley Kenney
Guest Star: Billy Halop

The Bunkers' breadwinner tries to avoid breaking the news that his union has called a strike.

Lear's writers and producers pioneered the multipart episode as a solution to the constraints imposed by the half-hour time slot. The extended format would rarely be used as effectively as in this four-part reflection on the short-term impact and long-range effects of an inflationary economy on the working-class Bunkers.

87   The Bunkers and Inflation—   September 21, 1974
      Archie Underfoot
Writers: Don Nicholl, Michael Ross, Bernie West
Director: H. Wesley Kenney

Tempers flare in the Bunker household when Archie finds himself with nothing to do but sit around the house.

88   The Bunkers and Inflation—   September 28, 1974
      Edith the Job Hunter
Writers: Don Nicholl, Michael Ross, Bernie West
Director: H. Wesley Kenney

When strike negotiations bog down, Archie grudgingly trades places with Edith and allows her to take a job at Jefferson's dry cleaners.

89   The Bunkers and Inflation—Archie's Raise   October 5, 1974
      Writers: Don Nicholl, Michael Ross, Bernie West
      Director: H. Wesley Kenney
      Guest Star: James Cromwell

Archie's union settles the strike, but under terms that effectively leave him worse off than he was before the walkout.

James Cromwell appears as Stretch Cunningham, the bard of the loading dock, who was often referred to, but until now seldom seen.

90   Lionel the Live-in   October 12, 1974
      Writer: Woody Kling
      Story: Jeffrey Mackowsky
      Director: H. Wesley Kenney

Lionel arrives to spend a few days with the Bunkers after a big blowup with his father.

91   Archie's Helping Hand   October 19, 1974
      Writers: Norman and Harriet Belkin
      Director: H. Wesley Kenney

The rising tide of feminism confronts Archie on all sides when Edith joins a women's group and Irene lands a job alongside him on the loading dock.

Edith's gradual awakening was inevitable. As Norman Lear observed, once the women's movement caught the writers' awareness, it wasn't long before Edith's consciousness was also raised. Her slow but steady evolution invested the series with a certain suspense: With each passing week, we wonder how long Archie can resist the rising tide of enlightenment that is springing up all around him.

92 Gloria's Shock October 26, 1974
Writer: Dixie Brown Grossman
Director: H. Wesley Kenney

Gloria is shocked when Mike announces that he doesn't plan on having children.

93 Where's Archie? (Part 1) November 2, 1974
Writers: Barry Harman, Harve Brosten
Director: H. Wesley Kenney
Guest Stars: Hector Elias, Charlotte Rae

Edith holds her first Tupperware party under a cloud of worry when Archie disappears on his way to a union convention in Buffalo.

This script was part of the producers' clever dodge to force the leading actor's hand after another contract dispute. When Carroll O'Connor failed to report to work at the start of the season, Lear taped this show without him. Then he vowed that Archie Bunker would be killed off in the very next episode—unless the actor returned to honor his contract.

Whether Norman Lear really had a plaid-jacketed, cigar-chomping stand-in for Archie Bunker waiting in the wings will never be known. By the third episode of this trilogy, O'Connor was back—at a substantially higher salary—and all was right on Hauser Street once more.

94 Archie Is Missing (Part 2) November 9, 1974
Writers: Lloyd Turner, Gordon Mitchell
Director: H. Wesley Kenney
Guest Stars: Allan Lurie, James Cromwell

With no word from Archie after twenty-four hours, the family faces the possibility that he might've run off with another woman.

95   The Longest Kiss (Part 3)   November 16, 1974
   Writers: Lou Derman, Bill Davenport
   Story: Dawn M. Stephens, Lou Derman, Bill Davenport
   Director: H. Wesley Kenney

Archie returns from his sorry adventure—he got sidetracked to a podiatrists' convention in Rochester—to find his friends and family celebrating his return with kissing contests, Hula Hoops, and ballroom dancing.

96   Archie and the Miracle   November 23, 1974
   Writers: Lloyd Turner, Gordon Mitchell
   Director: H. Wesley Kenney
   Guest Star: James Cromwell

After an accident on the loading dock brings Archie within inches of his life, he suddenly becomes a devout—if somewhat hypocritical—churchgoer.

97   George and Archie Make a Deal   November 30, 1974
   Writer: David P. Harmon
   Director: H. Wesley Kenney

George Jefferson seeks Archie's help when he runs for local political office.

98   Archie's Contract   December 7, 1974
   Writer: Ron Friedman
   Director: H. Wesley Kenney
   Guest Stars: Dennis Patrick, Mike Wagner, Ed Peck

Irene and the Jeffersons bail the Bunkers out after Archie buys two thousand dollars' worth of aluminum siding from a fast-talking salesman.

99   Mike's Friend   December 14, 1974
   Writers: Roger Shulman, John Baskin
   Director: H. Wesley Kenney
   Guest Star: Greg Mullavey

Gloria is made to feel like an intellectual outcast when she spends the evening with Mike and one of his graduate-school friends.

100 The Best of All in the Family (one hour) December 21, 1974
Writers: Bernie West, Michael Ross
Director: H. Wesley Kenney
Guest Star: Henry Fonda

Henry Fonda hosts an hour-long retrospective of high points from the show's first four years.

101 Prisoner in the House January 4, 1975
Writers: Bud Wiser, Lou Derman, Bill Davenport
Story: Bud Wiser
Director: H. Wesley Kenney
Guest Stars: Cliff Osmond, Sid Chute

A plumber's assistant causes Archie agony when he finds out the worker is a convict on a work-release program from Sing Sing.

102 The Jeffersons Move Up January 11, 1975
Writers: Don Nicholl, Michael Ross, Bernie West
Director: H. Wesley Kenney
Guest Stars: Paul Benedict, Franklin Cover, Berlinda Tolbert, Zara Cully

The Bunkers bid a fond farewell to the Jeffersons when their neighbors abandon Queens for the nouveau-riche life in a Manhattan high rise.

This episode was the pilot for the excruciatingly long-running spin-off series "The Jeffersons."

103 All's Fair January 18, 1975
Writers: Lloyd Turner, Gordon Mitchell
Director: H. Wesley Kenney

Gloria gives Edith a lesson in marriage assertiveness.

104 Amelia's Divorce January 25, 1975
Writers: Lou Derman, Bill Davenport
Director: H. Wesley Kenney
Guest Stars: George S. Irving, Elizabeth Wilson

Edith is surprised to discover that her cousin Amelia's ideal marriage is rotten to the core.

The writers made sure that O'Connor and Stapleton—masters of the comic take—had plenty of opportunity to practice their exquisite comic reactions on "All in the Family." When Amelia frankly confides her husband's preoccupation with sex, Edith's discomfited reactions are funnier than any lines she might utter. And the episode closes with a memorable nonverbal scene where Archie and Edith reaffirm the bond of their own marriage by clasping hands in a poignant silence that speaks volumes.

105 Everybody Does It   February 8, 1975
  Writers: Lou Derman, Bill Davenport, Susan Ware
  Director: H. Wesley Kenney

Archie steals a box of nails from work and finds himself at the center of a household debate on morality.

106 Archie and the Quiz   February 15, 1975
  Writer: Michael Morris
  Director: H. Wesley Kenney

Archie feels the weight of his own mortality after a magazine quiz on life expectancy gives him another seven years—tops.

107 Edith's Friend   February 22, 1975
  Writers: Barry Harmon, Harve Brosten
  Director: H. Wesley Kenney
  Guest Stars: Tim O'Conner, Jane Rose, Ruth Manning

Edith is reunited with her childhood sweetheart when she returns to her hometown for a wedding.

108 No Smoking   March 1, 1975
  Writers: Lou Derman, Bill Davenport
  Director: H. Wesley Kenney

The Bunker house is locked in a battle of wills after Mike vows he can go without food longer than Archie can abstain from smoking.

109 Mike Makes His Move   March 8, 1975
   Writers: Lou Derman, Bill Davenport
   Story: Robert Arnott
   Director: H. Wesley Kenney
   Guest Stars: Burt Mustin, Ruth McDevitt, Sherman Hemsley

After a fruitless search for new lodgings, Mike and Gloria agree to rent George Jefferson's old house—even though it means living next door to Archie.

1975/76   THE SIXTH SEASON

Year-End Rating: 30.1 (1st place)

A fresh stable of writers in the sixth year sets the stage for the family's most notable addition, Mike and Gloria's baby, little Joey Stivic. The nine-pound source of fresh story lines unites the Bunker clan as never before, as they embark on all-new debates over topics ranging from the baby's name to his religious upbringing.

An influx of experienced comedy veterans joins the show's creative staff in the sixth year, including story editors Milt Josefsberg, Larry Rhine, Phil Doran, and Douglas Arango; special program consultants Mel Tolkin and Ben Starr; and producers Lou Derman and Bill Davenport. Their first-rate scripts in the later seasons lack the passionate fire of the early shows, but the fine-tuned performances—and assured direction by Paul Bogart—guarantee well-crafted, if occasionally predictable, entertainment.

Woody Kling and Lou Derman serve as script supervisors; and Hal Kanter, Woody Kling, and Norman Lear share the executive producer's credit over the course of the year.

110 The Very Moving Day   September 8, 1975
   Writer: Hal Kanter
   Director: Paul Bogart

Gloria is nervous about announcing her unexpected pregnancy because of Mike's stubborn attitude toward overpopulation.

111 Alone at Last   September 15, 1975
   Writer: Hal Kanter
   Director: Paul Bogart

Teary farewells turn into fireworks when Mike hits Archie with five years of repressed rage, only to discover that he and Gloria can't move out for another week.

In the sixth season, Carroll O'Connor was able to bring in Paul Bogart as the series's new director. The star had known Bogart since the days of live television, and his arrival marked the beginning of the series's final, most tranquil period.

112   Archie the Donor   September 22, 1975
   Writers: Bill Davenport, Larry Rhine
   Director: Paul Bogart
   Guest Stars: J. A. Preston, Don Randolph, Sorrell Booke

Archie tries to impress his boss by making the maximum contribution to his favorite charity and unwittingly donates his body to medical science.

The producers aired four episodes at the start of the season in which Gloria didn't appear, after Sally Struthers sued to break her contract, which she felt was keeping her from a promising movie career. The problems were smoothed over, and judging by the first project she had to turn down—the ill-fated *Day of the Locust*—the producers probably did her a favor by keeping her tied to the show.

113   Archie the Hero   September 29, 1975
   Writers: Lou Derman, Bill Davenport
   Director: Paul Bogart
   Guest Stars: Lori Shannon, Sandy Kenyon, Billy Halop

Archie gets a rude shock when the tall, classy dame whose life he saved in a taxicab turns out to be a man.

Once again, the celebrated fireworks of Archie's reaction are no more than a theatrical contrivance compared to the script's real charm—the finely observed exchanges between Archie and Edith that authentically capture the tone of a couple who've been married to each other for twenty-six years.

114 Mike's Pains October 6, 1975
Writers: Lou Derman, Milt Josefsberg
Director: Paul Bogart
Guest Star: Francine Beers

Mike has second thoughts about natural childbirth when he gets queasy at the prospect of standing in the delivery room during Gloria's labor.

115 Chain Letter October 20, 1975
Writers: Lou Derman, Milt Josefsberg
Story: Lou Derman
Director: Paul Bogart
Guest Stars: Robert Guillaume, Beatrice Colen, Billy Halop

Archie's refusal to participate in a chain letter triggers a string of unlikely events.

116 Mike Faces Life October 27, 1975
Writers: Mel Tolkin, Larry Rhine
Director: Paul Bogart
Guest Stars: George Furth, Diane Shalet

Mike becomes the sole support of a growing family when Gloria loses her job because of her pregnancy.

117 Edith Breaks Out November 3, 1975
Writers: Lou Derman, Bill Davenport
Director: Paul Bogart
Guest Star: James Hong

Archie feels abandoned after Edith begins to volunteer part-time at the Sunshine Home for the Elderly.

118 Grandpa Blues November 10, 1975
Writers: Mel Tolkin, Larry Rhine
Story: John Rappaport
Director: Paul Bogart
Guest Stars: Sorrell Booke, John Zoller, Greg Mabrey, Tracy Bogart

Archie has difficulty keeping his blood pressure down for a company physical after the family launches into a heavy debate over the baby's name.

119   Gloria Suspects Mike   November 17, 1975
    Writers: Lou Derman, Milt Josefsberg
    Director: Paul Bogart
    Guest Star: Bernadette Peters

Gloria suspects hanky-panky when she meets the beautiful blonde Mike's been tutoring after school hours.

120   The Little Atheist   November 24, 1975
    Writer: Lou Derman
    Director: Paul Bogart

Thanksgiving dinner becomes a family battleground when Archie discovers that Mike and Gloria don't want to impose the family's religious beliefs on their baby.

121   Archie's Civil Rights   December 1, 1975
    Writers: Larry Rhine, Mel Tolkin
    Director: Paul Bogart
    Guest Stars: Paulene Myers, Frank Campanella, John Alvin, Charles Siebert

Archie gets a lesson in civil liberties when he's arrested for using outlawed tear gas to protect himself against a mugger.

The producers regularly trotted out episodes that were designed to offer piercing insights into social issues, such as this heavy-handed exploration of civil rights and unconstitutional police procedure. Unfortunately, most of these well-intentioned topical episodes were about as subtle as an episode of "Dragnet '68."

122   Gloria Is Nervous   December 8, 1975
    Writers: Milt Josefsberg, Ben Starr
    Director: Paul Bogart
    Guest Stars: Robin Wilson, Garn Stephens, Suzanne Astor, Madeleine Fisher

The baby is already nine days overdue, and the stress is turning Mike and Gloria into nervous wrecks.

Gloria's miraculous three-month gestation period is not uncommon to sitcom mothers. The medical breakthrough had been observed a full two decades earlier when Lucy Ricardo gave birth a scant six weeks after she first announced her pregnancy.

123 Birth of the Baby (Part 1)   December 15, 1975
  Writers: Lou Derman, Bill Davenport, Larry Rhine, Mel Tolkin
  Director: Paul Bogart
  Guest Stars: Herb Voland, Victor Rendina, Allan Melvin

Stuck in a phone booth in an Italian restaurant, Gloria goes into labor while Archie is busy rehearsing for his lodge's minstrel show.

Archie's blackface shenanigans were an unfortunate by-product of the writers' efforts to pad the episode out to two parts; the script also sets a new record for the show's long-standing—and inexplicable—fascination with bathroom humor: No less than three laughs are punched by the sound of a toilet's flush.

124 Birth of the Baby (Part 2)   December 22, 1975
  Writers: Milt Josefsberg, Ben Starr
  Director: Paul Bogart
  Guest Stars: Gene Blakely, Barbara Cason, Priscilla Morrill, Sudie Bond, Sharon Ullrick

Archie arrives at the hospital direct from his minstrel show—in blackface—just in time for Gloria's blessed event.

125 New Year's Wedding   January 5, 1976
  Writers: Lou Derman, Bill Davenport, Milt Josefsberg, Ben Starr
  Director: Paul Bogart
  Guest Stars: Billy Crystal, Eliot Reid, Joan Copeland, Elaine Princi, Michael Mann, Joe Bratcher, Nancy Stephens, Bibi Osterwald

The Stivics have a spat when Michael volunteers their living room for a wedding ceremony without even consulting Gloria.

126 Archie the Baby-sitter   January 12, 1976
  Writers: Lou Derman, Bill Davenport
  Director: Paul Bogart
  Guest Stars: Jack Somack, Joe Mantell, Ken Menard, Leslie Ackerman, Thad Geer

Archie's buddies form a lullaby quartet when Grandpa Bunker baby-sits Joey on his poker night.

Incredibly, this innocuous episode caused a furor when the network objected to a scene that called for total frontal nudity—the baby's! Despite the censor's objections, the producers trampled another TV taboo and ran Archie's diaper-changing sequence uncut.

127 Archie Finds a Friend   January 26, 1976
  Writers: Mel Tolkin, Larry Rhine
  Director: Paul Bogart
  Guest Star: Jack Gilford

Archie sees a chance to get rich quick when he befriends an old watchmaker who's got a surefire invention.

128 Mike's Move   February 2, 1976
  Writers: Milt Josefsberg, Ben Starr
  Director: Paul Bogart
  Guest Stars: Lee Bergere, David Downing

Mike's integrity is put to the test when he loses a teaching position to an equally qualified black candidate.

Archie extracts sweet revenge when he turns the tables on his bleeding-heart son-in-law with a hilarious reworking of the Emma Lazarus inscription on the Statue of Liberty. Archie's version begins, "Send me your poor, your deadbeats, your filthy . . . all of them free to live together in their own separate little sections where they feel safe and break your head if you go in there."

129 Archie's Weighty Problem   February 9, 1976
  Writers: Mel Tolkin, Larry Rhine
  Director: Paul Bogart
  Guest Stars: Burt Mustin, Billy Halop

Energetic Justin Quigley inspires Archie to stick with the strict diet his doctor has recommended.

130 Love by Appointment   February 16, 1976
  Writers: Lou Derman, Bill Davenport
  Director: Paul Bogart

Mike and Gloria's sex life suffers after they have to begin planning their encounters around the baby's feeding schedule.

In another funny and believable talk between mother and daughter,

Struthers shows us how the flighty postadolescent of the earliest shows has matured—first as a wife, then as a mother, until she finally emerges in later seasons as a woman who doesn't feel completely fulfilled in either of those roles.

131 Joey's Baptism   February 23, 1976
    Writers: Milt Josefsberg, Mel Tolkin, Larry Rhine
    Director: Paul Bogart
    Guest Star: Clyde Kusatsu

After Mike and Gloria refuse to have their son baptized, Archie stubbornly steals away to a church to douse the infant himself.

132 Mike and Gloria's Houseguests   March 1, 1976
    Writers: Larry Rhine, Mel Tolkin, Milt Josefsberg
    Director: Paul Bogart

A broken furnace forces Archie and Edith to spend a few nights under the Stivics' roof during a power blackout.

133 Edith's Night Out   March 8, 1976
    Writers: Lou Derman, Douglas Arango, Phil Doran
    Director: Paul Bogart
    Guest Stars: Doris Roberts, Scott Brady, Jason Wingreen

Edith abandons her stick-in-the-mud husband to liven things up on her own during an evening out at Kelcy's Bar.

Jason Wingreen would play Harry the bartender for the rest of the show's run, and he would be one of the few holdovers to survive the series's transition to "Archie Bunker's Place" at the end of the ninth season.

1976/77   THE SEVENTH SEASON

Year-End Rating: 22.9 (12th place)

The fury of the early years has largely evaporated by the seventh season as the writers exploit the rich personalities of the central cast in well-crafted character comedies that take full advantage of the show's rock-solid ensemble.

Mort Lachman joins the staff as executive producer for the show's last three seasons, and Milt Josefsberg takes over as producer. The pair also serve as script supervisors. Larry Rhine and Mel Tolkin are executive story editors, and Douglas Arango and Phil Doran are the seventh-year story editors.

134 Archie's Brief Encounter   September 22, 1976
    (Part 1—one hour)
  Writers: Mel Tolkin, Larry Rhine
  Director: Paul Bogart
  Guest Stars: Janis Paige, Scott Brady, Theodore Wilson, André Pavon

Edith leaves Archie when she finds out he dated a flirtatious waitress while she was volunteering at the Sunshine Home.

135 Archie's Brief Encounter (Part 2)   September 29, 1976
  Writers: Mel Tolkin, Larry Rhine
  Director: Paul Bogart
  Guest Stars: Scott Brady, Maxine Elliot, Bella Chronis, Harry Davis

Edith forgives Archie's indiscretion after Mike and Gloria bring the two together for an emotional reunion.

The events of this classic two-parter would color the Bunkers' relationship for some time to come. The subject would arise only on rare occasions—but in the aftermath of Archie's mistake, the couple shared a renewed tenderness that would carry them through the final three seasons.

136 The Unemployment Story (Part 1)   October 6, 1976
  Writers: Ben Starr, Chuck Stewart
  Director: Paul Bogart
  Guest Stars: Jinaki, F. Murray Abraham

Archie's self-esteem takes a beating when he loses his job on the loading dock.

137 The Unemployment Story (Part 2)   October 13, 1976
  Writers: Chuck Stewart, Ben Starr
  Director: Paul Bogart
  Guest Stars: Gerald Hiken, Neva Patterson, Eliza Garrett, Jeannie Linero, Ellen Travolta

A college grad threatens to commit suicide after he loses a janitor's job to Archie.

138   Archie's Operation (Part 1)   October 20, 1976
   Writers: Milt Josefsberg, Mort Lachman
   Story: Calvin Kelly, Jim Tisdale
   Director: Paul Bogart
   Guest Stars: Vinnette Carroll, Liz Torres, Milton Selzer

Archie's trip to the hospital is an ethnic nightmare: He's admitted by a Puerto Rican receptionist, treated by a Jewish physician, and is forced to accept a blood transfusion from a black doctor!

Liz Torres makes her first appearance as Teresa Betancourt, who would shortly become the Bunkers' boarder.

139   Archie's Operation (Part 2)   October 27, 1976
   Writers: Mel Tolkin, Larry Rhine
   Director: Paul Bogart
   Guest Stars: Vinnette Carroll, Frances Fong, Danny Dayton

Archie recuperates in record time after he's called back to work—with a raise and a promotion.

Danny Dayton appears as Hank Pivnik, one of Archie's pals who would frequent Kelcy's Bar and later, Archie's Place.

140   Beverly Rides Again   November 6, 1976
   Writers: Phil Doran, Douglas Arango
   Director: Paul Bogart
   Guest Stars: Lori Shannon, Eugene Roche, Phoebe Dorin, André Pavon

As a practical joke, Archie fixes up one of his drinking buddies with female impersonator Beverly LaSalle.

Lori Shannon returns for another round of tired theatrics as the showgirl Archie once saved with mouth-to-mouth resuscitation.

141   Teresa Moves In   November 13, 1976
   Writer: Michael Loman
   Director: Paul Bogart
   Guest Stars: Liz Torres, Alex Colon

The Bunkers take in a boarder to help revive their battered budget.

142   Mike and Gloria's Will   November 20, 1976
   Writers: Bill Richmond, Gene Perret
   Director: Paul Bogart

The Bunkers are stunned to hear that Mike and Gloria plan to appoint another couple as Joey's legal guardians in their will.

143   Mr. Edith Bunker   November 27, 1976
   Writers: Mel Tolkin, Larry Rhine
   Director: Paul Bogart
   Guest Stars: Priscilla Morrill, Phil Leeds, Florence Halop, James Greene, Maxine Elliot, Bella Chronis, Bob Duggan

Edith saves a man's life and becomes the toast of the town, but Archie isn't happy standing in the shadow of her limelight.

144   Archie's Secret Passion   December 4, 1976
   Writer: Michael Loman
   Director: Paul Bogart
   Guest Stars: Estelle Parsons, Mike Kellin

Edith discovers Archie once had a brief encounter with an old high school friend she's invited to dinner.

Estelle Parsons would be typecast as the show's lady of dubious virtue. After playing the woman with a checkered past in this episode, she returned in the ninth season as Barney Hefner's comically wayward wife.

145   The Baby Contest   December 11, 1976
   Writers: Larry Rhine, Mel Tolkin
   Story: Marion Zola, Ed Haas
   Director: Paul Bogart
   Guest Stars: Allan Melvin, Danny Dayton, Jason Wingreen

Archie enters Joey in a newspaper's beautiful-baby contest, against the express wishes of Mike and Gloria.

The series had become much less topical in later years, and many stories—like this one—revolved around the classic domestic situation of two married couples who are best friends and next-door neighbors. The show's occasional resemblance to "I Love Lucy"—albeit with the roles reversed and the focus now on the older couple—wasn't entirely coincidental. Many of "All in the Family's" current writers had formerly scripted the redhead's video misadventures. Lou Derman and Bill Davenport even wrote for Lucy's earliest radio sitcom, "My Favorite Husband," before joining Milt Josefsberg many years later on "Here's Lucy." And Bob Schiller and Bob Weiskopf, who joined "All in the Family" in the eighth season, were two-fifths of the writing team on the original "I Love Lucy."

146 Gloria's False Alarm   December 18, 1976
    Writers: Phil Doran, Douglas Arango
    Director: Paul Bogart
    Guest Star: Michael Mann

Gloria insists that Mike get the vasectomy he's talked about for years.

147 The Draft Dodger   December 25, 1976
    Writers: Jay Moriarty, Mike Milligan
    Director: Paul Bogart
    Guest Stars: Eugene Roche, Renny Temple, Liz Torres

Sparks fly when Mike invites a former draft resister to the Bunkers' Christmas dinner, where the guest of honor is the father of a vet who was killed in Vietnam.

The war returns as a topic of controversy in an unexpected homage to the kitchen-table fireworks of the earliest episodes but invested with the deeper emotional coloration typical of the show's later period. Instead of contributing to the predictable battle of clashing viewpoints, the bereaved father surprises everyone with an impassioned plea for amnesty.

Try as he might, even Archie can't remain unmoved. He agrees to mull the issue over in his mind and then, in frustration, retreats to the front porch to berate a festive chorus of carolers. But the singing continues, and in the final shot of this classic episode, Archie stands alone, a bewildered Scrooge unable to snuff out the last candle of hope.

148 The Boarder Patrol   January 8, 1977
    Writers: Larry Rhine, Mel Tolkin
    Director: Paul Bogart
    Guest Stars: Patrick Cronin, William Lanteau, Juan De Carlos

The Bunkers return home unexpectedly to find Teresa in bed with her boyfriend.

Much as the producers tried to establish Teresa as the Bunkers' surrogate daughter, the chemistry just wasn't there—and the boarder quietly moved out at the close of the season.

149 Archie's Chair   January 15, 1977
   Writers: Phil Doran, Douglas Arango
   Director: Paul Bogart
   Guest Stars: Michael Pataki, Allan Rich, Doug Robinson, Colin Hamilton, Tyler McVey

Archie's beloved easy chair ends up in an art museum after the repair shop accidentally sells it to a modern artist.

Archie's chair actually did end up in a museum, no less than the Smithsonian Institution. At the request of a congressional committee, Norman Lear donated the Bunkers' living-room ensemble to the Smithsonian's permanent collection at the close of the eighth season.

150 Mike Goes Skiing   January 22, 1977
   Writers: Ben Starr, Chuck Stewart
   Director: Paul Bogart
   Guest Stars: John Karlen, Rod Loomis, Tom Fitzsimmons, Mark Lonow

Mike asserts his independence by leaving Gloria behind while he joins his friends on a weekend skiing trip.

151 Stretch Cunningham, Good-bye   January 29, 1977
   Writers: Phil Doran, Douglas Arango, Milt Josefsberg
   Director: Paul Bogart
   Guest Stars: Charles Siebert, Jay Gerber

Archie reluctantly agrees to deliver Stretch Cunningham's eulogy, unaware that his departed friend was Jewish.

152 The Joys of Sex   February 5, 1977
   Writer: Erik Tarloff
   Director: Paul Bogart

Edith sneaks a peek at a best-selling sex manual and decides her romantic life could stand a little perking up.

Archie's squirming—and Edith's squeamishness—aside, "All in the Family" was the first TV series to openly acknowledge a healthy sexual relationship shared by a middle-aged couple. As incredible as it seems, before the Bunkers, television's married couples—young or old—always slept in twin beds.

153 Mike the Pacifist February 12, 1977
Writers: Phil Doran, Douglas Arango
Director: Paul Bogart
Guest Stars: Wynn Irwin, Nita Talbot, Sudie Bond, Richard Lawson, William Lanteau, William Pierson

Mike feels guilty for punching a man on the subway, even though he acted in defense of Gloria.

154 Fire February 19, 1977
Writers: Michael Loman, Larry Rhine, Mel Tolkin
Director: Paul Bogart
Guest Star: Roger C. Carmel

Archie tries to collect on a fraudulent insurance claim after a small fire breaks out in the upstairs bathroom.

155 Mike and Gloria Split February 26, 1977
Writers: Mel Tolkin, Larry Rhine
Story: Mort Lachman, Milt Josefsberg
Director: Paul Bogart

Mike spends a night with Archie after a fight with Gloria.

156 Archie the Liberal March 5, 1977
Writers: Ben Starr, Chuck Stewart
Director: Paul Bogart
Guest Star: James McEachin

When his lodge comes under fire for discrimination, Archie tries to knock off two quotas at once by courting a black Jew for membership.

157 Archie's Dog Day Afternoon March 12, 1977
Writers: Chuck Stewart, Ben Starr
Story: Mort Lachman, Milt Josefsberg
Director: Paul Bogart
Guest Stars: Bill Hunt, Vanda Barra, Tracy Bogart

Archie accidentally runs over Barney Hefner's dog.

1977/78   THE EIGHTH SEASON

Year-End Rating: 24.4 (4th place)

In what was originally conceived as the show's final season, the writers pull out all the stops to create a handful of the series's most memorable dramatic episodes—including the departure of Mike and Gloria at the season's end—many of them scripted by Bob Schiller and Bob Weiskopf, the veteran writing team who signed on as script consultants for the show's final two seasons.

In addition to contributions from the familiar bullpen—including story editors Mel Tolkin and Larry Rhine, and producer Milt Josefsberg—memorable scripts are written by Phil Sharp, Erik Tarloff, and Chuck Stewart and Ben Starr.

158   Archie Gets the Business (one hour)   October 2, 1977
   Writers: Mel Tolkin, Larry Rhine
   Director: Paul Bogart
   Guest Stars: Frank Maxwell, Norma Donaldson, Sid Conrad

Archie, desperate to realize his personal dream and buy Kelcy's Bar, forges Edith's signature on mortgage papers.

Archie's graduation from wage earner to entrepreneur opened up a wealth of new story possibilities, even as it changed the essential character of the show. No longer a downtrodden member of the working class, Archie the small businessman had less reason to vent his outrage than in days past and the show mellowed considerably in its final two seasons.

159   Cousin Liz   October 9, 1977
   Writers: Bob Schiller, Bob Weiskopf
   Story: Barry Harmon, Harve Brosten
   Director: Paul Bogart
   Guest Star: K Callan

At the funeral of Edith's cousin Liz, the Bunkers are shocked to learn that she'd been living with a lesbian roommate for years.

160   Edith's Fiftieth Birthday (one hour)   October 16, 1977
   Writers: Bob Schiller, Bob Weiskopf
   Director: Paul Bogart
   Guest Stars: David Dukes, Jane Connell, John Brandon, Ray Colella

Edith misses her birthday party when a rapist holds her at gunpoint in her own living room.

Schiller and Weiskopf faced built-in compromises when they chose to depict such a singularly violent crime within the confines of a television comedy, especially when the victim was one of the most beloved figures on prime time. Though the creators were justifiably applauded for their efforts, the episode wasn't entirely successful; the shocking drama and unsettling suspense of the first half hour makes for an uneasy blend with the head-thumping slapstick of Mike and Archie's ill-timed comic relief in the second half hour.

161 Unequal Partners   October 23, 1977
   Writers: Chuck Stewart, Ben Starr
   Director: Paul Bogart
   Guest Stars: Ian Wolfe, Merie Earle, Will Mackenzie

Edith ruins Archie's weekend fishing trip when she stages a wedding in the Bunkers' living room.

162 Archie's Grand Opening   October 30, 1977
   Writers: Larry Rhine, Mel Tolkin
   Director: Paul Bogart
   Guest Stars: Sorrel Booke, Joe Petrullo, Paul Larson, Sam Solito, Grace Lee

The family steps in to serve drinks and tend bar at Archie's tavern after his staff deserts him on opening night.

163 Archie's Bitter Pill (Part 1)   November 16, 1977
   Writers: Mel Tolkin, Larry Rhine, William C. Rader, M.D.
   Director: Paul Bogart
   Guest Stars: Arny Freeman, A. Martinez

Archie takes a few pep pills to keep pace with the increased demands of running his own business and winds up with an amphetamine addiction.

164 Archie's Road Back (Part 2)   November 23, 1977
   Writers: Mel Tolkin, Larry Rhine, William C. Rader, M.D.
   Director: Paul Bogart
   Guest Stars: A. Martinez, MacIntyre Dixon

A despondent Archie retreats to his bedroom, until Harry offers to bail him out with a partnership offer for the bar.

165   Archie and the Ku Klux Klan (Part 1)   November 27, 1977
   Writers: Bob Schiller, Bob Weiskopf, Mort Lachman, Milt Josefsberg
   Director: Paul Bogart
   Guest Stars: Dennis Patrick, Roger Bowen, Owen Bush

Archie is nominated for membership in a mysterious fraternal order that turns out to be the local branch of the KKK.

166   Archie and the Ku Klux Klan (Part 2)   December 4, 1977
   Writers: Bob Schiller, Bob Weiskopf
   Director: Paul Bogart
   Guest Stars: Dennis Patrick, Roger Bowen

Archie devises a plan to prevent the Klan from burning a cross on Mike and Gloria's lawn.

167   Mike and Gloria Meet   December 11, 1977
   Writers: Bob Schiller, Bob Weiskopf
   Director: Paul Bogart
   Guest Stars: Christopher Guest, Priscilla Lopez

A flashback explores Mike and Gloria's first blind date.

Rob Reiner would cast co-star Christopher Guest as one of the leads when he directed the 1984 rock'n'roll satire *This Is Spinal Tap*.

168   Edith's Crisis of Faith (one hour)   December 25, 1977
   Writers: Bob Schiller, Bob Weiskopf (first half hour)
   Erik Tarloff, Mel Tolkin, Larry Rhine (second half hour)
   Story: Erik Tarloff
   Director: Paul Bogart
   Guest Stars: Lori Shannon, Ron Vernan

Edith's religious faith is shaken after her friend female impersonator Beverly LaSalle is brutally murdered by street thugs at Christmas.

169 Archie and the Super Bowl   January 5, 1978
   Writers: Bob Schiller, Bob Weiskopf
   Director: Paul Bogart
   Guest Stars: Art Metrano, Louis Guss, Gloria LeRoy, J. J.
   Johnston, Raymond O'Keefe

Archie's Place is robbed on Super Bowl Sunday, the busiest day
of the year.

170 The Commercial   January 8, 1978
   Writers: Ben Starr, Ron Bloomberg
   Story: Ron Bloomberg
   Director: Paul Bogart
   Guest Stars: Alan Hamel, Frank Aletter, Darryl Hickman,
   Thomas Middelton

Edith is chosen to appear in a TV commercial but finds herself
unable to lie when she begins to doubt the quality of the sponsor's detergent.

171 Aunt Iola's Visit   January 22, 1978
   Writer: Albert E. Lewin
   Story: Michael Loman
   Director: Paul Bogart
   Guest Star: Nedra Volz

Archie refuses to let Edith's elderly aunt move into their spare
bedroom, even after she's been turned away by every other
relative.

172 Love Comes to the Butcher   February 5, 1978
   Writer: Phil Sharp
   Director: Paul Bogart
   Guest Stars: Theodore Bikel, Sarina C. Grant

Archie is jealous when a lonely butcher lavishes attention on
Edith.

173 Two's a Crowd   February 12, 1978
   Writer: Phil Sharp
   Director: Paul Bogart

Mike and Archie have a long talk after they find themselves
locked in the storeroom of Archie's Place.

Carroll O'Connor and Rob Reiner are splendid in this compelling exploration of their frequently tempestuous relationship. Locked in the quiet solitude of a cold cellar, each reveals a part of himself that's always been well guarded, and in the shadows of the dark basement, they begin to see each other in a new light. In Archie's touching monologue, he admits the reverent devotion he always felt toward his father and then dozes off in sorrow at the painful realization that he never earned the same respect from his own daughter. Michael doesn't say a word but quietly reaches over to cover him in the warmth of the cellar's lone blanket. The sleeping King Lear never stirs when he finally earns a small gesture of fatherly respect—bestowed not by a daughter—but by a son.

174   Stale Mates   February 19, 1978
Writers: Larry Rhine, Mel Tolkin
Director: Paul Bogart
Guest Stars: Judy Kahan, Terry Kiser

Mike and Gloria are sure the romance has gone out of their marriage when even a weekend in the Poconos fails to reignite the spark.

175   Archie's Brother   February 26, 1978
Writers: Larry Rhine, Mel Tolkin
Director: Paul Bogart
Guest Star: Richard Mackenzie

Archie's estranged brother returns, after twenty-nine years, to smooth things over before he enters the hospital for a serious operation.

176   Mike's New Job   March 5, 1978
Writers: Mel Tolkin, Larry Rhine
Director: Paul Bogart
Guest Star: Sherman Hemsley

The Stivics prepare to move to California after Mike is offered a teaching position in Santa Barbara.

177   The Dinner Guest   March 12, 1978
Writers: Mel Tolkin, Larry Rhine
Director: Paul Bogart

Edith is crushed when Mike and Gloria make other plans after she's prepared a special farewell dinner in their honor.

178 The Stivics Go West   March 19, 1978
   Writers: Bob Schiller, Bob Weiskopf
   Director: Paul Bogart
   Guest Star: Clyde Kusatsu

The Bunker house is the scene of tearful good-byes as Mike and
Gloria finally leave for California.

When the cast concluded taping this classic episode, there was hardly
a dry eye in the house, onstage or off. The sentimental ceremonies that
attended the season's final show were originally planned as a wrap party
for the entire series. When Reiner and Struthers first announced their
intention to leave at the end of the season, Norman Lear couldn't conceive of carrying on without them. "I'm confident you are watching the
last full season of 'All in the Family,' " he told reporters in January as
he made plans to leave television to return to the greener pastures of
feature-film production.

Carroll O'Connor was also adamant about his retirement. "Television's like a good neighborhood gone bad," he told columnist Marilyn
Beck, "and I'd like to get out." But that was before CBS stepped in with
an eleventh-hour offer to keep the ratings powerhouse going at least
one more year.

"I don't see why we should deprive the American public of one of
their favorite shows," was CBS president Bob Daly's public rationale for
luring Carroll O'Connor back to the fold with a salary that exceeded
$100,000 per episode, in addition to a lucrative production deal with the
network. The actor helped convince Jean Stapleton to return, and to
everyone's surprise, "All in the Family" entered a ninth and final season—without Mike, without Gloria, and without Norman Lear.

1978/79   THE NINTH SEASON

Year-End Rating: 24.9 (9th place)

The show's final—and not entirely unworthy—season is redeemed
by a handful of first-rate scripts, though the Bunkers almost never recover from the deadening pathos that arrives with the introduction of
a nine-year-old on Hauser Street. Even so, the writers manage to explore
the ever-deepening bond between Archie and Edith, who continue to
evolve as the most plausibly romantic couple on television.

Most ninth-year stories are scripted by a talented writing stable that
includes story editors Mel Tolkin and Larry Rhine, producer Milt Jo-

sefsberg, and story consultant Phil Sharp. Script consultants Bob Schiller and Bob Weiskopf once again contribute a number of memorable scripts, as do newcomers Patt Shea and Harriett Weiss.

179   Little Miss Bunker   September 24, 1978
   Writers: Mel Tolkin, Larry Rhine
   Director: Paul Bogart
   Guest Stars: Marty Brill, Bhetty Waldron, Santos Morales, Bern Bennett

Edith's cousin Floyd abandons his nine-year-old daughter, Stephanie, on the Bunkers' doorstep.

Danielle Brisebois, the littlest orphan in Broadway's *Annie*, joined the cast as Edith's niece, Stephanie Mills. The introduction of a child into the Bunker household created a dangerous breeding ground for gross sentimentality at a time when the show's critics were already lambasting the producers for letting Archie go soft in the show's old age. O'Connor later dismissed the criticism in the pages of *TV Guide* when he insisted, "We're not going to have him yell 'coon' every week just so we can keep up the reputation of a socially pungent show."

180   End in Sight   October 1, 1978
   Writer: Nate Monaster
   Director: Paul Bogart
   Guest Star: Phil Leeds

Archie spends a night wallowing in self-pity when an insurance physical reveals an ominous spot on his liver.

181   Reunion on Hauser Street   October 8, 1978
   Writers: Milt Josefsberg, Phil Sharp
   Director: Paul Bogart
   Guest Stars: Estelle Parsons, Glora LeRoy

The Bunkers attempt to reunite Blanche and Barney Hefner after her latest fling with an exterminator fizzles.

182   What'll We Do With Stephanie?   October 15, 1978
   Writers: Larry Rhine, Mel Tolkin
   Director: Paul Bogart
   Guest Star: Abbey Lincoln

The Bunkers decide to keep Stephanie after her father fails to reclaim her as promised.

183 Edith's Final Respects   October 22, 1978
 Writers: Bob Schiller, Bob Weiskopf
 Story: Sam Greenbaum
 Director: Paul Bogart
 Guest Stars: Howard Morton, Charles Siebert

Edith is the sole mourner at her Aunt Rose's funeral.

184 Weekend in the Country   October 29, 1978
 Writers: Phil Sharp, Milt Josefsberg
 Director: Paul Bogart
 Guest Star: Estelle Parsons

Once again, Archie and Edith try to preserve peace between Barney Hefner and his extremely wayward wife.

185 Archie's Other Wife   November 5, 1978
 Writers: Bob Schiller, Bob Weiskopf
 Director: Paul Bogart
 Guest Stars: Eugene Roche, Harvey Lembeck, Jonelle Allen, James J. Casino

At an American Legion convention, Archie awakens facing a beautiful black airline stewardess who swears they were married the night before.

186 Edith Versus the Bank   November 19, 1978
 Writers: Mel Tolkin, Larry Rhine
 Director: Paul Bogart
 Guest Star: John Harkins

Edith is disillusioned when her bank refuses to grant a loan without her husband's signature.

When she discovers her husband is as narrow-minded as the bank manager, Edith demands that Archie pay her a token five-dollars-a-week payment for her labors as a housewife. Using her own unique logic, she extracts exactly what she wants from Archie in the end, proving once more that in the realm of common sense, this dingbat has no peer.

187   The Return of the Waitress   November 26, 1978
   Writers: Milt Josefsberg, Phil Sharp
   Director: Paul Bogart
   Guest Star: Janis Paige

Edith finally confronts the waitress who tempted Archie's fidelity after Harry unwittingly hires her to work at Archie's Place.

Edith bears no malice toward the waitress but thanks her for helping to strengthen her union with Archie. He ends the episode with the observation, "Edith, you're a pip." The expression, employed as Archie's most disparaging put-down in the early years, suddenly rings with a tenderness as compelling as Ralph Kramden's classic declaration of devotion, "Baby, you're the greatest."

188   Bogus Bills   December 3, 1978
   Writers: Bob Schiller, Bob Weiskopf
   Director: Paul Bogart
   Guest Stars: Sandy Kenyon, John Finnegan, Charles Hallahan

Edith is arrested for passing phony ten-dollar bills she got from Archie's Place.

189   The Bunkers Go West   December 10, 1978
   Writers: Mel Tolkin, Larry Rhine
   Director: Paul Bogart

After Mike and Gloria cancel their trip home for Christmas, the Bunkers decide to travel west for the holidays.

190   California, Here We Are (one hour)   December 17, 1978
   Writers: Milt Josefsberg, Phil Sharp (first half); Bob Schiller, Bob Weiskopf (second half)
   Director: Paul Bogart
   Guest Star: Cory Miller

The Bunkers arrive in Santa Barbara for Christmas and soon discover that all is not right with Mike and Gloria.

More disturbing than the Stivics' heartbreaking announcement of their separation is Archie's reaction when he discovers that Gloria has been unfaithful to her husband: For the first time in nine years, he turns his back on his daughter and sides with Michael. The script, rife with disturbing details of the petty cruelties that have already poisoned the

Stivics' marriage, avoids the easy out of a tidy resolution. Mike and Gloria do effect a spontaneous reconciliation under the tree, but the tentative exchange lacks the conviction of a permanent reunion. They've been through enough to know, as we do, that the optimism of Christmas morning doesn't always stand up to the cold light of the new year.

The script's only nod toward romanticism is suggested by Edith and Archie, who never felt as thankful for the years they've shared together as they did on that eventful Christmas morning.

191   A Night at the PTA   January 7, 1979
Writers: Mel Tolkin, Larry Rhine
Director: Paul Bogart

When Edith develops laryngitis on the eve of her singing debut at Stephanie's PTA recital, Archie steps in to understudy the duet.

192   A Girl Like Edith   January 14, 1979
Writers: Bob Schiller, Bob Weiskopf
Director: Paul Bogart
Guest Stars: Theodore Bikel, Giovanna Pucci

Edith meets butcher Klemmer's new sweetheart, a woman who just happens to be her spitting image.

Edith's Teutonic double is played by Stapleton in a dual role, a technical stunt that would have been impossible to pull off while the show was still taped with a live crowd. The producers had done away with the live studio audience at the start of the ninth season to please O'Connor, who preferred to tape in a cold studio and dub in the laughs later.

193   The Appendectomy   January 21, 1979
Writers: Phil Sharp, Milt Josefsberg
Director: Paul Bogart
Guest Stars: George Wyner, Tracy Bogart

Edith and Archie rush Stephanie to the hospital for an emergency appendectomy.

194   Stephanie and the Crime Wave   January 28, 1979
    Writers: Larry Rhine, Mel Tolkin
    Director: Paul Bogart
    Guest Star: Davis Roberts

The Bunkers are at odds over Stephanie's punishment when they catch her stealing petty items from around the house.

195   Barney the Gold Digger   February 5, 1979
    Writers: Bob Schiller, Bob Weiskopf, Phil Sharp, Milt Josefsberg
    Story: Winston Moss
    Director: Paul Bogart
    Guest Star: Peggy Rea

Barney Hefner is suicidal after Blanche finally deserts him, until Archie fixes him up with an overweight but wealthy widow.

196   Stephanie's Conversion   February 18, 1979
    Writers: Patt Shea, Harriet Weiss
    Director: Paul Bogart
    Guest Stars: Clyde Kusatsu, Michael Mann

Archie is forced to reevaluate his religious prejudice after Stephanie tries to conceal the fact that she's Jewish.

197   Edith Gets Fired   February 25, 1979
    Writers: Patt Shea, Harriet Weiss
    Story: Mort Lachman
    Director: Paul Bogart
    Guest Stars: Angela Clarke, Dolores Sutton, Michael McGuire, Leonard Stone, Victor Killian, Gerald Castillo

Edith loses her job at the Sunshine Home after she honors an invalid woman's final wish to be allowed to die with dignity.

198   The Best of "All in the Family"   March 4, 1979
    (ninety-minute special)
    Director: Walter Miller
    Guest Star: Norman Lear

Norman Lear hosts an affectionate look at the high points of his ground-breaking TV series.

CBS didn't think anyone would accept Lucille Ball as the wacky wife of Desi Arnaz's Cuban bandleader, but their stubborn determination yielded "I Love Lucy," television's very first classic sitcom.

William Frawley, Desi Arnaz, and Vivian Vance are helpless observers of Lucy's frigid agony in an early "I Love Lucy" sight gag that's as painful as it's hilarious.

Lucy was visibly enceinte during much of the show's second year after the writers worked the star's real-life pregnancy into the storyline, despite objections from the sponsors and CBS.

Jackie Gleason, Audrey Meadows, Art Carney, Joyce Randolph—the cast of "The Honeymooners"—a classic that remains as funny on the third, fourth, even tenth viewing as it was the first time around.

A sense of dingy reality permeated every fibre of the series, from Norton's battered felt hat to the Kramden's depression-era kitchen. "Make it real," Gleason told his writers. "If it isn't credible, nobody's going to laugh."

BUY
SAVINGS BONDS
Payroll Savings Plan Today

Even stronger than the Kramden's conjugal ties—and perhaps more crucial to the show's chemistry—was the spiritual bond shared by lodge brothers Ralph and Ed.

Wiry, even-tempered, reasonably satisfied with his life, Art Carney's Ed Norton was everything Ralph Kramden was not—and yet, it was in Norton's childlike devotion that Kramden found strength.

Mary Tyler Moore, Dick Van Dyke, Larry Mathews—the Petries—on "The Dick Van Dyke Show," an undisputed masterpiece in the admittedly thin annals of television art.

"It was like a lovely party you never wanted to end," recalls Morey Amsterdam, pictured here with Rose Marie, Van Dyke, and Tyler Moore—the nucleus of one of TV's great ensembles.

The producers considered casting Johnny Carson, but finally chose Dick Van Dyke to play Rob Petrie because he seemed shy, like a writer. Mary Tyler Moore landed the role of Laura after Carl Reiner heard her say hello...like a real person.

Mary Tyler Moore as associate news producer Mary Richards. For the first time television showed us a beautiful young woman who was single by choice, not chance.

"The Mary Tyler Moore Show" family: Gavin MacLeod, Mary Tyler Moore, Ted Knight, Valerie Harper, Edward Asner, Cloris Leachman. In later seasons they were joined by Betty White and Georgia Engel (*right*). Each would probably agree that they did the best work of their careers on the series.

The episodes that defined and explored Mary's friendship with Rhoda Morgenstern—many of them scripted by women writers—often carried a sharp sting of truth.

Mary Richard's compassion for her boss set the stage for one of the most graceful love affairs in popular fiction: the unconsummated romance between Mary and Lou.

Mary looks on as Ted Baxter, played by Ted Knight, comforts Ed Asner's Lou Grant. Each member of the cast represented the perfect marriage of actor and role.

"All in the Family's" Jean Stapleton, Carroll O'Connor, Sally Struthers, and Rob Reiner as America's noisiest neighbors, the Archie Bunker clan of Queens, New York.

Long-suffering Edith Bunker appeals to Archie, who was once described by his creator as "basically a horse's ass." Somehow this incongruous pair made an absolutely convincing married couple.

It's hard to imagine two different actors as Gloria and Mike Stivic, but Struthers and Reiner were actually the third couple to play the parts.

The unkempt original cast of CBS's bawdy, brawling—and initially low-rated—antiwar comedy, "M*A*S*H" (*clockwise, from the left*): Larry Linville, Wayne Rogers, Gary Burghoff, MacLean Stevenson, Alan Alda, Loretta Swit.

Jamie Farr models another hand-me-down from the 20th Century-Fox wardrobe department. Klinger's efforts to get thrown out of the military were inspired by writer Larry Gelbart's recollection of how Lenny Bruce attempted a similar gambit to get discharged from the navy.

There was more sentiment than slapstick in later seasons, but after eleven years the 4077th staff had developed into TV's most fully defined character ensemble (*left to right, from the top*): William Christopher, Jamie Farr, Mike Farrell, Henry Morgan, Loretta Swit, David Ogden Stiers, Alan Alda.

The cast of "The Bob Newhart Show"—Marcia Wallace, Bob Newhart, Peter Bonerz, Suzanne Pleshette, Bill Daily—inhabitants of a surreal universe that frequently resembled Alice's Wonderland.

The Hartley's unabashed sexuality gave the series a distinctive, sophisticated edge, but writers admit they were equally tickled by the comic possibilities of the situation. Chuckled one of the show's creators, "It was funny to imagine Newhart in bed."

Tom Poston makes a guest appearance as Bob's old friend, the Peeper. The irony was that Bob's cast of crazies behaved as if they were the most well-adjusted characters on television.

Abe Vigoda's Detective Fish proved so popular that ABC (and Vigoda himself) insisted that his character be given a spin-off, a request that producer Danny Arnold resisted for two seasons.

The members of "Barney Miller's" detective squad—Jack Soo, Steve Landesberg, Ron Glass, Hal Linden, James Gregory, Max Gail, Ron Carey—were seldom afraid to share the spotlight with the host of bit players who gave the show its heart.

Unlike most TV supercops, the Twelfth Precinct detectives usually came up short in their struggles with the unrelenting stress of police work, a fact that caused law enforcement agencies to applaud "Barney Miller" as the most realistic show on television.

The first-season case of "Taxi," worthy heirs of the MTM legacy (*clockwise, from top left*): Randall Carver, Andy Kaufman, Judd Hirsch, Tony Danza, Danny DeVito, Jeff Conaway, Marilu Henner.

As Everyman Alex Reiger, Hirsch offers an impromptu English lesson to Kaufman's Latka Gravas, the cab company's stranger in a strange land.

Like Latka, Christopher Lloyd's Reverend Jim Ignatowski also hailed from a far distant reality—the 1960s.

Danny DeVito's Louie DePalma squares off with Marilu Henner's Elaine Nardo. Venal, disagreeable, dishonest, the pint-sized dispatcher quickly rose to the status of co-star in an ensemble loaded with memorable characters.

Funny, sophisticated, unpredictable, "Cheers" outlashed an initial season of dismal ratings to emerge as one of the top comedies of the 1980s (*left to right, from the top*): Shelly Long, Ted Danson, Woody Harrelson, Rhea Perlman, George Wendt, John Ratzenberger.

Nick Colasanto as the addled but avuncular coach Ernie Pantusso poses for this first-year portrait with the original gang working at Cheers: Danson, Long, and Perlman.

The most turbulent affair on prime time—the love story of Sam and Diane—offered a frequently harrowing look at the dark underside of modern romance.

199 The Return of Archie's Brother   March 11, 1979
    Writers: Bob Schiller, Bob Weiskopf
    Story: Bob Schiller, Bob Weiskopf, Tom Sawyer
    Director: Paul Bogart
    Guest Stars: Richard Mackenzie, Ellissa Leeds

Archie's brother, Fred, arrives with his latest wife—a child bride of eighteen.

200 The Family Next Door   March 18, 1979
    Writers: Mel Tolkin, Larry Rhine
    Director: Paul Bogart
    Guest Stars: Richard Ward, David Byrd, Isabel Sanford, Janet MacLachlan

Archie hits the roof when Edith rents out the old Jefferson house to a black couple.

201 The Return of Stephanie's Father   March 25, 1979
    Writers: Larry Rhine, Mel Tolkin
    Director: Paul Bogart
    Guest Stars: Ben Stack, Victor Kilian, Rick Plastina, Charles Wagenheim, Hugh McPhillips

Stephanie's father, Floyd, finally arrives with a devastating proposition for the Bunkers: They can keep Stephanie if they agree to pay him one thousand dollars cash!

202 Too-Good Edith   April 8, 1979
    Writers: Patt Shea, Harriet Weiss
    Director: Paul Bogart
    Guest Star: George Wyner

Archie is hurt and outraged when Edith tries to hide a serious illness from him.

There's a funny exchange between Archie and Edith in one of the very last episodes that reveals with pristine clarity the underlying optimism of the show. Archie is railing at the top of his lungs—dead-set against befriending the black family that's just moved in next door. Edith waits patiently for him to finish and continues preparing sandwiches for the new neighbors.

Miffed by her lack of sympathy, Archie moans, "You know damn well there's certain things about me I ain't never gonna change. But you keep asking me to make out like I'm gonna."

Edith pauses, then replies with a comical certainty, "That's right."

And so the series ends as it began, with Archie cursing the darkness, as Edith lights a candle and patiently waits for some small sign of progress. Things haven't really changed much since we first met the Bunkers at their twenty-second anniversary party so many years ago. Then, as now, Archie held forth in blustery ignorance as he demanded that Edith stifle herself at the first sign of rebuttal. And yet there is one small, but very encouraging difference: This time, it's Edith who gets in the last word.

By the time "All in the Family" left the air in 1979, the vast changes that had taken place during our nine years with the Bunkers appeared to be largely an illusion. The show dawned during the peak of Nixon's reign and ended as another Republican readied his own assault on the White House.

By the end of the decade, equal opportunity for blacks in television looked like just another program trend that had run its course. And for all the vaunted inroads "All in the Family" made in prime-time sophistication, by 1979 the most-watched show in the land was a slight comedy about a bachelor who shared a disarmingly platonic arrangement with a pair of buxom female roommates.

Of course, it was Norman Lear himself who warned against pinning too much hope on what was, after all, just a television show. As he admits, "If a couple thousand years of Judeo-Christian ethic have not solved the problems of bigotry and narrow-mindedness, I'd be a fool to think a little half-hour situation comedy is gonna do the trick."

EMMY AWARDS

The following is a complete listing of the Emmy Awards bestowed on "All in the Family" by the National Academy of Television Arts and Sciences.

1970/71   Outstanding Comedy Series
             Outstanding New Series
             Outstanding Continued Performance by an Actress in a
                Leading Role in a Comedy Series: Jean Stapleton

1971/72 Outstanding Series: Comedy
Outstanding Continued Performance by an Actor in a Leading Role in a Comedy Series: Carroll O'Connor
Outstanding Continued Performance by an Actress in a Leading Role in a Comedy Series: Jean Stapleton
Outstanding Performance by an Actress in a Supporting Role in Comedy: Sally Struthers (tied with Valerie Harper)
Outstanding Directorial Achievement in Comedy: John Rich, "Sammy's Visit"
Outstanding Writing Achievement in Comedy: Burt Styler, "Edith's Problem"

1972/73 Outstanding Comedy Series
Outstanding Writing Achievement in Comedy: Michael Ross, Bernie West, Lee Kalcheim, "The Bunkers and the Swingers"

1973/74 Outstanding Supporting Actor in a Comedy Series: Rob Reiner

1976/77 Outstanding Lead Actor in a Comedy Series: Carroll O'Connor

1977/78 Outstanding Comedy Series
Outstanding Writing in a Comedy Series: Bob Schiller, Bob Weiskopf, teleplay; Barry Harmon, Harve Brosten, story, "Cousin Liz"
Outstanding Directing in a Comedy Series: Paul Bogart, "Edith's Fiftieth Birthday"
Outstanding Continuing Performance by a Supporting Actor in a Comedy Series: Rob Reiner
Outstanding Lead Actress in a Comedy Series: Jean Stapleton
Outstanding Lead Actor in a Comedy Series: Carroll O'Connor

1978/79 Outstanding Lead in a Comedy Series: Carroll O'Connor
Outstanding Supporting Actress in a Comedy Series: Sally Struthers, "California, Here We Are"

"M*A*S*H"

·

War is hell. So is TV.
—LARRY GELBART

DR. RICHARD HORNBERGER figured that his profits from "M*A*S*H"—in surgeon's terms—came to about one gall bladder per episode.

Or about three hundred dollars a week which is what Twentieth Century–Fox Studios promised the small-town doctor—and part-time novelist—when they negotiated the television rights to "M*A*S*H" in 1971. Hornberger, who, under the pen name, Richard Hooker, had written the novel that spawned Fox's 1970 hit film *M*A*S*H*, thought it sounded like a fair deal, though he had no reason to believe the series would last more than a few weeks.

Fred Silverman was a great deal more optimistic. When William Self, the head of the Twentieth Century–Fox TV unit, called CBS to pitch his idea of spinning off a series from the popular *M*A*S*H* movie, the network programmer snapped it up. The network's recent success with "All in the Family" convinced Silverman that controversy was in. And what could be more controversial than a bawdy, bloody antiwar comedy?

Nothing. And that's what worried Gene Reynolds when he was assigned to produce and develop the project. He loved Robert Altman's irreverent movie, but he also knew how easily network meddling could emasculate a powder keg like *M*A*S*H*. Finally, after CBS promised him a free hand, he decided it was worth a try.

He flew to England to work out the details of the pilot script with Larry Gelbart, an expatriate American screenwriter then living in London. "We felt an obligation not to make the series a homogenized imitation of the film," Gelbart recalls. "CBS threw us a terrific curve. They agreed."

After Reynolds flew back to the States, the writer crafted a script that was a brilliant subversion of TV's traditional service comedy. The plot of his pilot script is familiar enough to anyone who's ever seen "McHale's Navy"—the fun-loving army surgeons stage a drunken bash that's foiled when a strict general drops by for a surprise inspection. But in Gelbart's version, the party doesn't end until the war begins.

The air fills with choppers carrying a precious cargo—the bodies of maimed and wounded men, fresh from the front lines. The hijinks end abruptly as the doctors scrub up to begin their cycle of insanity once again. They stitch and patch the broken soldiers until they're well enough to go back out to get shot at all over again. It was situation comedy as absurdist drama.

And it was also a thinly veiled satire of contemporary U.S. foreign policy. Taking a cue from the original film, Gelbart and Reynolds viewed the series as their contribution to the swelling antiwar movement. "We were doing a story about the Korean War, but it was really about Vietnam," explained Reynolds. "A lot of our stories were Vietnam stories."

CBS aired the pilot as the series's premiere episode in September 1972. The network's reaction was swift and far from favorable. Many executives objected to the show's dark ambiguities and at one point CBS suggested that the producers tone down the tense operating-room scenes so as not to offend viewers. That's when Reynolds and Gelbart knew it was time to assert themselves. "Gene and I decided to offend the network and put in as many such scenes as we could," says Gelbart.

But the series's mixed critical response and lackluster ratings certainly didn't help their case. After the show finished the season slumped in forty-sixth place, the "M*A*S*H" company was pleasantly surprised to hear that they'd been renewed for a second year.

The show had been saved by Fred Silverman, who was convinced that the series could make it, if only it could find its audience. To prove his point, he rescheduled the comedy to a slot where no one could miss it—Saturday nights, following the megahit "All in the Family." And sure enough, "M*A*S*H" became an instant—if somewhat belated—hit.

"As our ratings climbed," observed Gelbart, "corporate resistance fell." And he and Gene Reynolds wasted no time putting their creative liberties to good use. By the end of the third season, the show had tackled a raft of topics that were rarely broached on network TV— including homosexuality, interracial marriage, adultery, military genocide, and transvestism.

And as the content of the shows grew more sophisticated and varied, so did the personnel of the 4077th. Reynolds and his associate producer, former casting director Burt Metcalfe, assembled a powerful ensemble that included Alan Alda, McLean Stevenson, Gary Burghoff, Larry Linville, Wayne Rogers, and Loretta Swit. All of them were anxious to grow beyond the limitations their characters had inherited from the original film, but it was Hawkeye Pierce who emerged as the voice of the 4077th from the very start. Alan Alda radiated intelligence, sensitivity, and the incongruous charm of the class clown—a combination that made him a natural anchor for the series's sincere irreverence.

Gelbart confessed a special fondness for the character. "It was the first time that I ever tried writing a character who would speak as I do, act as I do—or at least as the idealized *I* do," he told reporter Marshall Berges. "After years of writing material that would conform with a performer's image, I was able to try molding one to my own."

Ironically, Alda's galvanizing effect on the series also brought about the show's first major rift, when Wayne Rogers made it clear that he wasn't pleased with Hawkeye's growing dominance. His repeated protests finally ended in a string of bitter, and ultimately unsuccessful, contract negotiations.

"I know who I am and where I'm going," the actor told *TV Guide*. "If both CBS and 20th Century–Fox burned down tomorrow, I'd retire to a small intellectual community and be a professional student for the rest of my life." At the close of the third season, Rogers walked away from the series and refused ever to look back.

The producers dealt with another contract dispute in a more ingenious fashion, when McLean Stevenson grew restless to break out on his own during the second and third years. "I'm tired of being one of six," he complained. "I want to be one of one."

When Stevenson made it clear he wouldn't be returning for a fourth year, the producers planned Colonel Blake's final appearance in absolute secrecy. When the actor got his copy of the complete script, he was shocked to discover that Colonel Blake was to be shot down over the Sea of Japan after his final appearance. "I felt it was vindictive," he told David Reiss, author of *M*A*S*H: The Exclusive, Inside Story of Television's Most Popular Show*, "that the real motive was to prevent me from doing a show where I might want to continue being Henry Blake,

M.D." But after his anger softened, he was forced to admit, "It did make one hell of a show."

To Gelbart and Reynolds, the circumstances presented a rare chance to make a statement about war that would carry a deep emotional impact that viewers wouldn't soon forget. "By killing a cherished character," Gelbart told *Newsweek*, "you can approximate the feeling of losing someone you love."

By the time new recruits Mike Farrell, Harry Morgan, and David Ogden Stiers signed on, there would be less outright silliness and robust sexuality as the producers moved the series away from the madcap antics of the original film.

"We couldn't just keep repeating war is hell, war is hell," Burt Metcalfe remarked after he and Alan Alda took over the show's supervision in later years. "So we started really exploring the characters and allowing them to evolve."

But as the staff of the 4077th grew more sympathetic in the show's later years, there was a danger that they'd sacrifice the comic bite that gave the series its edge. Margaret Houlihan left her "Hot Lips" moniker behind, only to emerge as an incongruous humanitarian in tailor-made dungarees; the show's creeping nobility turned Hawkeye into an insufferable "saint in surgical garb"—exactly the sort of windbag that would've been punctured with the business end of the surgeon's rapier in earlier shows. As Larry Gelbart observed in *People* long after his departure, "I'm not a big fan of commercial heart. In a comedy you also have to kick the character with heart in the ass. If you don't, you lose crispness, friction, conflict, drama . . . and comedy, too."

By the tenth season, the cast and writing staff openly acknowledged the creative strain that had set in. "Alan and I find it increasingly difficult to come up with story material," Burt Metcalfe TV columnist told Gary Deeb. "Some of us feel it would be a good idea to end the series while we're still on top in terms of both ratings and quality. But CBS and the studio would like to keep it going a lot longer."

At the end of the tenth year, the cast took a vote to decide the fate of "M*A*S*H." Jamie Farr, William Christopher, and Harry Morgan put thumbs up but found themselves outvoted by Alan Alda, David Ogden Stiers, Loretta Swit, and Mike Farrell—all of whom balked at returning for another year. It was decided. The tenth season would be the last year for "M*A*S*H."

But the executives at Twentieth Century–Fox and CBS approached Alan Alda with a counteroffer. If the actor could convince the cast to return for one final year, the network would allow them to film an abbreviated season of only sixteen episodes, with a grand finale that would be the most ambitious single TV show ever filmed—a final, feature-length farewell episode.

The gambit worked.

Alda couldn't resist the opportunity to cap the series with such an unprecedented farewell. At the last minute he swung his vote in favor of doing an eleventh, and unequivocably final, season.

The climactic two-and-one-half-hour episode, "Good-bye, Farewell and Amen," aired to unprecedented media hoopla and went on to become the single highest-rated program in television history, seen by an incredible 125 million viewers. The demise of the TV series received more attention than the actual Korean War ceasefire had, three decades earlier.

Which is an appropriate irony for a show that brought the war into our living rooms in a way that no wire service or news broadcast could hope to. "We weren't kidding ourselves, though," Alan Alda acknowledged after the series shut down. "We did enough research on war to know there's a vast difference between what we did on the show from 8:00 A.M. to 8:00 P.M. and the people who bled real blood."

But if the TV show was unable to bring us the wounds of battle in all their graphic horror, the series never flinched in its depiction of the equally violent wounds wrought by boredom, loneliness, and the sorrow that comes from an unending exposure to pain. And yet, even in the bleakest moments, the silliness of a practical joke—or the kindness of a shared affection—would pop up as a hopeful reminder of the indomitability of the human spirit. There were some things, we came to see, even more powerful than the ravages of war.

It was a complex message—both funny and sad. And the show's uncompromising treatment of these conflicting emotions provides a clue to the series's timeless appeal. In their finest half hours, the cast and creators of "M*A*S*H" didn't seem to care whether we laughed or cried—just so long as we never stopped watching.

A Critical Guide to All 251 Episodes

Captain Hawkeye Pierce	Alan Alda
Captain Trapper John McIntyre	Wayne Rogers
Lieutenant Col. Henry Blake	McLean Stevenson
Captain B. J. Hunnicut	Mike Farrell
Major Margaret "Hot Lips" Houlihan	Loretta Swit
Major Frank Burns	Larry Linville
Corporal Radar O'Reilly	Gary Burghoff
Colonel Sherman Potter	Harry Morgan
Major Charles Winchester	David Ogden Stiers
Corporal Max Klinger	Jamie Farr
Father John Mulcahy	William Christopher

FIRST-SEASON SUPPORTING CAST

Spearchucker Jones	Timothy Brown
Lieutenant Dish	Karen Philipp
Nurse Margie Cutler	Marcia Strassman
Lieutenant Ginger Ballis	Odessa Cleveland
General Hammond	G. Wood
Ho-John	Patrick Adiarte
Father Mulcahy (pilot episode)	George Morgan
Ugly John	John Orchard
Nurse Leslie Scorch	Linda Meiklejohn
Nurse Nancy Griffin	Lynnette Mettey
General Brandon Clayton	Herb Voland

SUPPORTING CAST

Nurse Kellye	Kellye Nakahara
Colonel Flagg	Edward Winter
Major Sidney Freedman	Allan Arbus
Sergeant Zelmo Zale	Johnny Haymer
Igor	Jeff Maxwell

253

Nurse Bigelow	Enid Kent
Luther Rizzo	G. W. Bailey
Lieutenant Colonel Donald Penobscott	Beeson Carroll, Mike Henry
Soon Lee	Rosalind Chao

STOCK COMPANY

Bobbie Mitchell, Patricia Stevens, Judy Farrell, Tom Dever, Dennis Troy, Abby Nelson, Soon Teck Oh, Jan Jorden, Val Bisoglio

Created by Larry Gelbart, Gene Reynolds
Theme song ("Suicide Is Painless") by Johnny Mandel
Directors of photography were William Jurgensen, Meredith Nicholson, Dominick R. Palmer
Principal directors were Gene Reynolds, Hy Averback, Jackie Cooper, Don Weis, William Jurgensen, Larry Gelbart, Burt Metcalfe, Charles S. Dubin, Alan Alda, George Tyne, Harry Morgan

1972/73   THE FIRST SEASON

Year-End Rating: 17.5 (46th place)

In their first season behind the lines of the Korean War, Hawkeye and Trapper John spend considerably more time chasing skirts than patching wounds in the operating room. But by the end of the year, producer Gene Reynolds and co-creator Larry Gelbart have evolved the bawdy and irreverent world of the 4077th mobile army surgical hospital into television's first true black comedy—a simultaneously grim and hilarious vision of war where laughter is the only potent weapon of defense.

In addition to executive story consultant Larry Gelbart's contributions, first-year scripts from Laurence Marks, Carl Kleinschmitt, and Sid Dorfman all help shape the series's early viewpoint. Burt Metcalfe is associate producer of the first four seasons, and William Jurgensen the director of photography for the first five. Stanford Tischler and Fred W. Berger are the show's regular editors for the first four years.

1 "M*A*S*H" Pilot   September 17, 1972
Writer: Larry Gelbart
Director: Gene Reynolds
Guest Stars: Karen Philipp, Patrick Adiarte, G. Wood, Timothy
Brown, Linda Meiklejohn, Laura Miller, George Morgan

Iconoclastic army surgeons Hawkeye Pierce and Trapper John
MacIntyre throw a drunken bash to raise money to send their
Korean houseboy to a U.S. college.

A remarkable episode that established the show's major characters
in a black comedy of absurd proportions. In one fell blow, the barracks
buffoonery of Sergeant Bilko and Gomer Pyle was rendered hopelessly
and shamefully irrelevant.

Karen Philipp appeared—briefly—as Lieutenant Dish, one of the
characters from the film who failed to survive the transition to the small
screen after the producers realized the limitations of a half-hour format
on such a large cast. Timothy Brown's Spearchucker Jones, the 4077th's
black surgeon, was also prominent in early episodes; he even bunked
with Hawkeye and Trapper John before he quietly shipped out midway
through the season. Writer Larry Gelbart maintains that the black doctor
was dropped after research revealed there just *weren't any* black surgeons
in Korea, but the writers clearly had no idea where to go with the blandly
written character from the very start.

2 To Market, to Market   September 24, 1972
Writer: Burt Styler
Director: Michael O'Herlihy
Guest Stars: G. Wood, Robert Ito, Jack Soo, John C. Johnson

Hawkeye hopes to replenish dwindling medical supplies when
he trades Henry's antique desk for a shipment of black-market
hydrocortisone.

Jack Soo plays a Korean black-marketeer here, though the late character actor would be better remembered as "Barney Miller's" Japanese
detective, Nick Yemena.

3 Requiem for a Lightweight   October 1, 1972
Writer: Bob Klane
Director: Hy Averback
Guest Stars: Marcia Strassman, Sorrell Booke, Mike McGirr

Trapper John is sorely mismatched when he faces a massive opponent in an intercamp boxing tournament.

Hawkeye and Trapper John both vie for the attention of Nurse Margie Cutler, whose tour of duty at the 4077th barely outlasts the first season.

4   Chief Surgeon Who?   October 8, 1972
Writer: Larry Gelbart
Director: E. W. Swackhamer
Guest Stars: Linda Meiklejohn, Jack Riley, Sorrell Booke, Timothy Brown, Odessa Cleveland, Jamie Farr

Jealous when Hawkeye is appointed chief surgeon, Frank summons a flabbergasted general to look in on the unorthodox leisure activities of the new head doctor.

There's a gag in this episode about a GI so desperate for a psychiatric discharge that he wears women's clothes—inspired, according to Larry Gelbart, by Lenny Bruce, who attempted a similar gambit to get thrown out of the navy. The sight gag would eventually blossom into financial security for bit player Jamie Farr, but it very nearly got left on the cutting-room floor. In director E. W. Swackhamer's first cut, he had Farr play the transvestite as an effeminate swish—a cliché that sent the producers scrambling for a retake. Reynolds did reshoot it. The second time the actor played it straight, the bit was much funnier and in no time at all, Corporal Max Klinger was a fixture on the series.

5   The Moose   October 15, 1972
Writer: Laurence Marks
Director: Hy Averback
Guest Stars: Paul Jenkins, Virginia Lee, Craig Jue, Barbara Brownell, Patrick Adiarte, Tim Brown

Incensed when a GI arrives with a Korean teenager he bought as a slave, Hawkeye conspires to emancipate the girl and restore her self-respect.

The writers often drew stories from actual historical detail. Here, a Korean family that still practices the ancient custom of indentured servitude propels the characters to action. The unstinting research paid off: Letters commending or correcting the show's accuracy began to pour in from veteran MASH doctors, most of whom were anxious to share their own wartime experiences. Over the years, these rich and detailed firsthand accounts of war would form the basis for some of the show's strongest episodes.

6 Yankee Doodle Doctor   October 22, 1972
Writer: Laurence Marks
Director: Lee Philips
Guest Stars: Ed Flanders, Bert Kramer, Herb Voland

The doctors rebel when they discover that the army plans to make a propaganda film glorifying the depressing conditions of war.

7 Bananas, Crackers, and Nuts   November 5, 1972
Writer: Burt Styler
Director: Bruce Bilson
Guest Star: Stuart Margolin

Hawkeye acts even crazier than usual after he's denied a weekend pass to Tokyo.

8 Cowboy   November 12, 1972
Writer: Bob Klane
Director: Don Weis
Guest Stars: Billy Green Bush, Alicia Bond, Rick Moses, Joe Corey

The 4077th copes with a shell-shocked helicopter pilot who turns to violence after Henry denies his discharge back to the States.

Don Weis, one of the first-season directors of "The Andy Griffith Show," would continue as a "M*A*S*H" director for four of the first six seasons.

9 Henry, Please Come Home   November 19, 1972
Writer: Laurence Marks
Director: William Wiard
Guest Star: G. Wood

When Colonel Blake's transfer to Tokyo leaves Frank Burns in command, Hawkeye and Trapper wage a campaign to get their beloved—and tolerant—commanding officer back in the fold.

10   I Hate a Mystery   November 26, 1972
   Writer: Hal Dresner
   Director: Hy Averback
   Guest Stars: Bonnie Jones, Linda Meiklejohn

Hawkeye decides to play detective when he becomes the chief suspect in a rash of petty thefts.

Hy Averback started out as a radio announcer before he distinguished himself as one of the most prolific television directors of the 1950s and 1960s. He would be the only early "M*A*S*H" director to continue with the show throughout its run.

The producers weren't as happy with some of the other first-year directors, most of whom had made their reputations directing a mixed bag of one-camera sitcoms during the 1960s. After a few run-ins with unsympathetic—or just plain confused—directors, Gelbart, and later Reynolds and Alda, added directing to their other duties. Together they would nurture the show through its first fledgling seasons, along with a handful of returning first-year directors, including Averback, Don Weis, William Wiard, and Jackie Cooper.

11   Germ Warfare   December 10, 1972
   Writer: Larry Gelbart
   Director: Terry Becker
   Guest Stars: Robert Gooden, Karen Philipp, Byron Chung

Frank is the unwitting donor in an emergency blood transfusion when Hawkeye extracts a pint from the major in his sleep.

12   Dear Dad   December 17, 1972
   Writer: Larry Gelbart
   Director: Gene Reynolds
   Guest Stars: Bonnie Jones, Lizabeth Deen, Gary Van Orman

During a lull in surgery, Hawkeye composes a Christmas letter to his dad describing the simple joys and endless dread of daily life in a war zone.

In one of his earliest efforts to stretch the narrative boundaries of situation comedy, Gelbart allowed the audience to look at life through the surgeon's eyes, as Hawkeye narrates the episode as a letter he's written to his dad. The script was more influential than anyone guessed at the time; it established Hawkeye as the show's empathetic voice just as Gelbart was first discovering his own voice in the character.

13 Edwina December 24, 1972
Writer: Hal Dresner
Director: James Sheldon
Guest Stars: Arlene Golonka, Linda Meiklejohn, Marcia Strassman

The nurses band together to find a date for an accident-prone nurse.

14 Love Story January 7, 1973
Writer: Laurence Marks
Director: Earl Bellamy
Guest Stars: Kelly Jean Peters, Indira Danks, Barbara Brownell, Jerry Harper

Trapper and Hawkeye offer Radar a crash course in music and literature when they fix him up with a nurse who's culturally inclined.

Though few people were aware of it at the time, four years earlier guest star Kelly Jean Peters had originated the role of Gloria in the first pilot for what would become "All in the Family."

15 Tuttle January 14, 1973
Writers: Bruce Shelly, David Ketchum
Director: William Wiard
Guest Stars: Herb Voland, Mary-Robin Redd, James Sikking

The medics create a fictitious captain so that they can donate his army salary to an orphanage.

16 The Ringbanger January 21, 1973
Writer: Jerry Mayer
Director: Jackie Cooper
Guest Stars: Leslie Nielsen, Linda Meiklejohn

Trapper and Hawkeye conspire to have an overzealous commander shipped back home to protect the troops from his military enthusiasm.

Nineteen-thirties child actor Jackie Cooper had grown up to star in two successful sitcoms of the 1950s, "The People's Choice" and "Hennesey," which he also produced. It was on the latter series that the actor-turned-producer gave another former child actor a break when he hired

Gene Reynolds to direct. Reynolds returned the favor on "M*A*S*H," and Cooper would eventually direct the majority of episodes in the series's second year.

17 Sometimes You Hear the Bullet January 28, 1973
Writer: Carl Kleinschmitt
Director: William Wiard
Guest Stars: James Callahan, Ronny Howard, Lynnette Mettey

Hawkeye mourns the sudden death of an old friend on his operating table.

Alan Alda cited this episode as the series's first real groundbreaker. "It was the first time on our show that a sympathetic and charming character had died," the actor wrote in *TV Guide*. It was a breakthrough that was lost on the confused executives at CBS, most of whom were unaccustomed to having death sprung on them between the toothpaste commercials of half-hour situation comedy. The producers held their ground and insisted that sudden and unexpected death was an entirely appropriate subject for a comedy set in war. When the episode finally aired, it drove yet another nail into the coffin of the superfluous situation comedy of the 1960s. At least for a time, anyway.

A decade earlier, writer Carl Kleinschmitt had been a prolific contributor to the original "Dick Van Dyke Show."

18 Dear Dad . . . Again February 4, 1973
Writers: Sheldon Keller, Larry Gelbart
Director: Jackie Cooper
Guest Stars: Alex Henteloff, Gail Bowman, Odessa Cleveland

In another letter home, Hawkeye explains how he survives the perverse insanity of war by staying just one step ahead of the butterfly net.

19 The Long-john Flap February 18, 1973
Writer: Alan Alda
Director: William Wiard
Guest Stars: Kathleen King, Joseph Perry

A coveted pair of long johns arrive during a Korean cold spell and find their way into more than one M*A*S*H footlocker before day's end.

A handful of TV actors had directed episodes of their own series before, and a few had even written scripts that could actually be filmed; but Alan Alda is probably the only actor ever to simultaneously direct, write, and star in a long-running television series. Not surprisingly, his early scripts reflect Gelbart's strong influence, but Alda quickly developed his own voice, both as a writer and as a director.

20 The Army-Navy Game February 25, 1973
Writer: Sid Dorfman
Story: McLean Stevenson
Director: Gene Reynolds
Guest Stars: Alan Manson, David Doyle, Tom Richards

The medics' enjoyment of the radio broadcast of the Army-Navy game is seriously compromised when an undetonated bomb lands in the middle of camp.

21 Sticky Wicket March 4, 1973
Writers: Laurence Marks, Larry Gelbart
Story: Richard Baer
Director: Don Weis
Guest Stars: Wayne Bryan, Lynnette Mettey, Bonnie Jones

Hawkeye accuses Frank of incompetent surgery, only to discover that one of his own patients is suffering a mysterious relapse.

22 Major Fred C. Dobbs March 11, 1973
Writer: Sid Dorfman
Director: Don Weis
Guest Star: Harvey J. Goldenberg

Frank is about to ship out of the 4077th, but Hawkeye and Trapper John trick him into staying on after they discover that his transfer doubles their workload.

The producers hadn't yet quite got their bearings, as this uncharacteristic episode proves. The script violates the basic premise of the characters in an inconsequential plot that veers dangerously into stock sitcom territory. Larry Gelbart would be so embarrassed by this episode that in later years he would remember it as simply "the worst."

23   Ceasefire   March 18, 1973
Writers: Laurence Marks, Larry Gelbart
Story: Larry Gelbart
Director: Earl Bellamy
Guest Star: Herb Voland

The 4077th makes premature plans to dismantle the camp when they hear rumors of a ceasefire.

The producers always kept an eye on the headlines as they fashioned their Vietnam allegory, so it's not entirely coincidental that this episode aired the same week the United States began withdrawing troops from Vietnam. Surprisingly, the end of the fighting in Southeast Asia had very little effect on the show. The ceasefire might have dulled the show's urgency, but it didn't blunt the message. As Hawkeye observed in a Gelbart script aired two years later, "Wars don't last forever, only war does."

24   Showtime   March 25, 1973
Writers: Robert Klane, Larry Gelbart
Story: Larry Gelbart
Director: Jackie Cooper
Guest Stars: Joey Forman, Harvey Goldenberg, Stanley Clay, Sheila Lauritsen, Oksun Kim

A USO song-and-dance man performs a comedy show in stark counterpoint to bleak business as usual in the operating room.

1973/74   THE SECOND SEASON

Year-End Rating: 25.7 (4th place)

The comedy's ratings skyrocket after CBS sandwiches it between "All in the Family" and "The Mary Tyler Moore Show" on their Saturday-evening lineup, and the show swiftly rises to the challenge set by such sterling company. Hawkeye continues to anchor the comic drama, but other characters also emerge as distinct and complex personalities in second-year scripts that reveal unexpected depth of feeling in Trapper John, Colonel Blake, and, perhaps most surprising of all, Hot Lips.

Producer Gene Reynolds is officially joined by Larry Gelbart as co-producer. Gelbart also continues to write or polish every script, along with the equally prolific story editor, Laurence Marks. Together and separately, the pair write the majority of the season's episodes, most of which are directed by Jackie Cooper, William Wiard, Don Weis, or Gene Reynolds.

25   Divided We Stand   September 15, 1973
   Writer: Larry Gelbart
   Director: Jackie Cooper
   Guest Star: Anthony Holland

The personnel of the 4077th are on their best behavior when they're visited by an army observer intent on reassigning the unit.

Gelbart and Reynolds designed this first show of the new season as a second pilot; the idea was to reintroduce the major characters for the benefit of all the new viewers who would join the series in its improved time slot.

26   Five O'Clock Charlie   September 22, 1973
   Writers: Larry Gelbart, Laurence Marks
   Story: Keith Walker
   Director: Norman Tokar

Frank is not amused when the camp starts placing bets on a bumbling enemy pilot's attempts to bomb an abandoned dump near the 4077th.

A rare directorial appearance from Norman Tokar, the director of "Leave It to Beaver" from 1957 to 1963.

27   Radar's Report   September 29, 1973
   Writer: Laurence Marks
   Story: Sheldon Keller
   Director: Jackie Cooper
   Guest Stars: Joan Van Ark, Allan Arbus, Tom Dever

There's a raving POW loose in the O.R., and an army psychiatrist tries to determine whether or not Klinger is certifiably nuts.

This is Allan Arbus's first appearance as army psychiatrist Major Freedman, who would be a frequent guest at the 4077th over the next decade.

28 For the Good of the Outfit   October 6, 1973
Writer: Jerry Mayer
Director: Jackie Cooper
Guest Star: Frank Aletter

After the army accidentally bombs a local village, Hawkeye and Trapper buck heads with a general when they refuse to cooperate in the military cover-up.

29 Dr. Pierce and Mr. Hyde   October 13, 1973
Writers: Alan Alda, Robert Klane
Director: Jackie Cooper

Hawkeye's behavior is unrestrained, even by *his* standards, when he refuses to slow his pace after a three-day marathon in the O.R.

30 Kim   October 20, 1973
Writers: Marc Mandel, Larry Gelbart, Laurence Marks
Director: William Wiard
Guest Stars: Leslie Evans, Edgar Raymond Miller, Ray Poss, Maggie Roswell, Momo Yashima

Trapper John decides to adopt an orphaned Korean refugee.

31 L.I.P (Local Indigeneous Personnel)   October 27, 1973
Writer: Carl Kleinschmitt
Director: William Wiard
Guest Stars: Corinne Camacho, Burt Young, Jerry Zaks

The doctors resort to blackmail to persuade a stubborn official who refuses to okay a young GI's marriage to a South Korean woman.

32 The Trial of Henry Blake   November 3, 1973
Writers: McLean Stevenson, Larry Gelbart, Laurence Marks
Director: Don Weis
Guest Stars: Hope Summers, Robert F. Simon, Jack Aaron

The hijinks of the 4077th fall under scrutiny when Colonel Blake faces a military hearing to determine whether he's fit for command.

Flashback sequences describe the 4077th in the throes of near-bacchanalian abandon. In these early shows, the doctors and nurses of the 4077th were an altogether randier bunch; their libidinous shenanigans were a chief refuge from the grim realities all around. It's a pity the medics' carnal urges were tamed as the series developed—their earthier desires usually provided the setting for some of the crew's funnier, and most authentic, wartime escapades.

33   Dear Dad . . . Three   November 10, 1973
   Writers: Larry Gelbart, Laurence Marks
   Director: Don Weis
   Guest Stars: Mills Watson, Sivi Aberg, Arthur Abelson

In another letter home, Hawkeye describes his efforts to remove a live grenade from a wounded soldier's chest; and the staff gathers for an impromptu screening of Henry's home movies.

A masterful piece of storytelling begins when the doctors assemble in Blake's office, all prepared to snicker at his quaint home movies. We're encouraged to laugh along with the wisecracking doctors as we watch Henry on-screen—a Midwestern rube posturing and clowning for the shaky camera.
   Then we look at the screen through Henry Blake's eyes for the first time. We see the clumsy shadows of a child's birthday celebration as he does—a sweet and poignant vision of a simple time that suddenly seems so far away.
   Blake fights back a tear, and it's hard not to join him. He's come to realize, as we have, that the carefree man dancing up there on the screen is already dead, an early casualty of war. In this short, elegiac sequence, writers Gelbart and Marks eloquently describe the worst war crime of all—the army's dreadful capacity to smother a man's spirit . . . very, very slowly.

34   The Sniper   November 17, 1973
   Writer: Richard M. Powell
   Director: Jackie Cooper
   Guest Stars: Teri Garr, Marcia Gelman, Dennis Troy

The sanctuary of the compound is threatened when the 4077th is besieged by a lone sniper.

Film actress Teri Garr has an early role as one of the nurses in this episode.

35   Carry On, Hawkeye   November 24, 1973
Writers: Bernard Dilbert, Larry Gelbart, Laurence Marks
Story: Bernard Dilbert
Director: Jackie Cooper
Guest Stars: Lynnette Mettey, Gwen Farrell, Marcia Gelman

Hawkeye and Hot Lips are the only medical personnel left standing after a flu epidemic hits the hospital

The shortage of qualified doctors requires the head nurse to perform surgical duties far beyond her training or abilities, all of which she tackles with patience and stamina. Before the day is done, she has saved a boy's life with her own hands—and gained the first shreds of self-respect that would soon spur major changes for Hot Lips Houlihan.

36   The Incubator   December 1, 1973
Writers: Larry Gelbart, Laurence Marks
Director: Jackie Cooper
Guest Stars: Robert F. Simon, Logan Ramsey, Vic Tayback

Hawkeye and Trapper follow the military chain of command to the very top in their determination to secure an incubator for the compound.

37   Deal Me Out   December 8, 1973
Writers: Larry Gelbart, Laurence Marks
Director: Gene Reynolds
Guest Stars: Pat Morita, Allan Arbus, Edward Winter, John Ritter

Frank tries to prevent the doctors from operating on a wounded military intelligence officer for fear he'll leak classified information while under sedation.

Edward Winter plays Captain Halloran, a prototype for Colonel Flagg, the malevolent patriot who would be a frequent visitor to the 4077th throughout the first five seasons.

38   Hot Lips and Empty Arms   December 15, 1973
Writers: Linda Bloodworth, Mary Kay Place
Director: Jackie Cooper

Fed up with the limited horizons of her life at the 4077th, Hot Lips requests a transfer to another unit.

Gelbart and Reynolds commissioned a pair of twenty-five-year-old novice writers to script what they'd slated as "Loretta's show." Linda Bloodworth and Mary Kay Place interviewed Loretta Swit for hours before they finally wrote a story that sees Margaret questioning her life, her career, and perhaps most of all, her barren relationship with Frank Burns. By the end of the episode, the first stage of Margaret's evolution is complete. The strident, two-dimensional army strumpet of the early shows has grown into a thinking, feeling, independent-minded woman.

Mary Kay Place would become better known as an actress, though Linda Bloodworth continued as a scripter for M*A*S*H and other television comedies. In 1986, Linda Bloodworth Thomason would create and write "Designing Women" for CBS, a series that would bear distinct echoes of her very first script.

39 Officers Only   December 22, 1973
   Writer: Ed Jurist
   Director: Jackie Cooper
   Guest Stars: Robert F. Simon, Robert Weaver, Clyde Kusatsu

Trapper and Hawkeye disagree with General Mitchell's limited admissions policy for the new officer's club he's opened at the 4077th.

40 Henry in Love   January 5, 1974
   Writers: Larry Gelbart, Laurence Marks
   Director: Don Weis
   Guest Stars: Katherine Baumann, Odessa Cleveland, Sheila Lauritsen

Henry returns from Tokyo smitten by a cheerleader half his age, convinced that it's the real thing.

41 For Want of a Boot   January 12, 1974
   Writer: Sheldon Keller
   Director: Don Weis
   Guest Stars: Michael Lerner, Suzanne Zenor, Johnny Haymer

Hawkeye exchanges favors with everyone in camp in his efforts to get a new pair of boots.

A classic episode that shows the 4077th as one big, happy family—except that in this clan, everyone's out for himself. The supply sergeant wants his teeth fixed in exchange for the precious boots; the dentist

demands a weekend pass for his services; and Radar barters his cooperation for a night with Nurse Murphy! Obviously, this episode occurred
before Radar became a virgin. The refreshing lack of sentiment in this
cynical roundelay typifies the sardonic humor that frequently infected
the series in the early seasons

42   Operation Noselift   January 19, 1974
   Writer: Erik Tarloff
   Story: Paul Richards, Erik Tarloff
   Director: Hy Averback
   Guest Star: Stuart Margolin

Hawkeye and Trapper enlist the aid of an army plastic surgeon
to perform a nose job on a deserving GI.

43   The Chosan People   January 26, 1974
   Writers: Laurence Marks, Sheldon Keller, Larry Gelbart
   Story: Gerry Renert, Jeff Wilheim
   Director: Jackie Cooper
   Guest Stars: Pat Morita, Clare Nono, Dennis Robertson, Jay Jay
Jue, Jerry Fujikawa

A Korean family tries to reclaim the land under the 4077th as
their own; and a young woman from the village declares Radar
the father of her child.

44   As You Were   February 2, 1974
   Writers: Larry Gelbart, Laurence Marks
   Story: Gene Reynolds
   Director: Hy Averback
   Guest Star: Patricia Stevens

The doctors agree to treat Frank's hernia during a lull in the
action, only to face a new deluge of wounded while Burns lies
incapacitated in postop.

45   Crisis   February 9, 1974
   Writers: Larry Gelbart, Laurence Marks
   Director: Don Weis
   Guest Stars: Jeff Maxwell, Alberta Jay

Tempers flare when the 4077th faces a supply shortage of food
and fuel during a frigid cold spell.

46 George   February 16, 1974
Writers: John Regier, Gary Markowitz
Director: Gene Reynolds
Guest Stars: Richard Ely, George Simmons

Hawkeye and Trapper scheme to prevent Frank from having a homosexual private drummed out of the corps.

47 Mail Call   February 23, 1974
Writers: Larry Gelbart, Laurence Marks
Director: Alan Alda
Guest Stars: Dennis Troy, Sheila Lauritsen

Hawkeye can't resist teasing Frank with bogus stock-market tips after the major brags about his keen investments.

48 A Smattering of Intelligence   March 2, 1974
Writers: Larry Gelbart, Laurence Marks
Director: Larry Gelbart
Guest Stars: Edward Winter, Bill Fletcher

It's spy versus spy when the CIA's Colonel Flagg decides to get the goods on an army intelligence agent who's been snooping around the 4077th.

1974/75   THE THIRD SEASON

Year-End Rating: 27.4 (5th place)

Larry Gelbart and Laurence Marks share third-season scripting chores with Jim Fritzell and Everett Greenbaum, notable additions to an overworked stable of writers that also includes Sid Dorfman and Simon Muntner, among others. Producers Gene Reynolds and Larry Gelbart bolster third-year story sessions with anecdotes and firsthand observations they gathered at the 43d Army Surgical Hospital in Korea.

49 The General Flipped at Dawn   September 10, 1974
Writers: Jim Fritzell, Everett Greenbaum
Director: Larry Gelbart
Guest Stars: Harry Morgan, Lynnette Mettey, Theodore Wilson, Brad Trumbull, Dennis Erdman

The doctors suspect their new spit-and-polish commander is missing a few marbles after he threatens to move the 4077th out onto the battlefield.

When Harry Morgan's crazed general was shipped off to the Pentagon at the end of this episode, no one guessed that the accomplished character actor would return to the series as Henry Blake's replacement the very next season.

50 Rainbow Bridge   September 17, 1974
  Writers: Larry Gelbart, Laurence Marks
  Director: Hy Averback
  Guest Stars: Mako, Leland Sun, Loudon Wainwright III

MacIntyre and Pierce abandon their planned furlough when they travel into enemy territory to retrieve a group of wounded GIs.

51 Officer of the Day   September 24, 1974
  Writer: Laurence Marks
  Director: Hy Averback
  Guest Stars: Edward Winter, Dennis Troy, Jeff Maxwell, Jerry Fujikawa, Tad Horino, Richard Lee Sung, Mitchell Sakamoto, Norman Hamano

While Henry vacations in Seoul, Hawkeye protects a wounded North Korean prisoner from Colonel Flagg, who wants to see the alleged spy executed.

52 Iron Guts Kelly   October 1, 1974
  Writers: Larry Gelbart, Sid Dorfman
  Director: Don Weis
  Guest Stars: James Gregory, Keene Curtis, Byron Chung

A visiting general suffers a fatal heart attack in the throes of passion on Hot Lips' bed, and his loyal aide schemes to give the commander a hero's funeral.

From the general's entrance—pearl-handled pistols at his side—to his final send-off in an ambulance packed with prostitutes, the sardonic script never falters in this black comedy that adds up to a simple but profound statement on the pathetic and dangerous folly of those who seek glory in war.

53 O.R. October 8, 1974
Writers: Larry Gelbart, Laurence Marks
Director: Gene Reynolds
Guest Stars: Allan Arbus, Bobbie Cleveland, Bobby Herbeck,
Orlando Dole, Jeanne Schulherr, Roy Goldman, Leland Sun

The staff faces an unrelenting day in the operating theater as
casualties continue to mount, with no end in sight.

Set entirely in the O.R., the story builds on the stark drama of life
and death as the doctors struggle to save those who can be saved and
move the rest out as quickly as possible. It's an uncompromising episode,
and though it's not without humor, it was one of the earliest episodes
aired minus a laugh track. Despite the network's early objection to scenes
set in the O.R., the producers steadfastly refused to sweeten those scenes
with recorded laughs. "It's hard to imagine the audience belly laughing
at bowel surgery," quipped Gelbart.

54 Springtime October 15, 1974
Writers: Linda Bloodworth, Mary Kay Place
Director: Don Weis
Guest Stars: Alex Karras, Mary Kay Place, Greg Mabrey

In spring, even an enlisted man's fancy turns to romance—a
maxim that's borne out when Radar and Klinger are both stung
by Cupid's arrow.

Writer Mary Kay Place scripted herself into this episode as Louise,
the willing object of Radar's affection. Place soon became a well-known
actress when she landed a long-running part on "Mary Hartman, Mary
Hartman."

55 Checkup October 22, 1974
Writer: Laurence Marks
Director: Don Weis
Guest Stars: Jeff Maxwell, Patricia Stevens

The camp throws a teary farewell party for Trapper John when
he discovers that his ulcer guarantees him a one-way ticket home.

Though a last-minute technicality spoils Trapper's clean break this
time, Hawkeye's stirring—if premature—farewell speech would have
to do. There would be no time for more formal good-byes a few weeks

later when Wayne Rogers's leave-taking forced his character's equally abrupt departure at the end of the season.

56   Life With Father   October 29, 1974
   Writers: Everett Greenbaum, Jim Fritzell
   Director: Hy Averback
   Guest Star: Sachiko Penny Lee

Henry suspects his wife may be having an affair; and Father Mulcahy officiates at an infant's circumcision.

This was the second "M*A*S*H" script from Everett Greenbaum and Jim Fritzell, veteran comedy team with impeccable credits—they'd scripted "Mr. Peepers" in the 1950s and written some of the finest early episodes of "The Andy Griffith Show" in the 1960s.

57   Alcoholics Unanymous   November 12, 1974
   Writers: Everett Greenbaum, Jim Fritzell
   Director: Hy Averback
   Guest Star: Bobbie Mitchell

In Henry's absence, Frank uses his executive powers to declare Prohibition at the 4077th.

58   There Is Nothing Like a Nurse   November 19, 1974
   Writer: Larry Gelbart
   Director: Hy Averback
   Guest Stars: Molli Benson, Leland Sun, Jeanne Schulherr, Loudon Wainwright III

The compound becomes more hellish than usual when the threat of enemy invasion forces the nurses to evacuate the 4077th.

59   Adam's Ribs   November 26, 1974
   Writer: Laurence Marks
   Director: Gene Reynolds
   Guest Stars: Basil Hoffman, Joe Stern, Jeff Maxwell

Fed up with army rations, Hawkeye places an order by shortwave to his favorite Chicago barbecue joint: forty pounds of ribs . . . to go.

60 A Full, Rich Day December 3, 1974
Writer: John D. Hess
Director: Gene Reynolds
Guest Stars: William Watson, Sirri Murad, Curt Lowens

Hawkeye's latest letter home describes a typical day at the 4077th: There's a mad Turk in the operating room, and the doctors have misplaced the body of an officer who may, or may not, be dead.

61 Mad Dogs and Servicemen December 10, 1974
Writers: Linda Bloodworth, Mary Kay Place
Director: Hy Averback
Guest Stars: Michael O'Keefe, Shizuko Hoshi, Arthur Song

Radar tries to find the potentially rabid dog who bit him; and the surgeons treat a corporal suffering from psychosomatic paralysis.

62 Private Charles Lamb December 31, 1974
Writers: Larry Gelbart, Sid Dorfman
Director: Hy Averback
Guest Stars: Ted Eccles, Titos Vandis, Gene Chronopolous

Radar almost sparks an international incident when he rescues a lamb from the skewer of a Greek regiment's Easter feast.

63 Bombed January 7, 1975
Writers: Everett Greenbaum, Jim Fritzell
Director: Hy Averback
Guest Stars: Louisa Moritz, Edward Marshall

The medics continue to operate on incoming wounded, despite a steady barrage that threatens to blow the camp apart at the seams.

64 Bulletin Board January 14, 1975
Writers: Larry Gelbart, Simon Muntner
Director: Alan Alda
Guest Star: Johnny Haymer

Posted camp activities include a picnic and a Shirley Temple movie.

65   The Consultant   January 21, 1975
Writers: Larry Gelbart, Robert Klane
Director: Gene Reynolds
Guest Stars: Robert Alda, Joseph Maher, Tad Horino

Hawkeye is deeply disappointed when a visiting specialist gets too drunk to perform a vital operation to save a soldier's leg.

Alan Alda's father joins him in this episode, a dramatic vehicle tailor-made for both generations of the acting clan.

66   House Arrest   February 4, 1975
Writers: Jim Fritzell, Everett Greenbaum
Director: Hy Averback
Guest Stars: Mary Wickes, Jeff Maxwell, Dennis Troy

Hawkeye nearly faces a court-martial after he gets carried away during one of his petty squabbles with Frank Burns.

67   Aid Station   February 11, 1975
Writers: Larry Gelbart, Simon Muntner
Director: William Jurgensen
Guest Star: Tom Dever

Margaret and Hawkeye provide emergency aid at the front lines when they're sent into battle with Corporal Klinger.

Klinger suits up in regular army fatigues when the chips are down, prefiguring the character's eventual position of responsibility much later in the series. Hot Lips, too, undergoes a change when she earns the men's respect with her cool performance under battle conditions. By the end of the episode, she and Hawkeye raise their mugs in a silent toast that only hints at the major changes that are yet to come.

68   Love and Marriage   February 18, 1975
Writer: Arthur Julian
Director: Lee Philips
Guest Stars: Soon Teck Oh, Dennis Dugan, Pat Li, Jerry Fujikawa

Trapper and Hawk attempt to unite one enlisted man with his pregnant wife and try to prevent another from marrying a Korean prostitute.

69 Big Mac   February 25, 1975
Writer: Laurence Marks
Director: Don Weis
Guest Stars: Graham Jarvis, Bob Courtleigh, Jeanne Schulherr,
Loudon Wainwright III

The camp prepares for a visit from Commanding General Douglas MacArthur.

70 Payday   March 4, 1975
Writers: John Regier, Gary Markowitz
Director: Hy Averback
Guest Stars: Jack Soo, Eldon Quick, Johnny Haymer, Mary
Katherine Peters, Leland Sun, George Holloway, Pat Marshall

Hawkeye is surprised when a military oversight nets him an extra
three-thousand-dollar paycheck.

71 White Gold   March 11, 1975
Writers: Larry Gelbart, Simon Muntner
Director: Hy Averback
Guest Stars: Edward Winter, Hilly Hicks, Stafford Repp

When valuable supplies of penicillin begin to disappear, the
doctors suspect the involvement of CIA operative Colonel Flagg.

72 Abyssinia, Henry   March 18, 1975
Writers: Everett Greenbaum, Jim Fritzell
Director: Larry Gelbart
Guest Stars: Kimiko Hiroshige, Virginia Lee, Cherylene Lee,
Ray Poss

With the memory of Colonel Blake's gala farewell party still fresh
in their minds, the 4077th is shocked to learn that the commanding officer's plane has just been shot down over the Sea
of Japan.

The producers weren't content simply to write Blake out of the series
after the actor voluntarily left the show. "Faced with the show business
reality of one of the star players wanting out," Larry Gelbart explained
in *The New York Times,* "we looked for a bold solution to his disappear-
ance consistent with the series's view of the wastefulness of war. Angry
viewers [later] accused us of trying to make them unhappy, as if the

warranty that came with their sets promised them only happy moments of viewing."

1975/76   THE FOURTH SEASON

Year-End Rating: 22.9 (14th place)

With the departure of Colonel Blake and Trapper John, the series enters a second, more subdued phase, as new recruits B. J. Hunnicutt and Colonel Sherman Potter are integrated into the tightly knit ensemble. The new characters are less zany than their predecessors, and far more noble—a development that gradually affects the tone of the show in this and in future seasons.

Larry Gelbart and the team of Jim Fritzell and Everett Greenbaum write most of the season's scripts, with significant contributions from Simon Muntner, Jay Folb, and Burt Prelutsky, among others. Associate producer Burt Metcalfe, cinematographer William Jurgensen, and actor Harry Morgan all make their directing debuts, though most fourth-season shows are directed by Alan Alda, Larry Gelbart, or Gene Reynolds.

73   Welcome to Korea (one hour)   September 12, 1975
    Writers: Everett Greenbaum, Jim Fritzell, Larry Gelbart
    Director: Gene Reynolds
    Guest Stars: Robert A. Karnes, Arthur Song, Shirlee Kong

Hawkeye returns from a weekend in Tokyo too late to bid farewell to Trapper, so he welcomes the surgeon's replacement, Captain B. J. Hunnicutt, instead.

We first see the new recruit at an airstrip, far from the familiar surroundings of the 4077th, as the producers wisely prevent any direct comparisons with his predecessor. In fact, Trapper John had almost nothing in common with his replacement. An outsider, Trapper was a strong-willed fighter and Hawkeye's chief partner in gambling, whoring, and insubordination.

Of course by then the show's emphasis had drifted away from the surgeons' carnal pursuits; there would be more humanism and less sleeping around from this point on. The new Hawkeye required a different sort of partner, someone who would complement, rather than compete with the undisputed anchor of the series. Enter B. J. A gentle family man from Marin County, California, he was undoubtedly one of the most sensitive men drafted into the Korean conflict. He and Hawkeye were a match made in story editors' heaven.

74 Change of Command   September 19, 1975
  Writers: Jim Fritzell, Everett Greenbaum
  Director: Gene Reynolds

Colonel Potter, the stern new commander of the 4077th, is eyed with suspicion until Hawkeye and B. J. convince him to exercise a certain flexibility in his leadership at the 4077th.

75 It Happened One Night   September 26, 1975
  Writers: Larry Gelbart, Simon Muntner
  Story: Gene Reynolds
  Director: Gene Reynolds
  Guest Stars: Christopher Allport, Darren O'Connor

On a bitterly cold night, Frank searches for love letters in Margaret's tent while the head nurse assists the surgeons in a marathon operation.

76 The Late Captain Pierce   October 3, 1975
  Writers: Glen Charles, Les Charles
  Director: Alan Alda
  Guest Stars: Richard Masur, Eldon Quick

After the army erroneously lists Hawkeye as killed in action, he's tempted to exploit the error for a ticket home.

Hawkeye's ever-widening streak of nobility gets its first clear definition in this episode. The once-irreverent surgeon follows his survival instinct and tries to turn a military error into a one-way ticket home. But his conscience gets the better of him, and at the first sound of arriving choppers carrying wounded, he abandons all common sense and returns to the call of duty in the operating room.

This was written by two brothers, Glen and Les Charles, who later became writer/producers of "Taxi" and, eventually, co-creators of "Cheers."

77   Hey, Doc   October 10, 1975
    Writer: Rick Mittleman
    Director: William Jurgensen
    Guest Stars: Frank Marth, Bruce Kirby, Ted Hamilton

The doctors demonstrate the fine art of wheeling and dealing when they perform a series of routine medical favors in exchange for a new microscope.

The tank commander is Frank Marth, a familiar face to "Honeymooners" fans. As one of Jackie Gleason's stock players, Marth played dozens of roles on the series throughout the mid-1950s.

78   The Bus   October 17, 1975
    Writer: John D. Hess
    Director: Gene Reynolds
    Guest Star: Soon Teck Oh

The men of the 4077th get stranded in enemy territory when their bus breaks down on the way back from a poker game.

While the other characters develop previously unseen depth and maturity, Frank Burns displays his unfailing selfishness by cowering in the bus and hoarding Hershey bars from the stranded company. Burns's craven character defied growth; whatever decent instincts he may have had were buried too deep in his psychosis for the writers to unearth. Despite Larry Linville's accomplished performance, Burns would remain a one-note character while the rest of the show outgrew him.

79   Dear Mildred   October 24, 1975
    Writers: Everett Greenbaum, Jim Fritzell
    Director: Alan Alda

The personnel of the camp bring gifts to their new commander as he writes a letter home to his wife on their wedding anniversary.

80   The Kids   October 31, 1975
    Writers: Jim Fritzell, Everett Greenbaum
    Director: Alan Alda
    Guest Stars: Ann Doran, Mitchell Sakamoto, Huanani Minn

The compound becomes a temporary refuge and maternity ward when a local orphanage is shelled.

81   Quo Vadis, Captain Chandler?   November 7, 1975
Writer: Burt Prelutsky
Director: Larry Gelbart
Guest Stars: Allan Arbus, Edward Winter, Alan Fudge

A guilt-plagued bombardier with a messiah complex arrives—
arousing the interest of both army psychiatrist Major Freedman
and the CIA's Colonel Flagg.

Major Freedman's reassuring voice of reason frequently contrasted
with the maniacal ravings of the chillingly dispassionate Colonel Flagg
in their joint appearances, though Freedman eventually proved a more
durable character. The army psychiatrist would figure prominently in
the series long after the writers retired the spy from active duty.

82   Dear Peggy   November 11, 1975
Writers: Jim Fritzell, Everett Greenbaum
Director: Burt Metcalfe
Guest Stars: Ned Beatty, Dennis Troy

In a letter to his wife, B. J. describes Hawkeye's attempt to break
the world record for jeep stuffing, and his own efforts to rescue
a patient from Frank's inept surgery.

83   Of Moose and Men   November 21, 1975
Writer: Jay Folb
Director: John Erman
Guest Stars: Johnny Haymer, Lois Foraker, Jeff Maxwell

Hawkeye's in deep when he splatters mud on an angry colonel;
and B. J. counsels Sergeant Zale after his stateside wife admits
a lapse in fidelity.

84   Soldier of the Month   November 28, 1975
Writer: Linda Bloodworth
Director: Gene Reynolds
Guest Star: Johnny Haymer

Colonel Potter sponsors a "soldier of the month" contest to
boost sagging morale; and Frank comes down with a raging
fever.

85   The Gun   December 2, 1975
Writers: Larry Gelbart, Gene Reynolds
Director: Burt Metcalfe
Guest Star: Warren Stevens

Frank steals a wounded colonel's vintage Colt .45.

86   Mail Call Again   December 9, 1975
Writers: Jim Fritzell, Everett Greenbaum
Director: George Tyne

Letters from home arrive with bad news for Frank: His wife
knows about Margaret.

87   The Price of Tomato Juice   December 16, 1975
Writers: Larry Gelbart, Gene Reynolds
Director: Gene Reynolds
Guest Star: James Jeter

Radar engages in elaborate negotiations to secure regular rations
of tomato juice for Colonel Potter.

88   Dear Ma   December 23, 1975
Writers: Everett Greenbaum, Jim Fritzell
Director: Alan Alda
Guest Stars: Redmond Gleeson, Byron Chung, John Fujioka

A camp-wide foot inspection is one of the subjects of Radar's
letter home.

89   Der Tag   January 6, 1976
Writers: Everett Greenbaum, Jim Fritzell
Director: Gene Reynolds
Guest Stars: Joe Morton, John Voldstad, George Simmons,
William Grant

Colonel Potter convinces Hawkeye and B. J. to treat Frank with
a touch of kindness.

90 Hawkeye   January 13, 1976
Writers: Larry Gelbart, Simon Muntner
Director: Larry Gelbart
Guest Stars: Philip Ahn, Shizuko Hoshi, June Kim, Susan
Sakimoto

Hawkeye seeks help from a family of uncomprehending Koreans
after he's wounded in a jeep accident on the road to camp.

Hawkeye has to stay alert until help arrives to treat his concussion,
so he embarks on a nonstop stream-of-consciousness monologue that
lasts the length of the program. Gelbart wasn't sure the one-man script
would play, but he later admitted he was excited by the risk, "For me,
the least satisfying episodes were the ones that we *knew* would work."
Apparently, this one did—the experiment earned Emmy Awards for
the writers and cinematographer William Jurgensen.

91 Some 38th Parallels   January 20, 1976
Writers: John Regier, Gary Markowitz
Director: Burt Metcalfe
Guest Stars: George O'Hanlon, Jr., Lynnette Mettey, Richard
Lee Sung, Ray Poss

A headstrong colonel insists on retrieving the bodies of soldiers
killed in action, regardless of the risk to those still living; and
Frank auctions off the camp garbage to local scavengers.

92 The Novocaine Mutiny   January 27, 1976
Writer: Burt Prelutsky
Director: Harry Morgan
Guest Stars: Ned Wilson, Johnny Haymer, Patricia Stevens

In temporary command during Colonel Potter's absence, Frank
lodges formal charges against Hawkeye for mutiny.

93 Smilin' Jack   February 3, 1976
Writers: Larry Gelbart, Simon Muntner
Director: Charles S. Dubin
Guest Stars: Robert Hogan, Dennis Kort, Michael A. Salcido,
Alba Francesca

The doctors try to ground a diabetic chopper pilot who's determined to set a military record for carrying in the greatest number
of wounded.

Inspired by their army research, the producers were anxious to emphasize the efforts of the chopper pilots. "They play a much bigger role than we realized," Gelbart observed on his return from a trip to Korea, "and they're more romantic than doctors." During the fourth year, the producers wove the helicopters into story lines—with a vengeance. They soon realized that the choppers were a device more wisely used sparingly, but not before it got to the point where the poor medics couldn't go to the latrine without getting buzzed by the untimely arrival of those damn choppers.

94   The More I See You   February 10, 1976
Writers: Larry Gelbart, Gene Reynolds
Director: Gene Reynolds
Guest Stars: Blythe Danner, Mary Jo Catlett

When his medical school sweetheart is transferred to the 4077th, Hawkeye is anxious to relive the exquisite pain all over again.

95   Deluge   February 17, 1976
Writers: Larry Gelbart, Simon Muntner
Director: William Jurgensen

An unexpected border advance by the Chinese results in a flood of casualties far beyond the capacity of the overworked 4077th.

96   The Interview   February 24, 1976
Writer: Larry Gelbart
Director: Larry Gelbart
Guest Star: Clete Roberts

A documentary look at the lives and work of the men and women of the 4077th, as seen through the eyes of a U.S. war correspondent.

Larry Gelbart was convinced he'd run out of story lines for the series, until Gene Reynolds suggested they create a quasi-documentary as the season's final episode. The writer fashioned a script based on the actors' actual responses to a series of questions about the war and then surprised them with additional, unrehearsed questions that were added after the cameras began to roll. Clete Roberts, a southern California newsman and former war correspondent, was enlisted to conduct the interview.

The results were edited, in black and white, into one of the show's most effective stylistic departures. A passionate and often chilling look at war through the eyes of reasonable men and women who find themselves stuck in a most unreasonable situation, "The Interview" sums up perfectly Gelbart's four years with the show. Gelbart retired from the series after this episode was finished, exhausted but proud.

1976/77   THE FIFTH SEASON

Year-End Rating: 25.9 (4th place)

In the fifth season, the show continues to explore the comic depths of military absurdity, but with a new seriousness of purpose. Margaret's marriage caps a season of major growth for most of the show's characters, with the notable exception of Frank Burns.

By now, the production values on the show exceed those of any sitcom in TV history; the lighting, editing, and cinematography are all first-rate, and the show looks more like a feature film than a weekly series. Still, die-hard fans would miss the grittiness of the early years and wonder if the high-gloss finish was really an improvement over the messy, often disjointed style that so perfectly fit the show's often messy and disjointed subject matter.

Burt Metcalfe signs on as producer, joined by Allan Katz and Don Reo. Gene Reynolds becomes executive producer, and writer Jay Folb handles story duties as the new executive story editor.

97 Bug Out (one hour)   September 21, 1976
   Writers: Jim Fritzell, Everett Greenbaum
   Director: Gene Reynolds
   Guest Stars: Richard Lee Sung, Frances Fong, Don Eitner, Barry Cahill, Peter Zapp, James Lough, Eileen Saki, Ko-Ko Tani

   Hawkeye, Radar, and Margaret are left behind to care for critical patients when the 4077th moves out to avoid a threatened invasion.

98 Margaret's Engagement   September 28, 1976
   Writer: Gary Markowitz
   Director: Alan Alda

   Margaret returns from Tokyo engaged, and the entire camp eagerly awaits Frank's response.

   Margaret's engagement came as a direct result of Loretta Swit's desire to develop her character's identity separate from Frank Burns. The producers acknowledged she'd outgrown her childish relationship with Burns by introducing her offscreen romance with Donald Penobscott—leaving poor Frank to fend for himself.

99   Out of Sight, Out of Mind   October 5, 1976
   Writers: Ken Levine, David Isaacs
   Director: Gene Reynolds
   Guest Stars: Tom Sullivan, Judy Farrell, Enid Kent, Dudley
Knight, Michael Cedar

Hawkeye sees the world with a clearer focus when he is temporarily blinded in an accident.

Ken Levine and David Isaacs were newcomers who had written numerous scripts for "The Jeffersons," "The Tony Randall Show," and "Joe and Sons." After two seasons as "M*A*S*H" story editors and three seasons on "Cheers," they would create Mary Tyler Moore's short-lived 1986 comeback series, "Mary."

100   Lieutenant Radar O'Reilly   October 12, 1976
   Writers: Everett Greenbaum, Jim Fritzell
   Director: Alan Rafkin
   Guest Stars: Sandy Kenyon, Johnny Haymer, Raymond Chao

Radar wins a promotion in a poker game, but finds that life as a lieutenant doesn't agree with him.

101   The Nurses   October 19, 1976
   Writer: Linda Bloodworth
   Director: Joan Darling
   Guest Stars: Linda Kelsey, Gregory Harrison, Mary Jo Catlett,
Carol Lawson Locatell, Patricia Sturges

Margaret discovers a gap between herself and the nursing staff when one of them defies her to spend the night with her newlywed husband.

This tale of Hot Lips's relationship with her nurses is a departure that draws attention to how few stories were told from the nurses' point of view. The situation improved somewhat as avowed feminist Alan Alda gained more creative control, but the circumstances of these women stranded in a forgotten corner of the war suggest a wealth of story possibilities that were strangely overlooked.

102 The Abduction of Margaret Houlihan   October 26, 1976
Writers: Allan Katz, Don Reo
Story: Gene Reynolds
Director: Gene Reynolds
Guest Stars: Edward Winter, June Kim, Le Quynh, Susan Bredhoff

When Major Houlihan ventures into the village to help deliver a baby, Frank causes a panic by announcing that she's been kidnapped.

Before they signed on as "M*A*S*H" writer/producers, Don Reo and Allan Katz had written or produced shows as disparate as "Mary Tyler Moore," "All in the Family," "Cher," "Laugh-In," a Lily Tomlin special, and "Rhoda."

103 Dear Sigmund   November 9, 1976
Writer: Alan Alda
Director: Alan Alda
Guest Stars: Allan Arbus, Charles Frank, Bart Braverman, Sal Viscuso, J. Andrew Kenny, Jennifer Davis

Psychiatrist Sidney Freedman tries to escape his deep depression by spending a few days observing the therapeutic antics of the 4077th at close range.

104 Mulcahy's War   November 16, 1976
Writer: Richard Cogan
Director: George Tyne
Guest Stars: Brian Byers, Ric Mancini, Richard Foronjy, Ray Poss

Father Mulcahy goes AWOL to experience battlefield conditions firsthand.

105 The Korean Surgeon   November 23, 1976
Writer: Bill Idelson
Director: Gene Reynolds
Guest Stars: Soon Teck Oh, Robert Ito, Larry Hama, Richard Russell Ramos, Dennis Troy

B. J. and Hawkeye cover up the identity of a skilled North Korean surgeon who's anxious to save lives on either side of the battle.

106   Hawkeye Get Your Gun   November 30, 1976
  Writer: Jay Folb
  Story: Gene Reynolds, Jay Folb
  Director: William Jurgensen
  Guest Stars: Mako, Richard Doyle, Jae Woo Lee, Thomas
  Botosan, Phyllis Katz, Carmine Scelza

Colonel Potter and Hawkeye wage their own war of ideals when
Pierce refuses to fire at enemy soldiers during an ambush.

In this story, Reynolds and Folb touch on the two seemingly irrec-
oncilable sides of Colonel Potter—the surgeon and the career soldier.
As a physician, he shares with his draftee doctors the common goal of
alleviating human suffering. Yet his rank and career status imply his
underlying acceptance of the military machinery that's at the root of the
suffering in the first place.

107   The Colonel's Horse   December 7, 1976
  Writers: Jim Fritzell, Everett Greenbaum
  Director: Burt Metcalfe

The doctors treat Margaret and the Colonel's horse when both
fall ill from very different maladies.

108   Exorcism   December 14, 1976
  Writer: Jay Folb
  Story: Gene Reynolds, Jay Folb
  Director: Alan Alda
  Guest Stars: Virginia Ann Lee, James Canning, Phillip Ahn

Everything that *can* go wrong *does* after Colonel Potter removes
a Buddhist good-luck talisman from the compound.

109   Hawk's Nightmare   December 21, 1976
  Writer: Burt Prelutsky
  Director: Burt Metcalfe
  Guest Stars: Allan Arbus, Patricia Stevens, Sean Roche

After a series of unsettling dreams, Hawkeye wonders if he hasn't
finally cracked up.

110 The Most Unforgettable Characters   January 4, 1977
   Writers: Ken Levine, David Isaacs
   Director: Burt Metcalfe
   Guest Star: Jeff Maxwell

Radar records his impressions for a correspondence course in creative writing; and B. J. and Hawkeye stage a feud for Frank's benefit on his birthday.

111 Thirty-eight Across   January 11, 1977
   Writers: Jim Fritzell, Everett Greenbaum
   Director: Burt Metcalfe
   Guest Stars: Dick O'Neill, Oliver Clark

Radar's signals get crossed when his shortwave call for help on a crossword puzzle summons a navy admiral expecting a dire emergency.

112 Ping-Pong   January 18, 1977
   Writer: Sid Dorfman
   Director: William Jurgensen
   Guest Stars: Richard Narita, Frank Maxwell, Sachiko Penny Lee

Colonel Potter confronts an old army buddy whose military incompetence has already cost too many lives on the battlefield.

113 End Run   January 25, 1977
   Writer: John D. Hess
   Director: Harry Morgan
   Guest Stars: Henry Brown, Johnny Haymer

Hawkeye tries to raise a former all-American football player's morale after the GI loses a leg; and Klinger and Sergeant Zale settle a feud in the boxing ring.

114 Hanky-Panky   February 1, 1977
   Writer: Gene Reynolds
   Director: Gene Reynolds
   Guest Star: Ann Sweeny

B. J. is plagued by guilt when his tender consolation of a nurse ends in a one-night stand.

115   Hepatitis   February 8, 1977
   Writer: Alan Alda
   Director: Alan Alda
   Guest Star: Barbara James

Father Mulcahy is quarantined with infectious hepatitis; and Hawkeye suffers psychosomatic back pain.

Alda's script was inspired by real life. Actor William Christopher's own bout with hepatitis caused him to miss a good many days' work that season.

116   The General's Practitioner   February 15, 1977
   Writer: Burt Prelutsky
   Director: Alan Rafkin
   Guest Stars: Edward T. Binns, Leonard Stone, Suesie Elene

Hawkeye chafes under his new appointment as personal physician to a general; and Radar copes with the unexpected arrival of a baby to a Korean war bride.

117   Movie Tonight   February 22, 1977
   Writers: Gene Reynolds, Don Reo, Allan Katz, Jay Folb
   Director: Burt Metcalfe
   Guest Stars: Enid Kent, Judy Farrell, Jeffrey Kramer

When technical problems beset the screening of Colonel Potter's favorite film, the camp improvises a talent show in defiance of the obstreperous projector.

118   Souvenirs   March 1, 1977
   Writer: Burt Prelutsky
   Story: Burt Prelutsky, Reinhold Weege
   Director: Joshua Shelley
   Guest Stars: Michael Bell, Brian Dennehy, Scott Mulhern

Frank buys a priceless antique vase from a shady junk dealer as a war memento.

119 Postop   March 8, 1977

    Writers: Ken Levine, David Isaacs
    Story: Gene Reynolds, Jay Folb
    Director: Gene Reynolds
    Guest Stars: Hilly Hicks, Sal Viscuso, Andy Romano

An acute shortage of blood complicates another marathon tour of duty for the doctors in O.R.

The chilling battle stories told by the recuperating soldiers were culled from firsthand accounts and interviews with veterans of both Vietnam and the Korean War. Producer Gene Reynolds acknowledged the series's debt to its sources: "At least 60 percent of the plots dealing with medical or military incidents were taken from real life. These guys gave us details we never would have thought of. They kept us honest."

120 Margaret's Marriage   March 15, 1977

    Writers: Everett Greenbaum, Jim Fritzell
    Director: Gene Reynolds
    Guest Stars: Beeson Carroll, Judy Farrell, Lynne Marie Stewart, Ray Poss, Kellye Nakahara

Donald Penobscott arrives at the 4077th to marry Margaret in an improvised ceremony that calls for something borrowed—a wedding dress from Klinger—and something blue—best-man Frank Burns.

As Margaret flies off on her honeymoon, blissfully unaware of the cruel tricks that fate—and the show's writers—have in store, it spells the end for Frank Burns. He could hardly continue on the series once Margaret's marriage altered permanently his one tenuous connection to reality.

Actor Larry Linville breathed a sigh of relief when he decided not to renew his contract. "I wasn't tired of playing Frank Burns," he explained, "I was tired of playing *only* Frank Burns."

"After Gelbart left," the actor told writer Suzy Kalter in *The Complete Book of M*A*S*H*, "it was easier to run Frank into a scene, dump on him, get a laugh, and run him out the door." It was quite a letdown for the actor who understood so well the character's dark function in the comedy of military absurdity. Linville once summed up Frank Burns in the pages of *TV Guide:* "He personified the psychosis of war itself—mindless, random, hostile one moment, silly the next."

1977/78   THE SIXTH SEASON

Year-End Rating: 23.3 (8th place)

The war continues for a sixth year of contained madness as the 4077th welcomes Major Charles Winchester III, a skilled surgeon and vituperative adversary for B. J. and Hawkeye. With the departure of Frank Burns, the ratio of slapstick to drama of the early years has reversed. Stories in this third phase of "M*A*S*H" often sacrifice belly laughs for the sake of the characters' emotional growth.

Gene Reynolds ceases day-to-day involvement to become a special creative consultant for the remainder of the run—a title he shares with Alan Alda, reflecting the actor's growing involvement behind the scenes. Burt Metcalfe continues as producer. Executive story editor Jay Folb oversees the sixth season's scripts, along with story editors Ken Levine and David Isaacs, and Ronny Graham, who signs on as a special program consultant.

121   Fade Out, Fade In (one hour)   September 20, 1977
   Writers: Jim Fritzell, Everett Greenbaum
   Director: Hy Averback
   Guest Stars: James Lough, Raymond Singer, Tom Stovall, Rick Hurst, Robert Symonds, William Flatley, Joseph Burns, Barbara James

Frank is shipped home after he goes bonkers in Tokyo, leaving the 4077th to wonder if his replacement—the skilled, articulate, and thoroughly strident Major Winchester is really an improvement.

Burt Metcalfe hired the classically trained David Ogden Stiers after spotting him on "The Mary Tyler Moore Show" when the actor played Mary's station manager during the final season. The producer knew immediately that he'd found the man to play the William F. Buckley of the 4077th. "David has this unique quality," he told *TV Guide*. "He can be lovably unlovable."

For all his pomposity, Winchester finally gains our sympathy when he musters a humble, if grudging, admiration for the skill of the 4077th's surgeons. The new doctor may be insufferable, but he's not unlikable. Metcalfe's hunch to replace Frank Burns with a more formidable adversary was a master stroke. With Winchester, the show's central triangle achieved a parity that made the balanced ensemble of the final years possible.

122   Fallen Idol   September 27, 1977
    Writer: Alan Alda
    Director: Alan Alda
    Guest Stars: Frances Fong, Robin Riker, Larry Gilman, Roy Goldman

Radar comes to the painful realization that Hawkeye is only human after the surgeon's performance is compromised by a hangover.

An ironic episode. By this point, Hawkeye had already lost many of the undesirable characteristics that made him so utterly human in the first place! In the remaining seasons, Alda and the writers gradually purged the doctor of his most offensive excesses: Hawkeye's womanizing was reduced to a series of halfhearted one-liners that rarely earned him more than a bemused smile from disinterested members of the nursing staff; his on-screen drinking would be cut by half; and even the selfish outrage that once fueled his most elaborate practical jokes was sublimated to the service of his occasional self-righteous antiwar protests.

123   Last Laugh   October 4, 1977
    Writers: Everett Greenbaum, Jim Fritzell
    Director: Don Weis
    Guest Stars: James Cromwell, Robert Karnes, John Ashton

The army questions B. J.'s medical credentials as a result of an elaborate practical joke staged by one of his old college chums.

124   War of Nerves   October 11, 1977
    Writer: Alan Alda
    Director: Alan Alda
    Guest Stars: Allan Arbus, Michael O'Keefe, Peter Riegert

Major Freedman arrives as a casualty, just in time to offer therapeutic advice to the squabbling staff of the 4077th.

125   The Winchester Tapes   October 18, 1977
   Writers: Everett Greenbaum, Jim Fritzell
   Director: Burt Metcalfe
   Guest Stars: Thomas Carter, Kimiko Hiroshige

Charles is the butt of B. J.'s merciless practical jokes, even as he dictates a letter pleading with his influential father to get him a transfer home.

There is a playful degree of heat generated when Margaret and Winchester discover their meeting of the minds, but of course, nothing comes of it. The writers are too smart to limit the characters with an ongoing romantic involvement.

126   The Light That Failed   October 25, 1977
   Writer: Burt Prelutsky
   Director: Charles S. Dubin
   Guest Stars: Enid Kent, Gary Erwin, Philip Baker Hall

The "M*A*S*H" crew play amateur sleuths when they try to determine whodunit in a mystery novel that arrives minus the final page.

127   In Love and War   November 1, 1977
   Writer: Alan Alda
   Director: Alan Alda
   Guest Stars: Kieu Chinh, Susan Krebs, Soorah Ahn, Enid Kent

Hawkeye finds a brief respite from the war when he romances an aristocratic South Korean woman who shelters the local orphans in her home.

In the final scene, Hawkeye and Margaret raise a toast to the flickering flame of romance in war. She drinks to a temporary reunion with her estranged newlywed husband, while Hawkeye raises his glass to a love he knows he'll never see again. It's a wistful moment that defines perfectly the romantic pessimism that would underlie many of the best shows in later seasons.

128 Change Day   November 8, 1977
Writer: Laurence Marks
Director: Don Weis
Guest Stars: Phillip Ahn, Noel Toy, Glenn Ash, Richard Lee Sung

Winchester concocts a scheme to profit from the hapless villagers when the army announces a scrip exchange.

129 Images   November 15, 1977
Writer: Burt Prelutsky
Director: Burt Metcalfe
Guest Stars: Susan Blanchard, Larry Block, John Durren

Against everyone's better judgment, Radar is determined to sharpen his image with a tattoo.

130 The M*A*S*H Olympics   November 22, 1977
Writers: Ken Levine, David Isaacs
Director: Don Weis
Guest Stars: Mike Henry, Michael McManus

Inspired by the 1952 Helsinki games, Potter organizes his own Olympics for the men and women of the 4077th.

Mike Henry appears as Margaret's husband, Lieutenant Colonel Donald Penobscott. The character's only other appearance on the show was at his wedding, when he was played by a different actor, Beeson Carroll.

131 The Grim Reaper   November 29, 1977
Writer: Burt Prelutsky
Director: George Tyne
Guest Stars: Charles Aidman, Jerry Hauser, Kellye Nakahara

Hawkeye is aghast at a military strategist's enthusiastic predictions of incoming casualty figures.

132 Comrades in Arms (Part 1)   December 6, 1977
Writer: Alan Alda
Director: Burt Metcalfe
Guest Stars: Jon Yune, James Saito

Lost behind enemy lines, Hawkeye and Margaret form a personal truce and seek shelter in a roadside hut.

This two-parter was the only episode of "M*A*S*H" to be jointly directed, by Alan Alda and Burt Metcalfe—though a Directors Guild rule required them each to take individual credit for one of the two separate episodes.

133 Comrades in Arms (Part 2) December 13, 1977
  Writer: Alan Alda
  Director: Alan Alda
  Guest Stars: Jon Yune, James Saito, Doug Rowe

Margaret and Hawkeye seek solace from enemy fire in each other's arms and end up, briefly, as lovers.

A pivotal episode for the head nurse. Her night with Hawkeye signaled the end of their comic enmity and foreshadowed her divorce from Penobscott, setting the stage for her final evolution in later shows as a confident and secure member of the 4077th family.

134 The Merchant of Korea December 20, 1977
  Writers: Ken Levine, David Isaacs
  Director: William Jurgensen
  Guest Star: Johnny Haymer

When B. J. and Hawkeye are unable to repay loans to Winchester, he extracts petty favors from the pair until they even the score over poker chips.

135 The Smell of Music January 3, 1978
  Writers: Jim Fritzell, Everett Greenbaum
  Director: Stuart Miller
  Guest Stars: Jordan Clarke, Nancy Steen, Lois Foraker, Richard Lee Sung

Hawkeye and B. J. wage a battle of wills with their bunkmate when they refuse to bathe until Winchester ceases his agonizing French-horn practice.

136 Patent 4077 January 10, 1978
  Writers: Ken Levine, David Isaacs
  Director: Harry Morgan
  Guest Stars: Keye Luke, Brenda Thomson, Harry Gold, Pat Stevens

Klinger loses Margaret's wedding ring; and the doctors commission a peddler of cheap jewelry to build a surgical clamp.

137   Tea and Empathy   January 17, 1978
       Writer: Bill Idelson
       Director: Don Weis
       Guest Stars: Bernard Fox, Neil Thompson, Sal Viscuso

Klinger and Father Mulcahy volunteer to retrieve a stolen cache
of penicillin from the black market.

138   Your Hit Parade   January 24, 1978
       Writer: Ronny Graham
       Director: George Tyne
       Guest Stars: Ronny Graham, William Kux, Ken Michelman

Radar plays disc jockey to keep spirits from sagging when the
4077th is deluged with an overflow of wounded from other
M*A*S*H units.

139   What's Up, Doc?   January 30, 1978
       Writer: Larry Balmagia
       Director: George Tyne
       Guest Stars: Charles Frank, Lois Foraker, Kurt Andon

Hawkeye performs delicate rabbit surgery to determine if Margaret is pregnant; and Klinger is the willing hostage of a mad GI
who demands passage to Ohio.

140   Mail Call Three   February 6, 1978
       Writers: Everett Greenbaum, Jim Fritzell
       Director: Charles S. Dubin
       Guest Stars: Oliver Clark, Jack Grapes, Carmine Scelza, Terri
       Paul

A tardy sack of mail brings a batch of misdelivered love letters
to Hawkeye and a Dear John letter for Klinger, from his wife,
Laverne.

The unfortunate corporal had married Laverne Esposito in a shortwave ceremony during the third season, but never did get to Toledo to
consummate the union.

141   Temporary Duty   February 13, 1978
     Writer: Larry Balmagia
     Director: Burt Metcalfe
     Guest Stars: George Lindsey, Marcia Rodd

The camp is enlivened by the arrival of a boisterous surgeon on temporary assignment to the 4077th.

142   Potter's Retirement   February 20, 1978
     Writer: Laurence Marks
     Director: William Jurgensen
     Guest Stars: George Wyner, Peter Hobbs, Ken White

Colonel Potter discovers that somebody down there doesn't like him when unflattering reports of his command are filed by someone in his own unit.

143   Dr. Winchester and Mr. Hyde   February 27, 1978
     Writers: Ken Levine, David Isaacs, Ronny Graham
     Director: Charles S. Dubin
     Guest Stars: Chris Murney, Joe Tornatore, Ron Max, Rod Gist

Winchester falls prey to drug abuse when he relies on self-prescribed amphetamines to help him through a long tour of duty.

144   Major Topper   March 27, 1978
     Writer: Allyn Freeman
     Director: Charles Dubin
     Guest Stars: Hamilton Camp, Andrew Bloch, Donald Blackwell, Peter Zapp, Paul Linke, John Kirby, Michael Mann, Kellye Nakahara

The doctors resort to placebos when the morphine supply is contaminated; and Klinger has competition when a new nut is introduced into the 4077th.

1978/79   THE SEVENTH SEASON

Year-End Rating: 25.4 (7th place)

The creative staff rises to the challenge of keeping the series fresh as the ensemble undergoes a slight, but perceptible shift. Actor Gary

Burghoff had chosen to limit Radar's involvement to thirteen appearances a year, and Alda occasionally spent more time behind the camera than in front of it. As the leading players regrouped, it naturally followed that supporting characters like Corporal Klinger and Father Mulcahy began to blossom during the later years of the show.

Executive story editors Ken Levine and David Isaacs write a third of the season's stories, with multiple script contributions from story editor Larry Balmagia, story consultant Ronny Graham, Alan Alda, Mitch Markowitz, and Tom Reeder.

145   Commander Pierce   September 18, 1978
   Writer: Ronny Graham
   Director: Burt Metcalfe
   Guest Stars: James Lough, Andrew Massett, Jan Jorden

The 4077th is astonished when Hawkeye becomes a petty tyrant and military bureaucrat after he's appointed temporary camp commander.

146   Peace on Us   September 25, 1978
   Writers: Ken Levine, David Isaacs
   Director: George Tyne
   Guest Stars: Kevin Hagen, Hugh Gillan

Hawkeye, frustrated by the lack of progress at the Panmunjom peace talks, decides to make a personal plea to the diplomats.

147   Lil   October 2, 1978
   Writer: Sheldon Bull
   Director: Burt Metcalfe
   Guest Stars: Carmen Mathews, W. Perren Page

Colonel Potter develops a more-than-casual interest in a spirited army nurse who visits the 4077th on an inspection tour.

Radar, ever the guardian of morality, keeps a watchful eye on the happily married colonel, as he did under similar circumstances for Henry Blake in the third season's "Henry in Love."

148 Our Finest Hour (one hour) October 9, 1978
  Writers: Ken Levine, David Isaacs, Larry Balmagia, Ronny Graham
  Director: Burt Metcalfe
  Guest Star: Clete Roberts

War correspondent Clete Roberts returns for a fresh documentary look at the lives of the doctors and nurses of the M*A*S*H 4077th.

This reprise of "The Interview" sums up the show's middle period, much as that previous pseudodocumentary put a cap on the first four years. Not surprisingly, there's very little new material that wasn't expressed with equal eloquence in the earlier show.

149 The Billfold Syndrome October 16, 1978
  Writers: Ken Levine, David Isaacs
  Director: Alan Alda
  Guest Stars: Kevin Geer, Allan Arbus

Major Sidney Freedman treats a shell-shocked medic who has completely forgotten who he was before the war.

150 None Like It Hot October 23, 1978
  Writers: Ken Levine, David Isaacs, Johnny Bonaduce
  Director: Tony Mordente
  Guest Stars: Ted Gehring, Johnny Haymer, Jan Jorden

Hawkeye and B. J. receive a mail-order bathtub during a heat wave and then try to keep a few dozen interlopers away from their portable oasis.

151 They Call the Wind Korea October 30, 1978
  Writers: Ken Levine, David Isaacs
  Director: Charles S. Dubin
  Guest Stars: Tom Dever, Paul Cavonis, Randy Stumpf

Klinger and Winchester provide emergency medical care to a truckload of wounded Greeks after a Manchurian windstorm strands them on the road to Seoul.

152   Major Ego   November 6, 1978
Writer: Larry Balmagia
Director: Alan Alda
Guest Stars: Greg Mullavey, David Dean, Frank Pettinger,
Phyllis Katz

Charles basks in the spotlight when his medical handiwork becomes the subject of a feature story in *Stars and Stripes*.

153   Baby, It's Cold Outside   November 13, 1978
Writer: Gary David Goldberg
Director: George Tyne
Guest Stars: Terry Wills, Teck Murdock, David Dramer, Jan
Jorden

Winchester is well insulated in a polar snowsuit as a GI fights
to survive overexposure during a record-breaking cold snap.

154   Point of View   November 20, 1978
Writers: Ken Levine, David Isaacs
Director: Charles S. Dubin
Guest Stars: Brad Gorman, Marc Baxley, Edward Gallardo, Jan
Jorden, Hank Ross, David Stafford, Paul Tuerpe

The efforts of the doctors and nurses of the 4077th are examined
from the perspective of a wounded soldier made mute by a
throat injury.

The writers' recent efforts to deepen the characters from the inside
out pay off splendidly in this classic episode that lets us see them from
the outside looking in. From the winning charm of Margaret's bedside
manner to the disarming compassion of Hawkeye's wisecracks, the dignity and warmth of the 4077th crew are revealed with a clarity uncolored
by the cloying sentimentality that would sink so many of the series's
later efforts in this vein.

155   Dear Comrade   November 27, 1978
Writer: Tom Reeder
Director: Charles S. Dubin
Guest Stars: Sab Shimono, Larry Block, Robert Clotworthy

A Communist spy goes undercover as Winchester's houseboy
to gather intelligence on the 4077th's superior record of medical
success.

156   Out of Gas   December 4, 1978
   Writer: Tom Reeder
   Director: Mel Damski
   Guest Stars: Justin Lord, Byron Chung, Johnny Haymer

Father Mulcahy and Winchester are the unlikely emissaries sent to barter for black-market supplies of much-needed sodium pentothal.

157   An Eye for a Tooth   December 11, 1978
   Writer: Ronny Graham
   Director: Charles S. Dubin
   Guest Star: Peter Palmer

When Father Mulcahy is passed over for promotion yet again, he decides to attract attention by sneaking off on an emergency chopper mission.

158   Dear Sis   December 18, 1978
   Writer: Alan Alda
   Director: Alan Alda
   Guest Stars: Lawrason Driscoll, Patrick Driscoll, Jo Ann Thompson, W. Perren Page

In a Christmas letter to his sister, Mulcahy laments his inability to help the GIs in more concrete ways than just the spiritual.

William Christopher, the actor who played Father Mulcahy, commented on the strength of the "M*A*S*H" ensemble when he told a reporter, "It's heartening to work on this show because I know my time will come each year and there will be a show in which my character is expanded." He hit a jackpot in the seventh year when these three consecutive episodes cast him in the spotlight.

159   B. J. Papa San   January 1, 1979
   Writer: Larry Balmagia
   Director: James Sheldon
   Guest Stars: Dick O'Neill, Mariel Aragon, Chao-Li Chi, Stephen Keep, Johnny Haymer, Richard Furukawa, Shizuko Hoshi

B. J. devotes himself to helping a destitute Korean family in an attempt to fill the void caused by his separation from his own wife and daughter.

160   Inga   January 8, 1979
Writer: Alan Alda
Director: Alan Alda
Guest Stars: Mariette Hartley, Phyllis Katz, Mark Favara

A twinge of jealousy quickly develops into pigheaded sexism when Hawkeye refuses to be outdone by a beautiful Swedish doctor.

Not surprisingly, this was one of Alan Alda's all-time favorite scripts. When it won an Emmy, the writer/actor/director gleefully cartwheeled to the podium to accept the award. Alda's confirmed feminism was never so pronounced, or frankly anachronistic, as in this story that revealed how far Hawkeye had come since the days of his amorous liaisons in the mattress-supply room—and how much further he had yet to travel.

161   The Price   January 15, 1979
Writer: Erik Tarloff
Director: Charles S. Dubin
Guest Stars: Miko Mayama, Yuki Shimoda, Ken Mochizuki, Dennis Sakamoto

Hawkeye and B. J. shield a young Korean draft dodger; and Potter's horse becomes a source of pride to an aged South Korean war hero.

162   The Young and the Restless   January 22, 1979
Writer: Mitch Markowitz
Director: William Jurgensen
Guest Star: James Canning

Elder statesmen Potter and Winchester are dazzled—and intimidated—by the accomplished surgical technique of a young army medical instructor.

163   Hot Lips Is Back in Town   January 29, 1979
Writers: Larry Balmagia, Bernard Dilbert
Story: Bernard Dilbert, Gary Markowitz
Director: Charles S. Dubin
Guest Stars: Peggy Lee Brennan, Walter Brooke, Jan Jorden

Major Houlihan, her sour marriage behind her, asserts her new independence when she rebuffs the advances of a general; and Radar is smitten by a new nurse.

164   C*A*V*E   February 5, 1979
   Writers: Larry Balmagia, Ronny Graham
   Director: William Jurgensen
   Guest Stars: Basil Hoffman, Mark Taylor, Charles Jenkins

The 4077th is driven underground, literally, when heavy shelling forces the camp to relocate temporarily in a cave.

165   Rally 'Round the Flagg, Boys   February 14, 1979
   Writer: Mitch Markowitz
   Director: Harry Morgan
   Guest Stars: Edward Winter, Neil Thompson, Bob Okazaki

Colonel Flagg returns to the 4077th to investigate Hawkeye's alleged Communist sympathies.

166   Preventive Medicine   February 19, 1979
   Writer: Tom Reeder
   Director: Tony Mordente
   Guest Stars: James Wainwright, Larry Jenkins

B. J. takes issue when Hawkeye prescribes unneccessary surgery for an overzealous commander to prevent him from jeopardizing the lives of more boys in battle.

The filming of this episode offers a glimpse into the writers' fluid approach to "M*A*S*H" story material. In the original script, both doctors colluded in the bogus appendectomy—a breach of medical ethics that actor Mike Farrell found morally reprehensible. Alda disagreed, and the actors launched into a heated onstage debate, which producer Metcalfe noted and later incorporated into the final script. As the producer observed, "It was better than what any writer alone could have done to improve the show."

167   A Night at Rosie's   February 26, 1979
   Writers: Ken Levine, David Isaacs
   Director: Burt Metcalfe
   Guest Stars: Keye Luke, Joshua Bryant, Joseph Di Reda

Hawkeye drowns his sorrows in an evening at Rosie's Bar, and one by one, the rest of the camp joins him.

Levine and Isaacs wrote this story "like a little play," just so they could place the characters in a fresh setting that everyone hadn't already seen a thousand times.

168 Ain't Love Grand March 5, 1979
Writers: Ken Levine, David Isaacs
Director: Mike Farrell
Guest Stars: Kit McDonough, Sylvia Chang, Eileen Saki,
Michael Williams, Judy Farrell

Charles develops an infatuation for an earthy Korean call girl; and Klinger is amazed to find himself the object of a new nurse's fancy.

169 The Party March 12, 1979
Writers: Burt Metcalfe, Alan Alda
Director: Burt Metcalfe

B. J. refuses to let an evacuation dampen plans for the grand party he's arranged for the staff's relatives back home in the States.

Burt Metcalfe's first "M*A*S*H" script gave the producer new respect for his scripters—he would compare writing to visiting the dentist. He and Alda dictated the entire second act of this episode into a tape recorder over an Italian dinner at Anna's restaurant in Los Angeles, a fertile watering hole that frequently hosted the writers' brainstorming sessions.

1979/80   THE EIGHTH SEASON

Year-End Rating: 25.3 (4th place)

Radar O'Reilly's decampment near the top of the eighth season sets the stage for Klinger's emergence as a more believable, three-dimensional central figure. The now fully balanced ensemble is poised for the series of rich character studies that will be at the heart of the final seasons' best episodes.

Burt Metcalfe is executive producer for the final four seasons, and Stanford Tischler the associate producer. John Rappaport and Jim Mulligan sign on as producers, and Dennis Koenig is the season's story editor. Thad Mumford and Dan Wilcox are the executive story editors. Ronny Graham continues as program consultant, and Charles S. Dubin is the staff director in season eight.

170   Too Many Cooks   September 17, 1979
   Writer: Dennis Koenig
   Director: Charles S. Dubin
   Guest Stars: John Randolph, Ed Begley, Jr.

The staff is forced to reevaluate their opinion of a bumbling foot soldier after he works wonders in the mess tent kitchen.

171   Are You Now, Margaret?   September 24, 1979
   Writers: Thad Mumford, Dan Wilcox
   Director: Charles S. Dubin
   Guest Stars: Lawrence Pressman, Jennifer Davis, Jeff Maxwell

A witch-hunting congressional investigator tries to uncover Communist sympathies in Margaret's youthful past.

Thad Mumford and Dan Wilcox had written scripts, together and separately, for "Maude," "Alice," "The Electric Company," "America 2-Night," as well as the miniseries "Roots II." The hardworking story editors would eventually become producers of the show's final two seasons.

172   Guerrilla My Dreams   October 1, 1979
   Writer: Bob Colleary
   Director: Alan Alda
   Guest Stars: Mako, Joshua Bryant, Huanani Minn, George Kee Cheung, Marcus Mukai, Connie Izay

Hawkeye tries to prevent a South Korean officer from interrogating a wounded woman being held at the 4077th as an enemy guerrilla.

173   Good-bye, Radar (Part 1)   October 8, 1979
   Writers: Ken Levine, David Isaacs
   Director: Charles S. Dubin
   Guest Stars: Marilyn Jones, Johnny Haymer, Michael O'Dwyer, Richard Lee-Sung, Tony Cristino, Arell Blanton

Radar returns from furlough to discover that he's been discharged so that he can help out at home after a family crisis.

Gary Burghoff decided to leave the series at the end of the seventh year, complaining that the monotony of the series had taken its toll. Though few tears were shed when the hotheaded actor finally left, CBS coerced him to return for this two-part farewell episode that was scheduled to take advantage of the November ratings sweeps period.

174   Good-bye, Radar (Part 2)   October 15, 1979
  Writers: Ken Levine, David Isaacs
  Director: Charles S. Dubin
  Guest Stars: Lee de Broux, Whitney Rydbeck, David Dozer

Radar's gala farewell party is upstaged by the unexpected arrival of incoming wounded, leaving the corporal to say his good-byes in silence to an empty camp.

Writers Levine and Isaacs avoid the potentially mawkish elements of Radar's farewell when they opt for a more compelling treatment that allows the little corporal only a muted last hurrah. The war arrives—an uninvited guest at his good-bye party—and suddenly everyone is back to the business of battle, with not a single tear shed. The character's final moments at the 4077th are moving, yet refreshingly devoid of gushing sentiment. Now, if only they hadn't dragged out that teddy bear for the final coda. . . .

175   Period of Adjustment   October 22, 1979
  Writers: Jim Mulligan, John Rappaport
  Director: Charles S. Dubin
  Guest Stars: Jeff Maxwell, Eileen Saki, Gwen Farrell

B. J. feels the sharp pangs of homesickness when he hears how his toddling daughter mistook Radar for her soldier daddy; and Klinger finds it rough going when he takes over as company clerk.

176   Nurse Doctor   October 29, 1979
  Writers: Sy Rosen, Thad Mumford, Dan Wilcox
  Story: Sy Rosen
  Director: Charles S. Dubin
  Guest Star: Alexandra Stoddart

The camp is in the midst of a drought, but Father Mulcahy finds himself in plenty of hot water when he rebuffs the affections of a young nurse.

177   Private Finance   November 5, 1979
   Writer: Dennis Koenig
   Director: Charles S. Dubin
   Guest Stars: Shizuko Hoshi, Denice Kumagi, Mark Kologi, Joey
   Pento, Philip Simma, Art Evans

Hawkeye debates whether to send a dead soldier's black-market
profits home to the boy's parents; and Klinger's offer of financial
support to a young Korean girl is misinterpreted by her mother.

178   Mr. and Mrs. Who?   November 12, 1979
   Writer: Ronny Graham
   Director: Burt Metcalfe
   Guest Stars: Claudette Nevins, James Keane

Charles returns from a lost weekend in Tokyo, stinging from a
hangover—and the possibility that he may have gotten married.

179   The Yalu Brick Road   November 19, 1979
   Writer: Mike Farrell
   Director: Charles S. Dubin
   Guest Stars: Soon Teck Oh, G. W. Bailey

After Klinger's Thanksgiving feast yields a harvest of food poi-
soning, Hawkeye and B. J. are sidetracked on the way back to
camp with the antibiotic antidote.

180   Life Time   November 26, 1979
   Writers: Alan Alda, Walter D. Dishell, M.D.
   Director: Alan Alda
   Guest Star: Kevin Brophy

The surgeons race the clock when a soldier's medical complications force them to complete his delicate heart operation within
twenty minutes.

An on-screen clock creates arresting suspense as it ticks off in real
time as the half hour progresses.
   The episode's script was co-written by Alda and Walter Dishell, the
show's medical adviser. The story is 100 percent medically plausible—
one of the more remarkable examples of the painstaking research that
went into almost every script. Dishell actually kept a 1953 medical text-
book in his office to ensure that the surgeons' procedures were never

anachronistic, and a registered army nurse was always on the set to oversee the accuracy of triage and O.R. sequences.

181   Dear Uncle Abdul   December 3, 1979
      Writers: John Rappaport, Jim Mulligan
      Director: William Jurgensen
      Guest Stars: Kelly Ward, Richard Lineback, Alexander Petale

With all his new responsibilities, Klinger barely has time to write a letter home to his family in Toledo.

182   Captains Outrageous   December 10, 1979
      Writers: Thad Mumford, Dan Wilcox
      Director: Burt Metcalfe
      Guest Stars: Eileen Saki, John Orchard, Sirri Murad, G. W. Bailey, Paul Cavonis, Momo Yashima, Jo Ann Thompson

Members of the staff tend bar after Rosie gets hurt during one of their brawls; and Father Mulcahy skeptically awaits news of his long-awaited promotion.

183   Stars and Stripe   December 17, 1979
      Writer: Dennis Koenig
      Director: Harry Morgan
      Guest Star: Joshua Bryant

B. J. and Winchester form a tempestuous partnership to write an article for a medical journal; and Hot Lips is reunited with a macho front-line boyfriend.

184   Yessir, That's Our Baby   December 31, 1979
      Writer: Jim Mulligan
      Director: Alan Alda
      Guest Stars: Howard Platt, William Bogert, Yuki Shimoda, Elizabeth Farley

The 4077th plays adoption agency when the staff tries to find a home for an unwanted Amer-Asian baby abandoned on their doorstep.

185 Bottle Fatigue   January 7, 1980
    Writers: Thad Mumford, Dan Wilcox
    Director: Burt Metcalfe
    Guest Stars: Shelley Long, David Hirokane, Shari Saba

Hawkeye's huge bar bill convinces him to go on the wagon; and Charles frets when his sister plans to marry beneath her station.

When he releases his grip on demon rum, Hawkeye questions his last boisterous, irredeemable, and purely selfish habit—and completes the final stages of his character's transformation. The lusty, hard-drinking, quick-witted, and utterly human doctor who'd been drafted eight seasons earlier has finally emerged as the walking, talking conscience of humanity—the Jiminy Cricket of the Korean War.

186 Heal Thyself   January 14, 1980
    Writer: Dennis Koenig
    Story: Dennis Koenig, Gene Reynolds
    Director: Mike Farrell
    Guest Star: Edward Herrman

Hawkeye and B. J. are delighted with a temporary surgeon who fills in for the ailing Winchester, until the new medic begins to crack under the strain.

187 Old Soldiers   January 21, 1980
    Writer: Dennis Koenig
    Director: Charles S. Dubin
    Guest Stars: Jane Connell, Sally Imamura, Jason Autajay

Colonel Potter drinks a toast to his old army buddies when he finds out he's the last survivor of his World War I battalion.

188 Morale Victory   January 28, 1980
    Writer: John Rappaport
    Director: Charles S. Dubin
    Guest Stars: James Stephens, G. W. Bailey, Connie Izay

Potter challenges B. J. and Hawkeye to boost camp morale; and Winchester tries to lift the spirits of a pianist who has a paralyzed hand.

189   Lend a Hand   February 4, 1980
   Writer: Alan Alda
   Director: Alan Alda
   Guest Stars: Robert Alda, Antony Alda, Daren Kelly, Shari Saba

Hawkeye volunteers for an emergency mission on the front lines and gets paired with an abrasive medical consultant he can't stand.

Robert Alda returns to reprise his role as the medical consultant Dr. Borelli, who previously appeared in the third year. Alan's brother, Antony, completes the family scene in a smaller role as the medic who referees the bickering physicians.

190   Good-bye, Cruel World   February 11, 1980
   Writers: Thad Mumford, Dan Wilcox
   Director: Charles S. Dubin
   Guest Stars: Clyde Kusatsu, Allan Arbus, Philip Bruns, James Lough, David Cramer

Dr. Freedman treats a wounded Asian-American war hero who would rather commit suicide than return home.

191   Dreams   February 18, 1980
   Writer: Alan Alda
   Story: Alan Alda, James Jay Rubinfier
   Director: Alan Alda
   Guest Stars: Ford Rainey, Robin Haynes, Catherine Bergstrom, Fred Stuthman, Kurtis Sanders, Ray Lynch, Connie Izay

The staff's worst fears and most desperate frustrations are explored as they daydream during short catnaps away from the rigors of surgery.

B. J.'s dream features the first appearance of his wife, Peg, played by Catherine Bergstrom.

192   War Co-Respondent   March 3, 1980
   Writer: Mike Farrell
   Director: Mike Farrell
   Guest Stars: Susan Saint James, Brad Wilkin, Calvin Levels

B. J. wrestles with his conscience when he nearly forsakes his marriage for an infatuation with an attractive war correspondent.

Susan Saint James is the reporter who tempts B. J. She was Rock Hudson's TV wife for six seasons of NBC's "McMillan and Wife" before she joined the sitcom camp as one-half of "Kate and Allie" on CBS in 1984.

---

193   Back Pay   March 10, 1980

Writers: Thad Mumford, Dan Wilcox, Dennis Koenig
Director: Burt Metcalfe
Guest Stars: Sab Shimono, Peter Kim, Jerry Fujikawa, G. W. Bailey, Richard Herd, Roy Goldman

Hawkeye bills the army $38,000 for his services to protest the profits civilian doctors are reaping by contributing to the war effort.

---

194   April Fools   March 24, 1980

Writer: Dennis Koenig
Director: Charles S. Dubin
Guest Stars: Pat Hingle, G. W. Bailey, Roy Goldman, Jennifer Davis

Potter warns the camp to be on their best behavior when a hard-boiled colonel schedules his inspection during the 4077th April Fool's Day festivities.

1980/81   THE NINTH SEASON

Year-End Rating: 25.7 (4th place)

After nearly two hundred episodes, the characters are superbly defined, but the irony is inescapable: As the years mount, these well-drawn, articulate characters are running out of things to say.

Dan Wilcox and Thad Mumford are the ninth season's executive script consultants, and Dennis Koenig is the executive story editor. John Rappaport returns as producer, and Gene Reynolds, Alan Alda, and Ronny Graham continue to serve as special creative and story consultants.

195 The Best of Enemies   November 17, 1980
    Writer: Sheldon Bull
    Director: Charles S. Dubin
    Guest Stars: Mako, Steven Lum

A North Korean soldier forces Hawkeye to perform an emergency roadside operation on his buddy.

196 Letters   November 24, 1980
    Writer: Dennis Koenig
    Director: Charles S. Dubin
    Guest Stars: Richard Paul, Eileen Saki, Larry Cedar, Michael Currie, Shari Saba

Members of the 4077th share their impressions of war in response to letters from fourth graders in Hawkeye's hometown.

197 Cementing Relationships   December 1, 1980
    Writers: David Pollack, Elias Davis
    Director: Charles S. Dubin
    Guest Stars: Joel Brooks, Alan Toy, Mel Harris

A jilted Italian soldier is smitten by Margaret; and Klinger pours a cement floor in the operating room to fight the spread of germs.

198 Father's Day   December 8, 1980
    Writer: Karen L. Hall
    Director: Alan Alda
    Guest Stars: Andrew Duggan, Jeffrey Kramer, Art Le Fleur, Roy Evans

Margaret has trouble pretending she's a chip off the old block when her dad, blood and guts "Howitzer" Al Houlihan, arrives for a visit.

199 Death Takes a Holiday   December 15, 1980
    Writer: Mike Farrell
    Director: Mike Farrell
    Guest Stars: G. W. Bailey, Keye Luke, Yoshiko Hoover

Christmas at the 4077th finds the surgeons struggling to keep a mortally wounded soldier alive, even if it's only through the holiday.

200 A War for All Seasons   December 29, 1980
  Writers: Dan Wilcox, Thad Mumford
  Director: Burt Metcalfe
  Guest Stars: Carl Freed, Laurie Bates, Jeff Maxwell

On New Year's Eve, the staff looks back on the highlights of 1951: The doctors invent an artificial kidney machine; Mulcahy plants a garden; and Margaret takes up knitting.

201 Your Retention, Please   January 5, 1981
  Writer: Erik Tarloff
  Director: Charles S. Dubin
  Guest Stars: Barry Corbin, Sam Weisman, Jeff Maxwell

Klinger is so depressed by news that his ex-wife plans to remarry, he reenlists for an additional six-year hitch.

By this time Klinger had already given up on his section-eight discharge, and with it, his wardrobe of Twentieth Century–Fox originals.

202 Tell It to the Marines   January 12, 1981
  Writer: Hank Bradford
  Director: Harry Morgan
  Guest Stars: Stan Wells, Michael McGuirre, Denny Miller, James Gallery

Winchester takes command during Potter's absence; and B. J. and Hawkeye try to convince the Marines to grant a hardship discharge to an immigrant soldier.

203 Taking the Fifth   January 19, 1981
  Writers: Elias Davis, David Pollack
  Director: Charles S. Dubin
  Guest Stars: Charles Hallahan, Judy Farrell, Margie Impert, Susan Berger

Hawkeye uses a bottle of vintage wine to lure unsuspecting nurses into his den; and Potter tries to secure a different sort of anesthetic when the army threatens to ban a painkiller.

Alda and the writers have a bit of fun with Hawkeye's bygone reputation as a ladies' man. Hawkeye, once the rooster of the henhouse, is reduced to posting a notice on the nurses' bulletin board practically begging for a volunteer.

204 Operation Friendship   January 26, 1981
Writer: Dennis Koenig
Director: Rena Down
Guest Stars: Tim O'Connor, Gwen Farrell

Klinger saves Winchester's life when an explosion rocks the operating room; and B. J. is reluctant to reveal the extent of his injuries after the blast.

205 No Sweat   February 2, 1981
Writer: John Rappaport
Director: Burt Metcalfe
Guest Stars: W. Perren Page, Jeff Maxwell, Kellye Nakahara

Margaret develops a case of prickly heat—just one of the indignities suffered by the 4077th staff during another unendurably hot night.

206 Depressing News   February 9, 1981
Writers: Dan Wilcox, Thad Mumford
Director: Alan Alda
Guest Stars: William Bogert, David Dozer, Albert Insinnia

Klinger's army newspaper reports on Hawkeye's monument to military stupidity: a giant tower made from a half million erroneously shipped tongue depressors.

207 No Laughing Matter   February 16, 1981
Writers: Elias Davis, David Pollack
Director: Burt Metcalfe
Guest Stars: Robert Symonds, Mae Hi, Nathan Jung

Hawkeye wagers that he can go a full day without a wisecrack; and Winchester finally confronts the major who exiled him to the 4077th.

208 Oh, How We Danced   February 23, 1981
Writer: John Rappaport
Director: Burt Metcalfe
Guest Stars: Yuki Shimoda, Arlen Dean Snyder, Catherine Bergstrom, Michael Choe, Jennifer Davis

Winchester is sent to inspect sanitary conditions on the front lines while the rest of the camp plans a surprise anniversary party for B. J.

209   Bottoms Up   March 2, 1981
   Writer: Dennis Koenig
   Director: Alan Alda
   Guest Stars: Gail Strickland, Shari Saba, Kellye Nakahara

One of Margaret's nurses tries to hide her severe drinking problem; and Hawkeye is scorned after a practical joke he plays on Winchester backfires.

210   The Red/White Blues   March 9, 1981
   Writers: David Pollack, Elias Davis
   Director: Gabriel Beaumont
   Guest Stars: Roy Goldman, Jeff Maxwell, Kellye Nakahara

Colonel Potter nearly blows his stack when his well-intentioned colleagues mollycoddle him in order to lower his blood pressure before his upcoming physical.

211   Bless You, Hawkeye   March 16, 1981
   Writers: Dan Wilcox, Thad Mumford
   Director: Nell Cox
   Guest Stars: Allan Arbus, Barry Schwartz

When Hawkeye can't stop a sneezing fit that has no apparent cause, psychiatrist Sidney Freedman digs into the surgeon's past for a clue to the unusual malady.

212   Blood Brothers   April 6, 1981
   Writers: Elias Davis, David Pollack
   Director: Harry Morgan
   Guest Stars: Patrick Swayze, Ray Middleton, G. W. Bailey

Hawkeye is overcome by the devotion of a terminally ill GI for his critically wounded buddy.

213   The Foresight Saga   April 13, 1981
   Writers: Elias Davis, David Pollack
   Director: Charles S. Dubin
   Guest Stars: Rummel Mor, Philip Sterling, Jeff Maxwell

The 4077th is given a gift of fresh-grown vegetables by a grateful Korean; and Potter questions the veracity of an upbeat letter from Radar.

214 The Life You Save   May 4, 1981
    Writers: John Rappaport, Alan Alda
    Director: Alan Alda
    Guest Stars: G. W. Bailey, Val Bisoglio

After Charles is nearly felled by a sniper's bullet, he develops a philosophical obsession with death.

1981/82   THE TENTH SEASON

Year-End Rating: 22.3 (10th place)

Stories in the tenth year again focus on the personalities of the central characters, who are forced, by the thinning plot lines, to explore situations that range from the mundane—poker games, petty thefts, and toothaches—to the bizarre—a goat swallows a $22,000 payroll.

The creative staff for the final two seasons includes John Rappaport, now the supervising producer; and Thad Mumford, Dan Wilcox, and Dennis Koenig, the new producers. Elias Davis and David Pollack are the executive script consultants, and Karen Hall is story editor in the tenth year and executive story editor for the final season.

215 That's Show Biz (one hour)   October 26, 1981
    Writers: Elias Davis, David Pollack
    Director: Charles S. Dubin
    Guest Stars: Gwen Verdon, Gail Edwards, Danny Dayton,
    Karen Landry, Amanda McBroom

A touring USO show brings an unexpected touch of vaudeville to the 4077th when the star showgirl requires an emergency operation.

216 Identity Crisis   November 2, 1981
    Writers: Dan Wilcox, Thad Mumford
    Director: David Ogden Stiers
    Guest Stars: Dirk Blocker, Squire Fridell, Joe Pantoliano

Father Mulcahy counsels a GI who is plagued by guilt.

217 Rumor at the Top   November 9, 1981
    Writers: David Pollack, Elias Davis
    Director: Charles S. Dubin
    Guest Stars: Nicholas Pryor, Jeff Maxwell, Roy Goldman

The latest scuttlebutt affects everyone's behavior when a visiting emissary is rumored to be recruiting for a new M*A*S*H unit.

218 Give 'Em Hell, Hawkeye   November 16, 1981
    Writer: Dennis Koenig
    Director: Charles S. Dubin
    Guest Stars: Stefan Gierasch, Ed Vasgersian, Tom Kindle

Hawkeye writes a heartfelt letter to President Harry Truman to protest the continued fighting in Korea.

219 Wheelers and Dealers   November 23, 1981
    Writers: Dan Wilcox, Thad Mumford
    Director: Charles S. Dubin
    Guest Stars: Anthony Charnota, Tony Becker, Chris Petersen

On the eve of a big poker game, B. J.'s pride is bruised when he finds out his wife is working as a waitress; and Potter takes driving lessons from Klinger.

220 Communication Breakdown   November 30, 1981
    Writer: Karen L. Hall
    Director: Alan Alda
    Guest Stars: James Saito, Byron Chung, Abby Nelson

Winchester infuriates the camp when he hoards his stateside newspapers; and Hawkeye reunites two Korean brothers who have been fighting on opposite sides of the war.

221 Snap Judgment (Part 1)   December 7, 1981
    Writer: Paul Perlove
    Director: Hy Averback
    Guest Star: Peter Hobbs

The military police think they've solved a rash of thefts at the 4077th when they apprehend Klinger with Hawkeye's stolen camera.

222   Snappier Judgment (Part 2)   December 14, 1981
   Writer: Paul Perlove
   Director: Hy Averback
   Guest Star: Peter Hobbs

B. J. and Hawkeye resolve to clear Klinger's name after he chooses
Winchester to defend him at his military court-martial.

223   'Twas the Day After Christmas   December 28, 1981
   Writers: David Pollack, Elias Davis
   Director: Burt Metcalfe
   Guest Stars: Michael Ensign, Leo Lewis, Val Bisoglio

To boost postyuletide morale on December 26, Potter has the
officers and enlisted men exchange jobs for the day.

224   Follies of the Living—Concerns   January 4, 1982
       of the Dead
   Writer: Alan Alda
   Director: Alan Alda
   Guest Stars: Kario Salem, Randall Patrick, Jeff Tyler

In a fever dream, Klinger communicates with the spirit of a dead
soldier who stays on to witness his own last rites.

225   The Birthday Girls   January 11, 1982
   Writer: Karen L. Hall
   Director: Charles S. Dubin
   Guest Stars: Jerry Fujikawa, Kellye Nakahara

Margaret's birthday plans are spoiled when she and Klinger get
stranded on a desolate roadside; and the surgeons assist in the
delivery of a calf.

226   Blood and Guts   January 18, 1982
   Writer: Lee H. Grant
   Director: Charles S. Dubin
   Guest Stars: Gene Evans, Brett Cullen, Stoney Jackson

Hawkeye is outraged when a sensationalistic war correspondent
reports irresponsible GI stunts as tales of military valor.

227   A Holy Mess   February 1, 1982
Writers: Elias Davis, David Pollack
Director: Burt Metcalfe
Guest Stars: Cyril O'Reilly, David Graf, Val Bisoglio

An AWOL soldier seeks sanctuary behind Father Mulcahy's robes.

228   The Tooth Shall Set You Free   February 8, 1982
Writers: Elias Davis, David Pollack
Director: Charles S. Dubin
Guest Stars: Tom Atkins, Jason Bernard, John Fujioka, Larry Fishburne

Charles faces a tooth extraction; and the doctors suspect prejudice when an inordinate number of black casualties are brought in from a single unit.

229   Pressure Points   February 15, 1982
Writer: David Pollack
Director: Charles S. Dubin
Guest Stars: Allan Arbus, John O'Connell, Gene Pietragallo, William Rogers, Roy Goldman

Potter sends for the army psychiatrist when he loses confidence in his surgical abilities; and Winchester loses patience with his bunkmates' sloppiness.

230   Where There's a Will, There's a War February 22, 1982
Writers: Elias Davis, David Pollack
Director: Alan Alda
Guest Stars: Dennis Howard, Larry Ward, Jim Borelli, James Emery

Hawkeye draws up a will under heavy shelling at the front lines.

231   Promotion Commotion   March 1, 1982
Writer: Dennis Koenig
Director: Charles S. Dubin
Guest Stars: John Matuszak, Jim Reid Boyce, Deborah Harmon, Cameron Dye, Richard Fullerton

Winchester, Pierce, and Hunnicutt find themselves in the sticky position of having to decide which enlisted men to recommend for promotion.

232 Heroes   March 15, 1982
   Writers: Thad Mumford, Dan Wilcox
   Director: Nell Cox
   Guest Stars: Pat McNamara, Earl Boen, Britt Leach, Matthew
   Faison

Hawkeye is the golden boy of the world press when he treats a
celebrity prize fighter for a stroke.

233 Sons and Bowlers   March 22, 1982
   Writers: Elias Davis, David Pollack
   Director: Hy Averback
   Guest Stars: Dick O'Neill, William Lucking, Roger Hampton

Hawkeye anxiously awaits word on his father's stateside operation as his cohorts engage the Marines in a bowling tournament.

234 Picture This   April 5, 1982
   Writer: Karen L. Hall
   Director: Burt Metcalfe
   Guest Stars: John Fujioka, Jeff Maxwell

Potter's attempts to assemble the crew for a family portrait are
thwarted by a feud between bunkmates Pierce, Hunnicutt, and
Winchester.

235 That Darn Kid   April 12, 1982
   Writer: Karen L. Hall
   Director: David Ogden Stiers
   Guest Stars: George Presnell, John P. Ryan, Tom Kindle

Klinger's goat eats the 4077th's $22,000 payroll, leaving paymaster
Hawkeye holding the bag.

1982/83   THE ELEVENTH SEASON

Year-End Rating: 22.6 (3d place)

With the show's research and story sources completely exhausted
after eleven years—and most of the cast restless to move on—the long-
running series calls it quits in one final season that culminates in the
most highly anticipated TV program of all time: the last episode of
"M*A*S*H."

236   Look Me Over   October 25, 1982
   Writer: Alan Alda
   Director: Susan Oliver
   Guest Stars: Kellye Nakahara, Peggy Feury, Perry Lang,
   Deborah Harmon

Hawkeye watches Nurse Kellye brighten a wounded GI's final
moments and comes to appreciate the nurses' vital contribution
to the healing process.

Kellye Nakahara had played Nurse Kellye since the very first year,
when she signed on as a background extra and never left.

The show kept a regular crew of actresses on the payroll to play the
various nurses who staffed the operating room with familiar faces from
week to week—and each got a crash course in actual triage and O.R.
techniques on their first day of shooting. Less obvious is the company
of recurring actors who played background GIs or wounded soldiers—
and sometimes both. More than one battlefield casualty reappears mi-
raculously in the mess tent in a later episode—a hungry Lazarus, cour-
tesy of the Screen Actors Guild.

237   Trick or Treatment   November 1, 1982
   Writer: Dennis Koenig
   Director: Charles S. Dubin
   Guest Stars: George Wendt, Richard Lineback, Andrew Clay,
   James Lough

The 4077th Halloween party hosts an unexpected guest after
Father Mulcahy works an apparent miracle during the reading
of a soldier's last rites.

George Wendt already seems typecast as a drunken reveler—the
rotund actor had just been cast to occupy a regular barstool at Sam's
place on NBC's "Cheers."

238   Foreign Affairs   November 8, 1982
   Writers: David Pollack, Elias Davis
   Director: Charles S. Dubin
   Guest Stars: Melinda Mullins, Jeffrey Tambor, Soon Teck Oh,
   Byron Chung

The army tries to get a North Korean pilot to defect; and Charles gets a rude shock when he falls for a French nurse with an unacceptable past.

239   The Joker Is Wild   November 15, 1982
   Writers: John Rappaport, Dennis Koenig
   Director: Burt Metcalfe
   Guest Stars: Clyde Kusatsu, David Haid

Hawkeye's guard is up when B. J. threatens to pull off the most elaborate practical joke in the compound's history.

The name of Trapper John MacIntyre, the 4077th's legendary practical joker, is invoked in a final, affectionate send-off to the long-departed charter member of the M*A*S*H roster.

240   Who Knew?   November 22, 1982
   Writers: David Pollack, Elias Davis
   Director: Harry Morgan
   Guest Stars: Kellye Nakahara, Enid Kent

Hawkeye volunteers to deliver the eulogy for a dead nurse and belatedly discovers her deep feelings for him.

The surgeon had dallied with the nurse on a few harmless evenings but never considered that her attraction for him would be fatal. His eulogy, colored by this guilt, makes for the strangest farewell of the entire season: The feminist Hawkeye bids adieu to the womanizing cad that was once Hawkeye Pierce.

241   Bombshells   November 29, 1982
   Writers: Dan Wilcox, Thad Mumford
   Director: Charles S. Dubin
   Guest Stars: Gerald O'Laughlin, Allen Williams, Stu Charno

Charles and Hawkeye start a rumor that Marilyn Monroe plans to visit the 4077th; and B. J. feels responsible when he's unable to rescue a wounded soldier.

242 Settling Debts   December 6, 1982
  Writers: Dan Wilcox, Thad Mumford
  Director: Mike Switzer
  Guest Stars: Guy Boyd, Jeff East

Hawkeye and the crew surprise Colonel Potter with a party to commemorate Mildred's final payment on the couple's mortgage.

243 The Moon Is Not Blue   December 13, 1982
  Writer: Larry Balmagia
  Director: Charles S. Dubin
  Guest Stars: Hamilton Camp, Sandy Helberg, Jan Jorden

With the camp facing prohibition and a severe medical-supply shortage during another heat wave, Hawkeye resolves to lift morale by importing a racy new movie.

244 Run for the Money   December 20, 1982
  Writers: Mike Farrell, David Pollack, Elias Davis
  Director: Nell Cox
  Guest Stars: Thomas Calloway, Mark Anderson, Phil Brock, William Schilling, Robert Alan Browne

When an Olympic runner assigned to the 4077th fails to materialize, Father Mulcahy must save the camp's honor in a high-stakes footrace against the 8063d.

245 U.N. the Night and the Music   January 3, 1983
  Writers: David Pollack, Elias Davis
  Director: Harry Morgan
  Guest Stars: George Innes, Kavi Raz, Dennis Holahan, David Packer

A United Nations delegation tours the 4077th—a Swede, a Hindu, and a British officer—and each leaves a lasting effect on the men and women of the camp.

The show's reputation for seamlessly blending comedy and drama began to suffer as the years advanced. Here, B. J.'s dramatic decision to amputate a young GI's leg—all dark lighting and slow, ponderous line readings—is awkwardly juxtaposed with a ludicrous slapstick sequence where Colonel Potter learns to stand on his head.

The on-screen sparks shared by Margaret and her handsome Swede ignited an offscreen romance that eventually led to the marriage of Loretta Swit and actor Dennis Holahan.

246   Strange Bedfellows   January 10, 1983
   Writer: Mike Farrell
   Director: Karen L. Hall
   Guest Stars: Dennis Dugan, Benjamin F. Wilson

The 4077th faces a sleepless night as Charles's snoring keeps B.J. and Hawkeye from counting sheep; and Colonel Potter discovers that his son-in-law has had an affair.

247   Say No More   January 24, 1983
   Writer: John Rappaport
   Director: Charles S. Dubin
   Guest Stars: John Anderson, Michael Horton, Chip Johnson, James Karen

A military strategist refuses to accept responsibility for the war games that have mortally wounded his own son; and Margaret develops laryngitis.

248   Friends and Enemies   February 7, 1983
   Writer: Karen L. Hall
   Director: Jamie Farr
   Guest Star: John McLiam

Colonel Potter must decide whether to blow the whistle on an old army chum whose military follies are costing boys their lives.

249   Give and Take   February 14, 1983
   Writer: Dennis Koenig
   Director: Charles S. Dubin
   Guest Stars: Craig Wasson, G. W. Bailey, Derek Wong

A wounded GI learns a painful lesson when he forms a recovery-room friendship with the enemy soldier he's critically wounded.

250   As Time Goes By   February 21, 1983
     Writers: Dan Wilcox, Thad Mumford
     Director: Burt Metcalfe
     Guest Stars: Rosalind Chao, G. W. Bailey, Michael Swan, Mark
     Herrier, Jeff Maxwell

Hawkeye and Margaret encapsulate the breadth of their wartime
experience when they bury souvenirs as a reminder for future
generations.

Actually the last episode filmed, "As Time Goes By" offers an economical alternative to the unwieldy behemoth that eventually closed the
series the following week. Margaret briefly, almost nostalgically, re-
emerges as the spitfire patriot who "sees the world through khaki-col-
ored glasses," and Hawkeye goes out, as always, the cynical romantic.
The pair bury their memories as they bury the hatchet in a classic episode
that strikes a near-perfect balance of sentiment, statement, and smiles.

251   Good-bye, Farewell and Amen   February 28, 1983
     (2½-hour special)
     Writers: Alan Alda, Burt Metcalfe, John Rappaport, Thad
     Mumford, Dan Wilcox, David Pollack, Elias Davis, Karen L.
     Hall
     Director: Alan Alda
     Guest Stars: Allan Arbus, Rosalind Chao, G. W. Bailey, Shari
     Saba, Jeff Maxwell, Gwen Farrell, Kellye Nakahara, Roy
     Goldman

The men and women of M*A*S*H discover that a peace treaty
doesn't vanquish the horrors of war overnight. Hawkeye suffers
a nervous breakdown when he tries to suppress memories of a
heinous atrocity; and Charles teaches a group of Chinese pris-
oners to play a Mozart quintet, only to see them killed in the
last gasp of fighting.

At last, the armistice is signed, and the weary medics regroup for
final farewells as they face their inevitable futures. Klinger makes plans
to stay in Korea with his native bride; Charles returns to Boston as he
bids Margaret adieu with a book of Browning and a kiss; and Hawkeye
and B. J. deliver their first—and only—full military salute to Colonel
Potter before each embarks on his own private journey back to a blessed
sanity.

Larry Gelbart envisioned a different scenario for the final episode. In the *Los Angeles Times*, he described what he saw as the only logical conclusion to so many seasons of televised war: "I wanted the camera to pull back and back and back, and I wanted to hear a director say, 'Cut,' and see the cast embrace and say goodbye." Then, Alan Alda would turn, face the camera, and say directly to the audience:

No matter how we tried, we could give you only an idea of what it was like. The blood was a pale imitation. This is only a show. War is not this manageable . . . or this entertaining.

Not surprisingly, that ending was never even considered.

EMMY AWARDS

The following is a complete listing of the Emmy Awards bestowed on "M*A*S*H" by the National Academy of Television Arts and Sciences.

1973/74   Outstanding Comedy Series
Outstanding Lead Actor in a Comedy Series: Alan Alda
Actor of the Year, Series: Alan Alda
Outstanding Directing in Comedy: Jackie Cooper, "Carry On, Hawkeye"

1974/75   Outstanding Directing in a Comedy Series: Gene Reynolds, "O.R."

1975/76   Outstanding Directing in a Comedy Series: Gene Reynolds, "Welcome to Korea"
Outstanding Film Editing for Entertainment Programming: Stanford Tischler, Fred W. Berger, "Welcome to Korea"

1976/77   Outstanding Continuing Performance by a Supporting Actor in a Comedy Series: Gary Burghoff
Outstanding Directing in a Comedy Series: Alan Alda, "Dear Sigmund"

1978/79   Outstanding Writing in a Comedy Series: Alan Alda, "Inga"

1979/80   Outstanding Supporting Actor in a Comedy Series: Harry Morgan
Outstanding Supporting Actress in a Comedy Series: Loretta Swit

1981/82   Outstanding Lead Actor in a Comedy Series: Alan Alda
Outstanding Supporting Actress in a Comedy Series: Loretta Swit

"THE BOB NEWHART SHOW"

*The show was so often
overlooked because it was
always in Mary's shadow.*
—GLEN CHARLES

MARY was a smash.

Her show was not just a hit, but a hit with class. And at CBS—the self-styled Tiffany's of television—class was valued almost as highly as ratings. That Mary Tyler Moore was able to deliver *both* made her very special, perhaps even one of a kind. And yet, who could blame the network for inquiring if there were any more at home like her?

"There was a strong feeling that if that show's working, there might be another one there," remembers Alan Wagner, the network's head of new program development during that fertile period in the early 1970s. "The place was bubbling with creative enthusiasm." Late in "Mary's" first year, the CBS executive casually approached two of the bubbliest of those creators to ask if they would be interested in writing a series of their own.

David Davis and Lorenzo Music were flattered—and excited. The prospect of creating a series of your very own is every TV writer's dream. But it would have to wait—they were too busy writing and producing "Mary Tyler Moore" to give much thought to anything but next week's show. The writers found themselves in the ironic position of having an open invitation to pitch a show to the network—and not a single idea for a series.

As their fateful appointment with Alan Wagner loomed closer, David Davis had an inspiration. "We don't have to come up with any ideas at all," he told his partner. "Let's just ask CBS what stars they've already signed for the fall. Then, we'll just volunteer to create a brand-new show for any one of them."

But as the writers sat down next to each other on the wide couch that faced the executive's swivel chair, they couldn't help but notice that he was already less enthusiastic than when they'd first met.

"Before we even start, I've gotta tell you—it's not a very good time for this meeting," began Wagner. "We've already spent this season's budget for new development, so even if I absolutely love it, there's no way we could act on your idea just now."

Music and Davis were relieved. "Oh, that's okay," answered Music, " 'cause we don't really have any ideas."

The executive leaned forward in his chair, suddenly intrigued. "Tell me more."

Davis explained how they hoped to create a brand-new series for one of CBS's contract stars, and Wagner stopped him midsentence. It was a good plan, but it had one flaw: The network hadn't signed a star to an exclusive contract in years. "We don't work that way anymore," he explained. But still, his curiosity piqued, he leaned back and posed a question. "If you *could* tailor a show to any star in the world—anyone you wanted—who would it be?"

It didn't take long for the writers to answer that one. Without a pause, they answered in unison.

"Bob Newhart."

The writers left the meeting with the network's go-ahead to write a pilot for a new series called "The Bob Newhart Show."

"We were very interested in Newhart," recalls Wagner. "I felt he was an essentially untried television performer with great potential. He'd tried one variety show ten years earlier—hardly enough to make a fair assessment." The executive was also aware that Newhart's manager, Arthur Price, had experienced great success with another of his clients who had done quite well in television—a perky actress named Mary Tyler Moore.

Even so, convincing the successful comic to settle down to the weekly grind of series television would not be easy. Newhart was an established nightclub star whose comedy albums sold in the millions. As for television, he still shuddered at the thought of his first series, an award-winning 1961 variety show that somehow failed to make it past a single season. The first ''Bob Newhart Show'' had convinced the star that weekly television was not for him.

But David Davis and Lorenzo Music were determined to prove him wrong.

In fact, they'd already tried twice before. One of the team's first scripts had been a ''Love, American Style'' episode that they'd custom-tailored to the button-down style of Bob Newhart. He turned it down. They later wrote a love-struck tax auditor into one of the earliest ''Mary Tyler Moore'' scripts—a plum role created especially for the accountant-turned-comic. Once again, Newhart passed, and the part went to Paul Sand.

''It wasn't that he didn't like our scripts,'' quipped Lorenzo Music. ''I think he just didn't want to learn all those lines.'' In fact, Newhart had long respected Music's ability to capture him on paper. When the comic was a guest on ''The Smothers Brothers Comedy Hour'' in the late 1960s, Music—along with Carl Gottlieb—created a monologue that featured Newhart as a harried air traffic controller. The star liked the piece so much, he bought it and used it in his nightclub act for years.

Davis and Music were confident they'd have no trouble creating a pilot that would fit the star's unique style. The hardest part would be finding the time to write it in between all their other duties as writer/producers on ''Mary Tyler Moore.'' At last, the writers decided their only hope was to head for the beach.

''We went to Santa Barbara to figure the show out, just to get away from the phones and the families,'' is how Lorenzo Music described the ordeal. ''We decided to take as long as it needed, and we set up a tough schedule. We'd get up at six in the morning and eat breakfast. Then we'd sit on the beach all day long and write. We wouldn't even eat— we just had Cokes for lunch. After four days, we'd written the pilot for 'The Bob Newhart Show.' ''

They brought the script back to Alan Wagner in Hollywood, who loved it. He asked the writers how soon they could start shooting it as the pilot for the new series. Very soon, they assured him. Just as soon as they talked Newhart into doing it.

Once again, Alan Wagner leaned back in his executive chair. ''Oh,'' he ventured slowly. ''I thought you had him already.''

''No,'' confessed Davis. ''Not yet. We didn't want to approach him until we had a series commitment. But *now* we've got something to offer him.''

As the writers turned to leave, the executive stopped them. ''Well, don't worry—we like this pilot. Even if you *can't* get Newhart, we'll still do the series. We'll just try to find someone else."

Finding a replacement for Bob Newhart was a casting quandary they would never have to face. The star liked their script as much as the network had. As Newhart recalled, "It was the first one I'd read where I didn't say, 'It's a good idea, but what do we do for show number two?' " The quality of the material, and the fact that Mary Tyler Moore had found such uncompromised success in the television medium, finally eased the star's lingering hesitations about signing on to do another series. "I kept saying no, it was kind of reflex," explained Newhart. "Then one day I asked myself why."

There was no arguing that the show Davis and Music created was different from anything the star had seen before. Bob played psychologist Robert Hartley, an occupation the writers chose after going through an entire telephone directory. "Luckily it was in Santa Barbara, and they've got a skinny little phone book," recalls Lorenzo Music. "When we found 'psychologist,' we thought it sounded right. We figured out that Bob listens funny, so we wanted to find a job where he could listen to all sorts of people. As a psychologist, Bob could still be the guy everyone knew him to be—an accountant from Chicago who was kinda Catholic and kinda shockable."

They even set his practice in Chicago—geographically, at least. For at times, the universe of "The Bob Newhart Show" more closely resembled Alice's Wonderland.

Bob and Emily Hartley lived in a jabberwocky world that wasn't bound by conventional laws of psychology or logic. You never quite knew what to expect. Ordinary take-out burgers might come swathed in an entire ream of butcher paper. An elevator door could open to reveal a black militant salesman with his Great Dane, Whitey; an empty shaft or a giggling family of all-Americans straight out of Norman Rockwell. And face a truckload of zucchini on this show, as one of Bob's patients had the misfortune to do, and you're as good as gone.

And somehow, all of this strange behavior was anchored in utterly believable characters whom we actually cared about. Like "The Mary Tyler Moore Show," the series was populated by witty, sincere people who daily faced the irrational realities of everyday life.

But the difference between Mary's Minneapolis and Bob's Chicago was far more than the breadth of Wisconsin. "Mary Tyler Moore" was offbeat, but "Bob Newhart" was positively surreal. Where Mary and her friends fought a valiant and invariably losing struggle to maintain sanity in an absurd world, Bob and his extended family accepted absurdity as the natural order of things. In many ways, Bob and his loonies were among the most well-adjusted characters on television.

The undercurrent of preposterous logic was actually an outgrowth of Newhart's own clearly defined comic persona. The performer whose nightclub act routinely included long-distance conversations with Abraham Lincoln, Sir Walter Raleigh, and King Kong was certainly no stranger to surrealism. "Comedy," Newhart once observed, "is my way of bringing logic to an illogical situation."

Of course, if all the show had to offer was quirky characters and bizarre situations, it probably wouldn't have lasted the season. Over the life of the series, the show's many creators understood that their incredible flights of fancy could work only if at least one part of Bob Hartley's life was rooted in a solid, wholesome reality—which is where the Hartleys' marriage came in. "Every one of the show's producers was committed to showing a good, sound, healthy adult marriage on television," commented long-time producer Michael Zinberg. And the casting of Suzanne Pleshette was crucial to that goal.

"We were trying to get away from the standard TV wife," David Davis recalled. To his surprise he and Music found the perfect candidate when they happened to see Pleshette as a guest on Johnny Carson's "Tonight Show." "There she was, just what we were looking for." Adds Music, "She was sharp and sexy and hip and outspoken, and we said that's the woman for Bob."

Her unabashed sensuality gave the show a distinctive, sophisticated edge. Not surprisingly, once the writers began to explore the realities of the couple's married life, it wasn't long before the Hartleys' king-size bed gently nudged one more prime-time taboo out the window by openly acknowledging that a couple on the far side of thirty could still enjoy a healthy, hearty sex life. It was grown-up comedy.

"We were selling class and charm and wit," David Davis told *TV Guide*'s Dwight Whitney. And the show didn't stray far from that principle throughout six seasons that saw contributions from some of television's most talented creators, including producers Tom Patchett and Jay Tarses, Martin Cohan, Gordon Farr and Lynne Farr, and Glen Charles and Les Charles; as well as directors Alan Rafkin, Peter Baldwin, Peter Bonerz, and Michael Zinberg.

Finally, after six years, Newhart decided to call it quits. "We hadn't slipped in any way," observed the star. "The show was still funny. Which was the time to get off."

Like "The Mary Tyler Moore Show" a year before, the series voluntarily left the air after contributing some of situation comedy's finest half hours. But unlike its more illustrious counterpart, the passing of "Bob Newhart" didn't launch a spate of news articles or a flood of awards. "I was very proud of our show," Newhart told *The New York Times*, "but chagrined that the show and the people on it were never truly acknowledged by the TV industry—not one Emmy."

Perhaps it would be some consolation to the star that producers Glen and Les Charles and Patchett and Tarses—along with a good many of the show's other writers and producers—went on to create some of the finest situation comedies of the following decade. "Taxi," "Cheers," and "Buffalo Bill" are just three top-grade comedies that owed a considerable debt to the off-kilter comic anarchy pioneered by the unassuming little show that was always in Mary's shadow.

But finally Newhart himself summed it up best when he paid tribute to the show's fine acting ensemble, though he might just as easily have been talking about any of the show's many creators. "We had so many good people—Suzanne Pleshette, Billy Daily, Marcia Wallace, Peter Bonerz, and the rest, and they all made it look too easy!"

And for a show with as much class as "The Bob Newhart Show," that was quite a trick.

A Critical Guide to All 142 Episodes

REGULAR CAST

Bob Hartley	Bob Newhart
Emily Hartley	Suzanne Pleshette
Howard Borden	Bill Daily
Jerry Robinson	Peter Bonerz
Carol Kester Bondurant	Marcia Wallace
Ellen Hartley	Pat Finley

THE PATIENTS

Elliot Carlin	Jack Riley
Lillian Bakerman	Florida Friebus
Emil Peterson	John Fiedler
Michelle Nardo	Renee Lippin
Victor Gianelli	Noam Pitlik
Edgar Vickers	Lucien Scott
Ed Herd	Oliver Clark
Craig Plager	Howard Hesseman
Leonard de Paolo	Cliff Osmond
Shirley Ullman	Millie Slavin

SUPPORTING CAST

Dr. Bernie Tupperman	Larry Gelman
Dr. Phil Newman	Howard Platt
Dr. Frank Walburn	Phillip R. Allen
Larry Bondurant	Will Mackenzie
Margaret Hoover	Patricia Smith
Cliff Murdoch, the Peeper	Tom Poston
Corrine Murdoch (the Peeper's wife)	Jean Palmerton
Junior Harrison (Emily's father)	John Randolph
Aggie Harrison (Emily's mother)	Ann Rutherford
Herb Hartley (Bob's father)	Barnard Hughes
Martha Hartley (Bob's mother)	Martha Scott

Gordon Borden (Howard's brother)	William Redfield
Debbie Flett (Carol's fill-in)	Shirley O'Hara
Eddie, the Mailman	Bill Quinn

Created by David Davis, Lorenzo Music
Music by Pat Williams
Theme song ("Home to Emily") by Lorenzo and Henrietta Music
Directors of photography were Paul Uhl, Edward E. Nugent (final year)
Principal directors were Alan Rafkin, Peter Bonerz, Peter Baldwin, Jay Sandrich, Michael Zinberg

1972/73   THE FIRST SEASON

Year-End Rating: 21.8 (16th place)

The life and times of Chicago psychologist Bob Hartley and his wife, Emily, are chronicled by series creators David Davis and Lorenzo Music, who serve as executive producers for the first three seasons. They are also the first-season producers, along with Bill Idelson. Michael Zinberg is the associate producer for the initial three years.

Primary directors in the premiere season are Jay Sandrich—on loan from "Mary Tyler Moore"—and Alan Rafkin, one of the show's most prolific directors. Freshman-year scripts are contributed by a handful of MTM's best writers, including Davis and Music, Charlotte Brown, Jerry Mayer, Martin Cohan, and Tom Patchett and Jay Tarses.

1   Fly the Unfriendly Skies   September 16, 1972
Writers: David Davis, Lorenzo Music
Director: Jay Sandrich
Guest Stars: Penny Marshall, Patricia Smith, Noam Pitlik, Jack Riley, Florida Friebus

Bob tries to help Emily overcome her paralyzing fear of planes by inviting her to join his "Fear of Flying" therapy group on a short flight to New York.

The series begins with a nod toward tradition, as Bob walks in the front door and doffs his hat, as sitcom husbands had been doing since the days when father knew best. And yet, over the course of our first short visit, things get curiouser and curiouser as we enter the peculiar universe of Bob Hartley, a rational man—a psychologist, no less—who finds himself moored in a surrealistic universe where the only prevailing logic is the serendipity of the absurd.

2   Tracy Grammar School,   September 23, 1972
    I'll Lick You Yet
Writers: Carl Gottlieb, George Yanock
Director: Jay Sandrich
Guest Stars: King Moody, Larry Gelman, Patricia Smith

Bob puts Emily's third graders to sleep when he attempts to explain the nuances of psychology on career day at Tracy Grammar School.

The episode hints at the show's casual attitude toward the Hartley's decidedly grown-up relationship. Always affectionate, and often demonstrative, Emily can't resist teasing her husband unmercifully. At one point she surprises Bob with a triple-strength kiss outside his office before she disappears into the elevator.

"It was funny to imagine Newhart in bed," chuckled writer Lorenzo Music, who quickly realized that the Hartleys' obvious physical attraction added a new dimension to Newhart's firmly established persona. "Bob could just as easily have been a loser on a date, but Emily gave him sexuality. If someone as hip and sexy as her saw something in him, he *must* have had something special. We didn't ever have to show it—you just knew it was there."

3   Tennis, Emily?   September 30, 1972
Writers: David Davis, Lorenzo Music
Director: Alan Rafkin
Guest Stars: Peter Brown, Barbara Barnett, Pat Lysinger

Bob treats a handsome tennis pro who complains that every woman he meets makes a pass at him—including Emily.

4   Mom, I L-L-Love You   October 7, 1972
Writers: Dick Clair, Jenna McMahon
Director: Alan Rafkin
Guest Stars: Martha Scott, Marilyn Child, Patricia Smith

Despite the difficulty he has talking to his mother, Bob finally resolves to tell her how much he cares for her.

5   Goodnight, Nancy   October 21, 1972
Writer: Susan Silver
Director: Jay Sandrich
Guest Stars: Penny Fuller, Richard Schaal, James B. Sikking,
Patricia Smith

Emily is surprised to find herself acting like a typical jealous wife
when one of Bob's old girlfriends pays a visit.

6   Come Live With Me   October 28, 1972
Writer: Jerry Mayer
Director: Alan Rafkin
Guest Stars: Eugene Troobnik, John Fiedler

Emily decides to get involved when Carol has trouble deciding
whether to move in with her new boyfriend.

John Fiedler makes his first appearance as the self-effacing Mr. Peterson.

7   Father Knows Worst   November 4, 1972
Writers: Tom Patchett, Jay Tarses
Director: Alan Rafkin
Guest Stars: Moosie Drier, Alice Borden

Howard is convinced he's failed as a father when Howie, Jr.,
begins spending most of his time with Jerry Robinson.

8   Don't Go to Bed Mad   November 11, 1972
Writer: Gene Thompson
Director: Alan Rafkin

The Hartleys spend a sleepless night after they agree not to rest
until they've settled a raging dispute over Bob's Monday-night
football habit.

The petty annoyances that continually dogged Bob and Emily's domestic life depicted the day-to-day struggles of real-life marriage with
perceptive, and always comic, accuracy. The Hartleys were as romantic
as any prime-time couple since Rob and Laura Petrie—but that didn't
mean they always had to get along. Come to think of it, Bob and Emily
probably aren't all that different from what Rob and Laura might have
been like ten years later—the approximate length of time between the
debut of "Dick Van Dyke" and "Bob Newhart's" premiere in 1972.

9   P-I-L-O-T   November 18, 1972
Writers: David Davis, Lorenzo Music
Director: Jay Sandrich
Guest Stars: Louise Lasser, Patricia Smith, William Redfield

Frustrated by their inability to conceive a child, the Hartleys decide to become adoptive parents.

This uncharacteristic episode is actually a reedited version of the show's pilot film, which bore very little resemblance to the characters and settings we came to know in the series. In the original pilot, Bob and Emily managed their apartment complex in addition to their other jobs; Howard Borden hadn't even been invented; and Jerry was a swinging psychologist who shared an office suite with Bob!

"We thought we needed other interests for Bob at home, so we made him manager of a condominium," explained creator Lorenzo Music. But the idea was dropped when CBS executives complained that people wouldn't know what a condo was. "We joked that they were afraid the public might get it confused with something high school boys buy at the drugstore to carry around in their back pockets. And they agreed!"

After the show began production, new scenes were edited into the original pilot incorporating Howard Borden along with the rest of the show's familiar elements. For obvious reasons, a more characteristic episode was substituted for the series debut, and this odd hybrid was quietly slipped in during the show's ninth week.

10   Anything Happen While I Was Gone?   November 25, 1972
Writer: Martin Cohan
Director: Jay Sandrich
Guest Star: Elaine Giftos

Jerry announces his engagement to a beautiful but domineering oral hygienist he's just met.

11   I Want to Be Alone   December 2, 1972
Writer: Jerry Mayer
Director: Alan Rafkin
Guest Stars: Archie Hahn, Bernie Kopell, Alan Hewitt, Patricia Smith

Howard is worried that the Hartleys are splitting up after Bob moves into a hotel room for a few days of peace and quiet.

This episode contains the brief final appearance of Patricia Smith as Emily's next-door neighbor, Margaret Hoover. The homespun mother of two was designed as a comic counterpoint to Emily—the wife with no kids. But she was dropped as a domestic contrivance. "There was so much going on down at the office that we didn't need her," writer Lorenzo Music confessed. "We couldn't get a Rhoda out of it."

12 Bob and Emily and Howard December 9, 1972
 and Carol and Jerry
Writer: Charlotte Brown
Director: Peter Baldwin

With Emily's help, Carol's momentary infatuation with Howard leads to a romance that ends almost before it begins.

13 I Owe It All to You . . . December 16, 1972
 But Not That Much
Writer: Martin Cohan
Director: Alan Rafkin

Bob gains a patient but loses a friend when Jerry suddenly decides to become a paying customer.

14 His Busiest Season December 23, 1972
Writers: David Davis, Lorenzo Music
Director: Peter Baldwin
Guest Stars: Harvey J. Goldenberg, Florida Friebus, King Moody, Ray Montgomery

Bob foolishly attempts to raise sagging holiday spirits by inviting his group to an impromptu Christmas party at his apartment.

15 Let's Get Away From It Almost January 6, 1973
Writers: Tom Patchett, Jay Tarses
Director: Jay Sandrich
Guest Stars: Chuck McCann, Joyce Van Patten, Allen Garfield

The Hartleys flee the city to get away from it all, only to spend the worst vacation of their life in a rundown ski lodge.

16   The Crash of Twenty-Nine Years Old   January 13, 1973
   Writer: Charlotte Brown
   Director: Alan Rafkin
   Guest Stars: Renee Lippin, Jack Bender, Dan Barrows

Depressed by the approach of her twenty-ninth birthday, Carol decides to quit her job and expand her horizons beyond the reception area.

During her three seasons with the series, Charlotte Brown would script some of the show's funniest moments, but her greatest contribution would be the keen insight she brought to the characterizations of the show's women—Emily; Bob's sister, Ellen; and especially Carol. In Brown's early scripts, Carol emerges as a vulnerable, impulsive, and painfully sincere young woman. More than any other character, Carol was capable of growth and change, and throughout her long journey of star-crossed romances and her countless attempts to break out of her receptionist's cage, we never stopped rooting for her.

17   The Man With the Golden Wrist   January 20, 1973
   Writer: Bill Idelson
   Director: Alan Rafkin
   Guest Stars: Larry Gelman, Mimi Torchin, Michael Lerner

Bob refuses to wear the expensive gold watch Emily gave him for his birthday after he discovers how much she paid for it.

18   The Two Loves of Dr. Hartley   January 27, 1973
   Writer: Gene Thompson
   Director: George Tyne
   Guest Star: Emmaline Henry

Emily is more than slightly concerned when one of Bob's patients falls hopelessly in love with him.

19   Not With My Sister You Don't   February 3, 1973
   Writer: Frank Buxton
   Director: Alan Rafkin
   Guest Stars: Heather Menzies, Mel Stewart

Howard does his best to hide his swinging life-style from his younger sister when she arrives to spend a week in the big city.

20 A Home Is Not Necessarily a House February 10, 1973
Writers: David Davis, Lorenzo Music
Director: Peter Baldwin
Guest Stars: Jenna McMahon, Dick Clair, Betty Palivoda

Howard is crestfallen when Bob and Emily make plans to move into their dream house.

MTM writers Jenna McMahon and Dick Clair make a cameo appearance as the other couple interested in the Hartley's house.

21 Emily, I'm Home—Emily?? February 17, 1973
Writer: Martin Cohan
Director: Rick Edelstein
Guest Star: Alma Beltran

Bob feels abandoned at home when Emily begins a full-time job at the Board of Education.

22 You Can't Win 'Em All February 24, 1973
Writer: Bill Idelson
Director: Jerry London
Guest Stars: Vern E. Rowe, Jim Watkins, Larry Gelman

Bob basks in reflected glory when he counsels the Chicago Cubs' star pitcher out of a losing streak.

By the time he signed on as producer of "The Bob Newhart Show," Bill Idelson was already a respected practitioner of quality TV comedy. At various times in his career, he has written scripts for such distinguished sitcoms as "Andy Griffith," "The Odd Couple," "M*A*S*H," and "The Dick Van Dyke Show"—where he also appeared as Sally's boyfriend, Herman Glimscher.

23 Bum Voyage March 3, 1973
Writers: Austin and Irma Kalish
Director: Martin Cohan
Guest Stars: Archie Hahn, Pat McCormick

Bob resists Emily's plans for a two-month cruise because he's convinced his group couldn't survive that long without him.

24 Who's Been Sleeping on My Couch? March 10, 1973
Writer: Jerry Mayer
Director: Alan Rafkin
Guest Stars: Renee Lippin, Herbie Faye

Jerry turns to Bob for solace in the aftermath of another failed romance, but it's a date with Carol that finally sets him straight.

1973/74 THE SECOND SEASON

Year-End Rating: 22.3 (12th place)

The peculiar logic of the Newhart universe continues to evolve as the offbeat individuals in Bob's therapy group emerge as a steady source of story ideas in the second year. Tom Patchett and Jay Tarses contribute the bulk of the season's scripts, along with Jerry Mayer and Charlotte Brown, among others.

Producer Martin Cohan is a key architect of this emerging universe, along with writers Patchett and Tarses, who serve as the season's story consultants. Peter Baldwin directs more than a third of the year's episodes, along with Jay Sandrich, George Tyne, Alan Rafkin, Jerry London, Peter Bonerz, and Don Bustany.

25 Last TV Show September 15, 1973
Writer: Charlotte Brown
Director: Jay Sandrich
Guest Stars: Jack Riley, Florida Friebus, John Fiedler, Renee Lippin, Noam Pitlik, Don Dandridge

Bob reluctantly accepts an invitation to hold a group session on live television.

The group insists that Bob schedule the TV appearance, and he bows to their will—only to find himself betrayed on live television when they freeze up, leaving him fifty-six minutes to fill with stories of his air force days, his stint as a soprano in the boys' choir, and those wonderful summers on his Uncle Ned's farm. It was a stock MTM situation—Mary Richards often found herself in similar straits—but no performer ever communicated the divine comedy of devastating anxiety quite so well as Bob Newhart.

26   Motel   September 22, 1973
Writers: Tom Patchett, Jay Tarses
Director: Jay Sandrich
Guest Stars: Zohra Lampert, Barbara Brownell

Bob gets an unexpected taste of Jerry's swinging life-style when the bachelor fixes him up with a local girl during an ill-fated trip to Peoria.

27   Backlash   September 29, 1973
Writer: Susan Silver
Director: George Tyne
Guest Star: Michael Conrad

Emily begins to wonder if they'll ever take a vacation when Bob calls off their trip to Mexico because of sudden back pain.

Emily is especially anxious to get away from it all, convinced that a few romantic nights south of the border will increase their odds of finally conceiving a baby. Her maternal yearnings surfaced in two or three of the earliest shows, but Newhart maintained that adding a child to the cast would dilute the show's adult appeal, and Emily's urgent longing was reduced to no more than a poignant subtext in later seasons.

28   Somebody Down Here Likes Me   October 6, 1973
Writer: Peter Myerson
Director: Jerry London
Guest Star: John McMartin

Bob feels responsible when the minister he's been treating decides to leave the church.

29   Emily in for Carol   October 13, 1973
Writer: Jerry Mayer
Director: Alan Rafkin
Guest Stars: Howard Platt, Rhoda Gemignani, Teri Garr

Despite Bob's strenuous objections, the doctors on his floor insist on hiring Emily as receptionist while Carol's on vacation.

30 Have You Met Miss Dietz? October 20, 1973
Writer: Bill Idelson
Director: George Tyne
Guest Stars: Mariette Hartley, David Fresco

Bob is caught in the middle of an unpleasant rivalry between his best friends when Emily's newly divorced girlfriend dates Howard and Jerry at the same time.

31 Old Man Rivers October 27, 1973
Writer: Martin Cohan
Director: Martin Cohan
Guest Stars: Jeff Corey, Don Fenwick

Carol thinks she's found happiness at last—with a doctor who's thirty years her senior.

Bob's receptionist is embarrassed to admit that she plans to have a butterfly tattoo removed from a place where no gentleman would see it anyway. But by a telepathy unique to the characters on "The Bob Newhart Show," both Howard and Jerry know about the tattoo without having to be told. How they came by such intimate knowledge is a provocative question that's never explained—and perhaps it's better that way.

32 Mister Emily Hartley November 3, 1973
Writer: Charlotte Brown
Director: Jerry London
Guest Stars: Bill Quinn, Claudette Nevins, Tom Patchett, Jay Tarses

Bob suffers from wounded pride when he discovers that Emily's IQ is a full twenty points higher than his.

Writers Patchett and Tarses, who began their careers as stand-up comics, make cameo appearances as a waiter and one of the guests at the cocktail party for geniuses.

33 Mutiny on the Hartley November 10, 1973
Writers: Tom Patchett, Jay Tarses
Director: Peter Baldwin
Guest Star: Henry Corden

Bob's therapy group stages a rebellion to protest a five-dollar rate increase.

34 I'm Okay, You're Okay,   November 17, 1973
        So What's Wrong?
Writer: Earl Barret
Director: George Tyne
Guest Star: Katherine Helmond

Bob and Emily consult a marriage counselor to help them through a lull in their married life.

35 Fit Fat and Forty-One   November 24, 1973
Writers: Bill Idelson, Harvey Miller
Director: Peter Baldwin
Guest Stars: Bruce Kirby, Lilyan Chauvin, Bob Ridgely, Ron Glass

Bob resolves to lose eight pounds by his forty-first birthday, but he quickly finds the regimen of dieting almost unbearable.

36 Blues for Mr. Borden   December 1, 1973
Writers: Tom Patchett, Jay Tarses
Director: Jerry London
Guest Stars: Moosie Drier, Julius Harris

Howard goes on a bender when he discovers that his ex-wife is engaged to be remarried—to a pilot.

The episode contains one of the series's most memorable throwaway gags, involving Jerry and a Great Dane. The high-strung dentist hears an imposing black man bark out the command to "Sit, Whitey!," which Jerry does—before he realizes the order was intended for the man's perversely named dog, Whitey.

37 My Wife Belongs to Daddy   December 8, 1973
Writer: Jerry Mayer
Director: Jerry London
Guest Stars: John Randolph, Ann Rutherford

Emily is delighted when her parents pay a visit, but Bob is discouraged when he discovers there's no way to compete with his charismatic father-in-law.

38 T. S. Elliot   December 15, 1973
Writers: Gerry Renert, Jeff Wilheim
Director: Peter Baldwin
Guest Stars: Shirley O'Hara, Robert Riesel, Shizuko Hoshi

Bob arranges for Carol to date Mr. Carlin—and they hit it off so
well that Elliot immediately begins making wedding plans.

39 I'm Dreaming of a Slight Christmas   December 22, 1973
Writers: Tom Patchett, Jay Tarses
Director: Peter Baldwin
Guest Stars: Gene Blakely, John Fiedler, Larry Gelman

A power failure traps Bob in his office on Christmas Eve.

40 Oh, Brother   January 5, 1974
Writer: Martin Cohan
Director: Peter Baldwin
Guest Star: Raul Julia

Jerry's brother arrives with a surefire plan for starting his own
dental practice—he'll steal his patients from his older brother.

41 The Modernization of Emily   January 12, 1974
Writer: Charlotte Brown
Director: Peter Baldwin
Guest Stars: Sharon Gless, Bill Miller, J. J. Barry

Emily is on a youth kick, convinced she can stave off the advancing years by donning an embarrassing new wardrobe of T-
shirts and tight blue jeans.

In a moment that's painfully funny but also very sad, Emily opens
a present bought at the House of Tacky—only to discover that Carol's
idea of a gag gift is a tasteless spangled T-shirt, the same one that Emily's
got on! Her insecurity and dread of encroaching middle age reveal a
chink in Emily's usually well-adjusted outlook, but the bittersweet humor
of Charlotte Brown's sympathetic script refuses to betray the character's
basic integrity. In the end, Emily forsakes the tacky fringes and denim
as she finally accepts the wisdom that comes along with the wrinkles.

42   The Jobless Corps   January 19, 1974
   Writers: Tom Patchett, Jay Tarses
   Director: Peter Baldwin
   Guest Stars: Millie Slavin, Howard Hesseman

Howard joins Bob's out-of-work workshop after he loses his job at the airline.

Under writers Patchett and Tarses, the series found some of its biggest laughs in the perversely comic outlook of the downtrodden and maladjusted members of Bob's group. In 1983, the writers carried their formula to sidesplitting extremes when they based an entire series around the most maladjusted protagonist in sitcom history—Buffalo Bill, a petty, egocentric, thoroughly reprehensible, and irresistibly hilarious talk-show host. Come to think of it, he might have fit into one of Bob's groups very nicely.

Howard Hesseman debuts as the out-of-work television writer, Mr. Plager.

43   Clink Shrink   January 26, 1974
   Writers: Paul B. Lichtman, Howard Storm
   Director: Peter Bonerz
   Guest Stars: Henry Winkler, Len Lessor

Bob wonders whether he should accept an expensive gift from his newest patient, a recently paroled ex-con who served time for armed robbery.

When supporting player Bonerz wasn't on camera, he was behind the scenes, observing the directors. "It sure beats waiting around drinking coffee," he once quipped. The producers finally sanctioned the actor's ambitions to step behind the camera with this episode. Bonerz adapted to his new role magnificently—he would eventually direct more "Bob Newhart" shows than any other director.

44   Mind Your Own Business   February 2, 1974
   Writers: Tom Patchett, Jay Tarses
   Director: Alan Rafkin
   Guest Stars: Ron Rifkin, Katharine Dunfee, Lou Cutell

Bob isn't sure he's cut out for the world of high finance after his new business manager puts him on a restricted budget of fifty dollars a week.

45 A Love Story   February 9, 1974
  Writer: Martin Cohan
  Director: Peter Bonerz
  Guest Stars: Pat Finley, Martha Scott, Renee Lippin

It's love at first sight when Howard meets Bob's sister, Ellen, despite one slight complication—she's already engaged to another man.

When Emily tries to coax the pair together, Bob observes—with deadpan accuracy—that her matchmaking has "sunk to a new low." But Howard's childlike determination wins out, and the befuddled bachelor experiences his finest triumph when the blushing bride interrupts his ironing with the news that she's called off her wedding.

46 By the Way . . . You're Fired   February 16, 1974
  Writers: Barbara Gallagher, Sybil Adelman
  Director: Peter Baldwin
  Guest Stars: Richard Schaal, Larry Gelman, Jill Jaress, Gene Blakely, Howard Platt

Carol's work suffers when she loses her head over her latest beau—a kook who recites half-baked epiphanies over lunch.

47 Confessions of an Orthodontist   February 23, 1974
  Writers: Tom Patchett, Jay Tarses
  Director: Peter Baldwin
  Guest Stars: Roger Perry, Teri Garr

Jerry surprises Bob with the startling confession that he's hopelessly in love with Emily.

48 A Matter of Principal   March 2, 1974
  Writers: Ray Jessel, Arnie Kogen
  Director: Don Bustany
  Guest Stars: Milton Selzer, Michael Conrad

Emily defies her school board by refusing to let an undeserving student skip a grade.

1974/75   THE THIRD SEASON

Year-End Rating: 22.4 (17th place)

The romance between Howard and Bob's sister, Ellen, provides fresh perspective in the domestic story line, as producers Tom Patchett and Jay Tarses usher the show into one of its most creative periods. Jerry Mayer is the season's story consultant, and Alan Rafkin directs many of the episodes—most of which are written by Patchett and Tarses, Charlotte Brown, and Jerry Mayer.

49 Big Brother Is Watching   September 14, 1974
   Writer: Charlotte Brown
   Director: Robert Moore
   Guest Star: Pat Finley

Bob puts a damper on Howard's blossoming romance with Ellen when he refuses to let his sister move in with the navigator.

50 The Battle of the Groups   September 21, 1974
   Writers: Tom Patchett, Jay Tarses
   Director: Alan Rafkin
   Guest Stars: Howard Hesseman, Daniel Travanti, Lenore Woodward, Millie Slavin

Bob has his hands full when he joins two therapy groups together for a marathon weekend session at a mountain retreat.

51 The Great Rimpau Medical Arts   September 28, 1974
       Co-op Experiment
   Writers: Coleman Mitchell, Geoffrey Neigher
   Director: George Tyne
   Guest Stars: Merie Earle, Larry Gelman, Howard Platt, Julie Payne, Tom Lacy

Jerry organizes a medical co-op so that the doctors can exchange services without charge, a plan that Bob discovers works better in conception than execution.

52   The Separation Story   October 5, 1974
   Writers: Tom Patchett, Jay Tarses
   Story: Bob Garland
   Director: Peter Bonerz
   Guest Stars: Richard Stahl, Carl Gottlieb

After Emily moves into a dormitory to bone up for her master's degree, rumors of the Hartleys' separation begin to buzz.

The inflatable-furniture salesman was played by Carl Gottlieb, the screenwriter of *Jaws* and *The Jerk*, and also one of the show's earliest writers.

53   Sorry, Wrong Mother   October 12, 1974
   Writer: Charlotte Brown
   Director: Jay Sandrich
   Guest Stars: Moosie Drier, Pat Finley, John Ritter

Even after she plies him with gifts and ice cream, Ellen can't seem to earn the approval of Howard's son.

The family tensions are played out in the unlikely setting of a razzle-dazzle strawhat ice-cream parlor, which is also the scene of one of Bob's most unforgettable comic nightmares, as towering plates of Hazelnut Hoohas, Hot 'n' Heavy Fandangoes, and Banana Fofana Splits are served up by an unrestrained waiter with the tableside manner of Rip Taylor. Hoping to avoid all the embarrassing hoopla, Bob orders an unassuming scoop of plain vanilla, only to find himself besieged by a cadre of singing waiters chanting, "Single scooper, single scooper, this man is a party pooper," as he tries to melt into the brightly checkered tablecloth.

54   The Gray Flannel Shrink   October 19, 1974
   Writer: Jerry Mayer
   Director: Peter Bonerz
   Guest Stars: John Anderson, Edward Winter, Jerry Fogel

Bob adandons his practice for the corporate world when he accepts a position as resident shrink for a major insurance company.

55   Dr. Ryan's Express   October 26, 1974
Writers: Tom Patchett, Jay Tarses
Director: Alan Rafkin
Guest Stars: Shirley O'Hara, Lucien Scott, Paula Victor, Maxine Stuart

Jerry hires a supremely incompetent temporary receptionist who makes a mess of Bob's well-ordered office routine.

56   Brutally Yours, Bob Hartley   November 2, 1974
Writer: John Rappaport
Director: Alan Rafkin
Guest Stars: Lawrence Pressman, Rose Gregario

Bob resolves to be completely honest and open with everyone he encounters, and in no time at all he's alienated his wife and most of his friends.

57   Ship of Shrinks   November 9, 1974
Writers: Coleman Mitchell, Geoffrey Neigher
Director: Alan Rafkin
Guest Stars: David L. Lander, Bobby Ramsen, Pat Finley

Bob is embarrassed to face his professional colleagues after a psychology article he wrote is published with revisions that he thinks make him look foolish.

58   Life Is a Hamburger   November 16, 1974
Writer: Jerry Mayer
Director: George Tyne
Guest Star: Richard Schaal

Carol happily announces her engagement to the oddball poet she's been dating, even though her friends are convinced he's a loser.

59   An American Family   November 23, 1974
Writer: Charlotte Brown
Director: Peter Bonerz
Guest Stars: Barnard Hughes, Martha Scott, John Randolph, Ann Rutherford

The Hartleys' plans for a festive Thanksgiving dinner are dashed when Bob's mother locks horns with Emily's dad.

60 We Love You . . . Good-bye   November 30, 1974
Writer: Charlotte Brown
Director: Peter Bonerz
Guest Stars: Rhoda Gemignani, Ann Weldon

Bob gets drummed out of his own women's consciousness-raising group after Emily reveals the truth about his less-than-enlightened behavior at home.

61 Jerry Robinson Crusoe   December 7, 1974
Writer: Erik Tarloff
Director: Alan Rafkin
Guest Star: Gail Strickland

The call of the wild beckons Jerry when a free-spirited girlfriend convinces him to chuck his practice and move to the South Seas.

62 Serve for Daylight   December 14, 1974
Writer: Jerry Mayer
Director: Alan Rafkin
Guest Stars: Larry Gelman, Howard Platt, Paula Shaw

Bob is determined to win the tennis trophy in the doctors' annual tournament but gets quickly discouraged when he's paired with Emily in a doubles match.

63 Home Is Where the Hurt Is   December 21, 1974
Writers: Tom Patchett, Jay Tarses
Director: Alan Rafkin
Guest Star: Bill Quinn

The Hartleys spend a dismal Christmas Eve as Carol shares her unhappy memories of past holidays.

64 Tobin's Back in Town   January 4, 1975
Writer: Michael Zinberg
Director: Peter Bonerz
Guest Stars: Fred Willard, Catherine Bacon

Howard worries that he might lose Ellen when her jilted fiancé returns to reclaim her.

Ellen's suede-and-leather Lothario is Fred Willard, best remembered for his stint as the dim-witted co-host of "Fernwood 2-Night."

65   Think Smartly—Vote Hartley   January 11, 1975
    Writers: Coleman Mitchell, Geoffrey Neigher
    Director: Bob Finkel
    Guest Stars: George Wyner, Lillian Garrett, Quinn Redeker

Emily's friends convince Bob to run for chairman of the school board.

66   The Way We Weren't   January 18, 1975
    Writer: Roger Beatty
    Director: James Burrows
    Guest Stars: Wayne Tippit, Joseph Sicari, Casey Connors, David Knapp

Emily is determined to figure out why Bob is so reluctant to discuss a mysterious former girlfriend.

67   A Pound of Flesh   January 25, 1975
    Writer: Jerry Mayer
    Director: Alan Rafkin
    Guest Stars: Merie Earle, Dick Wilson

Jerry is in a huff after Bob refuses to lend him money to buy a new motorcycle.

68   My Business Is Shrinking   February 1, 1975
    Writers: Arnie Kogen, Ray Jessel
    Director: Alan Rafkin
    Guest Stars: Phillip R. Allen, Timothy Blake, Ray Stewart, Mary Jo Catlett, Ron McIlwain

Bob joins another psychologist's therapy group to work his way through a temporary depression.

69   The New Look   February 8, 1975
    Writers: Gordon and Lynne Farr
    Director: Peter Bonerz
    Guest Stars: Cliff Norton, Marcia Lewis, Oliver Clark

Bob can't seem to find a comfortable spot in his own living room after Emily redecorates their apartment with antique furniture.

70 Bob Hits the Ceiling   February 15, 1975
   Writer: Phil Davis
   Director: Jay Sandrich
   Guest Stars: Cynthia Harris, Mike Henry, Al Stellone

Bob reluctantly agrees to counsel one of Emily's friends through her marital difficulties.

71 Emily Hits the Ceiling   February 22, 1975
   Writer: Jerry Mayer
   Director: James Burrows
   Guest Stars: George Wyner, Howard Hesseman, Susan Davis, Lillian Garrett, Tom Newman

The Hartleys are drafted into service as counselors when a group of Emily's friends decide to start a summer camp.

72 The Ceiling Hits Bob   March 8, 1975
   Writers: Tom Patchett, Jay Tarses
   Director: Alan Rafkin
   Guest Stars: Bill Quinn, Jess Nadelman, Lucien Scott, Pat Finley

The ceiling in Bob's office falls in—and the rest of his world threatens to follow when Ellen and Howard announce they're moving to New York, and Carol starts to look for a new job.

1975/76 THE FOURTH SEASON

Year-End Rating: 20.7 (26th place)

Bob welcomes two significant additions to the family in the fourth season—Tom Poston arrives as Cliff Murdoch in the first of the Peeper's many appearances; and Carol meets, courts, and marries travel agent Larry Bondurant, played by actor—and sometime director—Will Mackenzie.

Michael Zinberg is appointed producer in midseason, after producers Tom Patchett and Jay Tarses assume the duties of executive producers. Gordon and Lynne Farr are the season's story consultants; and Peter Bonerz, Michael Zinberg, and James Burrows are the most prominent of the season's directors.

73 The Longest Good-bye   September 13, 1975
Writers: Tom Patchett, Jay Tarses
Director: James Burrows
Guest Star: Tom Poston

Emily is less than impressed by Bob's legendary college chum, the Peeper—an inveterate jokester who arrives to spend a day and then stays a week.

74 Here's Looking at You, Kid   September 20, 1975
Writers: Gordon and Lynne Farr
Director: Peter Bonerz
Guest Stars: Pat Finley, Richard Balin, Vern E. Rowe, Don Nagel

Howard looks to Bob for moral support when he proposes to Ellen at a crowded restaurant.

Ellen didn't think the time was right for marriage, a decision shared by the show's producers. As Howard reclaimed his bachelor status in the final seasons, Bob's sister was reluctantly written out of the series.

75 Death of a Fruitman   September 27, 1975
Writers: Tom Patchett, Jay Tarses
Director: Peter Bonerz
Guest Stars: Renee Lippin, John Fiedler, Florida Friebus

The group is angry at Mr. Gianelli for missing their fourth anniversary party, until they find out he was crushed to death beneath a truckload of zucchini.

Noam Pitlik would meet a somewhat happier fate than his character when the actor cut back on his performing commitments to become the full-time director of "Barney Miller."

Gianelli's ludicrous demise foreshadowed the funeral of Chuckles the Clown on "The Mary Tyler Moore Show" the following month. Although the episodes have little in common beyond similarly silly treatment of the same subject matter, a comparison of the two offers a revealing look at how divergent the two shows really were. When WJM's kiddie show host was trampled by a rogue elephant, the newsroom came to a halt as the staff registered shock—and ultimately, laughter—at the ridiculous details of the clown's passing. The fruitman's death is no less absurd, and yet Bob and his group accept the circumstances of his demise with almost existential calm. On "The Bob Newhart Show," life itself was such an absurd proposition that death—*even death by zucchini*—was taken in stride.

76 Change Is Gonna Do Me Good October 4, 1975
   Writers: Gordon and Lynne Farr
   Director: John Erman
   Guest Star: Brian Byers

In an effort to shake Bob out of his domestic rut, Emily suggests they exchange household duties.

The husband-and-wife writing team of Gordon and Lynne Farr gave a boost to the continuing saga of the Hartleys in a series of fine fourth- and fifth-season scripts. "We wanted to develop Emily," recalled Lynne Farr, "so we made sure she spent as little time in the kitchen as possible."

77 The Heavyweights October 11, 1975
   Writers: Tom Patchett, Jay Tarses
   Director: Bob Claver
   Guest Stars: Cliff Osmond, Marcia Lewis, Larry Gelman

Carol gets roped into a date with an obnoxious tubbo from Bob's overweight workshop.

78 Carol's Wedding October 18, 1975
   Writers: Gordon and Lynne Farr
   Director: Michael Zinberg
   Guest Stars: Will Mackenzie, Robert Casper

Bob is skeptical when Carol announces that she's getting married to Larry Bondurant, a travel agent she met less than twelve hours earlier.

79   Shrinks Across the Sea   October 25, 1975
   Writers: Phil Doran, Douglas Arango
   Director: Bob Claver
   Guest Stars: Rene Auberjonois, Françoise Ruggieri, Richard
   Foronjy

Bob and Emily host a visiting French psychologist, who arrives
in the company of another man's wife.

80   What's It All About, Albert?   November 1, 1975
   Writer: Phil Davis
   Director: Michael Zinberg
   Guest Star: Keenan Wynn

Convinced that his psychological counseling has done none of
his patients a bit of good, Bob seeks inspiration from his old
college professor.

His college mentor is no help at all. But, grasping at straws, Bob
discovers a new approach to therapy in the movie *Born Free* and urges
his patients to follow the example of Elsa the lioness and return to their
wild state.

81   Who Is Mr. X?   November 8, 1975
   Writer: Bruce Kane
   Director: Peter Bonerz
   Guest Stars: Jennifer Warren, Alan Manson, Claudette Duffy

A seemingly innocuous talk-show host uses Bob as bait when
she decides to do a hatchet job on the entire field of psychology.

Once again, Bob finds himself humiliated before the unyielding gaze
of the entire city—and this time he's in trouble from the very start. Says
host Ruth Corley, by way of introduction, "It's been said that today's
psychologist is nothing more than a con man, a snake-oil salesman
flimflamming innocent people, peddling cures for everything from nail
biting to a lousy love life—and I agree. We'll ask Dr. Hartley to defend
himself after these messages."

82 Seemed Like a Good Idea at the Time   November 15, 1975
Writers: Tom Patchett, Jay Tarses
Director: Richard Kinon
Guest Stars: Titos Vandis, Ruth McDevitt, Phillip R. Allen

Bob forms an unlikely alliance when he goes into partnership with a well-heeled playboy psychologist.

83 Over the River and Through the Woods November 22, 1975
Writer: Bruce Kane
Director: James Burrows
Guest Stars: Janet Meshad, David Himes

When Emily flies home for Thanksgiving, Bob joins Jerry, Howard, and Mr. Carlin for a bachelor's feast of Chinese food and beer.

84 Fathers and Sons and Mothers   November 29, 1975
Writer: Arnold Kane
Director: James Burrows
Guest Stars: William Daniels, Martha Scott, Lucien Scott

Bob's mother drops by for an extended visit and begins to drive her son crazy within moments of her arrival.

85 The Article   December 6, 1975
Writer: Erik Tarloff
Director: Michael Zinberg
Guest Stars: Pat Finley, Ellen Weston, Bobby Ramsen, Jack O'Leary, Howard Platt

Bob and Jerry have second thoughts after they agree to let Ellen do a newspaper feature on the drama of life in a big-city medical building.

86 A Matter of Vice-Principal   December 13, 1975
Writers: Gordon and Lynne Farr
Director: Peter Bonerz
Guest Stars: Lawrence Pressman, Kristina Holland, Frances Lee McCain, Nora Marlowe

Emily suddenly finds herself embroiled in grammar school politics when she gets promoted to vice-principal ahead of a teacher with greater seniority.

87   Bob Has to Have His Tonsils Out,   December 20, 1975
         So He Spends Christmas Eve in the Hospital
Writers: Tom Patchett, Jay Tarses
Director: James Burrows
Guest Stars: Graham Jarvis, Merie Earle

Bob faces another depressing holiday when he's forced to undergo an emergency tonsillectomy on Christmas Eve.

88   No Sale   January 3, 1976
Writer: Michael Zinberg
Director: Eddie Ryder
Guest Star: Malcolm Atterbury

Bob and Jerry are investment partners in one of Carlin's shady real estate deals—this one hinges on evicting an old man from a slum tenement.

89   Carol at 6:01   January 10, 1976
Writer: Gordon and Lynne Farr
Director: Peter Bonerz
Guest Star: Will Mackenzie

Carol turns to Bob for help when she begins to feel smothered by her new husband's overly lavish attentions.

90   Warden Gordon Borden   January 17, 1976
Writers: Gordon and Lynne Farr
Director: James Burrows
Guest Stars: William Redfield, Pat Finley

Howard is upset by the arrival of his sibling rival, Gordon—his brother has always taken things from him, and now he's got his eye on Ellen.

William Redfield played Howard's possessive brother, Gordon. The actor had played the Hartleys' annoying next-door neighbor in the series's original pilot film—a role that was dropped, ironically, when the show was revamped to include the navigator next door, Howard Borden.

91 My Boy Guillermo   January 24, 1976
  Writer: Sy Rosen
  Director: Alan Myerson
  Guest Stars: Gail Strickland, Matthew Laborteaux

Jerry's globe-hopping girlfriend returns to tempt him out of his
rut with an offer of marriage and an instant family.

Story editors Gordon and Lynne Farr received this script in the mail
from a hopeful writer who was then working at a Palo Alto, California,
Goodwill Store. "We liked it so much we actually bought it—which was
almost never done," recalls Lynne Farr. "And then we invited him to
sit in on the rewrite, which was also never done. Afterward, we told
him we needed another story editor for the next season and asked him
if he was willing to leave his job at the Goodwill. His jaw nearly hit the
floor, he was so excited."

92 Duke of Dunk   January 31, 1976
  Writers: Douglas Arango, Phil Doran
  Director: Peter Bonerz
  Guest Star: Anthony Costello

Bob counsels an egocentric basketball superstar in the fine art
of team playing.

93 Guaranteed Not to Shrink   February 7, 1976
  Writer: Sy Rosen
  Director: James Burrows
  Guest Stars: Will Mackenzie, Claudia Bryar, Paul Bryar

Carol becomes an overnight psychoanalyst when she enrolls in
a night school psychology course.

This episode contains a priceless and hilariously authentic husband-
and-wife exchange when Bob plants his foot squarely in his mouth as
he starts to describe a brilliant old girlfriend who was such an underachiever that she finally settled, tragically, for an unchallenging job as
a mere *schoolteacher*. Of course, he barely finishes his sentence before
he's stopped cold by the withering glare of his wife—the schoolteacher.
Bob then bungles a tactful retreat by attempting to salvage the thought
midsentence when he amends it to "she finally settled for being a . . . a
school." By then, of course, it's already too late—and Bob spends the
rest of the episode in a doghouse of his own design.

94   Birth of a Salesman   February 14, 1976
   Writer: Sy Rosen
   Director: John C. Chulay
   Guest Star: Oliver Clark

After Bob counsels Mr. Herd to be more assertive, the milque-
toast takes the advice to heart and slaps him with a lawsuit.

95   The Boy Next Door   February 21, 1976
   Writer: Hugh H. Wilson
   Director: Peter Bonerz
   Guest Star: Moosie Drier

Howard's ex-wife grants him custody of their son, but Bob and
Emily end up spending more time with Howie than his dad does.

Hugh Wilson—a prolific second-generation MTM writer/producer—
would eventually distinguish himself as creator of "WKRP in Cincinnati"
in 1978.

96   Peeper—Two   February 28, 1976
   Writers: Tom Patchett, Jay Tarses
   Director: Michael Zinberg
   Guest Stars: Tom Poston, Veronica Hamel, Sally Stark, Barbara
   Ellen Levene

When the Peeper returns in sullen spirits after his wife leaves
him, Jerry decides to reacquaint Bob's old chum with the swinging singles scene.

1976/77   THE FIFTH SEASON

Year-End Rating: 19.0 (45th place)

Bob Hartley confronts another season of unparalleled comic anxiety
in fifth-year stories by Gordon and Lynne Farr, Hugh Wilson, Gary
David Goldberg, and Sy Rosen, who is also the season's story consultant.
Producers Gordon and Lynne Farr and Michael Zinberg return as cus-
todians of this fine madness, along with executive producers Tom Patchett and Jay Tarses.

97 Enter Mrs. Peeper September 25, 1976
Writers: Gordon and Lynne Farr
Director: Michael Zinberg
Guest Stars: Tom Poston, Jean Palmerton, Jay Tarses, Charles Thomas Murphy

Bob encounters an unexpected change in the Peeper when the incorrigible joker adopts a more serious outlook after his second marriage.

98 Caged Fury October 2, 1976
Writers: Gordon and Lynne Farr
Director: Michael Zinberg
Guest Star: Will Mackenzie

The Hartleys miss their own bicentennial party after Emily accidentally locks them in the basement storage room.

99 Some of My Best Friends Are . . . October 9, 1976
Writer: Hugh Wilson
Director: Alan Myerson
Guest Star: Leonard Stone

Howard undergoes a behavior-modification treatment to cure his unhealthy dependence on Bob and Emily.

The strange triangle of Bob, Emily, and Howard defied simple description. The perennially jet-lagged navigator was the Hartleys' best friend and neighbor, but also something more—as Bob discovers after one of his colleagues cures Howard's dependency by turning him into a joyless, self-sufficient bore.

Things just aren't the same without Howard around. Finally, Bob and Emily set a trap—with home-cooked mashed potatoes and roast beef as bait—to lure the old Howard back into blissful dependency, having come to the sobering conclusion that they need him as much as he needs them. Howard, the childlike dreamer, filled a void in the childless couple's life that gave the reciprocal devotion they shared an understated, and quite touching, subtext in the rich fabric of this deceptively simple show.

100   Still Crazy After All These Years   October 16, 1976
Writers: Pat Jones, Donald Reiker
Director: James Burrows
Guest Stars: Howard Hesseman, Florida Friebus, John Fiedler, Renee Lippin

Bob's group is stunned when Mr. Plager admits that he's a homosexual.

101   The Great Rent Strike   October 23, 1976
Writer: David Lloyd
Director: John C. Chulay
Guest Star: Jack Riley

Bob organizes a rent strike to protest abominable conditions in his high rise, only to discover that Mr. Carlin is the new owner of his building.

102   Et Tu, Carol   October 30, 1976
Writer: Gary David Goldberg
Director: Alan Myerson
Guest Stars: Shirley O'Hara, Larry Gelman, Howard Platt

Bob faces the nightmare of adjusting to a new secretary after Carol drops him from her work roster.

103   Send This Boy to Camp   November 6, 1976
Writer: David Lloyd
Director: Michael Zinberg
Guest Stars: Sorrell Booke, Michael LeClair, Tierre Turner

Bob and Jerry plan an exciting camping trip for a pair of orphans, but the foursome never gets any farther than a downtown parking lot.

104   A Crime Most Foul   November 13, 1976
Writer: Sy Rosen
Director: John C. Chulay
Guest Stars: Oliver Clark, Florida Friebus, John Fiedler

No one is above suspicion when Bob's expensive new tape recorder turns up missing—not even Emily.

Bob explains his obsession to recover the stolen recorder by rationalizing how he never got over the theft of his boyhood harmonica—the one he used when he played "Pop Goes the Weasel," just like Al of the Harmonicats. Bob's rambling autobiographical anecdotes rarely provided any real insight into the character's formative years, but the cockeyed wisdom and slippery irony of his anecdotes was the closest we'd come to a definition of the world according to Bob.

105   The Slammer   November 20, 1976
    Writers: Gordon and Lynne Farr
    Director: Michael Zinberg
    Guest Stars: Tom Poston, Bobby Ramsen, Lucy Lee Flippin,
    Jean Palmerton, David Himes, Kim O'Brien

A nostalgic visit to their old college bar turns sour when Bob and the Peeper are booked on vice charges by a pair of undercover policewomen.

106   Jerry's Retirement   November 27, 1976
    Writer: Hugh Wilson
    Director: Alan Myerson
    Guest Stars: John Randolph, Howard Morris

Bob questions the wisdom of Jerry's sudden decision to quit his practice and live off the profits of his real estate investments.

107   Here's to You, Mrs. Robinson   December 4, 1976
    Writers: Gordon and Lynne Farr
    Director: James Burrows
    Guest Stars: Lucy Landau, Fred D. Scott, Steve Anderson

The newly retired Jerry sets off on a worldwide quest to find his natural parents.

108   Breaking Up Is Hard to Do   December 11, 1976
    Writer: Sy Rosen
    Director: Peter Bonerz
    Guest Stars: John Holland, Martha Scott

Bob is shocked to discover his parents have separated after forty-seven years of married life.

109 Making Up Is the Thing to Do   December 25, 1976
   Writers: Gordon and Lynne Farr
   Director: Harvey Medlinsky
   Guest Stars: Barnard Hughes, Martha Scott, Will Mackenzie

Bob invites his feuding parents to Christmas dinner in the hope that the warm yuletide spirit will bring the pair back together.

110 Love Is the Blindest   January 8, 1977
   Writer: Gary David Goldberg
   Director: Will Mackenzie
   Guest Star: Mary Ann Chinn

Mr. Carlin invents a colorful string of tall tales about himself to impress his love-struck new secretary.

111 The Ironwood Experience   January 15, 1977
   Writer: Phil Davis
   Director: Peter Bonerz
   Guest Star: Max Showalter

Bob's lecture at the Ironwood Institute for Interpersonal Relationships gets off to an unexpected start when the audience arrives in the nude.

112 Of Mice and Men   January 22, 1977
   Writer: Bruce Kane
   Director: Peter Bonerz
   Guest Stars: John Fiedler, Oliver Clark, Betty Kean, Inga Neilsen

Bob invites Emily to participate in a role-playing session with the repressed men in his consciousness-raising group for henpecked husbands.

113 Halls of Hartley   January 29, 1977
   Writer: Michael Zinberg
   Director: James Burrows
   Guest Stars: Richard Libertini, Craig Wasson, Addison Powell, Tresa Hughes

Fed up with the pressures of urban life, Bob applies for a position on the faculty of a small rural college.

114   The Heartbreak Kidd   February 5, 1977
Writer: Sy Rosen
Director: Dick Martin
Guest Star: Tovah Feldshuh

An enthusiastic psychology major develops a schoolgirl crush on Bob during her student internship.

Dick Martin began a very successful career as a TV comedy director with this episode, after an auspicious start as one-half of Rowan and Martin, the comedy team that hosted NBC's "Laugh-In." He came to the series by way of Newhart, who introduced him to producer Michael Zinberg—with typical understatement—as "a friend of mine who wants to become a director."

115   Death Be My Destiny   February 12, 1977
Writer: Sy Rosen
Director: Michael Zinberg
Guest Stars: Oliver Clark, Lieux Dressler, Tom Patchett

Bob is convinced he's living on borrowed time after he narrowly escapes death in a freak elevator accident.

Producer Tom Patchett appears in a cameo as Mr. Death.

116   Taxation Without Celebration   February 19, 1977
Writer: Sy Rosen
Director: Peter Bonerz
Guest Stars: Vince Martorano, Will Mackenzie, Drew Michaels

Bob has a choice of honoring the income tax deadline *or* his anniversary, when he discovers they both fall on the same day.

117   Desperate Sessions   February 26, 1977
Writers: Michael Zinberg, Martin Davidson
Director: Dick Martin
Guest Stars: Robert Pine, Walker Edmiston

Bob is held hostage by an affable robber he befriended in the lobby of his bank.

118   The Mentor   March 5, 1977
   Writer: Gary David Goldberg
   Director: Michael Zinberg
   Guest Star: Will Mackenzie

Bob inspires Carol's husband to start his own travel agency, never suspecting Larry would set up shop right outside his office.

119   Shrinking Violence   March 12, 1977
   Writer: Sy Rosen
   Director: Peter Bonerz
   Guest Stars: Robert Ridgely, Florida Friebus, Oliver Clark

When Emily has difficulty venting her anger at a belligerent auto mechanic, Bob decides to show her how it's done.

120   You're Having My Hartley   March 19, 1977
   Writers: Gordon and Lynne Farr
   Director: Peter Bonerz
   Guest Stars: Tom Poston, Jean Palmerton, Bobby Ramsen

Bob has barely recovered from Carol's announcement that she's going to have a baby when he finds out that Emily is also expecting a visit from the stork.

This episode was written after Bob announced his intention to retire the series at the end of the fifth year. But by the time it was filmed, the star had decided to return for one final year—and a last-minute rewrite was required to explain away Emily's pregnancy as a dream.

"In the original story, she really was pregnant," recalls writer Lynne Farr. "Bob always said he wouldn't do a show with a baby, but when he announced he wasn't coming back for a sixth year, we decided to have some fun and see how far we could go before he changed his mind." Newhart—who long maintained the Hartleys could get along very nicely without children—cringed at the thought of introducing "baby humor" in the show's final year.

"When Bob first saw the script at the Monday-morning reading, he refused to do it as written—and all of a sudden we didn't have a script," remembers Farr. "We spent a frantic night trying to save the story before we finally just turned the whole thing into a dream. And even after all that, it was actually a pretty good show."

1977/78   THE SIXTH SEASON

Year-End Rating: 16.2 (67th place)

By the time Bob Newhart reconsidered his earlier decision to end the series after the fifth year, most of the show's longtime staff had already moved on to other projects. But despite the loss of so many key writers and producers, the show's final and most inconsistent season is redeemed by a handful of memorable and funny episodes.

Executive producer Michael Zinberg assembled a sixth-season staff that included producers Glen Charles and Les Charles, story editor Lloyd Garver, and executive script consultant Tom Tenowich. Directing chores are divided almost equally between Peter Bonerz, Michael Zinberg, and Dick Martin, who also serves as creative consultant in the show's final year.

121   Bob's Change of Life   September 24, 1977
Writers: Glen Charles, Les Charles
Director: Peter Bonerz
Guest Star: Martha Scott

Bob faces a midlife crisis when he and Emily decide to move to a new apartment.

122   Ex-Con Job   October 1, 1977
Writer: Ziggy Steinberg
Director: Michael Zinberg
Guest Stars: Bert Rosario, H. B. Haggerty, Allen Case, Taurean Blacque

Bob's newest therapy group has a unique set of problems—all five are freshly paroled ex-convicts.

123   A Jackie Story   October 8, 1977
Writer: Lloyd Garver
Director: Michael Zinberg
Guest Stars: Hope Alexander Willis, Sam Kwasman

Bob treats a schizophrenic ventriloquist and his dummy; and Jerry is convinced that his beautiful new girlfriend is too good for him.

124 Who Was That Masked Man?   October 15, 1977
    Writers: Glen Charles, Les Charles
    Director: Dick Martin
    Guest Stars: John Fiedler, Toni Lamond, Florida Friebus

After his wife kicks him out, Mr. Peterson finds an unlikely soul-mate in Mr. Carlin.

125 Carlin's New Suit   October 22, 1977
    Writer: Andrew Smith
    Director: Dick Martin
    Guest Stars: Loni Anderson, Mark Lenard, Sparky Marcus, Pat Cranshaw

Carlin decides to take advantage of a bogus paternity suit to pal around with the son he never had.

Loni Anderson would soon make waves as the sultry receptionist of MTM's "WKRP in Cincinnati."

126 A Day in the Life   October 29, 1977
    Writers: Kathy Donnell, Madelyn Dimaggio Wagner
    Director: Dick Martin
    Guest Stars: Richard Stahl, Bud Kenneally, Joan Kenneally, Rob Kenneally, Pamm Kenneally

Bob accepts a spur-of-the-moment invitation to Mardi Gras and then has but a single day to convince his patients that they can survive a week without him.

127 My Son the Comedian   November 12, 1977
    Writer: David Lloyd
    Director: Dick Martin
    Guest Stars: Moosie Drier, Bobby Ramsen, Elizabeth Kerr, Johnny West

Howard laughs at all his son's jokes, until Howie decides to quit high school to pursue a career as a professional comedian.

128 You're Fired, Mr. Chips   November 19, 1977
Writer: Lloyd Garver
Director: Peter Bonerz
Guest Stars: Ralph Bellamy, Richard Roat, Howard Witt

Bob hires his old college professor to help out with his practice and then faces the unenviable task of firing his mentor when things don't work out.

129 Shallow Throat   November 26, 1977
Writer: Earl Pomerantz
Director: Dick Martin
Guest Stars: Richard Libertini, Frank Maxwell, J. Jay Saunders, Lorrie Gia, Alan Haufrect, Julienne Wells

Bob convinces a close-mouthed patient to open up but wishes he'd left well enough alone when the man's confession makes him an accessory to larceny.

130 A Girl in Her Twenties   December 3, 1977
Writer: Laura Levine
Director: Peter Bonerz
Guest Stars: Mildred Natwick, Sondra Currie, J. J. Johnston, Macon McCalman

While Bob's away on business, Emily becomes better acquainted with an eccentric neighbor—an elderly woman who's perfectly content to live her life in the past.

As a condition of his return to the series's final year, Newhart's sixth-season contract allowed him to sit out four of the final twenty-two shows. Emily takes the spotlight in this episode, as well as in "Emily Carlin, Emily Carlin," "It Didn't Happen One Night," and "Crisis in Eduka-tion," while Bob makes only token appearances in all four.

131 Grand Delusion   December 17, 1977
Writer: Lloyd Garver
Director: Dick Martin
Guest Stars: Morgan Fairchild, F. William Parker, Michael Evans

On the evening of their tenth anniversary, Bob and Emily imagine how their lives might have been different had they each married someone else.

132   'Twas the Pie Before Christmas   December 24, 1977
   Writer: Phil Davis
   Director: Dick Martin
   Guest Stars: Florida Friebus, John Fiedler, Rik Pierce

Bob's group decides to boycott his Christmas party after they each discover a rate increase notice that was accidentally included with their Christmas cards.

133   Freudian Ship   January 7, 1978
   Writer: Earl Pomerantz
   Director: Peter Bonerz
   Guest Stars: John Crawford, Jeff Donnell

Even though he and Emily are supposed to be enjoying themselves on a ten-day pleasure cruise, Bob can't seem to resist solving other people's problems.

134   Grizzly Emily   January 14, 1978
   Writer: Laura Levine
   Director: Peter Bonerz
   Guest Stars: Barnard Hughes, Alice Nunn, Bob Yerkes

Emily is one disgruntled camper after Bob's father insists she stay behind to cook and clean while he and Bob go fishing.

135   Son of Ex-Con Job   January 21, 1978
   Writer: Emily Purdom Marshall
   Director: Michael Zinberg
   Guest Stars: Bert Rosario, Wyatt Johnson, Taurean Blacque, Norman Parker, Ric Mancini, Allen Case

Unable to find work on the outside, the parolees from Bob's ex-con therapy group decide to go into business for themselves.

136   Group on a Hot Tin Roof   January 28, 1978
   Writer: Andrew Smith
   Director: Michael Zinberg
   Guest Stars: Howard Hesseman, Jerry Devine, Florida Friebus, John Fiedler, Frank Ashmore, Ty Wilson, Lou Cutell, Amzie Strickland

Mr. Plager invites Bob's group to see his play—a turgid World War I drama with characters who bear more than a passing resemblance to the other members of the group.

137   Emily Carlin, Emily Carlin   February 4, 1978
    Writer: Laura Levine
    Director: Peter Bonerz
    Guest Stars: Karen Ericson, Michael Alldredge, Woody Skaggs,
Carole Shelyne Barry

Carlin convinces Emily to attend his high school reunion posing
as his wife, and then takes shameless advantage of the situation.

138   Easy for You to Say   February 11, 1978
    Writer: Andrew Smith
    Director: Dick Martin
    Guest Stars: Jerry Fogel, K. C. Martel, J. R. Miller

Bob treats Ralph Alfalfa, a stuttering radio personality who dreams
of hosting a children's TV show.

139   It Didn't Happen One Night   February 18, 1978
    Writer: Laura Levine
    Director: Dick Martin
    Guest Star: David Hedison

The Hartleys' friends assume the worst when Emily renews her
friendship with a handsome old boyfriend while Bob's away on
business.

140   Carol Ankles for Indie-Prod   March 4, 1978
    Writer: Lloyd Garver
    Director: Mark Tinker
    Guest Stars: Madeleine Fisher, John Terry Bell, Mert Rich, Joe
George

Bob and Jerry are shocked when Carol announces she's quitting
to accept a better job offer—working as personal assistant to
Mr. Carlin!

Director Mark Tinker, the son of MTM founder Grant Tinker, was
also associate producer of "Bob Newhart's" final two seasons. He would
later produce MTM's "The White Shadow" and "St. Elsewhere."

141   Crisis in Edukation   March 11, 1978
    Writer: Earl Pomerantz
    Director: Peter Bonerz
    Guest Stars: Edward Andrews, Robert Costanzo, Jan Fisher,
    Patricia Stevens, Bill Zuckert, Brian Miller, Delores Albin

Emily is left to fend off a group of irate parents after her principal
skips town to avoid the brewing protest.

142   Happy Trails to You   April 1, 1978
    Writers: Glen Charles, Les Charles, Lloyd Garver
    Directors: Michael Zinberg, Peter Bonerz
    Guest Stars: Bobby Ramsen, Bill Quinn, Florida Friebus, John
    Fiedler

Jerry, Howard, and Carol exchange tearful farewells at the Hartleys' good-bye party after Bob accepts a teaching job at a small
college in Oregon.

When the show went off the air, it seemed almost unimaginable that
Bob would trade in the hustle and bustle of the big city for the bucolic
pace of small-town life. And yet, four years later, Newhart reappeared
in a new MTM series set, coincidentally, in a small town. Before "Newhart" premiered in 1982, the star actually considered returning to his
former stamping grounds. "At one time," Newhart told *TV Guide*, "I
thought of simply picking up the old show four years later. I think it
might have worked."

Perhaps.

But for many of those who'd made "The Bob Newhart Show" a
regular part of their Saturday-night agenda for six years, the satisfying
finality of the last show sealed the wit and warmth of Bob, Emily, and
Howard forever into a single time and place. And then the show vanished, like a strange dream, with no imaginable postscript.

For them, it's consolation enough to know that sooner or later the
show will appear—mysteriously, and without warning—in reruns on
late-night television. And that when it does, it will never fail to bring a
smile in the darkness.

"BARNEY MILLER"

·

*That squad room was the end
result of twenty-six years of
analysis.*
—DANNY ARNOLD, "Barney
Miller" creator

THE FAILED PILOT for "Barney Miller" was already dead by the time
the president of ABC and his lieutenants sat down to lunch with the
hottest TV director in Hollywood. But John Rich was determined it
wouldn't stay buried.

Martin Starger, Barry Diller, and Michael Eisner—the reigning powers at ABC—had invited the director to their executive dining room to
woo him into their camp in time for the 1974 season. But Rich didn't
want to talk comedy. After four years at the helm of "All in the Family,"
he was in no hurry to lock himself into another series.

In fact, the only show he *would* talk about was a great pilot his friend
Danny Arnold had just made—a comedy about a compassionate New
York cop named Barney Miller.

Danny Arnold's quirky concept for a cop show had been around, in
one form or another, for years. At NBC in 1970, he pitched "Jacobi's
Turf"—a proposed vehicle for character actor Lou Jacobi, who would
play a bedraggled Jewish patrolman who served as protector and father
confessor to residents of a tough Manhattan precinct. The network thought
it sounded too ethnic. Despite Arnold's solid credits as a producer—
"That Girl," "Bewitched," and "My World and Welcome to It"—NBC
politely turned him down.

The producer put the concept on hold, but he never forgot about it. He was convinced that the cops 'n' robbers shoot-'em-ups that had been a staple of prime time since the 1950s barely scratched the rich vein of material that lurked just below the surface. "I wanted to turn the standard detective drama inside out," Arnold recalled, "I wanted to peer into the lives of cops who are stuck in an out-of-the-way precinct in a job that's really fundamentally boring."

It was fertile ground. And Danny Arnold wasn't the only one who thought so. In 1974 an agent introduced him to another writer who had an idea for a humanistic cop show of his own.

Ted Flicker, a comedy director best known for the dark satire of his 1968 feature, *The President's Analyst*, had been working on a concept for a police drama about a Jewish detective who operated in the sunny climes of California. Arnold, who by this time had secured a development deal with ABC, proposed a collaboration—but he insisted they drop the old concepts and start fresh. "They're not going to buy a Jewish detective in the San Fernando Valley any more than they bought him in New York."

They came up with a new half-hour pilot for ABC called "The Life and Times of Barney Miller." The detective was still Jewish, but the creators had decided not to draw attention to his background. "The name Miller was an attempt to be ethnic and nonethnic at the same time," recalled Arnold. ABC's insistence on casting all-American Abby Dalton as Barney's wife further obscured the detective's ethnic origins. But it didn't much matter whether he was Jewish or not—because ABC wasn't really interested in Barney.

Their research showed that Hal Linden—imported from New York for the title role—tested "dull." And besides, the precinct comedy had so many characters and story lines that it just seemed too confusing. The ABC executives aired the pilot once—buried late in the summer of 1974—and then promptly forgot about it.

Until John Rich brought the matter up during lunch.

Suddenly, the unsold pilot took on a new significance. In the eyes of Starger, Diller, and Eisner, "Barney Miller" had become the trump card in their plan to lure the most successful TV director in Hollywood over to their side.

And Martin Starger wanted Rich badly. For the network boss who let "All in the Family" slip through his fingers five years earlier, nabbing the director who shepherded that comedy through four hit seasons offered at least some consolation for the executive's wounded corporate pride. ABC would get John Rich, even if they had to revive a dead pilot to do it.

When Barry Diller commissioned four "Barney Miller" scripts, Danny Arnold was convinced ABC made the relatively small investment, in his words, "just to shut me up." So it came as a complete surprise to the producer when Michael Eisner called and asked him to start production on "Barney Miller" with two new episodes.

But there was a catch. The network insisted that John Rich direct.

"They really wanted John on the team," Danny Arnold remembered. "And I knew he was good. But I like to run my own show." The director had almost exactly the same reservations about the producer. Rich had worked with Arnold on "My World and Welcome to It" and knew the seasoned TV veteran as a brilliant, if slightly insane, producer. But the powerful director had also envisioned running his own show, not signing on as part of a network package deal with another creator who could be just as stubborn and single-minded as he. Rich finally agreed to direct the first two episodes on a trial basis, just to get the project off and running.

And, as expected, the creative sparks flew from the very first day of production. The director insisted on shooting the new comedy on videotape, straight through, like a one-act play—the technique he'd perfected on "All in the Family." "Danny went crazy," Rich remembered.

"I was horrified!" Arnold said with a laugh. The one-time film editor hated to lose the editing options that are sacrificed in a taping. "You had no control over moments you might want to extend. To do even minimal editing, we had to physically take the tape to this tiny facility that Rich had set up in some guy's apartment! Those first two shows were such a horrifying experience that I vowed never to shoot live on tape again."

The two sample episodes were hardly enough to boost the network's confidence in the fledgling series, but ABC finally gave "Barney Miller" the go-ahead anyway. Actually, they had little choice. ABC's 1974 lineup had been a disaster, and the network desperately needed new half-hour comedies to replace the early failures from the fall schedule. "Barney Miller," already primed and ready to roll into production, was hastily slated as a midseason replacement to debut in January 1975.

But the budget-conscious network made one firm demand: the show would continue to be shot on cost-effective videotape. ABC had no intention of footing the bill for the extravagance of film stock just to suit the aesthetic whims of Danny Arnold.

Arnold cringed. He knew he'd never be able to capture the dark, downbeat squalor of an urban squad room using the bright, flat lighting required for live video. He finally solved the problem by devising one of the most complex and unusual shooting techniques ever attempted for a TV situation comedy.

Instead of taping the whole show straight through, Arnold and his directors painstakingly adjusted the lighting for each separate scene, just as if they were shooting a movie. When they were satisfied they had recorded the best take of a scene, they would move on to the next shot. The live audience was superfluous to the process, since most of the real work was done after they'd already left. Eventually, the producer abandoned the use of a studio audience altogether.

The method produced striking results. "Barney Miller" would be justly celebrated for its moody, evocative atmosphere. But few realized that to achieve this look, the cast and crew labored under a grueling shooting schedule that frequently lasted far into the night. Actor Ron Glass remembered, "There were some days I didn't make it home until six the next morning."

The long hours didn't faze Danny Arnold. He approached the series with the enthusiasm of a man possessed, attacking every aspect of "Barney Miller's" production with fanatical attention to detail. "You have to live with a show all the time," he insisted. And there were long stretches when he did just that—working, eating, and sleeping in the studio for days at a time.

But his greatest obsession was writing. With his partner and co-producer, Chris Hayward, Arnold personally wrote—or rewrote, sometimes line by line—nearly every script provided during the first two seasons. Occasionally he even read the lines aloud, storming onto the set with his latest story revisions to act out all the parts himself. It was a performance for which Danny Arnold was particularly well suited.

"They're all a part of me," the writer confessed. "Barney was the compassionate, moral guy I always thought I should be. Wojo was well meaning, but sometimes pretty irresponsible. Harris's narcissism, Dietrich's sardonic point of view, Yemena's weakness for horses—all a part of my own private paranoia. My analyst, a big fan of the show, once told me, 'You don't know how thrilled I am that I protected your paranoia all these years.' "

To bring these characters to life, the producer hired an ensemble of seasoned veterans that included Linden, Abe Vigoda, Jack Soo, Barbara Barrie, and James Gregory, and paired them with relative newcomers Ron Glass, Max Gail, Greg Sierra, and eventually, Steve Landesberg and

Ron Carey. But fine as they were, the show frequently rested on the shoulders of the guest stars and bit players—that endless parade of kooks, con men, and lost souls that gave the series its heart.

"The show was a great platform," observed Arnold. "Anyone in the world could walk—or be dragged—into that station house." And in the simple democracy of the Twelfth Precinct, no one was ever denied a forum, no matter how unpopular—or absurd—his viewpoint.

There was the Indian who wanted to die in Central Park and the Gypsy who vandalized the novelty shop of a Nazi war criminal. The squad room hosted foot fetishists, spies, and librarians; mad bombers, prostitutes, and once even a werewolf.

They came to the Twelfth Precinct for different reasons—some demanding justice, others looking for hope, and still others who sought nothing more than a few moments' escape from their loneliness. But, no matter why they came, they rarely left unchanged.

"Barney Miller" was an instant hit with the critics, who applauded the show's slightly mocking approach to topics like teenage prostitution, urban terrorism, and mental illness—subjects that were seldom touched in prime time, and rarely with such wit and compassion. *Time* and *Newsweek* gave the series glowing write-ups, and before long, the show began to amass a faithful and ever-growing audience. By the end of its first full season, the series emerged as a consistent—though rarely spectacular—ratings winner.

In fact, "Barney Miller's" quiet success was one of the secrets of the show's surprising longevity. The show staked out a comfortable niche and as long as it delivered the same dependable ratings, ABC was content to leave it alone. They recognized that "Barney Miller" was in a class by itself—a situation comedy for connoisseurs.

Remarkably, the series weathered eight prime-time seasons. Even more remarkable is that, thanks to enormous creative contributions from writers Tony Sheehan, Chris Hayward, Reinhold Weege, Frank Dungan, and Jeff Stein—and director Noam Pitlik—the series never faltered in seven and a half years of production. When the station house was finally shuttered at the end of the eighth season, it wasn't for lack of ratings.

"We were a topical show that was running out of topics," confessed writer Jeff Stein. "We had the choice of floating on forever, like 'The Love Boat,' or going out with a little dignity. We decided to go out with dignity."

In the course of 168 well-crafted comic plays—each a model of clockwork precision that somehow looks effortless in execution—the cast and creators chronicled the entire range of human behavior in stories that could be hilarious or chilling, and were often both. In the depth of its wit and the breadth of its intelligence, "Barney Miller" attracted a loyal and discriminating following. And yet, even in reruns, the show's unfailing humor and affectionate view of humanity, in all of its colors, continues to attract new viewers almost every day.

Given time, it might just make connoisseurs of us all.

A Critical Guide to All 168 Episodes

REGULAR CAST

REGULAR CAST

Captain Barney Miller	Hal Linden
Detective Sergeant Phil Fish	Abe Vigoda
Detective Sergeant Chano Amenguale	Gregory Sierra
Detective Stan Wojciehowicz	Maxwell Gail
Detective Sergeant Nick Yemena	Jack Soo
Detective Sergeant Ron Harris	Ron Glass
Inspector Frank Luger	James Gregory
Detective Sergeant Arthur Dietrich	Steve Landesberg
Officer Carl Levitt	Ron Carey
Elizabeth Miller	Barbara Barrie
Elizabeth Miller (pilot episode)	Abby Dalton

SUPPORTING CAST

Lieutenant Scanlon	George Murdock
Marty	Jack DeLeon
Bernice Fish	Florence Stanley
Detective Janice Wentworth	Linda Lavin
Detective Roslyn Licori	Mari Gorman
Arnold Ripner	Alex Henteloff
Detective Maria Battista	June Gable
Inspector Kelly	Dick O'Neill
Detective Eric Dorsey	Paul Lieber
Officer Kogan	Milt Kogan
Detective Wilson	Rod Perry
Detective Mike Lovatelli	Art Metrano
Perlita Avilar (Luger's wife)	Carina Afable
Rachel Miller (Barney's daughter)	Anne Wyndham
David Miller (Barney's son)	Michael Tessier

Stanley Brock, Paul Lichtman, Richard Stahl, Philip Sterling, Phil Leeds, Jack Somack, Stuart Pankin, Kenneth Tigar, Miriam Byrd Netherly, Florence Halop, Phil Bruns, Candy Azzara, Doris Roberts, Oliver Clark, Ivor Francis, Stefan Gierasch, Michael Tucci, Walter Janowitz, Howard Platt, John Dullaghan, J. J. Barry, Peter Hobbs, Peggy Pope, Richard Libertini, Don Calfa, David Clennon, Ralph Manza, Dino Natali, Rod Colbin, Todd Susman, Walter Olkewicz

Created by Danny Arnold, Theodore J. Flicker

Music by Jack Elliot, Allyn Ferguson

Principal directors were Danny Arnold, Noam Pitlik

1974   THE PILOT EPISODE

Pilot   The Life and Times of Barney Miller   August 22, 1974
   Writers: Danny Arnold, Theodore J. Flicker
   Director: Theodore J. Flicker
   Guest Stars: Abby Dalton, Anne Wyndham, Val Bisoglio, Henry Beckman

A day in the life of Captain Barney Miller, a compassionate family man and chief detective in a colorful Greenwich Village precinct—where today he comes face-to-face with a gun-wielding junkie.

The series's original filmed pilot, it aired only once—as an unsold pilot on "Just for Laughs," an ABC summer anthology series. Abby Dalton is Barney's wife, Liz, the role played by Barbara Barrie when the script was rewritten—and reshot—for "Barney Miller's" debut five months later.

1975   THE FIRST SEASON

Year-End Rating: 14.7 (70th place)

The detectives of New York's Twelfth Precinct assemble for their first season under the exhaustive stewardship of executive producer Danny Arnold, who, along with producer Chris Hayward, would write the bulk of the stories during the first two seasons. Lila Garrett serves as executive script consultant during the first year, and associate producer duties and shared by Tim Steele and Mark Goode.

1 Ramon   January 23, 1975
Writers: Danny Arnold, Theodore J. Flicker
Director: Bill Davis
Guest Stars: Chu Chu Malave, Michael Moore, Buddy Lester,
John Hawker

Barney tries to reason with a frightened young junkie who holds
the Twelfth Precinct at bay with a small handgun.

Faced with a wild-eyed gunman, the first thing Barney does is introduce himself! He disarms the scared felon with a simple act of respect—standard procedure at the Twelfth Precinct, where for the next
eight seasons, lawbreaker and victim alike would be treated with an
empathy rarely seen on TV cop shows.

2 Experience   January 30, 1975
Writer: Steve Gordon
Director: Danny Arnold
Guest Stars: Jack DeLeon, Rod Perry, Alex Henteloff, Jane
Dulo, Ray Sharkey, Milt Kogan, Noam Pitlik

Fish worries that he's getting too old for his job; a mad bomber
leaves a live charge in the squad room; and the detectives arrest
a gay shoplifter.

Though Danny Arnold was credited as director of this episode, it
was actually the second—and final—episode directed by John Rich. "We
collaborated on that episode," explained Arnold. "And John's tough.
He knew what he wanted, and I knew what I wanted—but they weren't
always the same thing. In the end, John didn't think it represented his
work, so he chose not to have his name on it."
Actually the issue of who got final credit for writing and directing
various episodes would be a constant source of frustration for the producer. "Those credits were dictated by strict union rules," insists Arnold.
"In many, many cases, the writing and directing credits that appear on
'Barney Miller' have nothing to do with authorship or the actual work
that was done on the show. They give a false impression that is very
unfair to those who actually made substantial contributions to 'Barney
Miller.' "
The episode marks the first appearance of Alex Henteloff as Arnold
Ripner, the disreputable ambulance chaser who would plague the men
of the Twelfth for the next eight years; Jack DeLeon plays Marty, the
gay thief who would also make his share of return visits. Not so for Rod

Perry's Detective Wilson, a black member of the squad who failed to make the precinct's permanent roster.

3   Snow Job   February 6, 1975
Writers: Ron Friedman, Danny Arnold, Chris Hayward
Story: Dick Morgan
Director: Richard Kinon
Guest Stars: Ron Feinberg, Richard Stahl, Ted Noose, Paul Lichtman, Reid Cruickshanks

A department store entrusts their cash payroll to Wojo for safe-keeping during a blizzard; and a despondent flasher attempts suicide in the precinct's bathroom.

4   Graft   February 13, 1975
Writers: Danny Arnold, Chris Hayward
Story: Lila Garrett, Sanford Krinski
Director: Noam Pitlik
Guest Stars: Dick O'Neill, Buddy Lester, Derrel Maury

Chano investigates a rash of obscene phone calls; and Inspector Kelly arrives, intent on snooping out corruption in the Twelfth.

The episode contains one of a handful of scenes that took place in Barney's kitchen. Though the show had been designed to place equal emphasis on the policeman's home and work life, it quickly became apparent that the domestic scenes diluted the central focus of the squad room. In the early years, the writers made a few strained attempts to bring Liz down to the precinct. But, as producer Tony Sheehan observed, "There were only so many times we could have Liz drop in to have lunch or bring Barney a flower." With few exceptions, Barney's wife finally evolved into an off-screen presence throughout most of the series.

5   The Courtesans   February 20, 1975
Writers: Jerry Davis, Danny Arnold, Chris Hayward, Sybil Adelman
Story: Sanford Krinski, Jerry Davis
Director: Noam Pitlik
Guest Stars: Nancy Dussault, Naomi Stevens, Audrey Christie, Rosana Soto, Shannon Christie, Lavell Roby

Barney's daughter wants to move out on her own; and a call girl rejects Wojo's tender efforts to reform her.

6 Stakeout   February 27, 1975
Writer: Danny Arnold
Director: John Rich
Guest Stars: Lou Jacobi, Ed Barth, Brett Sommers, Vic Tayback,
Marjorie Bennett, Florence Stanley, Lucille Meredith, Jo Jo
Malone, Peter Carew

Fish, Barney, and Wojo are visited by a rash of curious neighbors
when they attempt a stakeout in an abandoned apartment.

Though broadcast as the seventh episode, this script, directed by
John Rich, was actually the first regular "Barney Miller" episode shot.

7 Bureaucrat   March 6, 1975
Writers: Richard Baer, Danny Arnold, Chris Hayward
Director: Bob Finkel
Guest Stars: David Wayne, Elliot Reid, Milt Kogan, Milton
Selzer, Claudio Martinez

A drunken bureaucrat finds himself behind bars; Wojo has the
local deli closed for minor health-code infractions; and Chano
nabs the twelve-year-old burglar who robbed his apartment.

8 Ms. Cop   March 13, 1975
Writers: Danny Arnold, Chris Hayward
Director: Noam Pitlik
Guest Stars: Linda Lavin, Howard Platt, Wynn Irwin

The detectives are put off by the determined lady cop who arrives
on temporary transfer to the Twelfth; and Chano gets the goods
on an obscene caller.

Linda Lavin's Detective Janice Wentworth would be reassigned to the
Twelfth for a stay of duty that lasted throughout the show's second year.

9 Vigilante   March 20, 1975
Writers: Danny Arnold, Chris Hayward
Story: Howard Albrecht, Sol Weinstein
Director: Noam Pitlik
Guest Stars: Titos Vandis, Gabe Dell, Marla Gibbs, Lee de
Broux, Milt Kogan, Nick Holt

An elderly vigilante defends his neighborhood against muggers;
Luger complains that Barney's squad isn't despised enough by
the citizenry; and Wojo arrests a transvestite teamster.

James Gregory's gruff but avuncular Inspector Luger was inspired by Danny Arnold's friend Barney Ruditsky, a roaring-twenties racket-buster whose life was immortalized on "The Lawless Years," an NBC cop show that ran from 1959 to 1961. Oddly enough, Jim Gregory played Ruditsky in that series as well.

10   The Guest   March 27, 1975
Writers: Danny Arnold, Chris Hayward, William Taub
Director: Noam Pitlik
Guest Stars: Herb Edelman, Jack DeLeon, Ed McCready, Milt Kogan

Wojo eats a poisoned sandwich that was intended for their prisoner, a nervous mob accountant; and Chano sets up a narcotics buy—with the detectives' own cash.

11   Escape Artist   April 10, 1975
Writers: Howard Leeds, Danny Arnold, Chris Hayward
Director: Noam Pitlik
Guest Stars: Roscoe Lee Browne, Leonard Frey, Danny Dayton, Judson Pratt, Reid Cruickshanks

The Twelfth plays host to a philosophical escape artist; Harris begins work on a police novel; and a crazy inventor attempts to fly.

Harris's literary leanings provide one of the show's most durable story lines—the eventual publication of *Blood on the Badge* in the sixth year would provide the author with both joy and anguish throughout the show's last three seasons.

12   Hair   April 17, 1975
Writers: Ron Pearlman, Danny Arnold, Chris Hayward
Story: Jerry Ross
Director: Allen Baron
Guest Stars: Michael Lembeck, Henry Beckman, Florence Stanley, Charles Fleischer

A long-haired loner from narcotics is transferred to the Twelfth Precinct; and Bernice is alarmed when Fish spends an afternoon investigating a massage parlor.

13 The Hero   May 1, 1975
Writers: Danny Arnold, Chris Hayward
Director: Noam Pitlik
Guest Stars: Todd Bridges, Cal Gibson

Chano is involved in a shoot-out with a pair of armed robbers; and Liz brings in a twelve-year-old who tried to rob her with a stick.

1975/76 THE SECOND SEASON

Year-End Rating: 19.0 (38th place)

As executive producer, Danny Arnold continues to perform and supervise a wide array of creative tasks in the second year. Arne Sultan joins Chris Hayward as producer for the show's first full season, and Noam Pitlik is established as the show's primary director, a distinction he will maintain throughout most of the series's run.

14 Doomsday   September 11, 1975
Writers: Danny Arnold, Chris Hayward, Arne Sultan
Director: Noam Pitlik
Guest Stars: William Windom, J. J. Barry, Steve Landesberg

A nervous human bomb threatens to blow himself up to protest the sorry state of Western civilization; the plumbing conks out; and Wojo arrests a bogus priest.

The guest cast is made up of friends, old and new. William Windom had starred in Danny Arnold's 1969 comedy "My World and Welcome to It"; J. J. Barry probably spent more time in the Twelfth Precinct's cage than any other actor; and Steve Landesberg would be invited back to play Sergeant Dietrich the following season.

15 The Social Worker   September 18, 1975
Writers: Danny Arnold, Chris Hayward, Arne Sultan
Director: Noam Pitlik
Guest Stars: Art Metrano, Herbie Faye, Alex Henteloff

The detectives book a master forger, but Barney is preoccupied with worry after Liz begins her new job as a social worker on the streets of the South Bronx.

16 The Layoff September 25, 1975
Writers: Danny Arnold, Chris Hayward, Arne Sultan
Director: Noam Pitlik
Guest Stars: Bob Dishy, Oliver Clark, Candy Azzara, Sandra Deel, Milt Kogan

New York City's cash crunch forces Barney to lay off Chano, Harris, and Wojo; a manicurist stabs her client; and an unemployed stockbroker turns purse snatcher.

17 Ambush October 2, 1975
Writers: Danny Arnold, Chris Hayward, Arne Sultan
Director: Noam Pitlik
Guest Stars: David Doyle, Dick O'Neill, Milt Kogan

Barney is offered a new job in Florida; and the men are shocked to discover that bystanders failed to assist after Yemena was shot in an ambush.

18 Heat Wave October 9, 1975
Writers: Danny Arnold, Chris Hayward
Story: Danny Arnold, Chris Hayward, Arne Sultan
Director: Noam Pitlik
Guest Stars: Linda Lavin, Janet Ward, Harold Oblong, Gloria Calomee, Paul Lichtman, Angelo Gnazzo

Wojo and Wentworth go undercover to lure a rapist into the open; and a wife reports her husband for assault and battery.

19 The Arsonist October 16, 1975
Writer: Tony Sheehan
Director: Noam Pitlik
Guest Stars: Roger Bowen, Jack Somack, Leonard Stone, Steve Franken

The detectives suspect arson after a rash of fires; and Chano arrests a man for shooting a subway candy machine.

The first script by Tony Sheehan, a prolific writer whose eventual contribution to the series would be incalculable. Sheehan was hired on the basis of a spec script he'd written for "M*A*S*H"—in longhand, on a legal pad—while still a student at UCLA. Larry Gelbart recommended him to Danny Arnold, who hired the talented young scribe as story editor. During his long tenure on the show, he would be a credited author on over sixty "Barney Miller" teleplays, and an uncredited contributor to scores of others.

20   Hotel   October 23, 1975
Writers: Danny Arnold, Chris Hayward, Arne Sultan
Story: Chris Hayward, Danny Arnold
Director: Noam Pitlik
Guest Stars: Linda Lavin, Robert Mandan, Adam Arkin,
Queenie Smith, Beatrice Colen, Joe Medalis, Arnold Soboloff

Wojo and Wentworth pose as a wealthy couple to flush out a burglary ring in a luxury hotel; and a college student is arrested for registering with his underage girlfriend.

The smoldering romance between Wojo and Wentworth was actually part of Danny Arnold's grand plan to please ABC's insatiable appetite for a spin-off series, preferably starring Fish. The producer refused— why jeopardize the chemistry of "Barney Miller" by pulling Fish out of the squad room for his own series? Instead, Arnold's novel solution proposed pulling *all of the detectives* out of the squad room—one at a time—for a separate anthology series that each week would examine the private life of a different member of the squad. Wentworth and Wojo's romance was projected as the basis for one story line; and alternating episodes might pick up Barney's life at home with Liz, or perhaps the camera would follow Fish home to a house full of wayward foster kids. Unfortunately, the producer abandoned the project as too ambitious for "Barney Miller's" already overworked staff, though he did salvage the latter story line as the basis for the "Fish" spin-off, which finally aired two years later.

21   Discovery   October 30, 1975
Writers: Tom Reeder, Danny Arnold, Chris Hayward
Director: Lee Bernhardi
Guest Stars: Jack DeLeon, Ray Stewart, Norman Rice, Philip Sterling

The department's computers declare Fish dead; and an impostor harasses neighborhood gays while posing as a detective from the Twelfth Precinct.

22   You Dirty Rat   November 13, 1975
Writers: Arne Sultan, Danny Arnold, Chris Hayward
Story: Arne Sultan
Director: Noam Pitlik
Guest Stars: Ned Glass, J. Pat O'Malley, Franklyn Ajaye, Val
Bisoglio, Del Vecchio

A hungry rat is the suspect when two pounds of marijuana come
up missing from the evidence locker; and a vagrant spends the
night in a department store.

23   Horse Thief   November 20, 1975
Writer: Tony Sheehan
Director: Noam Pitlik
Guest Stars: Ron Masak, Jack Dodson, Liam Dunn, Bruce
Solomon, Judy Cassmore

A hansom-cab driver's horse is stolen during the Bicentennial
celebration; and a canny streetwalker uses patriotic souvenirs
to mask her trade.

24   Rain   November 27, 1975
Writer: Tony Sheehan
Story: Danny Arnold, Chris Hayward
Director: Noam Pitlik
Guest Stars: Sidney Miller, Phil Leeds, Paul Lichtman

The squad room ceiling springs a leak; and the officers are forced
to put up with a steady stream of bad jokes from an incarcerated
comedian.

25   Fish   December 4, 1975
Writers: Danny Arnold, Chris Hayward, Herbert Baker
Director: Noam Pitlik
Guest Stars: Doris Belack, Steve Landesberg, Emily Levine,
Darryl Seman

Fish worries about his job when a new detective is assigned to
the precinct after his doctor puts him on restricted duty.

Stand-up comic Steve Landesberg debuts as Sergeant Arthur Dietrich, a one-shot tryout whose low-key appeal made him a natural for
the squad room ensemble. He was added to the precinct's permanent
roster the following season.

26   Hot Dogs   December 11, 1975
   Writer: Tony Sheehan
   Story: Arne Sultan, Danny Arnold, Chris Hayward
   Director: Lee Bernhardi
   Guest Stars: Jonelle Allen, Nellie Bellflower, David L. Lander,
   Howard Honig

A pair of eager lady cops makes an overzealous drug bust; and
a confused husband identifies his missing wife with a dime-store
photo of Jean Harlow.

27   Protection   December 18, 1975
   Writer: Tom Reeder
   Story: Danny Arnold, Chris Hayward, Tom Reeder
   Director: Noam Pitlik
   Guest Stars: Jack Somack, Ralph Manza, Ray Sharkey

A protection racket springs up amid rumors that the precinct is
about to be shuttered; and a local hood confesses to a crime
that can't be proven.

28   Happy New Year   January 8, 1976
   Writers: Danny Arnold, Chris Hayward, Arne Sultan
   Director: Bruce Bilson
   Guest Stars: Edith Diaz, Johnny Lamotta

The precinct hosts a suicidal man on New Year's Eve; and Wojo
delivers a pregnant shoplifter's baby.

Edith Diaz also played the very expectant Puerto Rican mother who
gave birth in a crowded elevator on "All in the Family" exactly four
years earlier.

29   Sniper   January 22, 1976
   Writers: Tom Reeder, Danny Arnold, Chris Hayward
   Director: Lee Bernhardi
   Guest Stars: Charlotte Rae, Jay Robinson, Sully Boyar

A space-age travel agent bilks a couple out of the cost of a round-
trip ticket to Saturn; and Wojo and Luger are targets of a sniper
outside the station house.

30   Fear of Flying   January 29, 1976
Writer: Reinhold Weege
Director: Lee Bernhardi
Guest Stars: Jack Riley, Valerie Curtin, Charles Murphy

Wojo must overcome his fear of flying when he's chosen to accompany an extradited bigamist to Cleveland.

Writer Reinhold Weege would become a major force in the show's middle years, first as a prolific writer and story editor, and finally as producer in the fifth year. He learned his lessons well; his 1984 NBC series, "Night Court," owed a considerable debt of inspiration to "Barney Miller."

31   Block Party   February 12, 1976
Writer: Tom Reeder
Director: Noam Pitlik
Guest Stars: Larry Bishop, Linda Lavin, George Murdock, Stanley Brock

Wentworth stops an assassin at a block party, but is frustrated when Chano gets all the credit.

32   Massage Parlor   February 19, 1976
Writer: Tony Sheehan
Director: Dennis Steinmetz
Guest Stars: Linda Lavin, Florence Halop, Meg Wyllie, Kenneth Tigar, Charles Frank, Janet Ruff, Opal Euard

Wentworth goes undercover in a massage parlor and gets the goods on a bewildered midnight cowboy; and an elderly woman is arrested for mugging.

This would be Linda Lavin's last appearance as Detective Wentworth. The actress left "Barney Miller" to star in "Alice," the long-running CBS series that premiered the following season.

33   The Psychiatrist   February 26, 1976
Writers: Tony Sheehan, Danny Arnold, Chris Hayward
Story: Greg Tiefer
Director: Noam Pitlik
Guest Stars: Fred Sadoff, Neil J. Schwartz, Martin Garner

Wojo's aggressive tendencies come under the scrutiny of a psychiatrist who insists that the officer is unfit to carry a gun.

34 The Kid   March 4, 1976
Writers: Tony Sheehan, Danny Arnold, Chris Hayward
Director: Stan Lathan
Guest Stars: Charles Murphy, Arny Freeman, Angelina Estrada,
Jose Flores

A good samaritan returns to retrieve the unclaimed cash he turned
in a month earlier; and Fish is smitten by the mother of a teenage
pickpocket.

35 The Mole   March 18, 1976
Writers: Danny Arnold, Chris Hayward, Reinhold Weege
Director: Mark Warren
Guest Stars: Dean Santoro, Richard Russell Ramos, Ron Carey,
Severn Darden

Fish agonizes over an upcoming operation; and Harris and Wojo
track a burglar through the sewers.

Ron Carey plays the subterranean thief who would return to the
precinct as the uniformed cop Officer Carl Levitt at the start of the
following season. The episode also marks the final appearance of Greg
Sierra's Chano. The actor eventually resurfaced in "AES Hudson Street,"
a short-lived attempt by "Barney Miller's" creators to duplicate the chemistry of the Twelfth Precinct in a hospital emergency room.

The producers were confident the series could withstand the loss of
major characters like Chano—and eventually, Fish. As Danny Arnold
observed, "The squad room itself is as much a personality as any of the
characters. Our audience buys the situation, and change is part of it."

1976/77   THE THIRD SEASON

Year-End Rating: 22.2 (17th place)

The third season sees the precinct's only major personnel shake-up,
when Chano and Wentworth leave the series to be replaced by new
recruits Dietrich and Levitt, and briefly, Detective Maria Battista. The
show's creative team also loses a major contributor when producer Chris
Hayward departs for greener pastures and, perhaps, shorter hours elsewhere.

Danny Arnold serves as producer in the show's third year. Story
editor Tony Sheehan is credited on most of the season's scripts; and

there are multiple submissions from Reinhold Weege, Tom Reeder, and Danny Arnold. Jerry Ross is the executive script consultant.

36 Evacuation   September 23, 1976
Writer: Danny Arnold
Story: Chris Hayward, Danny Arnold
Director: Noam Pitlik
Guest Stars: Joe Petrullo, Denise Miller, Paul Lichtman, Kenneth Mars

Wojo decides to beef up evacuation procedures for New York's eleven million citizens; and a young thief finds a friend in Fish.

37 Quarantine (Part 1)   September 30, 1976
Writer: Tony Sheehan
Director: Lee Bernhardi
Guest Stars: Paula Shaw, Jack DeLeon, Ray Stewart, Arthur Peterson, David Darlow, Michael Kerns, Dennis Spiegelman

The station house is filled to capacity when authorities place it under quarantine because an ailing burglar may have smallpox.

38 Quarantine (Part 2)   October 7, 1976
Writers: Tony Sheehan, Danny Arnold
Director: Noam Pitlik
Guest Stars: Paula Shaw, Jack DeLeon, Ray Stewart

The continued threat of smallpox forces an unlikely gathering of characters to spend the night in the Twelfth Precinct.

The underlying tension of a medical quarantine provides the ideal setting for a classic "Barney Miller" episode. The precinct emerges as a downtrodden Grand Hotel, with crackling dialogue flying nonstop among the disparate personalities suddenly forced together for a long night in very close quarters. Despite his initial resistance, Wojo comes to accept Marty and his gay lover; Inspector Luger learns to lighten up; and the writers even grant Fish a few privileged moments as the weary detective forms a tender platonic bond with an imperturbable prostitute—and for at least one night in his life, someone calls him Phil.

39 Bus Stop October 14, 1976
Writers: Tony Sheehan, Danny Arnold, Reinhold Weege, Jerry Ross
Story: Reinhold Weege, Chris Hayward, Danny Arnold
Director: Noam Pitlik
Guest Stars: Candy Azzara, Phil Bruns, Sal Viscuso, Florence Halop, Joe George, Howard Honig

A holdup man robs a busload of commuters and then faces their fury as they storm the precinct house.

40 The Election October 21, 1976
Writer: Tom Reeder
Director: Lee Bernhardi
Guest Stars: Brett Somers, Richard Venture, Gilbert Green, Steve Landesberg

On Election Day, a jailed shoplifter demands his right to cast a ballot; and the officers confront a husband who refuses to let his wife vote.

41 Werewolf October 28, 1976
Writers: Reinhold Weege, Tony Sheehan, Danny Arnold, Seymour Blicker
Story: Seymour Blicker, Tony Sheehan
Director: Noam Pitlik
Guest Stars: Kenneth Tigar, Janet MacLachlan, Queenie Smith, Jon Lormer

The usual loonies arrive during the full moon, including a man who swears he's turning into a werewolf.

42 The Recluse November 11, 1976
Writers: Reinhold Weege, Danny Arnold
Story: Chris Hayward, Reinhold Weege
Director: Bruce Bilson
Guest Stars: Arnold Soboloff, Ivor Francis, Florence Stanley, Denise Miller, John Cassisi

A doomsayer shares the cell with a recluse who hid in his apartment for three decades to avoid jury duty.

43 Noninvolvement   November 18, 1976
Writer: Reinhold Weege
Story: Chris Hayward, Danny Arnold, Reinhold Weege
Director: Bruce Bilson
Guest Stars: Mike Kellin, Ron Feinberg, June Gable, Oliver
Clark, Alex Henteloff, Lucille Meredith

Wojo arrests a man for refusing to interfere when he witnessed
a mugging in progress.

June Gable appears as Detective Maria Battista, a short-lived addition
to the precinct's ranks. "Every once in a while we'd bring in someone
new, to shake things up. But it never seemed to work out," explained
writer Tony Sheehan. "We had such a tight group that the newcomer always seemed like an outsider. It was very hard to get them past that point."

44 Power Failure   December 9, 1976
Writers: Tony Sheehan, Danny Arnold
Story: Rheinold Weege, Danny Arnold, Tony Sheehan
Director: Noam Pitlik
Guest Stars: Susan Brown, Arny Freeman, Stefan Gierasch,
Paul Lichtman

During a blackout, the station plays host to a suspect with a split
personality.

45 Christmas Story   December 23, 1976
Writers: Tony Sheehan, Reinhold Weege
Director: Bruce Bilson
Guest Stars: Nobu McCarthy, Jay Gerber, John Morgan Evans

Fish goes undercover as Santa Claus; Barney reluctantly invites
Luger to spend Christmas with his family; and Nick falls under
the spell of an Oriental call girl.

46 Hash   December 30, 1976
Writer: Tom Reeder
Director: Noam Pitlik
Guest Stars: Ed Peck, Walter Janowitz, George Perina, Michael
Tucci

It's a giddy evening at the Twelfth when the detectives sample
Wojo's girlfriend's brownies before anyone realizes her recipe
included an ample portion of hashish.

47 Smog Alert   January 6, 1977
Writer: Reinhold Weege
Story: Chris Hayward, Danny Arnold
Director: Bruce Bilson
Guest Stars: Lee Kessler, Alan Haufrect, June Gable

Fish bears up during a first-stage smog alert; and a suicidal woman strikes up a relationship with an obscene-graffiti artist.

48 Community Relations   January 13, 1977
Writers: Tony Sheehan, Dennis Koenig, Larry Balmagia
Story: Tony Sheehan, Winston Moss
Director: Noam Pitlik
Guest Stars: David Tress, Ralph Manza, Joseph Perry, Judson Morgan

A homeless old man confronts his former landlord with a musket; and a lawyer accuses Barney of harassment after he books a blind shoplifter.

49 The Rand Report   January 20, 1977
Writer: Reinhold Weege
Story: Roland Kibbee, Reinhold Weege
Director: Noam Pitlik
Guest Stars: Martin Garner, Anna Berger, John William Evans

Wojo resigns the force in protest after the department releases a critical study that recommends the detectives return to uniformed patrol.

50 Fire '77   January 27, 1977
Writer: Tony Sheehan
Director: Bruce Bilson
Guest Stars: Sal Viscuso, Howard Platt, K Callan, Russell Shannon

A suicidal couple is delighted when flames threaten to engulf the squad room after an arsonist sets fire to the station house.

51 Abduction   February 3, 1977
Writers: Tom Reeder, Tony Sheehan, Reinhold Weege
Director: Bruce Bilson
Guest Stars: Buddy Lester, Vivi Janiss, Rod Colbin, Jane Alice
Brandon, David Clennon, Buddy Lester, Florence Stanley

Nick's bookie is brought in; and a suburban couple turns to
Barney for help after they kidnap their daughter back from a
religious cult.

52 Sex Surrogate   February 10, 1977
Writers: Tony Sheehan, Dennis Koenig, Larry Balmagia
Story: Jerry Ross, Tony Sheehan
Director: Noam Pitlik
Guest Stars: Eugene Elman, Doris Roberts, Marilyn Sokol, Billy
Barty

A middle-aged woman shoots her husband for seeing a sexual
surrogate; and Harris suffers the ultimate indignity when he's
attacked by a gang of delinquents who ruin his suit.

53 Moonlighting   February 17, 1977
Writer: Reinhold Weege
Director: Noam Pitlik
Guest Stars: George Pentecost, Cal Gibson, John Dullaghan,
Jan Stuart Schwartz

Barney discovers Harris has been moonlighting; Dietrich arrests
a priest for fencing stolen goods; and a numbers racketeer uses
a retarded boy as a runner.

54 Asylum   February 24, 1977
Writers: Roland Kibbee, Tony Sheehan, Reinhold Weege,
Danny Arnold
Director: Alex March
Guest Stars: Ion Teodorescu, Michael Panaieff, David Clennon,
Louis Zito, Jack DeLeon

Wojo runs afoul of diplomatic protocol when he offers political
asylum to a Russian defector; and the squad room's old friend
Marty violates his probation with a half ounce of marijuana.

55 Group Home March 10, 1977

Writers: Tony Sheehan, Danny Arnold
Story: Dennis Koenig, Larry Balmagia
Director: Lee Bernhardi
Guest Stars: George Murdock, Don Calfa, Florence Stanley, John Cassisi

The squad tracks a mad bomber who's threatened to blow up an army recruiting office; and Fish has to dress as a woman when it's his turn for mugging detail.

The running joke of the mugging detail afforded the audience at least one good belly laugh every season, as each member of the squad took his turn in drag.

56 Strike (Part 1) March 24, 1977

Writer: Reinhold Weege
Story: Dennis Koenig, Larry Balmagia
Director: Jeremiah Morris
Guest Stars: Peter Hobbs, Peggy Pope

A woman is robbed by her computer date; and the detectives must decide whether to honor an unauthorized policeman's strike.

57 Strike (Part 2) March 31, 1977

Writers: Reinhold Weege, Tony Sheehan, Danny Arnold
Story: Dennis Koenig, Larry Balmagia
Director: Danny Arnold
Guest Stars: Peter Hobbs, Peggy Pope

Inspector Luger fills in for the striking detectives; and the woman who was robbed by her computer date refuses to press charges.

1977/78 THE FOURTH SEASON

Year-End Rating: 21.4 (17th place)

Fish retires from active duty at the top of the fourth season as the series moves into a very fertile middle period, with no creative drop-off in sight. Tony Sheehan is promoted to producer, and Reinhold Weege assumes the duties of story editor, though both will continue to write most of the show's scripts. Other memorable fourth-year stories are contributed by Dennis Koenig, Larry Balmagia, Tom Reeder, and executive producer Danny Arnold.

58   Good-bye, Mr. Fish (Part 1)   September 15, 1977
   Writers: Reinhold Weege, Danny Arnold
   Director: Danny Arnold
   Guest Stars: Stanley Brock, Arny Freeman, Jack Somack,
   Gregory V. Karliss

Barney tries to quell a neighborhood vigilante group; and Fish fails to arrive for work on his retirement day.

59   Good-bye, Mr. Fish (Part 2)   September 22, 1977
   Writer: Reinhold Weege
   Director: Danny Arnold
   Guest Stars: Larry Gelman, Timothy Jerome, Florence Stanley

Fish arrives for work as usual, refusing to acknowledge his forced retirement from the department.

The long-suffering detective had been dividing his time between the squad room and "Fish," the spin-off that began the previous February, despite resistance from Danny Arnold, who preferred to keep Abe Vigoda's blues bottled up as a potent source of laughter in the squad room. It was a decision Vigoda protested with vigor. "I found myself with a very unhappy actor on my hands," Arnold remembers. "Abe would walk around the set like a man in shock. Who was I to deprive an actor of his once-in-a-lifetime break? Finally I said, 'Okay—just stay through the third year of 'Barney Miller,' and we'll go with your show, too." With this episode, the senior detective retires to pursue his fortunes full-time in the spin-off that, ironically, lasted only thirty-four episodes.

60   Bugs   September 29, 1977
   Writers: Dennis Koenig, Larry Balmagia, Tony Sheehan
   Director: David Swift
   Guest Stars: Sammy Smith, Mari Gorman, Paula Shaw, Robert
   Costanzo, Lavell Roby

The detectives discover that someone has planted electronic bugs throughout the squad room.

61 Corporation   October 6, 1977
Writers: Lee H. Grant, Tony Sheehan, Danny Arnold
Story: Lee H. Grant
Director: Hal Linden
Guest Stars: David Dukes, Fran Ryan, Vernon Weddle

A vigilante environmentalist who's been sabotaging a chemical plant faces the corporation's high-powered lawyer.

62 Burial   October 20, 1977
Writer: Michael Russnow
Director: Danny Arnold
Guest Stars: Sy Kramer, Jack Kruschen, Abe Vigoda

After a suspect steals his best friend's corpse and refuses to tell anyone where he's hidden it, Fish returns to help Barney find the body.

63 Copy Cat   October 27, 1977
Writers: Douglas Wyman, Tony Sheehan
Director: Jeremiah Morris
Guest Stars: Don Calfa, Norman Bartold, Don Sherman, John Dullaghan

Prime time's cops and robbers provide inspiration for a criminal who mimics the felonies of TV police shows; and a drunk attempts armed robbery without a gun.

64 Blizzard   November 3, 1977
Writer: Tony Sheehan
Director: Danny Arnold
Guest Stars: Alex Henteloff, Lou Cutell, Lewis Charles, Tom Henschell

The officers are unable to remove a corpse from the station house during a blizzard; and an eccentric swears the snow is the start of a new ice age.

65 Chase November 17, 1977
Writers: Tom Reeder, Danny Arnold, Reinhold Weege
Director: Jeremiah Morris
Guest Stars: Luis Avalos, George Murdock, Marya Small, Joey Aresco, George Loros

Wojo wrecks a taxi that he borrows to chase a robbery suspect; and Lieutenant Scanlon enlists the help of a drug pusher to test the detectives' honesty.

66 Thanksgiving Story November 24, 1977
Writer: Reinhold Weege
Director: David Swift
Guest Stars: Ian Wolfe, George Skaff, Tom Lacy, Susan Davis, Anita Dangler, Kip King

The automat is the scene of a chaotic dinner when three mental patients sit down to a Thanksgiving feast.

67 Tunnel December 1, 1977
Writers: Tony Sheehan, Michael Russnow
Story: Michael Russnow
Director: David Swift
Guest Stars: Leonard Stone, J. J. Barry, Jay Gerber

Wojo gets buried underground on the trail of a burglar who's digging into the diamond exchange; and Harris looks desperately looks for a new apartment in Manhattan.

68 Atomic Bomb December 15, 1977
Writers: Tom Reeder, Reinhold Weege
Director: Noam Pitlik
Guest Stars: Phil Leeds, Karl Bruck, Stephen Pearlman, Al Ruscio, Will Seltzer, John Getz

The FBI arrives to investigate a college student who built a working nuclear bomb for his physics class project.

69 The Bank   January 5, 1978
Writer: Tony Sheehan
Director: Noam Pitlik
Guest Stars: Sandy Sprung, Peter Jurasik, Jodie Mann

A man with a vasectomy wreaks havoc when he accuses the owner of a sperm bank of destroying his only remaining sperm sample.

70 The Ghost   January 12, 1978
Writer: Reinhold Weege
Director: Lee Bernhardi
Guest Stars: Nehemiah Persoff, Titos Vandis, Kenneth Tigar, Caroline McWilliams

The detectives are skeptical of a man's claim that he's being pestered by a poltergeist, until a string of unexplainable occurrences give them pause.

71 Appendicitis   January 19, 1978
Writer: Tony Sheehan
Director: Noam Pitlik
Guest Stars: Jack Bernardi, Michael Durrell

An aging bounty hunter and a sugar addict are the precinct's latest guests; and Yemena is rushed to the hospital after an appendicitis attack.

72 Rape   January 26, 1978
Writer: Dennis Koenig
Director: Noam Pitlik
Guest Stars: Michael Pataki, Joyce Jameson, William Bogert, Dick Balduzzi, Linda Dano

A woman accuses her husband of raping her; Yemena is thrilled that New York has legalized offtrack betting; and a master of disguise embarks on a crime spree.

73   Eviction (Part 1)   February 2, 1978
Writers: Tom Reeder, Reinhold Weege
Director: Noam Pitlik
Guest Stars: Dave Madden, Rosana Soto, Felipe Turich

Barney refuses to comply with the court-ordered eviction of the impoverished residents of a condemned hotel.

74   Eviction (Part 2)   February 9, 1978
Writers: Tom Reeder, Reinhold Weege
Director: Noam Pitlik
Guest Stars: Dave Madden, George Kirby, John Clavin, Donna Bacalia

Barney intermediates when a SWAT team is dispatched to remove the stubborn occupants of a condemned hotel.

75   Wojo's Problem   February 23, 1978
Writer: Tony Sheehan
Director: Max Gail
Guest Stars: Ray Girardin, Henry Slate, Mari Gorman, Stanley Brock

Wojo's problem is a case of temporary impotence; the squad faces the jealous husband of their new female detective; and a wheelchair-bound shoplifter escapes.

Mari Gorman debuts as Detective Roslyn Licori. Like those of her predecessors, her assignment to the precinct would be temporary.

76   "Quo Vadis?"   March 2, 1978
Writer: Tony Sheehan
Story: Douglas Wyman, Tony Sheehan
Director: Alex March
Guest Stars: Ivy Bethune, Barbara Barrie

An irate woman demands the closing of an art gallery's nude-painting exhibit; and marital problems between Barney and Liz reach a standoff.

77 Hostage   March 23, 1978
Writer: Reinhold Weege
Story: Reinhold Weege, Chris Hayward
Director: Hal Linden
Guest Stars: Earle Towne, Oliver Clark, Don Calfa

A prisoner holds the precinct hostage; Harris finds an apartment
in the Village; and a ventriloquist is held responsible for his
dummy's lewd remarks.

78 Evaluation   May 4, 1978
Writer: Larry Balmagia
Director: Noam Pitlik
Guest Stars: Richard Libertini, Kay Medford, Eugene Elman

Barney must file an evaluation on each of the men; a mom-and-
pop porno store is vandalized; and Dietrich books a kook who
insists he has no name, only a number.

79 The Sighting   May 11, 1978
Writer: Tony Sheehan
Story: Reinhold Weege, Carol Gary
Director: Alex March
Guest Stars: Doris Roberts, Peter Hobbs, Jack Bannon

Wojo's excuse for tardiness is that he was up late the night before
tracking a UFO; and a woman reports her husband for turning
all their possessions into gold.

80 Inauguration   May 18, 1978
Writers: Reinhold Weege, Carol Gary
Director: Alex March
Guest Stars: Philip Sterling, Basil Hoffman, Florence Hallop

Harris has to decide whether to leave the squad after he's offered
a job in the mayor's office.

1978/79   THE FIFTH SEASON

Year-End Rating: 22.8 (15th place)

Fifth-year producers are Tony Sheehan and Reinhold Weege, who
also serve as the season's uncredited story editors. And once again,

Danny Arnold is the series's executive producer and uncredited script consultant. Notable additions to the show's small stable of writers include Wally Dalton and Shelley Zellman, and Frank Dungan and Jeff Stein, two prolific teams who make their initial contributions in the fifth year.

81 Kidnapping (one hour)   September 14, 1978
Writers: Reinhold Weege, Danny Arnold, Tony Sheehan
Director: Noam Pitlik
Guest Stars: Fred Sadoff, Beverly Sanders, Todd Susman, Barrie Youngfellow, Ralph Manza, John O'Connell

A department-store magnate is held for ransom by a political extremist; and Wojo arrests a prostitute and her john—an Arkansas traveler.

82 The Search   September 21, 1978
Writers: Bob Colleary, Tony Sheehan
Story: Bob Colleary
Director: Noam Pitlik
Guest Stars: Jenny O'Hara, Bruce Kirby, Arny Freeman

Television's Mr. Science is in the holding tank; Harris shaves his mustache for mugging detail; and the detectives help a woman find her father after twenty-eight years.

83 Dog Days   September 28, 1978
Writer: Reinhold Weege
Director: Noam Pitlik
Guest Stars: Rosalind Cash, Joseph Perry

Wojo is bitten by a possibly rabid German shepherd when he attempts to bust an illegal dogfight ring; and Barney has the blues over his impending separation.

84 The Baby Broker   October 5, 1978
Writer: Tony Sheehan
Director: Noam Pitlik
Guest Stars: Fredric Cook, Phoebe Dorin, Michael Durrell, Ivor Francis, Martine Getty

A couple tries to prevent a pregnant German girl from leaving the country by claiming that she's carrying *their* baby.

The intriguing premise of an unscrupulous lawyer's attempts to sell an as-yet-unborn infant to a childless couple—only to have the young mother change her mind—yields an archetypal "Barney Miller" situation: A question of morality is confused by the poignancy of human desire. And, not surprisingly, the law is a woefully ill-equipped arbiter. The jokes—and as always, there are plenty—each reveal something new about the characters and situation as the story dictates its own tentative, if far from happy, conclusion. The childless couple, now likely to remain that way, find some consolation in the pain they share; the single mother is offered scant encouragement by Dietrich; and, ironically, the lawyer who engineereed the whole mess is the only one to walk away scot-free. As in all the series's best scripts, the offbeat subject matter suggests no easy answers—and, refreshingly, the show's creators would never presume to impose any.

85 Accusation October 12, 1978
Writers: Wally Dalton, Shelley Zellman
Director: Max Gail
Guest Stars: George Murdock, Eugene Elman, Ruth Warshawsky, Michael Tucci, Miriam Byrd Netherly

A lonely woman accuses Dietrich of making indecent advances; and Yemena arrests a rabbi for running a gambling operation in his synagogue.

86 The Prisoner October 19, 1978
Writers: Reinhold Weege, Wally Dalton, Shelley Zellman
Director: Noam Pitlik
Guest Stars: Jeff Corey, Peggy Pope, Bruce Glover, Henry Jones

A newly released parolee discovers he was happier behind bars; and the detectives book a burglar's widow when she decides to carry on the family trade.

87 Loan Shark November 2, 1978
Writer: Tony Sheehan
Story: Judith Anne Nielsen, Richard William Beban, Mario Roccuzzo, Bob Colleary
Director: Noam Pitlik
Guest Stars: Boris Aplon, Lewis Charles, Larry B. Scott, Mario Roccuzzo

After twenty years on the force, Yemena unexpectedly rebels; a tattoo artist refuses to remove his handiwork from a timid client; and Harris counsels a savvy teenage loan shark.

88 The Vandal November 9, 1978
Writers: Dennis Koenig, Tony Sheehan
Director: Noam Pitlik
Guest Stars: Jay Gerber, Howard Honig, Christopher Lloyd

A disgruntled TV fan assaults a network programmer in a coffee shop; and Levitt is the detectives' chief suspect when the squad room is vandalized.

The psychopathic vandal is played by Christopher Lloyd, soon to make his debut as "Taxi's" Reverend Jim Ignatowski.

89 The Harris Incident November 30, 1978
Writers: Wally Dalton, Shelley Zellman, Reinhold Weege
Director: Noam Pitlik
Guest Stars: Ed Peck, Michael Lombard, Marilyn Chris, Rick Waln

Harris is shot at by a pair of prejudiced patrolmen who assume he's a felon because of his skin color; and a stockbroker is arrested for panhandling.

90 The Radical December 7, 1978
Writer: Tony Sheehan
Story: Lee H. Grant
Director: Noam Pitlik
Guest Stars: Corey Fischer, Stuart Pankin, Craig Richard Nelson

Inspector Luger locks horns with a radical fugitive from the 1960s underground; and Harris collars a rotund and very defensive burglar.

91 Toys   December 14, 1978
   Writers: Wally Dalton, Shelley Zellman, Tony Sheehan
   Story: Wally Dalton, Shelley Zellman
   Director: Noam Pitlik
   Guest Stars: Zachary Berger, Barbara Barrie, Walter Janowitz,
   Sidney Lassick

Barney has little cause to be jolly as he faces his first holiday
since his separation from Liz with a claustrophobic thief and a
pair of feuding toymakers.

The long-running story line that ended in Barney's trial separation
from Liz didn't sit well with a sizable portion of the show's loyal audience, and they made their opinions known. Producer Tony Sheehan
recalls, "We got letters telling us, 'Don't do this! They have the best
marriage on television.' But the funny thing is, she wasn't even *on* the
show anymore! We came up with the separation story line to bring
Barbara back—because we liked her and loved using her character—
but before that, they hadn't seen Liz in years! And still we got all these
letters about what a wonderful marriage they had."

92 The Indian   January 4, 1979
   Writer: Reinhold Weege
   Story: Richard William Beban, Judith Anne Nielsen, Reinhold
   Weege
   Director: Noam Pitlik
   Guest Stars: Charles White Eagle, Phil Leeds, Richard Stahl,
   Dino Natali

A foot fetishist steals a woman's shoes right off her feet; and
Wojo befriends an aged Indian who wants to be allowed to die
quietly in Central Park.

Wojo, easily the most openly compassionate of all the detectives,
refuses to abandon the old man at Bellevue. Instead, he returns to the
park, where he sits with the Indian in silent vigil, until, at last, the brave
dies—as he wished, in peace. When the detective later explains how he
defied procedure, Barney can't help but forgive him. Wojo broke the
rules but respected a higher order, and, as the Captain realizes, there
are some things that just aren't covered in the police manual.

93   Voice Analyzer   January 11, 1979
Writers: James Bonnet, Reinhold Weege
Story: James Bonnet
Director: Noam Pitlik
Guest Stars: George Murdock, Phil Roth, Allan Rich, Barry Pearl

Suspicious Lieutenant Scanlon tries to root out corruption with the aid of a voice-activated lie detector; and a furrier files a fraudulent burglary report.

94   The Spy   January 18, 1979
Writer: Tony Sheehan
Director: Noam Pitlik
Guest Stars: Philip Sterling, Estelle Omens, Stanley Brock, Flip Reade

A mime is charged with disorderly conduct; and an unemployed—and extremely paranoid—spy holds the squad room hostage.

95   Wojo's Girl (one hour)   January 25, 1979
Writers: Tony Sheehan, Danny Arnold
Director: Noam Pitlik
Guest Stars: Darlene Parks, Michael Conrad, Philip Bruns,
Lewis Arquette, Peter Hobbs, Doris Roberts

A man threatens to leave his wife to become a soldier of fortune; and Wojo moves in with his new girlfriend, a reformed prostitute.

96   Middle Age   February 1, 1979
Writers: Reinhold Weege, Danny Arnold
Story: Wally Dalton, Shelley Zellman
Director: Noam Pitlik
Guest Stars: Nehemiah Persoff, Richard Libertini, Raleigh
Bond, Kres Mersky

Barney worries about his encroaching middle age; a Hassidic diamond trader is robbed; and a decathlon hopeful is arrested for disorderly conduct.

97 The Counterfeiter February 8, 1979
Writers: Frank Dungan, Jeff Stein, Reinhold Weege
Director: Max Gail
Guest Stars: Jack Riley, J. Pat O'Malley, George Pentecost,
Susan Davis

Harris is delighted by the story potential of a colorful old counterfeiter; and a man assaults the plastic surgeon who operated
on his wife.

98 Open House February 15, 1979
Writers: Wally Dalton, Shelley Zellman, Tony Sheehan
Director: Noam Pitlik
Guest Stars: Allan Miller, Christopher Lloyd, David Fresco,
Carmen Filipi

A psychiatrist refuses to divulge the name of a known arsonist
in his care; and the Twelfth Precinct holds an open house that
attracts only vagrants.

99 Identity March 1, 1979
Writer: Tom Reeder
Director: Noam Pitlik
Guest Stars: Jack Somack, Don Calfa, David Clennon, Kip King

The Justice Department requests immunity for a thief who's been
given a new identity in a witness-relocation program; and Dietrich saves Harris's life.

Harris, burdened by the enormity of his debt to Dietrich, blows off
steam by admonishing a subway crazy with a terse outline of the precinct's minimum requirement for its guests: "I don't care if you're psy-
chotic—just don't *whine* about it."

100 Computer Crime March 15, 1979
Writer: Calvin Kelly
Story: Calvin Kelly, Dennis Koenig
Director: Max Gail
Guest Stars: Mabel King, Barry Gordon, Rod Colbin, Roger
Brown

Dietrich apprehends a white-collar embezzler; and Harris is flabbergasted by a black doctor who claims to be cursed by voodoo.

101 Graveyard Shift   May 10, 1979
    Writer: Tony Sheehan
    Director: Noam Pitlik
    Guest Stars: Paul Lawrence Smith, Raymond Singer, Lee
    Kessler

Late-night visitors to the precinct include an irate tourist and an insomniac who's convinced he'll be possessed by a succubus once he dozes off.

102 Jack Soo, a Retrospective   May 17, 1979
    Writers: Various
    Director: Noam Pitlik

The cast offers an affectionate tribute to the late Jack Soo by reviewing Sergeant Nick Yemena's more memorable moments at the Twelfth Precinct.

Producer Danny Arnold had known the Korean-American actor since they both performed stand-up on the same Midwestern nightclub circuit in the late forties—before Soo made his Broadway splash in *Flower Drum Song* in the fifties. The producer's loyalty to the recently departed actor was so great that he refused to authorize a new photo to commemorate the show's fifth anniversary after Jack had gone into the hospital. "Nothing goes out without Jack," the producer insisted. "Use the old shots."

1979/80   THE SIXTH YEAR

Year-End Rating: 20.9 (21st place)

The show moves smoothly into a sixth year, despite major behind-the-scenes upheavals. After suffering a heart attack late in the fifth season, executive producer Danny Arnold would strictly curtail his active involvement for the duration of the sixth and seventh years. Director Noam Pitlik joins Tony Sheehan as producer, and associate producer Gary Shaw takes on the duties of co-producer for the remainder of the series's run. The team of Frank Dungan and Jeff Stein contributes most of the year's scripts—along with Tony Sheehan, when they sign as the new story editors.

103　Inquisition　　　　　　　　　　September 13, 1979
Writer: Tony Sheehan
Story: Jim Tisdale, Calvin Kelly
Director: Noam Pitlik
Guest Stars: George Murdock, Dino Natali, Norman Bartold, Peter Jurasik, David Darlow

An angry citizen takes an ax to a department-store Muzak machine; and Scanlon starts a witch-hunt to root out an anonymous gay officer in the Twelfth Precinct.

104　The Photographer　　　　　　September 20, 1979
Writer: Bob Colleary
Director: Noam Pitlik
Guest Stars: Sal Viscuso, Kenneth Tigar, Phil Leeds, Anita Dangler

A charming mugger poses as a photographer to lure his victims; and a would-be messiah scolds the Eighth Avenue pimps for debasing the harlots.

The detectives calmly accept the arrival of a streetwise Christ with healthy skepticism—though none are prepared to dismiss the possibility that he might *actually be* what he claims. It's a tacit acknowledgment that not even miracles are outside the realm of possibilities in the Twelfth Precinct.

105　Vacation　　　　　　　　　　September 27, 1979
Writers: Frank Dungan, Jeff Stein
Director: Noam Pitlik
Guest Stars: Bruce Kirby, Jack Bernardi, Ben Slack

Nobody's very happy when Barney posts the annual vacation schedule; and two brothers feud when one refuses to donate a kidney to his ailing sibling.

106　The Brother　　　　　　　　　October 4, 1979
Writers: Wally Dalton, Shelley Zellman
Director: Noam Pitlik
Guest Stars: Gary Imhoff, John Christy Ewing, Elise Caitlin

A monk suspects foul play when one of his novitiates vanishes during a weekend in New York; and it's Dietrich's turn to cross-dress for mugging detail.

107   The Slave   October 18, 1979
Writers: Frank Dungan, Jeff Stein
Director: Noam Pitlik
Guest Stars: Manu Tupou, Sumant, Peg Shirley, Stanley Kamel

The detectives are shocked to discover that a chauffeur involved in a minor traffic accident is actually a slave indentured to a Burmese diplomat.

108   Strip Joint   November 1, 1979
Writers: Jaie Brashar, Frank Dungan, Jeff Stein
Director: Noam Pitlik
Guest Stars: Todd Susman, Rosana Soto, Walter Janowitz, Diana Canova, James Cromwell

A man is convinced that he's overdue to explode in spontaneous combustion; and a bookseller complains that a new strip joint is ruining his business.

109   The Bird   November 8, 1979
Writers: Frank Dungan, Jeff Stein
Story: Frank Dungan, Jeff Stein, Richard Beban, Judith Nielsen
Director: Noam Pitlik
Guest Stars: Michael Lombard, Martin Garner, Miriam Byrd Netherly

Harris's publisher insists that he obtain signed releases from the detectives; Wojo's new parrot dies; and a suicide hot-line operator decides to end it all.

110   The Desk   November 22, 1979
Writers: Frank Dungan, Jeff Stein
Director: Noam Pitlik
Guest Stars: Don Calfa, Jeff Corey, Alex Henteloff, Fred Sadoff

A partial lobotomy turns a master thief into a mindless zombie; and an Amish man is unable to use the telephone to call for help after he's been mugged.

111   The Judge   December 6, 1979
Writers: Frank Dungan, Jeff Stein, Tony Sheehan
Director: Noam Pitlik
Guest Stars: Peggy Pope, Philip Sterling

A judge assaults an attorney with his gavel; and a confused daytime-drama devotee reports dastardly deeds from TV soap operas as if they really happened.

112   The DNA Story   December 13, 1979
Writer: Rich Reinhart
Story: Rich Reinhart, Jaie Brasher
Director: Noam Pitlik
Guest Stars: Kay Medford, Jack Kruschen, A. Martinez, Stefan Gierasch, Raymond Singer

A dangerous disease culture is missing from a research lab; and a woman insists that her husband has been replaced by a clone.

113   The Dentist   December 27, 1979
Writers: Frank Dungan, Jeff Stein
Director: Noam Pitlik
Guest Stars: Oliver Clark, Jenny O'Hara, Arthur Malet, Estelle Omens

A dentist is accused of taking advantage of his female patients; and Wojo books a man accused of disturbing the peace by making noises with his hands.

114   People's Court   January 3, 1980
Writers: Frank Dungan, Jeff Stein
Director: Noam Pitlik
Guest Stars: Michael Tucci, Howard Honig, Rod Colbin, Ralph Manza, Helen Verbit

A census taker breaks into an apartment to count the uncooperative residents; and a burglar is kept locked in a basement cell by a vigilante tenants' group.

115   Vanished (Part 1)   January 10, 1980
   Writers: Tony Sheehan, Frank Dungan, Jeff Stein
   Director: Noam Pitlik
   Guest Stars: Elaine Giftos, John Dullaghan

Harris mysteriously vanishes during his undercover assignment as a vagrant; and a woman seeking a man to father her child considers candidates Dietrich and Wojo.

This episode contains a delightful exchange typical of writers Dungan, Stein, and Sheehan. Barney and Dietrich decide to have their first meaningful conversation, but within ten seconds their dialogue gets mired in small talk. The characters conclude, with keen insight, that the secret of their intimacy is in the distance they keep; when they face life and death together every day, what's the point in discussing philosophy?

116   Vanished (Part 2)   January 17, 1980
   Writers: Tony Sheehan, Frank Dungan, Jeff Stein
   Director: Noam Pitlik
   Guest Stars: Leonard Frey, David Fresco, Elaine Giftos, John Dullaghan, Ralph Olivia

Harris uncovers the secret of the shanghaied hobos; and Luger accepts a demotion in order to stay on the force past his official retirement date.

117   The Child Stealers   January 24, 1980
   Writers: Frank Dungan, Jeff Stein
   Director: Noam Pitlik
   Guest Stars: Joanna Miles, Ray Stewart, Jack DeLeon, Dino Natali, Richard Libertini

A divorced father reclaims custody of his son by kidnapping him; and the precinct is visited by a man who claims to be from the twenty-first century.

118   Guns   January 31, 1980
   Writers: Rich Reinhart, Tony Sheehan, Frank Dungan, Jeff Stein
   Director: Noam Pitlik
   Guest Stars: Jack Dodson, Madison Arnold, Mario Roccuzzo, David Paymer

Luger is despondent with his new assignment in the Twelfth; a man robs a liquor store with a duelist's pistol; and a citizen steals a TV from the police vault.

119 Uniform Day February 7, 1980
Writers: Richard Beban, Judith Nielsen
Director: Noam Pitlik
Guest Stars: Leonard Stone, Michael Alaimo, Stuart Pankin

Natty Sergeant Harris refuses to buckle under to a department edict that requires all detectives to dress in full uniform one day a year.

120 Dietrich's Arrest (Part 1) February 28, 1980
Writers: Tony Sheehan, Frank Dungan, Jeff Stein
Director: Noam Pitlik
Guest Stars: George Murdock, Candice Azzara, Peter Hobbs

A lottery winner causes a riot by tossing money from a window; and Dietrich is arrested for participating in an antinuclear protest rally.

121 Dietrich's Arrest (Part 2) March 6, 1980
Writers: Tony Sheehan, Frank Dungan, Jeff Stein
Director: Noam Pitlik
Guest Stars: George Murdock, Kay Medford, Allan Miller

Harris books Dietrich for his participation in the illegal protest; and a nuclear engineer is arrested for splashing atomic water on the demonstrators.

"With Dietrich, you're never quite sure just who he is or why he does things," Tony Sheehan told *TV Guide*. Despite his unflappable wit and carefully guarded irreverence, Dietrich surprised no one when he willingly faced a jail sentence in support of his principles. The writers merely cultivated the enigmatic quality that deadpan Steve Landesberg brought to the role, and as a result, the precinct's resident intellectual remained something of a paradox right to the end of the series. "We kind of like it that way," confessed Sheehan.

122   The Architect   March 27, 1980
   Writers: Tony Sheehan, Frank Dungan, Jeff Stein
   Story: Calvin Kelly, Jim Tisdale
   Director: Noam Pitlik
   Guest Stars: Paul Lieber, Chu Chu Malave, Norman Bartold,
   Jesse Aragon, David Clennon

An architect, unhappy with the changes carried out on a building
he designed, threatens to bomb the structure.

As the clock ticks away on the time bomb, the squad room is a
pressure cooker. And, as the producers had long since discovered, tension in a life-or-death situation creates the perfect climate for black humor.
When a pair of hapless gunmen storm into the precinct at the height of
the bomb scare, Barney patiently explains that he's busy, and that they'll
just have to sit down and wait their turn.

123   The Inventor   May 1, 1980
   Writers: Frank Dungan, Jeff Stein, Tony Sheehan
   Director: Noam Pitlik
   Guest Stars: Ben Piazza, Arny Freeman, Dan Frazer

Wojo tries to recall the details of a forgotten case while under
hypnosis; and an inventor is accused of stealing the plans for
his own invention.

124   Fog   May 8, 1980
   Writers: Frank Dungan, Jeff Stein, Tony Sheehan
   Story: Mark Brull
   Director: Noam Pitlik
   Guest Stars: J. J. Barry, Sidney Lassick, Robert Levine, William
   Dillard

A street musician assaults a string quartet that tried to move in
on his corner; and once again, Barney is turned down for deputy
inspector.

A thick fog enshrouds the station for one of the most downbeat
episodes of the entire series. His optimism spent after another rejection
for the deputy inspector's rank, Barney finally faces the grim futility of
his job. "It's getting harder and harder to keep a sense of purpose around
here," he grieves. "We bring people in, we ship 'em out. Nothing
changes." After the other detectives fail to raise his bitter spirits, it's

finally the mournful melody of the street musician's slow blues that draws the detective away from his gloom. As the sublime melancholy of the lonely horn fills the corners of Barney's own private dread, he rises to join his fellow detectives in the squad room. While outside his window, the fog only grows thicker.

1980/81   THE SEVENTH SEASON

Year-End Rating: 18.4 (33d place)

The sixth-season creative team—producers Pitlik and Sheehan and story editors Dungan and Stein—reprises their roles in the seventh year, with an able assist in the script department from newcomers Jordan Moffett and Nat Mauldin.

125   Homicide (Part 1)   October 30, 1980
   Writers: Frank Dungan, Jeff Stein
   Director: Noam Pitlik
   Guest Stars: Harold J. Stone, Marjorie Bennett, Jack Somack,
   Allyn Ann McLerie, Al Ruscio, Tricia O'Neill

The detectives book a man who admits he killed his barber after a bad haircut; and a woman decides to cancel the murder contract she put out on her husband.

126   Homicide (Part 2)   November 6, 1980
   Writers: Frank Dungan, Jeff Stein
   Director: Noam Pitlik
   Guest Stars: Ben Piazza, Tricia O'Neill, Harold J. Stone, Allyn
   Ann McLerie, Michael Alaimo, Jack Somack

The detectives attempt to find the hapless husband before the hit man does; and Harris makes a pass at the station's new crime photographer.

The Twelfth Precinct's temporary reassignment as a homicide-only squad created a near-panic among the show's most vocal fans. "Boy, did we get letters on that," writer Frank Dungan recalls. "People were so scared it was going to be permanent."

127 The Delegate   November 13, 1980
Writer: Jim Tisdale
Director: Noam Pitlik
Guest Stars: Phil Leeds, Bob Dishy, Bonnie Bartlett, Don Sherman, Tom Henschel

The precinct discovers an impostor in their ranks; and a vagrant claims he came to town as a delegate to the 1976 Democratic Convention and never left.

128 Dorsey   November 27, 1980
Writer: Tony Sheehan
Director: Noam Pitlik
Guest Stars: Paul Lieber, Michael Lombard, Darrell Zwerling, Cal Gibson, Andrew Bloch

The squad's new member insinuates that the detectives are all on the take; and a refugee from a no-smoking clinic complains that their methods are hazardous to his health.

Paul Lieber—previously seen as one of the gunmen in "The Architect" episode—arrives as Dorsey, yet another short-lived addition to the squad's roster.

129 Agent Orange   December 11, 1980
Writer: Tony Sheehan
Director: Noam Pitlik
Guest Stars: Paul Lieber, Peter Hobbs, Doris Roberts, Michael Currie, Joe Regalbuto, Louis Giambalvo, Lyman Ward, Robert Phalen

A woman complains when her apartment building goes nudist; and a confused vet blames his condition on exposure to the residue of germ warfare in Vietnam.

130 Call Girl   December 18, 1980
Writers: Frank Dungan, Jeff Stein
Director: Noam Pitlik
Guest Stars: Paul Lieber, Arthur Malet, Paul Kent, Tasha Zemrus, Sarina C. Grant, Nancy Bleier

Dorsey plays big brother to a young prostitute; Harris solicits stock tips from a well-heeled call girl; and Dietrich explores the new celibacy.

131 Resignation January 8, 1981
  Writers: Frank Dungan, Jeff Stein
  Director: Noam Pitlik
  Guest Stars: Allan Rich, Steve Franken, Peter Elbling, Mario
  Roccuzzo

Dietrich is plagued by guilt after he's forced to use his gun to
stop a robbery; and a playwright assaults an incompetent actor.

Unlike most TV supercops, the very human detectives of the Twelfth
often came up short in their struggle against the unrelenting stress of
police work. And yet, law enforcement agencies everywhere applauded
the series as the most realistic cop show on television. The New York
Police Department even conferred honorary membership on Barney's
squad, prompting the unintended irony of Los Angeles police chief Daryl
Gates's quip, "We view 'Barney Miller' as a comedy, but my colleagues in New York think of it as a documentary."

132 Field Associate January 15, 1981
  Writer: Jordan Moffet
  Director: Noam Pitlik
  Guest Stars: Jeffrey Tambor, Ned Glass, Florence Halop

Someone in the precinct has been leaking incriminating information to Internal Affairs; and a burglar celebrates his fiftieth
year in crime.

133 Movie (Part 1) January 22, 1981
  Writers: Frank Dungan, Jeff Stein
  Director: Noam Pitlik
  Guest Stars: Arny Freeman, Dino Natali, George Murdock,
  Dennis Howard

A veteran radio journalist roughs up an insipid TV news anchor;
and Harris scripts a porno-movie spectacular as part of an undercover vice operation.

134 Movie (Part 2) January 29, 1981
  Writers: Frank Dungan, Jeff Stein
  Director: Noam Pitlik
  Guest Stars: Jay Gerber, Ralph Manza, J. J. Barry, Norman
  Bartold

Harris proudly screens his overbudget hard-core spectacular; a blind man is mugged; and an overzealous charity collector stages a holdup.

135 The Psychic   February 5, 1981
Writers: Tony Sheehan, Frank Dungan, Jeff Stein
Director: Noam Pitlik
Guest Stars: Kenneth Tigar, Fred Sadoff, Rod Colbin, Larry Hankin, Robert Burgos

A linguist vandalizes a billboard to protest improper grammar in advertising; and a psychic foils a purse snatcher—*before* the crime is committed.

136 Stormy Weather   February 12, 1981
Writer: Nat Mauldin
Director: Noam Pitlik
Guest Stars: Phyllis Frelich, Robert Costanzo, Seymour Bernstein, Peter Wolf

Wojo plunges into the Hudson in pursuit of a looter; and Barney confronts a deaf woman with an unusual occupation—she's a hooker.

137 The Librarian   February 19, 1981
Writers: Tony Sheehan, Frank Dungan, Jeff Stein
Director: Noam Pitlik
Guest Stars: Allan Miller, Titos Vandis, Miriam Byrd Netherly, Zachary Berger, James Gallery

A librarian employs artillery to enforce order in her reading room; and a Gypsy is arrested for continually harassing the owner of a novelty store.

In one of the series's most chilling images, the kindly old man who sells whoopee cushions and dribble glasses is identified as a Nazi war criminal—even as a set of windup teeth chatter away on the desk. As always, the bizarre juxtaposition is not without humor—but when Harris finally reaches down to snap the toy teeth shut, there is no laugh track to break the eerie pall of silence that blankets the squad room.

On "Barney Miller," even canned laughter was used as a creative element in the producers' palette. The series hadn't been taped before a live studio audience since the third year, when the show's creators decided they could more carefully orchestrate their curious blend of comedy and drama without the wild card of audience reaction—as this particular episode certainly bears out.

138 Rachel   February 26, 1981
Writers: Tony Sheehan, Frank Dungan, Jeff Stein
Director: Homer Powell
Guest Stars: Anne Wyndham, Stanley Brock, Alex Henteloff, Chu Chu Malave

The owner of a sports store rigs a lethal trap to catch a burglar; shyster Arnold Ripner sues Harris for libel; and Wojo asks Barney's daughter for a date.

139 Contempt (Part 1)   March 12, 1981
Writers: Frank Dungan, Jeff Stein
Director: Noam Pitlik
Guest Stars: Dale Robinette, Larry Gelman, William Windom, Maggie Brown, John Dullaghan

Barney is charged with contempt of court when he refuses to name an informant; and a man complains he was refused service at a restaurant because he's ugly.

140 Contempt (Part 2)   March 19, 1981
Writers: Frank Dungan, Jeff Stein
Director: Noam Pitlik
Guest Stars: Jack Murdock, Maggie Brown, J. J. Barry, John Dullaghan

Harris assumes command of the precinct after Barney is jailed for his contempt citation.

141 The Doll   March 26, 1981
Writer: Tony Sheehan
Story: Jordan Moffet, Nat Mauldin
Director: Noam Pitlik
Guest Stars: A. Martinez, Philip Bruns, Oliver Clark, Dee Croxton

An expensive antique doll is kidnapped for ransom; a naive optician buys a bogus ticket to ride the NASA space shuttle; and Luger puts Barney in his will.

142 Lady and the Bomb					April 9, 1981
Writer: Lee H. Grant
Director: Noam Pitlik
Guest Stars: Abe Vigoda, Peggy Pope, Howard Mann, Judson Morgan, James Murtaugh, Ben Freedman

Sergeant Fish drops in for a visit; Arnold Ripner wins his libel suit against Harris; and a woman threatens to blow up the precinct with a homemade bomb.

143 Riot					April 30, 1981
Writers: Frank Dungan, Jeff Stein
Story: Greg Giangregorio
Director: Noam Pitlik
Guest Stars: Nehemiah Persoff, Howard Platt, Susan Tolsky, Victor Brant, Pat McNamara

A group of Hasidic Jews rally to protest the department's ineffectiveness; and a pair of urban survivalists are found living in steam tunnels beneath the city.

144 The Vests					May 7, 1981
Writer: Nat Mauldin
Director: Noam Pitlik
Guest Stars: Don Calfa, Alice Hirson, Warren Munson

The detectives are issued bulletproof vests; and Luger collects background information for the detectives' official obituaries.

145 The Rainmaker					May 14, 1981
Writers: Frank Dungan, Jeff Stein
Story: Paul Hunter, Frank Dungan, Jeff Stein
Director: Noam Pitlik
Guest Stars: J. Pat O'Malley, Beatrice Colen, Leonard Stone

An eccentric stages a rainmaking ceremony in Washington Square; and Wojo, Harris, and Dietrich all eye an opening in the vice squad.

146 Liquidation   May 21, 1981
   Writers: Frank Dungan, Jeff Stein
   Director: Noam Pitlik
   Guest Stars: Alex Henteloff, Walter Olkewicz, Martin Garner,
   James Cromwell

Harris liquidates everything he owns to pay off the $320,000 judgment Arnold Ripner was awarded in his libel suit against the detective.

1981/82   THE EIGHTH SEASON

Year-End Rating: 15.7 (54th place)

After seven and a half seasons, Danny Arnold decides to retire the Twelfth Precinct at the conclusion of the eighth season, marking the end of one of the longest unbroken streaks of top-flight writing, acting, and direction in the history of the situation comedy.

Producers Frank Dungan and Jeff Stein continue as story editors in the eighth season, and their considerable story contributions are augmented by memorable scripts from Nat Mauldin, Jordan Moffett, and Tony Sheehan, among others. Gary Shaw continues as co-producer; Gennaro Montanino, Danny Arnold, Lee Lochhead, and Bruce Bilson direct most of the year's episodes; and Roland Kibbee joins Danny Arnold as executive producer for the final year.

147 Paternity   October 29, 1981
   Writer: Nat Mauldin
   Director: Danny Arnold
   Guest Stars: Rebecca Holden, Dana Gladstone, Stephan
   Gierasch

A beauty queen has her purse snatched; an angry moviegoer vandalizes a theater for showing snuff films; and Wojo is slapped with a paternity suit.

148 Advancement   November 5, 1981
   Writers: Frank Dungan, Jeff Stein
   Director: Danny Arnold
   Guest Stars: Martin Garner, Anna Berger, Howard Honig,
   Mario Roccuzzo, Philip Simms

Luger asks for Barney's help in composing a letter to his prospective wife; Harris signs another book deal; and a lottery winner threatens the couple who lost his winning ticket.

149   The Car   November 12, 1981
Writer: Nat Mauldin
Director: Bruce Bilson
Guest Stars: Joseph Regalbuto, Patrick McNamara, Larry Gelman, Alice Backes

An overzealous sanitation officer pulls a gun on a litterbug; Levitt performs an act of heroism; and a car thief confesses—twenty-five years after the fact.

150   Possession   November 19, 1981
Writers: Tom Reeder, Roland Kibbee
Director: Bruce Bilson
Guest Stars: Kenneth Tigar, Susan Peretz, Allan Miller, Phil Rubenstein

A police chaplain performs an impromptu exorcism; and a full-figured wife assaults her husband for forcing her into a pair of designer jeans.

151   Stress Analyzer   November 26, 1981
Writer: Nat Mauldin
Director: Bruce Bilson
Guest Stars: Florence Halop, Phil Leeds, James Cromwell, Ann Guilbert, James Murtaugh, Rod Colbin

A Peace Corps recruiter goes berserk at a job fair; and Barney is distraught when an electronic stress analyzer indicates Dietrich has been shot in action.

152   Games   December 10, 1981
Writer: Jordan Moffet
Director: Gennaro Montanino
Guest Stars: Philip Sterling, Carol Rossen, Vernon Weddle, Trinidad Silva, Warren Munson, John O'Leary, Sarah Kennedy

A WAC supplements her meager army salary by soliciting in Greenwich Village; and a video-game chip manufacturer is accused of spying for the KGB.

153 Homeless   December 17, 1981
  Writers: Jordan Moffet, Frank Dungan, Jeff Stein
  Director: Lee Lochhead
  Guest Stars: Stanley Brock, Don Calfa, Ben Piazza, David
  Clennon, Paul Stolarsky, Zane Buzby, Mari Gorman, Walter
  Janowitz

The homeless flock to the Twelfth Precinct at Christmas; a livid
greeting-card writer loses his job; and a local merchant rousts
a vagrant with a cattle prod.

154 The Tontine   January 7, 1982
  Writer: Nat Mauldin
  Story: Nat Mauldin, Dick Wesson
  Director: Homer Powell
  Guest Stars: Ivor Francis, Ian Wolfe, Jay Robinson, Jane Dulo,
  Lou Cutell, Dennis Lipscomb

One of the last two survivors of an old-world tontine decides to
do himself in so that his cousin can enjoy the benefits of the
pact.

155 Examination Day   January 14, 1982
  Writer: Jordan Moffet
  Director: Gennaro Montanino
  Guest Stars: Jack Kruschen, Lyman Ward, Louis Giambalvo

The detectives are forced to go back into uniform while the rest
of the force takes the sergeant's exam.

156 The Clown   January 21, 1982
  Writer: Sam Simon
  Director: Alan Bergmann
  Guest Stars: Walter Olkewicz, Howard Platt, Philip Bruns, J. J.
  Barry, Michael Tucci

A mugger singles out street clowns; and a bureaucrat alleviates
jail overcrowding by quietly releasing a hundred inmates on
Madison Avenue in the dead of night.

A pair of story lines that could have come straight from the screaming
headlines of the New York tabloids—and probably did. "We got a lot
of ideas from the *New York Post* and the *Daily News*," writer Jeff Stein

confessed. "We'd look at the other papers, but we never found much we could use in *The New York Times*."

157   Chinatown (Part 1)   February 4, 1982
   Writers: Frank Dungan, Jeff Stein
   Director: Danny Arnold
   Guest Stars: Chao-Li Chi, George Murdock, Fred Sadoff, Joanna Barnes, Leonard Stone

Lieutenant Scanlon falls for a wealthy mugging victim; a restaurateur breaks into his own restaurant; and a Chinese waiter is an uncooperative witness to murder.

158   Chinatown (Part 2)   February 11, 1982
   Writers: Frank Dungan, Jeff Stein
   Director: Danny Arnold
   Guest Stars: Chao-Li Chi, Joanna Barnes, Phil Diskin, Peter Pan, George Murdock

Dietrich and Harris stake out their murder suspect at a Chinese restaurant.

159   Hunger Strike   February 18, 1982
   Writer: Tony Sheehan
   Story: Tony Sheehan, Stephen Neigher
   Director: Tony Sheehan
   Guest Stars: Nora Meerbaum, Larry Gelman, Stanley Kamel, Ion Teodorescu

A prisoner stages a hunger strike to end nuclear arms; Dietrich aids an elderly psychiatric patient; and Barney refuses another nomination for deputy inspector.

160   Arrival   February 25, 1982
   Writer: Jordan Moffett
   Director: Lee Lochhead
   Guest Stars: Carina Afable, Andrew Bloch, Alan Oppenheimer

Luger finally meets the Manilan he's been courting by mail; a genius turns to petty crime; and a man is mugged by an elderly woman.

161 Obituary   March 11, 1982
Writer: Nat Mauldin
Director: Gennaro Montanino
Guest Stars: Barney Martin, Richard Stahl, Phil Diskin, Will
Seltzer, Peggy Pope

An angry citizen complains when the newspaper prints his premature obituary; and a modern-day Robin Hood steals surplus
chickens from a government warehouse.

162 Inquiry   March 26, 1982
Writers: Frank Dungan, Jeff Stein
Director: Gennaro Montanino
Guest Stars: Michael Lombard, Bonnie Bartlett, Allan Rich,
Barry Gordon

An angry parent assaults the admissions director of a private
kindergarten; and Wojo faces a police inquiry for using excessive
force in a recent arrest.

163 Old Love   April 2, 1982
Writer: Philip Jayson Lasker
Director: Hal Linden
Guest Stars: Sharon Spelman, Mitch Kreindel, Ben Hammer,
Mario Roccuzzo, Audrey Christie

A former child star assaults his agent with a telephone; a good
samaritan is charged with assault; and Dietrich spends the afternoon with a college sweetheart.

164 Altercation   April 9, 1982
Writer: Tony Sheehan
Director: Alan Bergmann
Guest Stars: Alex Henteloff, Todd Susman, Miriam Byrd
Netherly, Rod Colbin, Robert Pastorelli

Harris punches Arnold Ripner when the lawyer threatens another libel suit; and a mugging victim reveals that she's carried
the torch for Barney since 1966.

165 Bones   April 29, 1982

    Writers: Jordan Moffet, Nat Mauldin
    Story: Jordan Moffet, Nat Mauldin, Lee H. Grant
    Director: Max Gail
    Guest Stars: Howard Platt, Ivor Francis, Pancito Gomez, Mark Banks, Luis Avalos

The precinct's plumbing goes out again; a scoutmaster apprehends a mugger; and a militant Indian retrieves his tribe's ancestral bones from a museum exhibit.

166 Landmark (Part 1)   May 6, 1982

    Writer: Tony Sheehan
    Director: Tony Sheehan
    Guest Stars: Susan Tolsky, Philip Sterling, James Gallery, Al Ruscio

The Twelfth is declared a national landmark; a former political hostage decides to emigrate back to South America; and an unemployed man is robbed at an automatic teller machine.

167 Landmark (Part 2)   May 13, 1982

    Writers: Frank Dungan, Jeff Stein
    Director: Danny Arnold
    Guest Stars: Helen Verbit, Florence Halop, James Murtaugh, Carina Afable

Dietrich arrests the head of a professional crime school, along with a pair of his unlikely graduates; Luger tries to squirm out of his marriage commitment; and the Twelfth Precinct is sold to a real estate developer.

168 Landmark (Part 3)   May 20, 1982

    Writers: Frank Dungan, Jeff Stein, Tony Sheehan
    Director: Danny Arnold
    Guest Stars: Carina Afable, George Murdock, Walter Janowitz, Ray Stewart, John Dullaghan, Jack DeLeon, Mari Gorman, Stanley Brock, J. J. Barry, Earl Boen, Oliver Clark, Ralph Manza, Meshach Taylor, Judson Morgan, F. William Parker

The squad room fills with familiar faces who arrive to pay last respects to the departing detectives; and Barney bids a fond farewell to the men and women—past and present—who made up the illustrious roster of the Twelfth Precinct.

Producer Danny Arnold once singled out the station house itself as the most important personality in the drama of "Barney Miller." And indeed, of all the sad farewells in that final episode, no single image evoked the sense of passing as eloquently as the sight of those dingy old walls, now stripped bare and waiting for the first inevitable blow of the rehabber's hammer.

During their time together, the detectives of the Twelfth Precinct endured the ravages of fire, death, depression, and maddening bureaucracy. They were laid off, arrested, seduced, shanghaied, and even haunted; they survived bomb threats, snipers, rabid dogs, and corrupt politicians. But in the show's final—and fitting—irony, after eight years, the ol' one-two was done in by a real estate speculator.

It was a fate that could happen only in New York.

EMMY AWARDS

The following is a complete listing of the Emmy Awards bestowed on "Barney Miller" by the National Academy of Television Arts and Sciences.

1979/80   Outstanding Writing in a Comedy Series: Bob Colleary, "The Photographer"

1981/82   Outstanding Comedy Series

"TAXI"

·

It was NOT a lotta one liners
about crazy New York cabbies.
It was about lives, the human
condition.
—JUDD HIRSCH

A FEW WEEKS before "Taxi's" premiere, Ed. Weinberger made a bold prediction. "I think we're going to deliver a hit."

In the business of TV comedy, such prophecy is always risky conjecture. And yet, coming from one of four producers who'd just shepherded Mary Tyler Moore through seven seasons of prime time, his brash optimism was something more than a boast. For James L. Brooks, Stan Daniels, David Davis, and Ed. Weinberger, it was a declaration of independence.

Until recently, the four writers had formed the inner circle of MTM Productions' creative brain trust. At least one of them had been involved in the creation of practically every series produced by the company during its glory days, including "Mary Tyler Moore," "Bob Newhart," "Rhoda," and "Lou Grant." But by 1978, they'd left to start their own independent production unit at Paramount Studios.

"It was a staggering blow," MTM president Arthur Price told journalist Paul Weingarten. "None of those guys ever came and said we're a group now, and this is what we want to do, can you match it? I just got a phone call, we'd like to come up and see you, and they came up and they laid it on us and they were gone."

"They felt like the sons had betrayed them, and I understand those feelings," recalled Ed. Weinberger. James Brooks also acknowledged the difficulty of leaving the shop where he and his partners had experienced so much creative freedom. "I can't tell you how perfect it was there, and it couldn't stay that way."

After the team retired "Mary Tyler Moore"—a tough act to follow, even for its creators—Ed. Weinberger and his partner, Stan Daniels, sat back and waited for something to happen. "We had no plans after 'Mary,'" explained Weinberger, "and nobody made us any offers. So we went to see our agents, who proposed we go to ABC and see if we could pick up some commitments. Somewhere along the line, Jim and Dave came along, and we all joined together. It was as simple as that."

Of course, the producers' decision to branch out was motivated by financial considerations as much as any creative factors. "The people with the greatest desire to see us move were our agents," admitted Brooks. Which isn't surprising, since the talent brokers stood to profit immensely from their clients' independence. As co-owners of the shows they wrote and produced, the profits that would accrue to Brooks, Weinberger, Daniels, and Davis after syndication could be astounding.

And so, after the inevitable split, the producers moved onto the Paramount backlot. They hung up a shingle that read John Charles Walters Productions—no such person existed, but they thought it sounded classy—and signed a contract with ABC, which guaranteed that at least two of their new series would go on the air, without pilots.

Brooks, Daniels, Davis, and Weinberger had done all right for themselves. They had their own production facility and as much creative freedom as they could hope for. All they needed now was an idea for a hit comedy.

And Jim Brooks had one, though at that point it was really little more than a hunch.

"All I had was a magazine article and an idea. Nothing else," Brooks recalled. But he figured it was a start, so he got the network on the phone and pitched his idea. "They liked it. They bought it."

Within twenty-four hours, four of the best creative minds in television were hard at work on a new comedy called "Taxi."

The idea of a TV series set in a taxi garage actually originated about a year earlier, when Brooks and Jerry Belson—co-creator of ABC's "Odd Couple," and a regular writer on the original "Dick Van Dyke Show"—convinced MTM to option an article they'd seen in *New York* magazine. The story mentioned the Dover Cab Company, a New York taxi garage that served as a way station for aspiring actors, writers, and other creative types who were waiting for their dreams to come true.

Brooks and Belson thought they might develop the material into a one-camera show that could be shot on actual New York locations. But, eventually, they both moved on to other projects, and "Taxi" was all but forgotten—until Jim Brooks revived it as the perfect vehicle for the creative talents at John Charles Walters.

Daniels, Davis, and Weinberger warmed to the idea instantly. For one thing, the show would be about men.

Of course, the guys had nothing against women on television. But after seven seasons of "Mary Tyler Moore" and another half dozen concurrent seasons of "Phyllis" and "Rhoda," they were growing weary of the comical struggles of modern single women in a middle-class milieu. "We felt we'd explored that world," explained Ed. Weinberger. "But 'Taxi' was a blue-collar situation, and it was about guys. That really appealed to us."

As anxious as they were to get started, there was still one slight hitch. Before they could proceed, the producers had to consult their old boss. Technically, MTM had a prior claim to the concept, since they still held the rights to the original magazine piece that had inspired the series. But after a quick phone call, MTM's Grant Tinker gave "Taxi" his blessings, and—with customary generosity—sold Brooks and company the rights to the article for fifteen hundred dollars, exactly what MTM paid for it in the first place.

The series quickly took shape as the producers began their search for a suitable leading man. As the sympathetic anchor for most of the show's action, he would have to be a strong character actor who could handle the comedic as well as dramatic demands of the series.

It didn't take long to narrow the choice down to one—Judd Hirsch.

"We wrote the part of Alex Reiger with Judd Hirsch in mind," recalled Ed. Weinberger. But convincing the successful film and stage actor to return to television would not be easy. "I told my agent to pass the offer by," Hirsch confided. "I'd *done* TV, you know?" The actor was referring to the bitter taste left by CBS's cancellation of "Delvecchio"—Hirsch's well-regarded 1976 cop show—after barely a season.

The producers continued to court the actor, and he continued to play hard to get. But finally, after he got a look at the show's first script, Hirsch needed little encouragement. Just as the producers had hoped, the actor responded to quality.

Drawing from a wide palette of inspiration, the creators had taken the intelligent humanism they'd perfected on "Mary Tyler Moore," added a dollop of the surreal wackiness that Dave Davis favored on "The Bob Newhart Show," and then dropped the strange brew into a blue-collar setting that could easily have been stamping grounds for Ralph Kramden. The potent blend that resulted fused the hip sophistication of MTM-style humor with the broad physical comedy of more traditional shows like "The Honeymooners."

And at the center of it all was Alex—the cab company's resident Everyman and the only practical thinker in the entire garage. Like any good cabbie, he had a philosophical observation to relieve any situation that might confront his beleaguered colleagues—though he was usually at a loss when it came to facing one of his own dark quandaries.

But philosophical questions didn't plague everyone at the Sunshine Cab Company. Louie DePalma was rarely bothered by angst. The well-adjusted dispatcher was disagreeable, venal, dishonest—and he in charge. He sat in his cage, far above the rabble, and like a malevolent Wizard of Oz, bluffed everyone into thinking he was far more omniscient than his pint-sized stature could ever allow.

The character actually began his life as a much smaller supporting role. But that changed the minute casting director Joel Thurm read the script and cautioned the producers, "Don't cast that part until you meet Danny DeVito!"

"Danny and the material met head-on," declared Ed. Weinberger, as he recalled the actor's first audition. "Before he even got to his car, we were on the phone to his agent. And his part eventually grew from a page and a half in the first script until he became, in effect, the show's co-lead."

The producers rounded out their talented ensemble with a cast that included Marilu Henner, Tony Danza, Jeff Conaway, Randall Carver, and, most memorably, comedian Andy Kaufman.

Brooks, Daniels, Davis, and Weinberger carefully built an equally talented behind-the-scenes crew as well. Former MTM staffer James Burrows was signed to direct the series, and Glen and Les Charles were lured over from MTM to produce the show and head the writing staff.

Before long, "Taxi" attracted some of the finest writing talent in the industry. And the show continued to develop a new stable of young writers, many of whom eventually carried the show's tradition of quality with them when they went on to produce some of the best TV comedy of the 1980s. As Les Charles observed, "It was a terrific group of writers. Probably as good as any show has ever had at one time."

With a nucleus of creative talent like that, the producers thought, there was no reason why the show shouldn't be a resounding success. And, for a time at least, it was.

Buoyed by an advantageous time slot on ABC's powerhouse Tuesday comedy night, the series finished its first two seasons in the top twenty. But after ABC moved the show to Wednesday night, the network was surprised to notice a sharp drop in ratings during the third season. They eventually shuttled the series to Thursday, where it did even worse.

By the end of the fourth year, the series had slumped its way into fifty-third place, after ABC canceled the show—despite the fact that "Taxi" had won the Emmy for best comedy series in each of its first three seasons. Of course, no one argued that the show lacked quality; the network simply felt the series had lost the power to pull in the big numbers.

And then, just when it looked as if "Taxi" had run its course, an odd thing happened. Very important people suddenly began to take a keen interest in the show's survival.

And, by a strange twist of fate, one of them was Grant Tinker.

By 1981, Tinker had left MTM to accept a job as head of the NBC network, where he shook things up by inaugurating a downright radical policy of quality programming. After ABC orphaned "Taxi," Tinker declared that his network would give the series a second chance. He topped a competing bid from the Home Box Office pay-TV channel—which also coveted the prestigious comedy—and "Taxi" parked at NBC for its fifth year.

Alas, the show's renaissance would be short-lived. The comedy's ratings didn't show much improvement on NBC, and it was unceremoniously canceled at the end of the season.

But even after two cancellations, "Taxi" was still not easily forgotten.

The following September, the Academy of Television Arts and Sciences once again honored the show with a cluster of Emmy Awards, as it had during each of the show's previous four seasons, prompting Judd Hirsch to quip, "Don't they know we've been canceled?" When he rose to accept his own award as best actor in a comedy, Hirsch introduced a note of rancor to the stately proceedings by criticizing the priorities of an industry that chose to honor a series it couldn't afford to keep alive.

"If you can't get it out of your mind," he intoned, "if you have to keep giving laurels to us, then you should put it back on the air."

But this time, there would be no last-minute reprieve.

Even so, the show's creators certainly had no cause for regret. In "Taxi," they had crafted something pretty rare—a television comedy with heart and humor, and a genuine point of view. "Taxi" placed a high premium on the value of dreams but never let us forget that there's more to life than chasing rainbows.

It was a philosophy Brooks, Daniels, Davis, and Weinberger must've taken to heart. The four writers set out with a dream—to deliver a hit series. But, five seasons and 113 episodes later, it was obvious they had finally accomplished a great deal more.

A Critical Guide to All 113 Episodes

Alex Reiger	Judd Hirsch
Louie DePalma	Danny DeVito
Elaine Nardo	Marilu Henner
Bobby Wheeler	Jeff Conaway
Jim Caldwell Ignatowski	Christopher Lloyd
Tony Banta	Tony Danza
Latka Gravas	Andy Kaufman
Simka Dahblitz Gravas	Carol Kane
Zena Sherman	Rhea Perlman
John Burns (1st season)	Randall Carver
Jeff Bennett	J. Alan Thomas

SUPPORTING CAST

Tommy, the Waiter	T. J. Castronova
Jason Nardo (Elaine's son)	Michael Hershewe, David Mendenhall
Jennifer Nardo (Elaine's daughter)	Melanie Gaffin
Phyllis Consuelos (Alex's ex-wife)	Louise Lasser
Cathy Consuelos (Alex's daughter)	Talia Balsam
Greta Gravas (Latka's mother)	Susan Kellermann
Tom Caldwell (Jim's brother)	Walter Olkewicz
Ivan Reiger (Alex's father)	Jack Gilford

Created by James L. Brooks, Stan Daniels, David Davis, Ed. Weinberger
Music and theme song ("Angela") by Bob James
Directors of photography were Edward E. Nugent, Ken Peach
Principal directors were James Burrows, Noam Pitlik

1978/79 THE FIRST SEASON

Year-End Rating: 24.9 (9th place)

"Taxi's" ragtag ensemble springs to life in first-season stories that detail the aspirations and frustrations of the colorful gang at New York's Sunshine Cab Company. First-season scripts are written under the watchful eyes of executive producers James L. Brooks, Stan Daniels, David Davis, and Ed. Weinberger, with significant contributions from producers Glen Charles and Les Charles, and writers Earl Pomerantz and Barry Kemp, among others.

James Burrows directs practically all premiere-season episodes, as he will continue to do throughout most of the show's first four years. Bud Cherry is the first year's associate producer, and creator James L. Brooks receives a credit as executive consultant.

1   Like Father, Like Daughter   September 12, 1978
Writers: James L. Brooks, Stan Daniels, David Davis, Ed.
Weinberger
Director: James Burrows
Guest Stars: Talia Balsam, Jill Jaress

With all the cabbies in tow, Alex drives to Miami for a surprise reunion with the daughter he hasn't seen in fifteen years.

One of the best-written—and most economical—opening episodes ever devised for a situation comedy. In the space of a single half hour, the writers skillfully introduce each fully developed character in the cast of seven, with time left over for the touching sequence where Alex finally meets his estranged teenage daughter in the lobby of the Miami airport. Father and daughter attempt to compress the scattered emotions of fifteen lost years into a few short minutes in a wholly satisfying blend of comedy and pathos that would be the hallmark of this most sophisticated situation comedy.

2   One-Punch Banta   September 19, 1978
Writer: Earl Pomerantz
Director: James Burrows
Guest Stars: Carlos Palomino, Allan Arbus

Tony's lucky punch during a sparring round earns him a once-in-a-lifetime bout with World Champion Carlos Navarone.

Actor Tony Danza had actually been a struggling New York middleweight before he turned to acting. Ironically, his greatest success in the ring came after he'd hung up his gloves to join "Taxi," when a canny promoter arranged for the celebrity to box his last match in New York's Madison Square Garden after the conclusion of the show's first season.

3 Blind Date September 26, 1978
Writer: Michael Leeson
Director: James Burrows
Guest Star: Suzanne Kent

Alex, stuck on a date with an overweight and overbearing woman, refuses to let her bitterness spoil their evening.

4 Bobby's Acting Career October 5, 1978
Writers: Ed. Weinberger, Stan Daniels
Director: James Burrows
Guest Stars: Taurean Blacque, John Lehne, Michael Mann, Robert Phalen

Bobby's self-imposed deadline to land an acting job is about to expire, and the struggling actor has no prospects in sight.

5 Come As You Aren't October 10, 1978
Writers: Glen Charles, Les Charles
Director: James Burrows
Guest Stars: Andra Akers, William Bogert, Paula Victor, Clyde Kusatsu, Treva Silverman

Elaine convinces Alex to be her date at a fancy party and then insists that he not tell anyone they both work as cabbies at night.

The shy young woman who leaves the party on Latka's arm is actually Emmy Award–winning writer Treva Silverman in a rare cameo appearance.

6 The Great Line October 17, 1978
Writer: Earl Pomerantz
Director: James Burrows
Guest Stars: Ellen Regan, Dolph Sweet, Sheila Rogers

John develops second thoughts after he gets married to a girl he met at Mario's the night before.

7 High School Reunion October 24, 1978
Writer: Sy Rosen
Director: James Burrows
Guest Stars: Joanna Cassidy, Arlene Golonka, Sandy Holt, Pierrino Mascarino

Ashamed of what his classmates might think of him, Louie convinces Bobby to attend his twentieth high school reunion in his place.

8 Paper Marriage October 31, 1978
Writers: Glen Charles, Les Charles
Story: Barton Dean
Director: James Burrows
Guest Stars: Christopher Lloyd, Rita Taggart, James Randolph

Latka gets a disillusioning view of American mating rituals when he marries a call girl to qualify for U.S. citizenship.

The ceremony is presided over by the Reverend Jim Ignatowski, an ordained minister and bona fide relic of the 1960s, who is recruited from Mario's Bar and Grill. "He wasn't intended to be a permanent character," recalled writer Glen Charles. "But," adds executive producer Ed. Weinberger, "from the first minute Christopher Lloyd hit the stage, he was destined to stay. That very night, we all agreed we had to get him on the show."

9 Money Troubles November 14, 1978
Writer: Earl Pomerantz
Director: James Burrows
Guest Star: Ellen Regan

After John's wealthy in-laws move to Florida, he and his new wife turn to Alex for a friendly—and sizable—loan.

Ellen Regan returns as John's young wife, Suzanne.

10 Men Are Such Beasts November 21, 1978
Writers: Ed. Weinberger, Stan Daniels
Director: James Burrows
Guest Stars: Gail Edwards, George Reynolds

Tony tries to dump his possessive girlfriend after she takes a job at the cab company just to be near him.

11   Cab 804 (Part 1)   November 28, 1978
   Writer: Barry Kemp
   Director: James Burrows
   Guest Stars: Scoey Mitchell, Rod Browning, Chris Barnes

After John wrecks cab 804, the cabbies pay tribute to the beloved taxi with fond recollections of memorable shifts spent behind its wheel.

12   Cab 804 (Part 2)   December 5, 1978
   Writer: Barry Kemp
   Director: James Burrows
   Guest Stars: Tom Selleck, Mandy Patinkin, Regie Baff

The cabbies' vigil continues as Elaine recalls an unusual date she had in 804, and Alex recounts how the cab once served as a makeshift maternity ward.

Elaine's handsome stranger is played by Tom Selleck, in a role that predated his prime-time success in "Magnum, P.I." by two years.

The sequence where Alex delivers a baby in the backseat of cab 804 while the anxious dad peers over his shoulder demonstrates the show's wide emotional range. The story effortlessly switches gears from high comedy to a moment of utterly believable drama without missing a beat.

The nervous papa was played by Mandy Patinkin, a New York actor who had been the producers' first choice for the role of "Taxi's" struggling thespian long before Jeff Conaway landed the part. Patinkin turned it down, perfectly content to remain in Manhattan, where he achieved continued success onstage and in feature films.

13   A Full House for Christmas   December 12, 1978
   Writer: Barry Kemp
   Director: James Burrows
   Guest Star: Richard Foronjy

Alex and Louie team up in a high-stakes poker game against the dispatcher's disreputable brother, Nick.

Richard Foronjy was a last-minute replacement in the role of Louie's brother. In the show's most disastrous week, Andy Kaufman had been set to play Nick DePalma in the guise of lounge-lizard Tony Clifton. Clifton was an alter-ego Kaufman used as a warm up in his nightclub act, and as part of the joke, the conceptual performer maintained that he and Tony were actually two different people. It seemed a harmless-enough hoax. But it took an ugly turn when, on the first day of rehearsal, Kaufman refused to drop the obnoxious character, onstage or off.

As spoiled nightclub performer Tony Clifton, Kaufman ordered cases of liquor delivered to his trailer on the Paramount lot, where he holed up with a pair of ladies he'd brought along for companionship. By the third day, he refused to show up for rehearsals—venturing out of his trailer just long enough to heap abuse on fellow actors, stagehands, and anyone else who dared cross his supposedly temperamental path.

Executive producer Ed. Weinberger finally summoned Kaufman to his office, where the comic meekly suggested that Tony Clifton be fired, preferably on the soundstage and in front of the entire crew—a request to which the producer gladly complied. "It was all part of Andy's theater," remembers producer Glen Charles. "But it was not as much fun as it sounds. It was a very troubled week."

14 Sugar Mama   January 16, 1979
  Writers: Glen Charles, Les Charles
  Director: James Burrows
  Guest Stars: Ruth Gordon, Herb Vigran, Aharon Ipale

Alex's conscience bothers him after he accepts cash and extravagant gifts from an eccentric old woman who rides his cab for companionship.

15 Friends   January 30, 1979
  Writer: Earl Pomerantz
  Director: James Burrows
  Guest Stars: Liz Miller, J. Alan Thomas

Tony ends his friendship with Bobby after the irresponsible actor accidentally allows Tony's beloved pet goldfish to die.

16 Louie Sees the Light   February 6, 1979
  Writer: Ruth Bennett
  Director: James Burrows
  Guest Stars: John Dukakis, Fay Hauser

Louie resolves to mend his irascible ways after he survives a nerve-racking operation.

17　Elaine and the Lame Duck　　　　　February 13, 1979
Writers: Glen Charles, Les Charles
Director: James Burrows
Guest Stars: Jeffrey Tambor, Susan Heldfond, Rusdi Lane

Alex fixes Elaine up with an inept congressman, convinced that an evening with the fiery redhead will do wonders for the legislator's sagging confidence.

Elaine eventually decides to sleep with the hapless politician, only to face an awkward morning-after scene when she realizes that her therapeutic solution has caused more problems than it's solved. The series's depiction of Elaine as a single, sexually independent woman was a refreshing breakthrough for situation comedy. Unfortunately, television tastes were receding so rapidly that the show's mature sophistication would have little direct impact on the increasingly childish sitcoms of the era.

18　Bobby's Big Break　　　　　February 15, 1979
Writer: Barry Kemp
Director: James Burrows
Guest Stars: Amanda McBroom, Michele Conaway

Bobby tears up his hack license after he lands a part on a soap opera, but his grandiose exit soon proves premature.

19　Mama Gravas　　　　　February 27, 1979
Writers: Glen Charles, Les Charles
Director: James Burrows
Guest Star: Susan Kellermann

Latka demands that Alex marry his mother after the cabbie's date with the lusty Brunhilde ends in an evening of spirited "nik nik."

The garage's peculiar mechanic was largely the creation of Andy Kaufman, who was cast in the show after the producers saw him hold a nightclub audience spellbound in his persona as a stuttering, painfully shy immigrant. They threw a pair of white coveralls on the character, named him Latka Gravas, and wrote him into the very first show. Writers would be especially fond of Latka, whose strange language and behavior offered unlimited opportunities to explore a surreal world of their own devising.

20 Alex Tastes Death and Finds   March 6, 1979
    a Nice Restaurant
Writer: Michael Leeson
Director: James Burrows
Guest Stars: James Staley, Byron Webster

After Alex is nearly killed by a mugger, he abandons the garage to become a waiter in a four-star restaurant.

21 Hollywood Calling   May 8, 1979
Writers: Glen Charles, Les Charles
Director: James Burrows
Guest Stars: Martin Mull, Joey Aresco

The cabbies are starstruck when a Hollywood producer arrives to absorb background for a movie based on life in a New York taxi garage.

Comedian Martin Mull was fondly remembered for his portrayal of twin brothers Garth and Barth Gimble on Norman Lear's "Mary Hartman, Mary Hartman" and its spin-offs, "Fernwood 2-Night" and "America 2-Night."

22 Substitute Father   May 15, 1979
Writer: Barry Kemp
Director: James Burrows
Guest Stars: Michael Hershewe, David Knapp, Suzanne Carney

The cabbies become substitute daddies when Elaine leaves her nine-year-old in their care after she's suddenly called out of town.

This episode marked the final appearance of cabbie John Burns. The character was dropped as the producers pared the ensemble in preparation for the arrival of Jim Ignatowski in the second season. As producer Ed. Weinberger observed, "We just had too many people. We couldn't write for everybody."

1979/80   THE SECOND SEASON

Year-End Rating: 22.4 (13th place)

Louie and Latka each discover romance in season two, and the cabbies recruit Jim Ignatowski into their ranks in the year's third episode.

Once again, producers Glen Charles and Les Charles contribute some of the season's finest scripts, along with Earl Pomerantz, executive script consultant Barry Kemp, and program consultant Ken Estin. Ian Praiser and Howard Gewirtz are the story editors, and Richard Sakai is associate producer for the second and third seasons. James L. Brooks, Stan Daniels, and Ed. Weinberger serve as executive producers for the remainder of the show's run.

23 Louie and the Nice Girl   September 11, 1979
    Writer: Earl Pomerantz
    Director: James Burrows
    Guest Star: Rhea Perlman

Louie is petrified at the prospect of falling in love with a girl he's sure is too good for him.

Kindhearted candy girl Zena Sherman was played by Rhea Perlman, DeVito's real-life girlfriend. Louie's romance with Zena barely lasted through season four, but the real-life couple finally did tie the knot three years later in an impulsive ceremony conducted during a "Taxi" lunch break.

24 Honor Thy Father   September 18, 1979
    Writers: Glen Charles, Les Charles
    Director: James Burrows
    Guest Stars: Jack Gilford, Ian Wolfe, Richard Beauchamp

Alex is strangely unmoved by news of his father's heart attack.

25 Reverend Jim: A Space Odyssey   September 25, 1979
    Writers: Glen Charles, Les Charles
    Director: James Burrows
    Guest Star: Kenneth Kimmins

The cabbies help a refugee from the 1960s find sanctuary behind the wheel of a taxi.

The Reverend Jim Caldwell Ignatowski—he added Ignatowski to his family name, we later discovered, because he thought it meant "Star Child"—was a comic creation of practically unlimited potential. There was no concept too bizarre, no drug too potent, and no experience too outlandish for Jim. He had experienced life in ways the other cabbies could barely imagine, yet he remained an innocent who drew our sympathy as easily as our laughter. When Tony angrily confronts Jim with the bitter accusation that he fought in Vietnam so that burnouts like him could stay home and get loaded at protest rallies, the philosophical Ignatowski can only stammer a heartfelt, and utterly sincere, "thank you."

26 Nardo Loses Her Marbles   October 2, 1979
Writer: Earl Pomerantz
Director: James Burrows
Guest Stars: Tom Ewell, Paula Victor, Mary Woronov, Robert Picardo, William Callaway

Alex suggests Elaine seek professional help when the stress of holding down two jobs while raising a pair of kids begins to take a toll on her sanity.

In a low moment, Elaine decides that sleeping with Alex might be the most expedient form of therapy—an offer that he shuns, to his instant regret. The sexual tension that developed over the course of their relationship was rarely addressed with such candor, though it remained a compelling subtext that colored their friendship throughout the life of the series.

27 Wherefore Art Thou, Bobby?   October 16, 1979
Writer: Barry Kemp
Director: James Burrows
Guest Star: Michael Horton

Bobby is stunned when an inexperienced actor fresh off the bus lands a plum role on his very first audition.

28 The Lighter Side of Angela Matusa   October 23, 1979
Writer: Earl Pomerantz
Director: James Burrows
Guest Stars: Suzanne Kent, Phil Rubenstein, Dick Miller

Alex's overweight blind date returns, now a hundred pounds thinner and ready for serious romance.

29   A Woman Among Friends   October 30, 1979
  Writer: Ken Estin
  Director: James Burrows
  Guest Star: Constance Forslund

Tony and Bobby compete for the attentions of a woman who seems to have fallen for both of them.

30   The Great Race   November 6, 1979
  Writer: Glenn Gordon Caron
  Director: James Burrows
  Guest Stars: James Hong, Jean Owens Hayworth, Fred Stuthman, Scott Brady, Craig T. Nelson, Bob Levine, Julie Payne, Milt Oberman, Kres Mersky

The cabbies place their bets when Louie and Alex compete to see who can book the most money in a single shift.

Writer Glenn Gordon Caron would eventually mastermind "Moonlighting," the cross-genre detective spoof that premiered on ABC in 1985.

31   The Apartment   November 13, 1979
  Writer: Barry Rubinowitz
  Director: James Burrows
  Guest Stars: Nancy Steen, Dick Butkus, Mike Binder

Latka blows his entire life savings on a luxury penthouse after he assumes that the three-thousand-dollar monthly rent is a one-time charge.

32   Alex's Romance   November 20, 1979
  Writers: Ian Praiser, Howard Gewirtz
  Director: Ed. Weinberger
  Guest Star: Dee Wallace

Alex surprises everyone—including himself—when he falls in love with an out-of-work actress.

Actress Dee Wallace would find plenty of work in feature films, including a starring role in Steven Spielberg's *E.T.*

33 Latka's Revolting   November 27, 1979
Writers: Glen Charles, Les Charles
Director: James Burrows
Guest Star: Lenny Baker

Latka hears the patriotic call to duty when revolution breaks out in his homeland.

34 Elaine's Secret Admirer   December 4, 1979
Writer: Barry Kemp
Director: James Burrows
Guest Star: Michael Delano

Elaine is determined to find out which of the cabbies has been leaving anonymous love poems in her locker.

35 Louie Meets the Folks   December 11, 1979
Writer: Barry Kemp
Director: James Burrows
Guest Stars: Rhea Perlman, Camila Ashland, John Becher

Nervous at the prospect of meeting Zena's parents for the first time, Louie pays Alex five hundred dollars to come along for moral support.

36 Jim Gets a Pet   December 18, 1979
Writer: David Lloyd
Director: James Burrows

Jim makes a killing at the track and then buys the winning horse to take home as a pet.

37 Reluctant Fighter   December 25, 1979
Writer: Ken Estin
Director: James Burrows
Guest Stars: Marc Danza, Armando Muniz, Michael V. Gazzo

Tony has a chance to fight the retired champ but loses heart when he discovers his opponent has dedicated his victory to a crippled boy.

38   Tony and Brian   January 8, 1980
   Writer: Ken Estin
   Director: James Burrows
   Guest Star: Marc Danza

Tony wants to adopt his foster child officially, but the canny youngster would rather take his chances with a wealthy couple.

Tony's foster child was played by Danza's real-life eight-year-old, Marc Antony Danza.

39   Guess Who's Coming for Brefnish   January 15, 1980
   Writer: Barry Kemp
   Director: James Burrows
   Guest Stars: Carol Kane, Frank Ashmore

Latka's whirlwind romance with a strange girl from his home country sours after he discovers she's from a socially inferior class.

When actress Carol Kane was hired to play Simka, Andy Kaufman invited her to dinner so they could practice Latka-language and then refused to let her speak English during the meal. "It is the perfect way to learn a language," observed the actress. "Andy made it up and got a very specific sound to it. You just open your mouth and dive in."

40   What Price Bobby?   January 22, 1980
   Writer: Ken Estin
   Director: James Burrows
   Guest Star: Susan Sullivan

Bobby hits it off with an influential agent who seems more confident of his talents in bed than on the stage.

41   Shut It Down (Part 1)   January 29, 1980
   Writers: Mark Jacobson, Michael Tolkin
   Director: James Burrows

Shop steward Elaine faces a dilemma after Louie agrees to meet the cabbies' labor demands—in exchange for a date.

42 Shut It Down (Part 2)   February 5, 1980
  Writers: Mark Jacobson, Michael Tolkin
  Director: James Burrows

Elaine's date with Louie goes as badly as expected, until the dispatcher surprises her with an uncharacteristic display of human feelings.

43 Alex Jumps Out of an Airplane   February 26, 1980
  Writer: Ken Estin
  Director: James Burrows

After he survives a death-defying ski jump, Alex develops a dare-devil's addiction to thrills.

44 Art Work   March 4, 1980
  Writers: Glen Charles, Les Charles
  Director: James Burrows
  Guest Star: Marvin Newman

Elaine convinces the cabbies to pool their money to bid on un-dervalued artwork at a gallery auction.

45 Fantasy Borough (Part 1)   May 6, 1980
  Writer: Barry Kemp
  Director: James Burrows
  Guest Stars: Eric Sevareid, Herve Villechaize, Warren Munson

A visit from ''Fantasy Island's'' Herve Villechaize prompts each of the cabbies to share their own private fantasies.

46 Fantasy Borough (Part 2)   May 13, 1980
  Writer: Barry Kemp
  Director: James Burrows
  Guest Stars: Herve Villechaize, Lassie

Alex has difficulty imagining a fantasy with a happy ending; and Elaine envisions herself belting a Broadway showstopper in the dreary garage.

Lassie makes a cameo appearance as Louie's pet collie in the dis-patcher's farfetched fantasy that he's wealthy and well liked.

1980/81   THE THIRD SEASON

Year-End Rating: 17.1 (53d place)

"Taxi" rolls into a third strong season under the guidance of executive producers James L. Brooks, Stan Daniels, and Ed. Weinberger, and producers Glen Charles and Les Charles, who continue to contribute noteworthy scripts, along with David Lloyd, executive script consultant Barry Kemp, and executive story editor Ken Estin.

47 Louie's Rival   November 19, 1980
  Writer: Ken Estin
  Director: James Burrows
  Guest Stars: Rhea Perlman, Richard Minchenberg

Louie is crushed when Zena drops him for the bartender at Mario's.

48 Tony's Sister and Jim   November 26, 1980
  Writer: Michael Leeson
  Director: James Burrows
  Guest Stars: Julie Kavner, Andrew Block

Tony tries to match Alex with his wacky sister—who only has eyes for Jim.

Tony's sister was played by Julie Kavner, best remembered for her stint as Brenda Morgenstern, the title character's younger sister on "Rhoda."

49 Fathers of the Bride   December 3, 1980
  Writer: Barry Kemp
  Director: James Burrows
  Guest Stars: Louise Lasser, Talia Balsam, Carlo Quinterio

Alex—enraged that he wasn't invited to his daughter's New York wedding—crashes the fancy reception and confronts his estranged wife.

In addition to hosting one of the brightest acting ensembles in television history, "Taxi" also managed to attract some of Hollywood's finest character players as recurring guest stars. Carol Kane, Jack Gilford, and Andrea Marcovicci were all well established before they made repeat appearances on the series, as was Louise Lasser, who would return as Alex's loopy ex-wife in a handful of later episodes.

50 Elaine's Strange Triangle   December 10, 1980
  Writer: David Lloyd
  Director: James Burrows
  Guest Star: John David Carson

Alex and Tony fix Elaine up with a handsome stranger, only to discover that her new beau is actually more attracted to Tony.

51 Going Home   December 17, 1980
  Writers: Glen Charles, Les Charles
  Director: James Burrows
  Guest Stars: Victor Buono, Barbara Deutsch, Walter Olkewicz, Dick Yarmy

Jim's wealthy father dispatches a private eye to the garage to coax his son into a long-overdue reconciliation.

52 The Ten Percent Solution   January 7, 1981
  Writer: Pat Allee
  Director: James Burrows
  Guest Stars: Sarina C. Grant, Ed. Weinberger, Jim Staskell

Bobby decides to manage Tony's budding acting career on a lark, but soon develops a bad case of professional jealousy.

Series creator Ed. Weinberger has a brief cameo as—what else?—one of the producers at Tony's audition.

53 The Call of the Mild   January 21, 1981
  Writer: Katharine Green
  Director: James Burrows
  Guest Star: Harvey Vernon

Inspired by Bobby's rugged beer commercial, the cabbies retreat to the wilderness for a survival weekend.

54   Latka's Cookies   February 5, 1981
Writers: Glen Charles, Les Charles
Director: James Burrows
Guest Star: Wally "Famous" Amos

Latka decides to market his own line of cookies using a special old-world recipe that includes at least one highly illegal ingredient.

55   Thy Boss's Wife   February 12, 1981
Writer: Ken Estin
Director: James Burrows
Guest Stars: Eileen Brennan, Stephen Elliot

Louie has difficulty resisting temptation when the boss's wife casts a lustful eye in his direction—even though he knows the affair may cost him his job.

56   The Costume Party   February 19, 1981
Writer: David Lloyd
Director: James Burrows
Guest Stars: Hector Britt, Louie Guss, Michael Klingher

The cabbies plan to hobnob with the stars when they crash what they assume is Woody Allen's masquerade ball.

57   Elaine's Old Friend   February 26, 1981
Writers: Susan Linder, Nancy Lane
Director: Jeff Chambers
Guest Stars: Martha Smith, John Considine

Elaine makes a date with her old high school rival and then cons Alex into posing as her imaginary boyfriend—a worldly Columbia University professor.

58   Out of Commission   March 12, 1981
Writer: Sam Simon
Director: James Burrows
Guest Stars: Carmine Caridi, Al Ruscio, Jesse Goins, Jimmy Lennon

Tony refuses to abandon his career in the ring, even after the boxing commission revokes his license.

59   Zen and the Art of Cab Driving   March 19, 1981
   Writers: Glen Charles, Les Charles
   Director: Will Mackenzie
   Guest Stars: Nicholas Hormann, Michael Mann

The cabbies are mystified when Jim embarks on a mysterious quest for absolute perfection.

Jim spends the profits of his efforts to set up an elaborate bank of TVs and satellite receivers in his small apartment—a foolhardy extravagance that causes the other cabbies to scoff. And yet, none of them can resist the hypnotic lure of Jim's video Medusa, and the show closes with a curious meditation on our own love-hate relationship with the tube, as each of the cabbies sits frozen, staring at their world through Jim's electronic windows.

60   Louie's Mother   March 26, 1981
   Writer: Katharine Green
   Director: James Burrows
   Guest Star: Julia DeVito

Louie throws a party to celebrate his independence after his elderly mother moves out to enter a retirement home.

Louie's spry mom was played by Julia DeVito, the actor's real-life mother.

61   Bobby's Roommate   April 9, 1981
   Writer: Earl Pomerantz
   Director: James Burrows

Alex and Tony suspect Bobby's motives when he offers to let Elaine stay at his apartment after she loses her own place.

62   Louie Bumps Into an Old Lady   April 16, 1981
   Writer: David Lloyd
   Director: James Burrows
   Guest Stars: Iris Korn, Sam DeFazio, Jay F. Riley, Lane Brody, Joe Medalis

Louie is slapped with a million-dollar lawsuit by the kindly old woman he accidentally ran down with his cab.

63   Bobby and the Critic   April 30, 1981
Writer: Barry Kemp
Director: James Burrows
Guest Star: John Harkins

Bobby performs a turgid one-man show for a vengeful theater critic who carries a personal grudge against the actor.

64   On the Job (Part 1)   May 7, 1981
Writers: Dennis Danziger, Ellen Sandler
Director: James Burrows
Guest Stars: Robert Balderson, Bill Wiley, John O'Leary, Carmine Caridi, Alice Hirson, John Petlock, Robin Pearson Rose

A month after the cab company goes bankrupt, the drivers reunite to exchange tales of their employment experiences in the outside world.

Tony lands a job as a loan shark's enforcer; Elaine finds work as a legal secretary; and, as a door-to-door salesman, Jim nearly destroys a condo when he attempts to demonstrate a new high-powered vacuum cleaner.

65   On the Job (Part 2)   May 14, 1981
Writers: Dennis Danziger, Ellen Sandler
Director: James Burrows
Guest Stars: Clint Young, Claire Malis, Al Lewis, Michael McGuire, Dana Halsted

The cabbies continue to recount harrowing tales of their new jobs.

Before they return to the shelter of the garage, Louie discovers his calling in the stock market; Bobby plays the Easter Bunny at children's birthday parties; and Alex lands a job as a night watchman.

66   Latka the Playboy   May 21, 1981
Writers: Glen Charles, Les Charles
Director: James Burrows
Guest Stars: George Wendt, Robin Klein

Tired of striking out with the ladies, shy Latka adopts the split personality of smooth-talking ladies' man Vic Ferrari.

1981/82   THE FOURTH SEASON

Year-End Rating: 15.8 (53d place)

Fourth-season producers Ken Estin, Howard Gewirtz, and Ian Praiser write many of the year's scripts, along with executive script consultant David Lloyd, executive story editor Sam Simon, and Glen Charles and Les Charles, who are credited as executive consultants in the fourth year. Richard Sakai is co-producer, and James L. Brooks is billed as executive creative consultant.

67   Jim the Psychic   October 8, 1981
   Writer: Barry Kemp
   Story: Holly Holmberg Brooks
   Director: James Burrows
   Guest Stars: Diane Peterson, Kiva Dawson

The cabbies prepare for the worst when Jim's latest premonition foretells doom for Alex.

This episode was based on a story submitted by Holly Holmberg Brooks, the wife of executive producer James L. Brooks.

68   Vienna Waits   October 15, 1981
   Writer: Ken Estin
   Director: Howard Storm
   Guest Stars: Reuven Bar-Yotam, Gary Phillips, Warwick Sims, Cassandra Gava, Patch Mackenzie

Alex is worried that Elaine might cramp his style during a trip to Europe, but she ends up adapting to the romantic climate far better than he does.

Alex and Elaine's occasional attraction resurfaces in a lovely scene where they both agree that, after four years of helping each other through good times and bad, their bond may actually be strong enough to withstand a single night as lovers.

69   Mr. Personalities   October 22, 1981
   Writers: Ian Praiser, Howard Gewirtz
   Director: Howard Storm
   Guest Stars: Barry Nelson, Bernadette Birkett, Wendy Goldman

The cabbies convince Latka to see a psychiatrist after his playboy persona threatens to take over his entire personality.

70   Jim Joins the Network   October 29, 1981
   Writer: David Lloyd
   Director: Noam Pitlik
   Guest Stars: Martin Short, Melendy Britt

A spineless network executive taps Jim as a silent partner after the cabbie's programming hunches prove unerringly correct.

71   Louie's Fling   November 5, 1981
   Writer: Sam Simon
   Director: James Burrows
   Guest Stars: Andrea Marcovicci, Rhea Perlman

Louie takes advantage of Zena's girlfriend Emily—an emotional wreck on the rebound from a disastrous love affair.

After he exploits Emily, Louie still can't resist entertaining the fantasy that she's in love with him—a dream that comes tumbling down when, like Chaplin's drunken benefactor in *City Lights*, she sobers up in the cold morning light to declare him disgusting. And yet, despite Louie's despicable behavior, our sympathy goes out to this misguided devil who is brave—or foolish—enough to act out his own mischievous fantasies.

72   Like Father, Like Son   November 12, 1981
   Writer: David Lloyd
   Director: James Burrows
   Guest Stars: Jack Gilford, Barbara Babcock

Alex gets involved in a bizarre triangle when he finds himself in romantic competition with his own irrepressible father.

73   Louie's Mom Remarries   November 19, 1981
   Writer: Earl Pomerantz
   Director: James Burrows
   Guest Stars: Julia DeVito, Jerry Fujikawa

Louie hits the roof when his mother asks his blessing for her marriage to an elderly Japanese man.

74 Fledgling   November 26, 1981
  Writer: Ken Estin
  Director: James Burrows
  Guest Star: Paul Sand

Elaine tries to convince a severely agoraphobic artist to venture
outside his studio for the first time in years.

75 Of Mice and Tony   December 10, 1981
  Writers: Glen Charles, Les Charles
  Director: James Burrows
  Guest Stars: Ernie Hudson, John Christy Ewing

Tony's dream of managing an up-and-coming young boxer crum-
bles when a syndicate of well-to-do doctors makes his fighter a
better offer.

Writers Ian Praiser and Howard Gewirtz make cameo appearances
as two of the well-heeled doctors.

76 Louie Goes Too Far   December 17, 1981
  Writer: Danny Kallis
  Director: Michael Lessac
  Guest Stars: Allen Williams, Noni White

Louie's days at the Sunshine Cab Company appear numbered
when Elaine files charges against him for spying on her through
a peephole in the ladies' room.

77 I Wanna Be Around   January 7, 1982
  Writers: Glen Charles, Les Charles
  Director: James Burrows
  Guest Star: J. Alan Thomas

Louie prepares for an imagined apocalypse by recruiting a survival squad for his bomb shelter.

78 Bobby Doesn't Live Here Anymore   January 14, 1982
  Writers: Glen Charles, Les Charles
  Director: James Burrows
  Guest Star: Jeff Conaway

Bobby returns to suffer Louie's taunts one last time as he prepares to move on to brighter horizons in Hollywood.

79   Nina Loves Alex   January 21, 1982
   Writer: David Lloyd
   Director: Joan Darling
   Guest Stars: Charlaine Woodard, John Mengatti, Audrey
   Berindey

An optimistic cabbie launches a romantic campaign to attract
Alex, who finds himself fiercely uninterested in the ingratiating
young actress.

A superb comic script that captures the essence of Alex's tragic inability to synchronize head and heart. At his most caustic, he dismisses
his would-be companion as a naive fool, "She's like every actress or
Hindu I've ever met!" The inevitable turnaround comes when Alex con-
soles Nina after her first defeat, and he finally senses an attraction to
her despair. He inspires her to strike out on her own, only to find himself
standing alone once again at the top of the stairs.

80   Tony's Lady   January 28, 1982
   Writer: Ken Estin
   Director: Michael Zinberg
   Guest Stars: Rebecca Holden, Joel Brooks, John Calvin

Tony lands a job as chauffeur for a wealthy young woman and
soon finds himself falling in love with the untouchable beauty.

81   Simka Returns   February 4, 1982
   Writers: Ian Praiser, Howard Gewirtz
   Director: Michael Zinberg
   Guest Star: Carol Kane

Latka discovers an unlikely rival for Simka's affections when she
falls under the spell of his alter-ego, Vic Ferrari.

Carol Kane had already appeared in more than a dozen films when
she approached Jim Brooks for advice on whether she should do television. The executive producer's response was to offer her the role of
Latka's girlfriend in a third-year episode. "It went through the roof,"
he remembers, which brought about Simka's reprise in this episode—
an appearance that earned the actress an Emmy.

82 Jim and the Kid   February 11, 1982
Writer: David Lloyd
Director: Michael Zinberg
Guest Stars: Tony La Torre, Rebecca Clemons, Mark Harrison

After Tony brings a runaway into the Sunshine garage, Jim decides to raise the wayward kid as his own son.

83 Take My Ex-Wife, Please   February 18, 1982
Writers: Ian Praiser, Howard Gewirtz
Director: Noam Pitlik
Guest Stars: Louise Lasser, Candi and Randi Brough, Alex Rodine

Alex is frantic when his ex-wife develops an unexplainable attraction to Louie DePalma.

84 The Unkindest Cut   February 25, 1982
Writer: Sam Simon
Story: Barbara Duncan
Director: Noam Pitlik
Guest Stars: Ted Danson, Gela Jacobsen, Karen Anders

Louie and Alex extract revenge on a snooty hairdresser who has bilked Elaine out of $225 for a perfectly hideous hairstyle.

During a lull in shooting, staff director Jim Burrows huddled with guest star Ted Danson long enough to interest him in reading for a part in a new series he was developing with Glen and Les Charles. The show was called "Cheers," and Danson walked off with the lead role.

85 Tony's Comeback   March 4, 1982
Writer: Sam Simon
Director: Michael Lessac
Guest Stars: Bubba Smith, Naomi Stevens

An unemployed pro football player inspires Tony to attempt a boxing comeback.

86   Elegant Iggy   March 18, 1982
   Writer: Ken Estin
   Director: Noam Pitlik
   Guest Stars: Fran Ryan, Nina Van Pallandt, Robert Denison

Elaine prepares for the most embarrassing night of her life when Jim escorts her to an elegant dinner party hosted by an influential society matron.

87   The Wedding of Latka and Simka   March 25, 1982
   Writers: Howard Gewirtz, Ian Praiser
   Director: James Burrows
   Guest Stars: Carol Kane, Dr. Joyce Brothers, Susan Kellermann, Vincent Schiavelli, Peter Elbing

Latka and Simka's marriage plans fall in doubt when the pair fails to pass the bizarre rituals of their old-world wedding ceremony.

88   Cooking for Two   April 8, 1982
   Writers: Ken Estin, Sam Simon
   Director: James Burrows

Jim proves a most unwelcome houseguest when he sleeps through a fire that reduces Louie's apartment to cinders.

89   The Road Not Taken (Part 1)   April 29, 1982
   Writers: Sam Simon, Ken Estin
   Director: James Burrows
   Guest Stars: J. Pat O'Malley, Wendy Phillips, Tom Hanks, Eugene Roche, Charles Cioffi, Michael A. Salcido

The cabbies recall the crucial turning points of their lives when they help Elaine face a momentous decision of her own.

Tom Hanks has a role as one of Jim's college chums in a hilarious flashback that reveals the cabbie's first fateful brush with mind-expanding drugs.

90   The Road Not Taken (Part 2)   May 6, 1982
Writers: Ian Praiser, Howard Gewirtz
Director: James Burrows
Guest Stars: Susan Kellermann, Max Wright, Jill Jaress, David
Mendenhall, Melanie Gaffin, Matthew Faison

Despite all the well-meaning advice from her fellow cabbies,
Elaine still can't decide whether she wants to pull up stakes and
move to Seattle.

Flashbacks reveal Latka's tearful farewell to his frigid homeland on
the eve of his emigration to America, and a second vignette reveals
Alex's final confrontation with the petty tyranny of office politics.

1982/83   THE FIFTH SEASON

Year-End Rating: 13.2 (73d place)

As the show moves to NBC for a fifth season, producers Ken Estin,
Sam Simon, and Richard Sakai attempt to rejuvenate the series by introducing new romantic interests for Louie, Tony, and Elaine. But despite their efforts, the show is canceled at the close of the fifth year.

David Lloyd is executive script consultant in the final season, and
Katharine Green serves as the season's executive story editor. Harvey
Miller signs on as executive consultant, and James L. Brooks continues
as executive creative consultant and executive producer, along with Stan
Daniels and Ed. Weinberger.

91   The Shloogel Show   September 30, 1982
Writers: Ken Estin, Sam Simon
Director: Noam Pitlik
Guest Stars: Marcia Wallace, Carlene Watkins, Wallace Shawn,
Anne DeSalvo, Murphy Cross

Latka and Simka attempt to match each of the cabbies with their
ideal partner when they stage a massive blind date at Mario's.

Jim finally meets Marcia Wallace—his TV idol since her days as a co-
star of "The Bob Newhart Show." The actress played herself in the
producers' sly homage to that classic comedy.

Three of the cabbies' blind dates resurfaced in later episodes of the
season. Anne DeSalvo would return as Tony's streetwise girlfriend,
Vicki; Elaine later introduced bookish Arnie—played by Wallace Shawn—

to the kids; and Murphy Cross played Louie's date, Judy, the irrepressible blind girl whose sight would be restored by the end of the season.

92   Jim's Inheritance   October 7, 1982
    Writer: Ken Estin
    Director: Noam Pitlik
    Guest Stars: Dick Sargent, F. William Parker

Jim stands to inherit millions from his father's estate, but only
if he can legally prove his sanity.

93   Alex Goes off the Wagon   October 14, 1985
    Writer: Danny Kallis
    Director: Noam Pitlik

Alex falls prey to his old gambling addiction after a lucky night
in Atlantic City, and Jim is the only one who can help.

94   Scenskees From a Marriage (Part 1)   October 21, 1982
    Writers: Ian Praiser, Howard Gewirtz
    Director: Noam Pitlik
    Guest Stars: Allyce Beasley, Peter Elbing, Vincent Schiavelli

After spending the night snowbound with a woman cabbie, Latka
lands in hot water when Simka discovers how the pair managed
to stay warm.

95   Scenskees From a Marriage (Part 2)   October 28, 1982
    Writers: Ian Praiser, Howard Gewirtz
    Director: Noam Pitlik

To even the score with her wayward husband, old-world tradition dictates that Simka must choose a lover from among Latka's
workmates.

96   Crime and Punishment   November 4, 1982
    Writer: Katharine Green
    Director: Stan Daniels
    Guest Stars: J. Alan Thomas, Allen Goorwitz, Martin Garner

Louie persuades Jeff to cover for him after the boss discovers
his petty thievery, a favor that costs the hapless junior dispatcher
his job.

97 Alex the Gofer   November 11, 1982
  Writer: David Lloyd
  Director: Michael Lessac
  Guest Stars: Matthew Laurence, David Paymer, Caren Kaye

Alex is thrilled to land a job in show business, even though he winds up as no more than an errand boy for a pair of arrogant young producers.

98 Louie's Revenge   November 18, 1982
  Writer: Sam Simon
  Director: Stan Daniels
  Guest Stars: Andrea Marcovicci, Charlie Stavola

Louie plans to extract revenge on Emily—the unbalanced woman who turned on him after their ill-fated fling—but ends up falling for her all over again.

99 Travels With My Dad   November 25, 1982
  Writer: Barton Dean
  Director: Michael Zinberg
  Guest Stars: Donnelly Rhodes, Dick Miller, Wendell Wright

Tony's seafaring father returns from his travels to offer his son a job on a Chinese freighter.

100 Elaine and the Monk   December 2, 1982
  Writer: David Lloyd
  Director: Danny De Vito
  Guest Star: Mark Blankfield

Elaine falls for a guy who's fun-loving, sensitive, and bright— and also due back at the monastery in exactly one week.

As he prepares to renew his vows of silence, Elaine and her beau share a last dance—choreographed by Debbie Allen, one of the stars of TV's "Fame."

101 Zena's Honeymoon December 9, 1982
Writer: David Lloyd
Director: Richard Sakai
Guest Stars: Rhea Perlman, Peter Jurasik

Louie is brokenhearted to hear that Zena is getting married, especially since he always hoped she'd come crawling back to him.

Zena Sherman's exit from "Taxi" was inevitable after Rhea Perlman moved to a neighboring Paramount soundstage to begin her new life as "Cheers's" irascible waitress Carla Tortelli.

102 Get Me Through the Holidays December 16, 1982
Writers: Ken Estin, Sam Simon
Director: Michael Zinberg
Guest Star: Louise Lasser

Alex's ex-wife attempts a holiday reconciliation to dispel her yuletide loneliness.

103 Louie Moves Uptown January 22, 1983
Writer: David Lloyd
Director: Michael Zinberg
Guest Stars: Gayle Hunicutt, Penny Marshall, Nelson Welch, Lois DeBanzie

Louie plans to move into an exclusive Manhattan co-op apartment, if he can win the approval of a panel of pompous tenants.

"Laverne and Shirley" star Penny Marshall plays herself in a delightful cameo where she tries to convince the co-op board that acting in a situation comedy is a legitimate profession.

104 Alex's Old Buddy January 29, 1983
Writers: Ken Estin, Sam Simon
Director: Richard Sakai
Guest Stars: Judith Marie Bergan, John Hancock

Alex comes to terms with the imminent death of his oldest friend— his aged family dog, Buddy.

105   Sugar Ray Nardo   February 5, 1983
   Writer: Katharine Green
   Director: Danny DeVito
   Guest Stars: David Mendenhall, Brad Kester, Michael Alldredge

Elaine is upset when her son abandons his oboe lessons to study boxing with Tony.

106   Celebration of "Taxi" (one hour)   March 23, 1983
   Writers: Various
   Directors: Various

A retrospective of highlights from the first four seasons of "Taxi."

107   Alex Gets Burned by an Old Flame   March 30, 1983
   Writer: Barton Dean
   Director: Harvey Miller
   Guest Star: Cathie Shiriff

Alex falls for a lady lawyer who still carries the torch for Jim.

108   Louie and the Blind Girl   April 6, 1983
   Writer: Larry Anderson
   Director: Noam Pitlik
   Guest Stars: Murphy Cross, David Young

Louie's blind girlfriend has her sight restored, but the dispatcher worries that she may have second thoughts about him once she sees what he looks like.

Over five seasons, it became necessary to soften Louie's rough edges from time to time. It's too horrible to imagine what might have happened if the leering, slobbering Louie from the show's first year had been left at the bedside of a blind girl! But even at his sweetest, Louie oozed a palpably disreputable charm—there was always that sly twinkle in Danny DeVito's eyes that warned you not to trust him.

109   Arnie Meets the Kids   April 13, 1983
   Writer: John Markus
   Director: Richard Sakai
   Guest Stars: Wallace Shawn, Melanie Gaffin, David Mendenhall, Wendy Jewell

Elaine's new beau tries to win her kids' affection by bribing them with cash and gifts.

110　Tony's Baby　　　　　　　　　　　　　　April 20, 1983
　　Writer: Dari Daniels
　　Director: Richard Sakai
　　Guest Stars: Anne De Salvo, Keenan Wynn

On the eve of a big match, Tony is shocked to learn that his girlfriend is expecting a baby.

111　Jim's Mario's　　　　　　　　　　　　　　May 18, 1983
　　Writers: Ken Estin, Sam Simon
　　Director: Danny DeVito
　　Guest Star: Walter Olkewicz

The cabbies pitch in to make a success of Mario's after Jim buys the restaurant against his family's better judgment.

112　A Grand Gesture　　　　　　　　　　　　May 25, 1983
　　Writers: Ken Estin, Sam Simon
　　Director: Noam Pitlik
　　Guest Stars: Jeff Thomas, Vincent Schiavelli, Scatman Crothers, Tom Villard, Tracey Walter, Melanie Gaffin

Jim concocts a novel plan to share the wealth when he offers each of the cabbies a thousand-dollar bill to be given away to whomever he or she sees fit.

113　Simka's Monthlies　　　　　　　　　　　June 15, 1983
　　Writer: Holly Holmberg Brooks
　　Director: Harvey Miller

Latka worries when Simka's behavior suddenly grows erratic on the eve of her final meeting at the Bureau of Immigration.

This would be the last first-run episode of "Taxi."

Despite the protests of Judd Hirsch and other cast members, the series quietly expired in the late spring of 1983—a tragic victim of audience indifference. "The show still had a lot of life in it," producer Ed. Weinberger maintains. "We probably could have gone another two years."

Maybe so. But times were changing.

By the early 1980s, the progressive era that spawned Archie Bunker, Hawkeye, and Mary Richards had already faded from the public consciousness. Given the country's shifting tastes, perhaps it's best that "Taxi" ran out of gas when it did—before the free-spirited misfits of the Sunshine garage fell completely out of step with the times. At least this way, Jim Ignatowski would never have to face the indignity of mandatory drug testing.

In any event, there was very little chance of another revival for a show that had already been canceled by two networks. In the end, die-hard fans would find their only consolation in syndicated reruns—where, freed from the pressures of network ratings battles, the show would flourish. And now that everyone's stopped paying so much attention to the meter, "Taxi" just may run forever.

EMMY AWARDS

The following is a complete listing of the Emmy Awards bestowed on "Taxi" by the National Academy of Television Arts and Sciences.

1978/79 Outstanding Comedy Series
Outstanding Lead Actress in a Comedy for a Continued or Single Performance in a Regular Series: Ruth Gordon, "Sugar Mama"
Outstanding Achievement in Film Editing: M. Pam Blumenthal, "Paper Marriage"

1979/80 Outstanding Comedy Series
Outstanding Directing in a Comedy Series: James Burrows, "Louie and the Nice Girl"
Outstanding Achievement in Film Editing: M. Pam Blumenthal, "Louie and the Nice Girl"

1980/81 Outstanding Comedy Series
Outstanding Lead Actor in a Comedy Series: Judd Hirsch
Outstanding Supporting Actor in a Comedy Series: Danny DeVito
Outstanding Directing in a Comedy Series: James Burrows, "Elaine's Strange Triangle"
Outstanding Writing in a Comedy Series: Michael Leeson, "Tony's Sister and Jim"
Outstanding Achievement in Film Editing: M. Pam Blumenthal, Jack Michon, "Elaine's Strange Triangle"

1981/82   Outstanding Lead Actress in a Comedy Series: Carol Kane, "Simka Returns"

Outstanding Supporting Actor in a Comedy Series: Christopher Lloyd

Outstanding Writing in a Comedy Series: Ken Estin, "Elegant Iggy"

1982/83   Outstanding Lead Actor in a Comedy Series: Judd Hirsch

Outstanding Supporting Actress in a Comedy Series: Carol Kane

Outstanding Supporting Actor in a Comedy Series: Christopher Lloyd

"CHEERS"

·

*In "Cheers," nobody slips on
the banana peel.*
—JIM BURROWS, director and
executive producer of "Cheers"

GLEN AND LES CHARLES didn't like to leave the house on Saturday night.

In the glory days of 1974, the benevolent programmers at CBS had scheduled "All in the Family," "M*A*S*H," and *both* the "Bob Newhart" and the "Mary Tyler Moore" shows back-to-back on Saturday night, and there was simply no better place to be than in front of the TV. For confirmed fans of situation comedy, it was an inspiring two hours of television. For the two brothers who would one day mastermind "Cheers," watching that lineup of television was the start of a new career.

Back then, Glen was an advertising copywriter, and Les worked part-time as a junior high school teacher. They had no experience in television, but both recognized the quiet revolution that was taking place in our living rooms in the early 1970s. After a mindless decade of witches, genies, and talking horses, television suddenly seemed capable of delivering bright, literate comedy you could laugh at without feeling ashamed. It was a time when many of the industry's funniest writers were scripting—not for movies or Broadway—but for television. To Glen and Les Charles, writing for TV just seemed to make sense. Getting paid lots of money to write scripts that made people laugh—well, how hard could that really be?

And with no more preparation than that, they sat down and began to write.

"We were so eager to get into the business," recalled Les Charles, "we wrote a script for every comedy on the air. Then we started in on the *dramas*." Within a few months they had submitted full scripts— unsolicited, on speculation—to every major program supplier in Hollywood. "We blanketed the town with spec scripts."

Glen Charles later remarked, incredulously, "We even wrote a spec script for 'Gunsmoke'!"

Their story took a fairy-tale twist when their efforts actually landed them a job. One of their scripts found its way to a story editor's desk at MTM Productions, where there were a couple of immediate openings on "Phyllis"—a troubled "Mary Tyler Moore" spin-off that had recently undergone a major format overhaul. The brothers were hired to write for the show and before long they found themselves producing the series.

On their first major assignment, the writers had lucked into a golden opportunity to learn the TV business from the inside out. As fate would have it, one of the key directors on "Phyllis" was Jim Burrows, a soft-spoken man who shared the brothers' low-key sense of humor. And by odd coincidence, he, too, had been lured to Hollywood by the siren song of "The Mary Tyler Moore Show."

The son of Pulitzer Prize–winning playwright Abe Burrows, James Burrows had stage-managed Mary Tyler Moore's ill-fated 1967 Broadway debut in *Holly Golightly*. Years later, after Mary returned to television in her own hit series, Burrows wrote a letter of congratulations for her new success. The letter found its way to the desk of Mary's husband, Grant Tinker, who was then running MTM. Always on the lookout for new talent, the executive remembered the bright young stage manager and offered him a job as a novice director at MTM.

Tinker's instincts proved correct. Burrows proved to be a quick study— before long he was directing episodes of MTM's top comedies, including "Phyllis," "Rhoda," and "The Bob Newhart Show." His work drew compliments from the company's top creators, including James L. Brooks, Ed. Weinberger, Stan Daniels, and David Davis—all of whom were about to split off from MTM to produce shows under their own banner. When they left, they asked Burrows—and the Charles brothers—to come along to help write, produce, and direct a new comedy series called "Taxi."

One of the finest comedies of the 1970s, "Taxi" proved a worthy heir to the MTM legacy—due, in no small part, to the contributions of Burrows and the Charles brothers. "It was a great experience," Les Charles remembered. Between them, Burrows and the Charles brothers wrote, produced, or directed nearly every episode of the show's first three seasons. But finally, the talented threesome longed to move on.

"It just wasn't *our* show," Les Charles explained. "We felt we were ready to do something of our own."

Apparently, so did Brandon Tartikoff. The young NBC programming chief fancied himself a connoisseur of TV comedy and he made it a point to keep careful tabs on the best comedy creators in the business. When he heard that the director and head writers of "Taxi" had formed their own production company, he urged his boss to grab them—before somebody else did.

Fred Silverman took his top programmer's advice. He snagged Charles, Burrows, and Charles by offering to finance their first series—with a guarantee that NBC would buy at least thirteen episodes, regardless of the show's initial ratings. It was a promise the executive would not personally carry out. In 1981—no longer the golden boy of network television—Fred Silverman was ousted from the presidency of NBC.

In his place, the network appointed Grant Tinker.

"We're looking for *quality*" was the new president's edict to NBC programmers and producers alike. After a decade of producing many of the finest shows in prime time, Tinker declared his intention to apply those same high standards to the program practices of an entire broadcast network. And Charles, Burrows, and Charles were delighted when the executive chose to inaugurate his new policy by giving the green light to a show they'd been brainstorming for well over a year—a comedy set in a bar called "Cheers."

"We wanted to do an ensemble show, like 'M*A*S*H' or 'Taxi,' rather than a family story," Glen Charles told *TV Guide*. "At first we thought of setting it in a hotel, to bring a lot of different types of people together." But when they realized that most of the action would take place in the bar, they dropped the hotel and moved the show to a neighborhood saloon in Boston. As Les Charles observed, "It's much easier to write when you put all your characters in one room. Anytime you need a joke, you've got someone there who can do it."

On "Taxi," Burrows and the brothers Charles had learned how important atmosphere was to character comedy and so they were determined that "Cheers" would look, sound—and even smell—just like a genuine neighborhood watering hole. Glen Charles even traveled to the

Bull and Finch—an actual tavern on the Boston Commons—to find a model for the working bar they would construct on a soundstage at Paramount Studios.

The ensemble cast was assembled with the same attention to detail. The denizens of "Cheers" would be a cast of experienced players—most of them new to series television—who formed an immediate close-knit ensemble. Rhea Perlman, who'd been Louie DePalma's girlfriend for three years on "Taxi," landed the part of the bar's wisecracking waitress Carla. George Wendt and John Ratzenberger were cast as "Cheers's" steadiest customers—Norm, a rotund and harmless boozer; and Cliff, a proud U.S. Mail carrier who dazzled no one with his bottomless font of useless knowledge. Finally, Nick Colasanto was chosen to play Coach Ernie Pantusso, the addled but avuncular bartender who gave the usually sardonic proceedings an irresistibly soft center.

But it was the central relationship played out by Shelley Long and Ted Danson that provided the producers with their greatest challenge. "We wanted to create a show around a Katharine Hepburn/Spencer Tracy–type relationship," Burrows told a *New York Times* reporter. But, ironically, in creating the discordant pairing of Sam and Diane, the producers were actually inspired by the benign friendship of Mary Richards and Lou Grant.

As longtime fans of "The Mary Tyler Moore Show," Glen and Les Charles were always frustrated that the news director and his associate producer never allowed their passion to surface over the seven seasons of that classic series. "Lou and Mary were essentially the same at the end as they were at the beginning. We didn't want that," Les Charles insisted. "Our key concern was not to get stuck in a rut. We didn't want to set up a situation and just ride it out for however long the show was on."

There was certainly no danger of that. From their very first meeting in "Cheers's" premiere episode, it's almost impossible to keep up with Sam and Diane as they set off on the maddeningly convoluted path the producers have mapped out for them.

Abandoned at Cheers while her fiancé goes off to find a wedding ring, Diane is both repelled and enchanted by the uncouth bartender whose girlfriends casually call to remind him that he's "a magnificent pagan beast." The evening doesn't end until Diane has spent what is easily the most hellish—and exciting—night of her life.

When she finally faces the harsh truth—that her would-be suitor *has* stranded her at Cheers—the prim English-lit. major reverts into just another poor wretch "with no one in the world to turn to but some stranger who mixes drinks." Naturally, Sam takes advantage of the opening to launch the first assault in what will become prime time's most protracted seduction. Leaning over the bar, he tenders a job offer, confident she'll accept, since the phrase "magnificent pagan beast" has never left her mind.

And, despite her protests, there's a glint in Diane's eye that tells us he's right—it hasn't.

It was a remarkable beginning. Funny, unpredictable, sophisticated—and a dismal failure in the ratings. "It looked pretty bleak for a while," Glen Charles commented, recalling the show's early ratings. "The one encouraging thing was that the people at the network were very much fans of the show."

Grant Tinker and Brandon Tartikoff were still convinced that NBC could capture an audience by taking the high road to prime time. For them "Cheers" had become a source of personal, as well as professional pride. Both executives *watched* the show. They both *liked* the show. So, despite barely measurable ratings, there was no way they could *cancel* the show—not after the quality-programming campaign they'd pitched to their eager affiliate stations.

In October the executives held their breath and ordered the nine additional episodes needed to round out a full season of "Cheers." They were confident that the show would find its audience by the end of the season. It had to.

Eventually, it did—if only by a nose.

Buoyed by a barrage of favorable press and excellent word of mouth—once viewers finally did tune in, they almost invariably became loyal, nearly evangelical fans—"Cheers" inched its way up the Nielsen chart throughout the rest of the season, a few agonizing points at a time. Finally, in August, after a flood of Emmy nominations proffered the industry's official endorsement, the series was vindicated by the popular audience as well. To the amazement of skeptics throughout the industry, "Cheers" finally broke into Nielsen's top ten.

But for Jim Burrows and the brothers Charles, the ratings breakthrough and the cartload of Emmy nominations the series gathered for its first season represented only one measure of success. Not long after they began production on the show's second season, Glen and Les Charles discovered a very different—but no less significant—indication that they must be doing something right.

They noticed a large pile of "Cheers" sample scripts stacked near their secretary's desk. Many had been submitted—on spec—from hopeful young writers who had obviously watched the show and been inspired enough to take a crack at writing an episode themselves. Getting paid lots of money to write scripts that made people laugh—well, how hard could that really be?

The two brothers, who certainly knew the answer, could only chuckle as they returned to work on the next "Cheers" script.

A Critical Guide to the First 95 Episodes

REGULAR CAST

Sam Malone	Ted Danson
Diane Chambers	Shelley Long
Coach Ernie Pantusso	Nick Colasanto
Carla Tortelli	Rhea Perlman
Norm Peterson	George Wendt
Cliff Clavin	John Ratzenberger
Frasier Crane	Kelsey Grammer
Woody Boyd	Woody Harrelson

SUPPORTING CAST

Nick Tortelli	Dan Hedaya
Loretta Tortelli	Jean Kasem
Alan	Alan Koss
Larry	Larry Harpel
Al	Al Rosen
Tim	Tim Cunningham
Steve	Steve Gianelli
Greg	Paul Willson
Jack	Jack Knight
Fred	John Fielder
Paul	Paul Vaughn
Harry	Harry Anderson
Andy Andy	Derek McGrath

Created by Les Charles, James Burrows, Glen Charles
Music by Craig Safan
Theme ("Where Everybody Knows Your Name") by Judy Hart
  Angelo, Gary Portnoy, sung by Gary Portnoy
Director of photography is John Finger
Principal director is James Burrows

475

1982/83   THE FIRST SEASON

Year-End Rating: 13.1 (75th place)

The friendliest bar in Boston opens its doors to a comic assortment of chronic misfits and eccentric regulars in a first year written under the careful supervision of Glen Charles, Les Charles, and first-year co-producers Ken Levine and David Isaacs. Along with executive story editor David Lloyd, they will contribute the bulk of scripts for the first season.

The freshman year is produced by Glen Charles, James Burrows, and Les Charles. Burrows also directs every episode, as he will—with a single exception—for each of the seasons to follow. Tim Berry is the series's associate producer.

1   Give Me a Ring Sometime   September 30, 1982
Writers: Glen Charles, Les Charles
Director: James Burrows
Guest Stars: Michael McGuire, John P. Navin, Jr., Erik Holland, Ron Frazier

On the eve of her intended elopement, Diane Chambers sits on a barstool at Cheers and watches her entire life crumble before her eyes.

"Where better than here to study life in all its facets?" Diane asks, rationalizing why she has stooped to accept Sam's offer of a job as a cocktail waitress. "People meet in bars, they part, they rejoice, they suffer, they come here to be with their own kind."

It's a flimsy rationale from a perennial student who suddenly realizes that her entire life has prepared her for nothing more challenging than serving drinks in a bar. In her shallow appraisal of Cheers, she even misses the irony that Sam and the gang at Cheers have offered her sanctuary—even though they have just met—while the man she planned to spend the rest of her life with didn't think twice about dumping her on their doorstep. Though she complains that her stay at Cheers is a form of purgatory, Diane, too, has come to Cheers to be with her own kind. She just doesn't know it yet.

2   Sam's Women   October 7, 1982
Writer: Earl Pomerantz
Director: James Burrows
Guest Stars: Donna McKechnie, Donnelly Rhodes, Angela Aames

Diane chides Sam for dating women of limited intellect; and a visitor to Cheers demands to speak to the former owner.

The producers were well acquainted with writer Earl Pomerantz from his frequent contributions to "Taxi" during their long tenure on the series.

3 The Tortelli Tort   October 14, 1982
Writer: Tom Reeder
Director: James Burrows
Guest Stars: Ron Karabatsos, Stephen Keep

Sam is slammed with a lawsuit after Carla assaults an outspoken Yankees fan who dared to wander into Cheers.

4 Sam at Eleven   October 21, 1982
Writers: Glen Charles, Les Charles
Director: James Burrows
Guest Stars: Fred Dryer, Harry Anderson, Rick Dees, Julie Brown

During a TV interview with a local sportscaster, Sam reveals how much he misses the spotlight of his major-league days.

The loudmouth sportscaster was played by Fred Dryer, who, along with film star William Devane, had been a contender for the role of Sam Malone in "Cheers's" original casting sessions.

5 The Coach's Daughter   October 28, 1982
Writer: Ken Estin
Director: James Burrows
Guest Stars: Allyce Beasley, Philip Charles MacKenzie, Tim Cunningham

Coach meets his daughter's fiancé, an obnoxious salesman who's so thoroughly detestable that even the Coach can't stand him.

Philip Charles MacKenzie would become better known as the flighty Donald on "Brothers," cable TV's first sitcom; and Allyce Beasley found much greater renown as Miss DiPesto, the gal Friday of "Moonlighting."

6   Any Friend of Diane's   November 4, 1982
Writers: Ken Levine, David Isaacs
Director: James Burrows
Guest Stars: Julia Duffy, Macon McCalman

An old school chum of Diane's arrives at Cheers hankering for an afternoon of lustful abandon with Sam.

Julia Duffy, who along with film star Lisa Eichhorn was one of the actresses considered for the part of Diane in the series's early development, soon landed the plumb role of Stephanie, the self-absorbed maid on "Newhart."

7   Friends, Romans, Accountants   November 11, 1982
Writers: Ken Levine, David Isaacs
Director: James Burrows
Guest Stars: James Read, Kenneth Kimmins, Peter Van Norden

After a disastrous office party at Cheers, Norm tries to score points with his boss by fixing him up with Diane.

Norm succeeds only in losing his job—which helps explain how he was able to spend so much time at the bar. Norm, "Cheers's" all-purpose underachiever, was based on a real-life guzzler Les Charles remembered from his days as a bartender in college.

8   Truce or Consequences   November 18, 1982
Writers: Ken Levine, David Isaacs
Director: James Burrows
Guest Star: Jack Knight

Carla calls a truce with Diane to reveal a shocking secret.

9   The Coach Returns to Action   November 25, 1982
Writer: Earl Pomerantz
Director: James Burrows
Guest Star: Murphy Cross

Sam participates in an unwitting rivalry with Coach when both have designs on the same woman.

10   Endless Slumper   December 2, 1982
  Writer: Sam Simon
  Director: James Burrows
  Guest Stars: Christopher McDonald, Anne Haney

Sam becomes an accident-prone wreck after he lends his good-luck charm to a Red Sox pitcher who's stuck in a slump.

11   One for the Book   December 9, 1982
  Writer: Katharine Green
  Director: James Burrows
  Guest Stars: Boyd Bodwell, Ian Wolfe

An aging doughboy holds a lonely World War I reunion in Cheers; and a novice monk comes looking for one last night of debauchery before he checks into the monastery.

12   The Spy Who Came in for a Cold One   December 16, 1982
  Writer: David Lloyd
  Director: James Burrows
  Guest Stars: Ellis Rabb, Robert Evan Collins, Kurtis Woodruff

The gang at Cheers copes with an inveterate liar who's convinced Diane that he's a poet, while Carla is certain he's really a spy.

13   Now Pitching: Sam Malone   January 6, 1983
  Writers: Ken Levine, David Isaacs
  Director: James Burrows
  Guest Stars: Barbara Babcock, Luis Tiant, Richard Hill, Paul Vaughn

Sam feels used when an attractive theatrical agent lands him a string of lucrative commercial endorsements in exchange for his romantic favors.

After Diane and Sam debate the barkeeper's next move, Coach arrives to offer Sam his own no-nonsense solution—along with a well-placed kick in the pants. For all his confusion, the simple-minded Coach was often the only person in Cheers capable of straightforward thought. Glen and Les Charles admitted that their model for Coach Ernie Pantusso was baseball's legendary Yogi Berra, who was also well known for the peculiar logic of his public utterances.

14   Let Me Count the Ways   January 13, 1983
  Writer: Heide Perlman
  Director: James Burrows
  Guest Stars: Mark King, Jack Knight, Steve Hanafin

Diane mourns the death of her housecat but discovers there are no shoulders to cry on at Cheers during a Celtics game.

The script, the first of many written by Rhea Perlman's sister, Heide, opens with a precredit "teaser" scene, as did every episode of the series. Here, Diane arrives, bursting with enthusiasm after attending an Indian film festival—only to leave screaming in abject defeat a moment later, after Coach and Carla describe their own favorite Indian film, *Fort Apache*. Given the soap-operatic overtones of the show's continuing narrative line, the producers designed the opening teaser as a hook that provided an instant introduction to the show and its characters in order to entice the uninitiated—a useful weapon in the uphill ratings battle the series faced during the first year.

15   Father Knows Last   January 20, 1983
  Writer: Heide Perlman
  Director: James Burrows
  Guest Stars: Mark King, Jack Knight

Diane attempts to prevent an injustice when Carla schemes to convince an unwitting computer programmer that he's the father of her baby.

16   The Boys in the Bar   January 27, 1983
  Writers: Ken Levine, David Isaacs
  Director: James Burrows
  Guest Stars: Alan Autry, Harry Anderson, John Furey, Michael Kearns, Kenneth Tigar, Lee Ryan, Jack Knight, Tom Babson

After Sam publicly supports an old teammate who has just come out of the closet, the regulars are convinced that Cheers is turning into a trendy gay hangout.

17 Diane's Perfect Date   February 10, 1983
   Writer: David Lloyd
   Director: James Burrows
   Guest Stars: Derek McGrath, Gretchen Corbett, Doug Sheehan

Sam unwittingly fixes Diane up with a man who was just released from a prison for the criminally insane.

The date begins when the ex-offender refuses to eat in an Italian restaurant where he once killed a waitress—and goes downhill from there. Andy Andy would return to Cheers about once a year over the next few seasons.

18 No Contest   February 17, 1983
   Writer: Heide Perlman
   Director: James Burrows
   Guest Stars: Charlie Stavola, Renee Gentry, Paul Vaughn, Thomas "Tip" O'Neill, Tessa Richarde, Sharon Peters

Diane attempts to sabotage the Miss Boston Barmaid contest after she discovers Sam entered her in the competition without her knowledge.

The cameo appearance of Bostonian "Cheers" fan, Speaker of the House Thomas "Tip" O'Neill, was a stunt designed to draw attention—and viewers—to the show during the first fledgling season.

19 Pick a Con . . . Any Con   February 24, 1983
   Writer: David Angell
   Director: James Burrows
   Guest Stars: Harry Anderson, Reid Shelton

Sam convinces Cheers's resident con man to stage an elaborate sting to get the Coach's money back from a traveling card shark.

Stand-up comic and magician Harry Anderson—soon to be the star of "Night Court"—was typecast as Harry the con man.

20 Someone Single, Someone Blue   March 3, 1983
   Writer: David Angell
   Director: James Burrows
   Guest Stars: Glynis Johns, Duncan Ross, Dean Dittman, Paul Willson

Diane and Sam plan a marriage of convenience to protect her mother's fortunes from a bizarre legal stipulation in her late father's will.

Diane's mother is played by British stage and film actress Glynis Johns, in the first script by David Angell, who would become one of the show's chief contributors.

21   Showdown (Part 1)   March 24, 1983
Writers: Glen Charles, Les Charles
Director: James Burrows
Guest Stars: George Ball, Alan Koss, Paul Vaughn, Deborah Shelton

Sam can't conceal his resentment of his visiting brother—a rich and talented charmer with something to offer everyone, especially Diane.

22   Showdown (Part 2)   March 31, 1983
Writers: Glen Charles, Les Charles
Director: James Burrows
Guest Stars: Lois DeBanzie, Helen Page Camp, Peggy Kubena

Sam's brother sweeps Diane off her feet with an invitation to Paris, but the waitress finds it harder to leave Cheers than she imagined.

"We didn't want to have two people just flirting with each other ad infinitum," explained Les Charles, so he and his brother, Glen, planned this season's finale—a quirky cliff-hanger that ends with the lovers poised on the brink of consummating their season-long tryst. It's an unlikely romantic encounter that begins when Sam pledges his feelings under duress—Diane has threatened to run her fingernails on the chalkboard if he doesn't—and ends with the lovers locked in a violent embrace. At least for the time being.

1983/84   THE SECOND SEASON

Year-End Rating: 16.6 (34th place)

Sam and Diane's well-contained passion finally bubbles to the surface when the pair form a tentative romantic alliance during the second season. Once again, the producers are Glen Charles, James Burrows, and Les Charles. The second-year story editors are David Angell and Heide Perlman, and David Lloyd serves as executive script consultant, as he does for each of the years that follow.

23   Power Play   September 29, 1983
   Writers: Glen Charles, Les Charles
   Director: James Burrows
   Guest Stars: Alan Koss, Paul Vaughn

The gang at Cheers doesn't hold much hope for Sam and Diane's newly blossomed romance after Sam returns to Cheers early on the night of their first date.

"You've made my life a living hell," Sam complains, brushing aside the stuffed toys that litter the scene of their intended carnal pleasure. "I didn't want you to think I was easy," Diane retorts, setting the comic tone for the bumpy romance that ensues throughout the second season. The show's loyal fans were delighted to see Sam and Diane in each other's arms at last, but their petty insecurities and power plays nearly doom the affair before it's begun.

24   Little Sister, Don'tcha   October 13, 1983
   Writer: Heide Perlman
   Director: James Burrows
   Guest Stars: Paul Vaughn, Paul Willson, Jerry Prell

Cliff falls for Carla's identical twin, a mousy woman who's actually more like her sister than anyone guesses.

Early on, Coach proclaims Cheers, "a romantic bar. As many people fall in love here as get sick." But before the night is over, it's Cliff and Norm who declare their devotion—to each other! After Norm warns Cliff away from Carla's sister, the bewildered postman confesses that Normie is the best friend he's ever had—though the two do stop short of actually hugging. As Cliff points out, it's not like Norm pulled him from a burning car or anything. Rhea Perlman also plays Carla's twin sister, Annette Lozupone.

25 Personal Business   October 20, 1983
Writer: Tom Reeder
Director: James Burrows

Norm and Diane both decide to expand their horizons, but for very different reasons.

26 Homicidal Ham   October 27, 1983
Writer: David Lloyd
Director: James Burrows
Guest Stars: Severn Darden, Derek McGrath, Paul Vaughn, Alan Koss

Andy Andy returns to Cheers with a new career goal—he wants to be an actor.

Diane's criminally maladjusted blind date is up to his old tricks when he performs a strikingly realistic interpretation of the murder scene from *Othello*, with Diane as his unsuspecting Desdemona.

27 Sumner's Return   November 3, 1983
Writer: Michael J. Weithorn
Director: James Burrows
Guest Star: Michael McGuire

To compete with Diane's brainy former beau, Sam tries to finish *War and Peace* in four days.

28 Affairs of the Heart   November 10, 1983
Writer: Heide Perlman
Director: James Burrows
Guest Star: Don Amendolia

Carla rebuffs her latest suitor, convinced that any guy who's interested in her must have *something* wrong with him.

29 Old Flames   November 17, 1983
Writer: David Angell
Director: James Burrows
Guest Stars: Fred Dryer, Elizabeth McIvor

An overbearing sportscaster wagers he can put an end to Sam and Diane's romance within twenty-four hours.

30 Manager Coach   November 24, 1983
Writer: Earl Pomerantz
Director: James Burrows
Guest Stars: Herb Mitchell, Elliott Scott, Corey Feldman,
Martin Davis

Coach undergoes a startling personality transformation when he volunteers to manage a Little League team.

31 They Called Me Mayday   December 1, 1983
Writer: David Angell
Director: James Burrows
Guest Stars: Dick Cavett, Walter Olkewicz, Ed Quinlan

Dick Cavett inspires Sam to write his memoirs; and Norm fumes when Vera dates his old high school rival.

Broke, unemployed, and homeless after his separation from Vera, Norm has evolved into an almost heroically pathetic character. At his lowest ebb, he actually moves into his home-away-from-home when he secretly camps out in Sam's office after closing hours.

32 How Do I Love Thee, Let Me   December 8, 1983
         Call You Back
Writer: Earl Pomerantz
Director: James Burrows
Guest Star: Harry Anderson

Diane insists on a week's separation from Sam to allow them both time to reevaluate the depth of their commitment.

33 Just Three Friends   December 15, 1983
Writer: David Lloyd
Director: James Burrows
Guest Star: Markie Post

Diane refuses to believe that her best friend finds Sam completely irresistible.

34   Where There's a Will   December 22, 1983
  Writer: Nick Arnold
  Director: James Burrows
  Guest Stars: George Gaynes, Alan Koss

The gang at Cheers lifts the gloom of a terminally ill customer, for which he leaves them ten thousand dollars in a hastily scrawled will.

35   Battle of the Exes   January 5, 1984
  Writers: Ken Estin, Sam Simon
  Director: James Burrows
  Guest Stars: Dan Hedaya, Jean Kasem

Carla's insensitive ex-husband invites her to his wedding, which she attends with Sam in tow.

Dan Hedaya gives flesh to the previously imagined horrors of Carla's ex-husband, Nick Tortelli, who would soon develop semiregular status in the Cheers cosmos.

36   No Help Wanted   January 12, 1984
  Writer: Max Tash
  Director: James Burrows
  Guest Star: Barbra Horan

Feeling sorry for Norm, Sam reluctantly hires the unemployed accountant to do Cheers's income tax return.

37   And Coachie Makes Three   January 19, 1984
  Writer: Heide Perlman
  Director: James Burrows
  Guest Star: Eve Roberts

When Coach begins to spend his every waking moment with Sam and Diane, they decide to fix him up with an eligible woman of his own.

38   Cliff's Rocky Moment   January 26, 1984
  Writer: David Lloyd
  Director: James Burrows
  Guest Stars: Sam Scarber, Peter Iacangelo

Tired of hearing Cliff's opinions on everything under the sun, a Cheers patron finally challenges the verbose mailman to a fight.

39 Fortune and Men's Weights   February 2, 1984
Writer: Heide Perlman
Director: James Burrows
Guest Star: Tim Cunningham

Diane worries that the uncanny predictions of an antique fortune-teller's scale might end the spell—and spell the end—for
her and Sam.

The couple convince themselves that their fate rests on the very next
card drawn from the fortune-teller's slot, but the cryptic legend reads,
"Machine empty. Order more fortunes today." The screen goes black
before they have time to comprehend the message, and we are left on
our own to ponder their fate—at least for another week.

As the comedy traces the peaks and valleys in the continuing saga
of Sam and Diane, their epic courtship begins to take on nearly operatic
proportions. The show's creators admit a far greater debt to soap opera
than Wagner, but still insist they never planned to carry the romance
to such extremes when they started. "Initially there was no master plan,"
Glen Charles confessed, "but when it began to look like the show might
actually stay on the air a second year, we knew we'd have to chart their
relationship over a period of time. Now, at the start of every year, we
sit down and figure out where we want Sam and Diane to be at the
beginning, the middle, and the end of the season."

40 Snow Job   February 9, 1984
Writer: David Angell
Director: James Burrows
Guest Star: James Gallery

Cliff is jealous of Norm's new friendship; and Sam concocts a
farfetched story so that he can slip away for a weekend skiing
trip in Vermont.

41 Coach Buries a Grudge   February 16, 1984
Writer: David Lloyd
Director: James Burrows

Coach mourns the passing of an old friend until he discovers
the cad was once romantically involved with his wife.

42   Norman's Conquest   February 23, 1984
Writer: Lissa Levin
Director: James Burrows
Guest Star: Anne Schedeen

The guys egg Norm into making a play for an attractive woman who's hired him to audit her books.

43   I'll Be Seeing You (Part 1)   May 3, 1984
Writers: Glen Charles, Les Charles
Director: James Burrows
Guest Stars: Christopher Lloyd, Steve Gianelli

A temperamental artist offers to paint Diane's portrait, convinced that he can reveal the inner turmoil that Sam has inflicted on her soul.

Christopher Lloyd, late of "Taxi," is Philip Semenko, the haughty painter who comes between Sam and Diane.

44   I'll Be Seeing You (Part 2)   May 10, 1984
Writers: Glen Charles, Les Charles
Director: James Burrows
Guest Star: Christopher Lloyd

Diane jeopardizes her relationship with Sam when she poses for a portrait by the mad artist against Sam's express wishes.

Once again, the Charles brothers script a darkly funny season finale. This one ends with the lovers pitched in a nose-pulling, slapstick stand-off that's as harrowing as it is hilarious. "This is it!" Diane declares in comic desperation. "We have sunk as low as two human beings can sink. There is no degradation left!" Only after she's stormed out of Cheers for good does Sam allow himself to be taken in by the fragile melancholy of her oil portrait. In the episode's final, sad moment, the barman—who rebelled so violently against Diane's cultural superiority—now finds his only solace in the quiet appreciation of a work of art.

1984/85   THE THIRD SEASON

Year-End Rating: 19.7 (13th place)

"Cheers's" love story forms a triangle in the third season when Kelsey Grammer is introduced as Diane's new beloved, Dr. Frasier Crane.

Producers for the third year are Ken Estin and Sam Simon; Heide Perlman is the season's executive story consultant; and David Angell serves as executive story editor. Glen Charles, James Burrows, and Les Charles will serve as executive producers for the remainder of the series's run.

45 Rebound (Part 1)   September 27, 1984
  Writers: Glen Charles, Les Charles
  Director: James Burrows
  Guest Stars: Kelsey Grammer, Duncan Ross

Coach tries to reunite Sam and Diane after he sees the shambles their lives have become in the wake of their soured romance.

In flashback, Cliff reveals how Sam and Diane spent their summer vacation: Sam went back to the bottle and has emerged a boorish drunk; while Diane spent her hiatus in a rest home after a nervous breakdown. Though alcoholism and mental instability seem unlikely subjects for comedy, the wisecracking gang at Cheers keeps the bleaker aspects of this latest wrinkle in comic perspective.

46 Rebound (Part 2)   October 4, 1984
  Writers: Glen Charles, Les Charles
  Director: James Burrows
  Guest Stars: P. J. Soles, Kelsey Grammer

Diane's analyst helps Sam get back on the wagon; and Diane reluctantly returns to Cheers.

Diane also reveals a newly blossomed romance with her hapless psychoanalyst, Frasier Crane, played by Kelsey Grammer—who makes his debut as "Cheers's" latest regular character in this episode.

47 I Call Your Name   October 18, 1984
  Writers: Peter Casey, David Lee
  Director: James Burrows
  Guest Star: Sam Scarber

Frasier turns the tables on his patient when he seeks advice from Sam; and Cliff faces the wrath of a vengeful co-worker.

48   Fairy Tales Can Come True   October 25, 1984
Writer: Sam Simon
Director: James Burrows
Guest Star: Bernadette Birkett

Cliff attends a masquerade party dressed as a suave ladykiller
and discovers that sometimes clothes *do* make the man.

49   Sam Turns the Other Cheek   November 1, 1984
Writer: David Lloyd
Director: James Burrows
Guest Stars: Kim Lankford, Carmen Argenziano

Sam accidentally shoots himself in the rear while tussling with
an irate husband and then builds his blunder into a tale of barside
valor.

50   Coach in Love (Part 1)   November 8, 1984
Writer: David Angell
Director: James Burrows
Guest Stars: Bette Ford, Ellen Regan

Coach and Sam make a play for a mother and daughter who
wander into Cheers—and by the end of the evening, Coach finds
himself engaged.

51   Coach in Love (Part 2)   November 15, 1984
Writer: David Angell
Director: James Burrows
Guest Star: Bette Ford

Coach refuses to believe his new fiancée has dumped him just
because she won a fortune in the state lottery.

52   Diane Meets Mom   November 22, 1984
Writer: David Lloyd
Director: James Burrows
Guest Star: Nancy Marchand

Diane encounters unexpected wrath when she meets Frasier's
mother for the first time.

53 An American Family   November 29, 1984
Writer: Heide Perlman
Director: James Burrows
Guest Stars: Dan Hedaya, Jean Kasem

Carla is unexpectedly cooperative when her loutish ex-husband returns to demand custody of their daughter.

54 Diane's Allergy   December 6, 1984
Writer: David Lloyd
Director: James Burrows

Diane is convinced that the source of her sudden acute allergy can only be Frasier.

55 Peterson Crusoe   December 13, 1984
Writer: David Angell
Director: James Burrows
Guest Stars: Howard Goodwin, Michael Griswold, John Marzilli

Diane bests Carla in an extemporaneous waitress competition; and Norm decides to chuck it all and start a new life in Bora Bora.

56 A Ditch in Time   December 20, 1984
Writer: Ken Estin
Director: James Burrows
Guest Stars: Carol Kane, Larry Harpel

Despite Diane's warnings, Sam gets involved with an unbalanced young woman who makes marriage plans after their very first date.

57 Whodunit?   January 3, 1985
Writer: Tom Reeder
Director: James Burrows
Guest Stars: James Karen, Kelsey Grammer, Ernie Sabella

Frasier is appalled when one of his most respected colleagues admits that he's smitten with Carla.

After rebuffing the professor's advances and, finally, his proposal of marriage, the flinty barmaid offers a sad and sweet description of the white knight she's certain will one day walk through Cheers's door.

Sweet, because it reveals the Tasmanian devil of a waitress as a misty-eyed dreamer; and sad, because—with a few minor adjustments—the man she describes could be Sam.

58   The Heart Is a Lonely Snipe Hunter   January 10, 1985
   Writer: Heide Perlman
   Director: James Burrows
   Guest Stars: Alan Koss, Tim Cunningham, Kelsey Grammer

Diane pressures the guys into taking Frasier along on a camping trip, where they can't resist having a little fun at the gullible psychiatrist's expense.

59   King of the Hill   January 24, 1985
   Writer: Elliot Shoenman
   Director: James Burrows
   Guest Stars: John Hancock, David Paymer, Larry Harpel, Steve Giannelli

Sam reveals a vicious competitive streak when he returns to the mound in a charity ball game and then wages a marathon Ping-Pong match with Diane.

60   Teacher's Pet   January 31, 1985
   Writer: Tom Reeder
   Director: James Burrows

While Coach studies diligently for a night school course, Sam discovers that his grade-point average rises sharply once he begins dating the teacher.

61   The Mail Goes to Jail   February 7, 1985
   Writer: David Lloyd
   Director: James Burrows
   Guest Stars: Debi Richter, Troy Evans, Nick De Mauro, Al Rosen

Norm is charged with postal theft after he substitutes on Cliff's route as a favor to the ailing postman; and Diane gets wedged into a broken heating vent.

Trapping Diane in an air duct was one of the more creative solutions concocted to conceal Shelley Long's blooming pregnancy. The producers toyed with the idea of making Diane Chambers an unwed mother in the third season, until reason prevailed. "I don't think America would have stood for it," explained Glen Charles. "We figured Sam had to be the father, and the more we considered *that*, the *less* acceptable it seemed."

62 Behind Every Great Man   February 21, 1985
  Writers: Ken Levine, David Isaacs
  Director: James Burrows
  Guest Star: Alison La Placa

For his latest conquest, Sam sets his sights on an attractive reporter who's doing an in-depth survey of the Boston singles scene.

63 If Ever I Would Leave You   February 28, 1985
  Writers: Ken Levine, David Isaacs
  Director: James Burrows
  Guest Stars: Dan Hedaya, Jean Kasem

After his new wife dumps him to go on tour with a singing group called the Grinning Americans, Carla's ex-husband turns over a new leaf to win the waitress back.

64 The Executive Executioner   March 7, 1985
  Writer: Heide Perlman
  Director: James Burrows
  Guest Stars: Richard Roat, Larry Harpel

After Norm is charged with the task of firing one of his fellow employees, he discovers his hidden talent as a corporate hatchet man.

65 Bar Bet   March 14, 1985
  Writer: Jim Parker
  Director: James Burrows
  Guest Stars: Michael Richards, Laurie Walters, Thomas W. Babson

In the aftermath of a long-forgotten drunken bet, Sam stands to lose Cheers unless he can meet—and marry—Jacqueline Bisset by midnight.

66   Cheerio Cheers   April 11, 1985
    Writer: Sam Simon
    Director: James Burrows

Diane decides to leave Cheers when Frasier is offered a job at
the University of Bologna.

In a scene that generated more erotic heat than is usually registered
on a situation comedy, the pair say farewell with a good-bye embrace
that neither is anxious to release. Though the abrupt separation of Sam
and Diane bears all the markings of great melodrama, Diane's sudden
trip to Europe was actually motivated by the writers' desire to conceal
the actress's problematic pregnancy. "We thought it would be easier to
sit her down behind sidewalk cafés," confided producer Glen Charles.

67   The Bartender's Tale   April 18, 1985
    Writer: Sam Simon
    Director: James Burrows
    Guest Stars: Lila Kaye, Camilla More, Rhonda Shear, Tim
    Cunningham

To avoid any more on-the-job romantic entanglements, Carla
insists that Sam hire a dowdy older woman as Cheers's new
waitress.

68   The Belles of Saint Clete's   May 2, 1985
    Writer: Ken Estin
    Director: James Burrows
    Guest Stars: Camila Ashland, Kate Zentall

Carla is hot for revenge when the high school teacher who once
made her life miserable wanders into Cheers.

69   Rescue Me   May 9, 1985
    Writer: Ken Estin
    Director: James Burrows
    Guest Stars: Martin Ferrero, James V. Christy, Dan Galliani,
    Susan Kase

Diane calls from Europe, hoping Sam will talk her out of ac-
cepting Frasier's sudden marriage proposal.

1985/86   THE FOURTH SEASON

Year-End Rating: 23.7 (5th place)

In the fourth year, Woody Harrelson joins "Cheers's" staff as the new bartender, Woody Boyd. Peter Casey and David Lee are the season's producers, along with Heide Perlman and David Angell, and writers Cheri Eichen and Bill Steinkellner are the executive story consultants for season four.

70   Birth, Death, Love, and Rice   September 26, 1985
Writer: Heide Perlman
Director: James Burrows
Guest Star: Woody Harrelson

Sam tracks Diane to a convent, where she's taken to scrubbing floors in penance for the reckless debauchery of her recent European spree.

Frasier Crane, dumped by Diane and now at *his* lowest ebb, has finally earned a place at Cheers, where he will spend the better part of the fourth season nursing his wounds.

71   Woody Goes Belly Up   October 3, 1985
Writer: Heide Perlman
Director: James Burrows
Guest Star: Amanda Wyss

Woody begins a mysterious eating binge after his hometown girlfriend pays a surprise visit.

After Nick Colasanto's death in the third season, the producers tackled the delicate challenge of replacing the well-loved actor who had become firmly identified with the role of Cheers's bartender. Newcomer Harrelson's Woody Boyd bore little outward resemblance to Colasanto. Yet, like the Coach before him, the new bartender provided "Cheers" with a marshmallow center that took the sting off the show's occasionally bitter sarcasm. As Les Charles observed, "Our humor tends to have a hard edge. On 'Cheers,' if you take that sweet and innocent guy away, it gets a little dark in the bar."

72   Someday My Prince Will Come   October 17, 1985
Writers: Tom Seeley, Norman Gunzenhauser
Director: James Burrows
Guest Star: Frank Dent

After she creates a lively fantasy life about the owner of a lost jacket, Diane rashly arranges a blind date to meet her Prince Charming.

73   The Groom Wore Clearasil   October 24, 1985
Writers: Peter Casey, David Lee
Director: James Burrows
Guest Stars: Timothy Williams, Mandy Ingber, John Ingle, Sherilyn Fenn

Carla hopes the allure of Sam's bachelor life-style will dissuade her teenage son from his premature marriage plans.

74   Diane's Nightmare   October 31, 1985
Writer: David Lloyd
Director: James Burrows
Guest Stars: Derek McGrath, Nancy Cartwright

Diane dreams that the ex-con who once tried to strangle her is hiding out in Cheers's cellar.

The long-running saga of Andy Andy apparently comes to an end when the maladjusted murderer returns to Cheers as a healthy and honorable citizen. Alas, as it turns out, the unlikely events are merely part of a dream-within-a-dream that also features Diane's unlikely fantasy of Sam as a culture vulture with a pipe and smoking jacket.

75   I'll Gladly Pay You Tuesday   November 7, 1985
Writers: Cheri Eichen, Bill Steinkellner
Director: James Burrows
Guest Star: William Lanteau

Sam is understandably upset when Diane borrows five hundred dollars to squander on an Ernest Hemingway first edition.

76   2 Good 2 Be 4 Real   November 14, 1985
    Writers: Peter Casey, David Lee
    Director: James Burrows
    Guest Stars: Michael Alaimo, Don Lewis

The guys concoct an imaginary lonely hearts pen pal for Carla, but the ruse backfires when she rejects her only real prospect to wait for her dream date.

77   Love Thy Neighbor   November 21, 1985
    Writer: David Angell
    Director: James Burrows
    Guest Stars: Miriam Flynn, Ernie Sabella, John F. Dryer, Carolyn Ann Clark

Norm and his neighbor's wife jump to conclusions about their spouses; and Diane is incensed when Sam describes her as his "former love bunny" on a radio show.

Even when confronted with his wife's adultery, Norm maintains his usual aplomb, though he does eventually leave his barstool—a sure sign of emotional upheaval for the uncommonly sedentary drinker. The burly accountant actually reveals a wistful side when he tells Woody a tender anecdote about the football game where he first set eyes on the cheerleader he would one day marry. But Woody is more interested in who won the game—a gag, typical of "Cheers," that undercuts the sentiment at the precise moment before it grows leaden.

David Angell's script is refreshing in another way. Somehow, he's fashioned a script about adultery without resorting to any of the idiotic clichés that have rescued errant sitcom wives from their husband's wrath since the dawn of the cathode ray tube: Vera *wasn't* secretly planning Norm's surprise party; she *wasn't* mistakenly overheard rehearsing lines from a play; nor was the man she'd been seeing really a TV producer planning to spotlight Norm on "This Is Your Life." She actually *was* planning to cheat on poor Norm, but everything is resolved so that Norm, Vera, and the neighbor's wife are all allowed their full measure of dignity.

78   From Beer to Eternity   November 28, 1985
    Writers: Peter Casey, David Lee
    Director: James Burrows
    Guest Star: Joel Polis

When Woody freezes up during the crucial frame of the Cheers bowling tournament, Diane takes it upon herself to rescue the bar's wounded pride.

79   The Barstoolie   December 5, 1985
Writers: Andy Cowan, David S. Williger
Director: James Burrows
Guest Stars: Dick O'Neill, Claudia Cron

Diane joins Sam and his new girlfriend on their first date; and Cliff is reunited with his long-lost father.

80   Don Juan Is Hell   December 12, 1985
Writer: Pheof Sutton
Director: James Burrows
Guest Stars: Kenneth Tigar, Steve Minor

Sam is flattered when Diane's psychology class observes him as a case study in modern human sexuality.

81   Fools and Their Money   December 19, 1985
Writer: Heide Perlman
Director: James Burrows
Guest Stars: Paul Willson, Al Rosen

Inspired by his success in the Cheers football pool, Woody bets his entire life savings on an impossible long shot.

82   Take My Shirt, Please   January 9, 1986
Writer: David Lloyd
Director: James Burrows
Guest Stars: Robert Symonds, Frances Bey

Sam's ego takes a beating when he donates his retired baseball jersey to a charity auction—and no one bids on it.

83   Suspicion   January 16, 1986
Writer: Tom Reeder
Director: James Burrows
Guest Star: Hamilton Camp

As part of her latest psychology experiment, Diane dupes the gang at Cheers—and then faces the anxiety of awaiting their certain revenge.

84   The Triangle   January 23, 1986
  Writer: Susan Seeger
  Director: James Burrows

To lift Frasier's sagging spirits from a deep depression, Sam and Diane agree to pose as lovers once more—with dire consequences.

85   Cliffie's Big Score   January 30, 1986
  Writer: Heide Perlman
  Director: James Burrows

Cliff's in double trouble when Diane and Carla both consent to be his date for the mailman's ball.

86   Second Time Around   February 6, 1986
  Writers: Cheri Eichen, Bill Steinkellner
  Director: Tom Lofaro
  Guest Stars: Jennifer Tilly, Bebe Neuwirth, Lou Fant

Sam's campaign to salvage Frasier's shrinking self-respect takes an unexpected turn after the bartender fixes him up with a woman who is guaranteed to be a sure thing.

87   The Peterson Principle   February 13, 1986
  Writers: Peter Casey, David Lee
  Director: James Burrows
  Guest Stars: Chip Zien, Daniel Davis

Norm discovers that a co-worker is having an affair with the boss's wife and wonders if he should use the information to gain a promotion.

88   Dark Imaginings   February 20, 1986
  Writer: David Angell
  Director: James Burrows
  Guest Stars: Pamela Bach, Tim Dunigan, Christine Dickinson, Lisa Vice, Jeré Fields

Sam refuses to acknowledge he's not as spry as he once was, until he lands in the hospital from injuries he got on the racquetball court.

89   Save the Last Dance for Me   February 27, 1986
Writer: Heide Perlman
Director: James Burrows
Guest Stars: Dan Hedaya, Jean Kasem, Hal Landon, Jr., Nick Dimitri, Sinara Stull

Carla wants to win a dance contest in her old neighborhood so badly that she's willing to consider a temporary reunion with her ex-husband, Nick Tortelli.

The writers frequently alluded to Carla's Terpsichorean passion—an enthusiasm shared by actress Rhea Perlman, who regularly devoted one lunch hour a week to tap-dance lessons on the studio lot.

90   Fear Is My Co-Pilot   March 13, 1986
Writers: Cheri Eichen, Bill Steinkellner
Director: James Burrows
Guest Star: Joseph Whipp

Sam and Diane get a chance to live dangerously when a daredevil pilot abandons them at the controls of his plane in midair.

91   Diane Chambers Day   March 20, 1986
Writer: Kimberly Hill
Director: James Burrows

To brighten Diane's spirits, the gang at Cheers grudgingly attends an evening at the opera.

92   Relief Bartender   March 27, 1986
Writer: Miriam Trogdon
Director: James Burrows

Sam takes on a new bartender and then reluctantly gives Woody notice when he discovers he can't afford to keep them both.

93   Strange Bedfellows (Part 1)   May 1, 1986
Writer: David Angell
Director: James Burrows
Guest Stars: Kate Mulgrew, David Paymer, Max Wright, Brad Burlingame, Carolyn Ann Clark, Mike Hagerty

Carla and Diane are both concerned when Sam's fling with a brash lady politician starts to develop into something more serious.

Diane had good reason to fret: Kate Mulgrew's Janet Eldridge was the first woman to pose a real threat to her relationship with Sam. "We wanted Sam genuinely involved with someone other than Diane," explained writer Glen Charles. "Rather than just having them *say* they loved each other, we let it run three episodes so that it would mean a little more."

94   Strange Bedfellows (Part 2)   May 8, 1986
Writer: David Angell
Director: James Burrows
Guest Stars: Kate Mulgrew, David Paymer, Max Wright,
Senator Gary Hart

Janet reveals a jealous streak when she insists that Sam fire Diane and sever his ties with Diane once and for all.

The character of strong, confident Janet Eldridge reveals colors we hadn't seen before in Diane—or in Carla either. Rarely have our sympathies for Diane been so deeply felt as when we spy her huddling under the bar after she overhears Sam's resolution to dump her—abandoned and suddenly painfully alone. Oddly, Sam echoes the same emotion in the show's closing moments. After Diane has made the first of her grand exits, he cranes his neck for one last, longing glance at the woman who has haunted his every waking hour for the previous four years.

95   Strange Bedfellows (Part 3)   May 15, 1986
Writer: David Angell
Director: James Burrows
Guest Stars: Kate Mulgrew, David Paymer

After Sam and Diane create a public scene during Janet's press conference, the councilwoman develops serious doubts about her future with the bartender.

Diane stages her most grandiose exit yet in a scene that slyly encapsulates the slapstick sadomasochism that has plagued their relationship from the start. As the TV cameras roll, she storms out of the bar—dragging Sam after her by the neck—and then abruptly slams the door on him—and Cheers—forever.
Or at least until the start of the next season.
In the show's final moments, Sam picks up the phone to tender a weary marriage proposal to the unseen voice on the other end. Of course,

the cliff-hanger leaves us dangling—but few fans of the show were surprised at the top of the fifth year when Sam greeted Diane to replay for another season the sublime agony that only those two seem to understand.

By the 1986/87 television season, "Cheers," now five years old, had already earned a niche in TV history. The success of the series helped pave the way for the situation-comedy resurgence of the mid-1980s, which includes such well-regarded examples of the form as "Newhart," "Family Ties," "The Golden Girls," and the staggeringly popular "Cosby."

Of course, it's appropriate that "Cheers" should usher in television's most recent sitcom renaissance. As the latest in a long line of classic comedies, the success of "Cheers" is as much a testament to the talent and sly wit of its creators as it is to the rich mother lode of unforgettable television comedy that inspired them.

As the men and women of "Cheers" assume their place in the company of so many bona fide TV classics, it's not hard to imagine Sam Malone standing up at the end of his bar to lead a toast.

Raise your mugs, he might propose, and toast the Ricardos and the Kramdens; the Petries, the Bunkers, and the Hartleys. To all the TV families who, in good times or bad, left the porch light burning and the front door ajar so we could drop in whenever we felt like a visit.

To the cabbies at Sunshine Taxi and the staff at the WJM Six O'Clock News; to the die-hard detectives of the Twelfth Precinct and the tireless surgeons at the 4077th. To all the misfits and miscreants who invited us to join their gang on those nights when we had nothing better to do. It was an invitation we found hard to resist—even when we *did* have better things to do.

And, finally, a toast to all those sitting at the bar. To tomorrow's classics and all those reruns yet to come.

Cheers.

EMMY AWARDS

The following is a listing through 1985/86 of the Emmy Awards bestowed on "Cheers" by the National Academy of Television Arts and Sciences.

1982/83 Outstanding Comedy Series
Outstanding Lead Actress in a Comedy Series: Shelley Long

Outstanding Directing in a Comedy Series: James Burrows, "Showdown (Part 2)"

Outstanding Writing in a Comedy Series: Glen Charles, Les Charles, "Give Me a Ring Sometime"

Outstanding Individual Achievement/Graphic Design and Title Sequences: James Castle, Bruce Bryant

1983/84 Outstanding Comedy Series

Outstanding Supporting Actress in a Comedy Series: Rhea Perlman

Outstanding Writing in a Comedy Series: David Angell, "Old Flames"

Outstanding Film Editing for a Series: Andrew Chulack, "Old Flames"

1984/85 Outstanding Supporting Actress in a Comedy: Rhea Perlman

Outstanding Live and Tape Sound Mixing and Sound Effects for Series: Douglas Gray, Michael Ballin, Thomas Huth, Sam Black, "The Executive Executioner"

1985/86 Outstanding Supporting Actress in a Comedy: Rhea Perlman

Outstanding Sound Mixing for a Comedy Series: Michael Ballin, Robert Douglas, Douglas Gray, Thomas Huth, "Fear Is My Co-Pilot"

Appendix A

The Critics' Choice Poll

In early 1985, forty-five professional television critics were polled by the author to determine the classic comedies that would become the subject of this book. Here are the results of that poll, listed in order of the critics' preferences.

THE TOP TV SITCOMS OF ALL TIME AS DETERMINED BY THE NATION'S TV CRITICS—1985

1 "The Mary Tyler Moore Show"
2 "All in the Family"
3 "I Love Lucy"
4 "M*A*S*H"
5 "The Dick Van Dyke Show"
6 "The Honeymooners"
7 "Barney Miller"
8 "Cheers"
9 "The Bob Newhart Show"
10 "Taxi"

RUNNERS-UP

11 "The Phil Silvers Show"
12 "The Andy Griffith Show"
13 "Get Smart"
14 "Soap"
15 "United States"

Appendix B

Critical Choices

The following is a complete list of the critics who responded to the Critics' Choice Poll, along with their newspaper or syndicate affiliation at the time of the poll, and a complete list of their choices for the best—and worst—situation comedies of all time.

GLENN ALBIN/*Interview* Magazine (New York, N.Y.)

BEST   "Green Acres," "The Burns and Allen Show," "Mary Hartman, Mary Hartman," "Get Smart," "Bewitched"

WORST   "Happy Days," "Three's Company," "Welcome Back, Kotter," "Family Ties," "Facts of Life"

JON ANDERSON/*Chicago Tribune* (Chicago, Ill.)

BEST   "I Love Lucy," "The Honeymooners," "The Dick Van Dyke Show," "The Mary Tyler Moore Show," "Mr. Peepers"

WORST   "My Mother the Car," "Rango," "The Munsters," "We Got It Made," "AKA Pablo"

KEN BECK/*The Tennessean* (Nashville, Tenn.)

BEST   "The Andy Griffith Show," "Car 54, Where Are You?," "Sanford and Son," "Get Smart," "The Mary Tyler Moore Show"

WORST   "Family Affair," "The Partridge Family," "Sugar Time," "The Doris Day Show," "Maude"

JEFF BORDEN/*The Columbus Dispatch* (Columbus, Ohio)

BEST   "Barney Miller," "M*A*S*H," "Cheers," "I Love Lucy," "The Associates"

WORST   "Three's Company," "The Jeffersons," "My Mother the Car," "Carter Country," "Ball Four"

RUTH BUTLER/*Grand Rapids Press* (Grand Rapids, Mich.)

BEST   "M*A*S*H," "The Mary Tyler Moore Show," "The Phil Silvers Show," "The Dick Van Dyke Show," "Barney Miller"

WORST   "Laverne and Shirley," "Three's Company," "AKA Pablo," "The Jeffersons," "The Hathaways"

STUART D. BYKOFSKY/*Philadelphia Daily News* (Philadelphia, Pa.)

BEST   "The Mary Tyler Moore Show," "All in the Family," "I Love Lucy," "Get Smart," "Barney Miller"

WORST   "Laverne and Shirley," "Joanie Loves Chachi," "The Ropers," "The Ted Knight Show," "Three's Company"

JOHN CARMAN/*Atlanta Journal and Constitution* (Atlanta, Ga.)

BEST   "The Mary Tyler Moore Show," "The Honeymooners," "The Bob Newhart Show," "Cheers," "United States"

WORST   "The Roller Girls," "The Ropers," "Punky Brewster," "Gilligan's Island," "Coed Fever"

KENNETH R. CLARK/*Chicago Tribune* (Chicago, Ill.)

BEST   "The Mary Tyler Moore Show," "The Dick Van Dyke Show," "All in the Family," "The Honeymooners," "I Love Lucy"

WORST   "Open All Night," "Gimme a Break," "Ozzie and Harriet," "The Flying Nun," "Gilligan's Island"

JERRY COFFEY/*Fort Worth Star-Telegram* (Fort Worth, Tex.)

BEST   "The Dick Van Dyke Show," "All in the Family," "I Love Lucy," "The Honeymooners," "M*A*S*H"

WORST   "The Tammy Grimes Show," "The Debbie Reynolds Show," "Mr. T and Tina," "Me and the Chimp," "Lotsa Luck"

JEAN COLLOHAN/*American Film Magazine* (Washington, D.C.)

BEST "All in the Family," "I Love Lucy," "Dobie Gillis," "The Odd Couple," "The Mary Tyler Moore Show"

WORST "Punky Brewster," "The Ted Knight Show," "Bosom Buddies," "Me and the Chimp," "Hello Larry"

DAVID CUTHBERT/*New Orleans Times-Picayune-States-Item* (New Orleans, La.)

BEST "I Love Lucy," "The Mary Tyler Moore Show," "The Bob Newhart Show," "The Dick Van Dyke Show," "All in the Family"

WORST "When Things Were Rotten," "The Brady Bunch," "Family Affair," "I Married Joan," "Hogan's Heroes"

GARY DEEB/*News America Syndicate* (Chicago, Ill.)

BEST "The Honeymooners," "Barney Miller," "All in the Family," "The Mary Tyler Moore Show," "I Love Lucy"

WORST "Three's Company," "Joanie Loves Chachi," "Flo," "Mr. T and Tina," "What's Happening"

MICHAEL DOUGAN/*San Francisco Examiner* (San Francisco, Calif.)

BEST "All in the Family," "M*A*S*H," "The Mary Tyler Moore Show," "Paul Sand in Friends and Lovers," "The Dick Van Dyke Show"

WORST "We Got It Made," "Three's Company," "My Mother the Car," "Petticoat Junction," "The Flying Nun"

DAVID DRAKE/*Columbus Citizen-Journal* (Columbus, Ohio)

BEST "The Dick Van Dyke Show," "The Honeymooners," "The Mary Tyler Moore Show," "The Andy Griffith Show," "The Bob Newhart Show"

WORST "Roller Girls," "CPO Sharkey," "Mr. T and Tina," "Hello Larry," "Coed Fever"

RICK DU BROW/*Los Angeles Herald Examiner* (Los Angeles, Calif.)

BEST "The Honeymooners," "Barney Miller," "All in the Family," "The Mary Tyler Moore Show," "The Phil Silvers Show"

WORST "Hello Larry," "Me and the Chimp," "Camp Runamuck," "The Mothers-in-Law," "Blansky's Beauties"

MIKE DUFFY/*Detroit Free Press* (Detroit, Mich.)

BEST "The Honeymooners," "The Phil Silvers Show," "The Mary Tyler Moore Show," "Taxi," "Bosom Buddies"

WORST "Hello Larry," "My Mother the Car," "The Jeffersons," "Three's Company," "I'm Dickens, He's Fenster"

PETER FARRELL/*The Oregonian* (Portland, Ore.)

BEST "M*A*S*H," "Cheers," "All in the Family," "Barney Miller," "United States," "Soap"

WORST "Mr. Smith," "Three's Company," "Condo," "The New Odd Couple," "Laverne and Shirley"

JUDY FLANDER/*United Features Syndicate* (New York, N.Y.)

BEST "The Mary Tyler Moore Show," "Buffalo Bill," "The Cosby Show," "I Love Lucy," "United States," "All in the Family"

WORST "The Ropers," "Three's Company," "The Jeffersons," "Carter Country," "Hogan's Heroes"

BARRY GARRON/*Kansas City Star* (Kansas City, Mo.)

BEST "All in the Family," "M*A*S*H," "The Mary Tyler Moore Show," "Odd Couple," "The Dick Van Dyke Show"

WORST "The Brian Keith Show," "The McLean Stevenson Show," "Joanie Loves Chachi," "Ozzie's Girls," "My Mother the Car"

TONY GENTILE/*Newsday* (Long Island, N.Y.)

BEST "I Love Lucy," "The Honeymooners," "The Mary Tyler Moore Show," "All in the Family," "Taxi"

WORST "Mr. T and Tina," "My Mother the Car," "The Dumplings," "The Montefuscos," "Mama Malone"

MARC GUNTHER/*Hartford Courant* (Hartford, Conn.)

BEST "The Honeymooners," "The Mary Tyler Moore Show," "M*A*S*H," "I Love Lucy," "All in the Family"

WORST "We Got It Made," "The Flying Nun"

RICHARD HACK/*Hollywood Reporter* (Hollywood, Calif.)

BEST "The Mary Tyler Moore Show," "Cheers," "I Love Lucy," "The Courtship of Eddie's Father," "M*A*S*H"

WORST "My Mother the Car," "Punky Brewster," "Me and the Chimp," "Welcome Back, Kotter," "United States"

KEN HOFFMAN/*Phoenix Gazette* (Phoenix, Ariz.)

BEST "Cheers," "Taxi," "The Honeymooners," "Police Squad," "All in the Family"

WORST "Roller Girls," "The Pruitts of Southampton," "The McLean Stevenson Show," "Facts of Life," "Joanie Loves Chachi"

BARBARA HOLSOPPLE/*Pittsburgh Press* (Pittsburgh, Pa.)

BEST "M*A*S*H," "The Mary Tyler Moore Show," "All in the Family," "Barney Miller," "The Lucy Show"

WORST "Me and the Chimp," "Blansky's Beauties," "Mr. T and Tina," "The Mothers-in-Law," "My Mother the Car"

NOEL W. HOLSTON/*Orlando Sentinel* (Orlando, Fla.)

BEST "Barney Miller," "The Mary Tyler Moore Show," "The Bob Newhart Show," "M*A*S*H," "The Andy Griffith Show"

WORST "Mr. T and Tina," "The Ropers," "Coed Fever," "Baby, I'm Back," "Lotsa Luck"

TOM JICHA/*Miami News* (Miami, Fla.)

BEST "All in the Family," "Cheers," "The Honeymooners," "M*A*S*H," "Soap"

WORST "The Hathaways," "The McLean Stevenson Show," "The Ropers," "Three's a Crowd," "Rango"

BILL LANE/*World News Syndicate* (Los Angeles, Calif.)

BEST "Archie Bunker's Place," "I Love Lucy," "The Jeffersons," "Amos n' Andy," "Sanford and Son," "The Bill Cosby Show"

WORST "Baby, I'm Back," "Barney Miller," "Alice" (without Flo), "Bridget Loves Bernie," "The Monkees"

SYLVIA F. LAWLOR/*Allentown Call-Chronicle* (Allentown, Pa.)

BEST "The Mary Tyler Moore Show," "All in the Family," "The Dick Van Dyke Show," "M*A*S*H," "Barney Miller," "Cheers"

WORST "San Pedro Beach Bums," "Holmes and Yoyo," "Busting Loose," "In the Beginning," "90 Bristol Court"

JIM LYNCH/*JDL Syndicate* (Boca Raton, Fla.)

BEST "Barney Miller," "All in the Family," "Cheers," "The Dick Van Dyke Show," "Taxi"

WORST "Laverne and Shirley," "Three's Company," "Mr. Ed," "Gilligan's Island," "Bosom Buddies"

JACK MAJOR/*Providence Journal-Bulletin* (Providence, R.I.)

BEST "The Dick Van Dyke Show," "The Bob Newhart Show," "I Love Lucy," "Barney Miller," "Fernwood 2-Night"

WORST "Don't Call Me Charlie," "Mama Malone," "In the Beginning," "Apple Pie," "Ball Four"

LEE MARKSBURY/*Fresno Bee* (Fresno, Calif.)

BEST "I Love Lucy," "M*A*S*H," "The Mary Tyler Moore Show," "Laverne and Shirley," "The Andy Griffith Show"

WORST "Filthy Rich," "I Dream of Jeannie," "Three's Company," "My Mother the Car," "CPO Sharkey"

JOHN D. MILLER/*South Bend Tribune* (South Bend, Ind.)

BEST "M*A*S*H," "I Love Lucy," "The Dick Van Dyke Show," "All in the Family," "Soap"

WORST "The Ropers," "The Beverly Hillbillies," "My Mother the Car," "We Got It Made," "Hello Larry"

WALLY PATRICK/*Asbury Park Press* (Asbury Park, N.J.)

BEST "All in the Family," "Buffalo Bill," "The Mary Tyler Moore Show," "Taxi," "Leave It to Beaver"

WORST "Mr. T and Tina," "The ABC Evening News with Barbara Walters and Harry Reasoner"

JON-MICHAEL REED/*United Features Syndicate* (New York, N.Y.)

BEST "The Mary Tyler Moore Show," "Kate and Allie," "The Dick Van Dyke Show," "The Burns and Allen Show," "The Bob Newhart Show"

WORST "AfterM*A*S*H," "Jennifer Slept Here," "Hello Larry," "Car 54, Where Are You?" "The Hathaways"

HAROLD SCHINDLER/*Salt Lake City Tribune* (Salt Lake City, Utah)

BEST "Barney Miller," "You'll Never Get Rich (The Phil Silvers Show)," "M*A*S*H," "F-Troop," "The Dick Van Dyke Show"

WORST "Buffalo Bill," "Detective School," "Fish," "My Mother the Car," "The New Odd Couple"

TOM SHALES/*Washington Post* (Washington, D.C.)

BEST "I Love Lucy," "The Honeymooners," "All in the Family," "You'll Never Get Rich (The Phil Silvers Show)," "The Mary Tyler Moore Show"

WORST "Buffalo Bill," "Just Our Luck," "My Little Margie," "Gimme a Break," "Hello Larry"

RICK SHEFCHIK/*Saint Paul Pioneer Press-Dispatch* (Saint Paul, Minn.)

BEST "The Dick Van Dyke Show," "M*A*S*H," "The Mary Tyler Moore Show," "I Love Lucy," "Green Acres"

WORST "It's About Time," "Hello Larry," "The Tammy Grimes Show," "Coed Fever," "Benson"

DWIGHT SILVERMAN/*San Antonio Light* (San Antonio, Tex.)

BEST "The Honeymooners," "All in the Family," "Get Smart," "The Mary Tyler Moore Show," "M*A*S*H"

WORST "My Mother the Car," "The Brady Bunch," "The Flying Nun," "Gilligan's Island," "The Partridge Family"

STEVE SONSKY/*Miami Herald* (Miami, Fla.)

BEST "All in the Family," "The Mary Tyler Moore Show," "I Love Lucy," "The Honeymooners," "The Bob Newhart Show"

WORST "The McLean Stevenson Show," "Condo," "My Mother the Car," "Hogan's Heroes," "Hello Larry"

VINCE STATEN/*Louisville Times* (Louisville, Ky.)

BEST "The Mary Tyler Moore Show," "The Andy Griffith Show," "The Dick Van Dyke Show," "The Phil Silvers Show," "M*A*S*H"

WORST "Alice," "Mama Malone," "The Ropers," "The Waverly Wonders," "My Mother the Car"

GUS STEVENS/*San Diego Tribune* (San Diego, Calif.)

BEST "Barney Miller," "Taxi," "WKRP in Cincinnati," "M*A*S*H," "The Mary Tyler Moore Show"

WORST "Hello Larry," "My Mother the Car," "Mr. T and Tina," "Car 54, Where Are You?" "The Girl With Something Extra"

KARL VICK/*Saint Petersburg Times* (Saint Petersburg, Fla.)

BEST "The Andy Griffith Show," "The Dick Van Dyke Show," "The Mary Tyler Moore Show," "All in the Family," "Cheers"

WORST "Ball Four," "The Six O'Clock Follies," "Carter Country," "Brothers and Sisters," "Far Out Space Nuts"

KEITH WATSON/*Houston Post* (Houston, Tex.)

BEST "I Love Lucy," "All in the Family," "Cheers," "The Dick Van Dyke Show," "Taxi"

WORST "The Brady Bunch," "Webster," "Punky Brewster," "Petticoat Junction," "It's Not Easy"

RON WEISKIND/*Pittsburgh Post-Gazette* (Pittsburgh, Pa.)

BEST "All in the Family," "M*A*S*H," "The Mary Tyler Moore Show," "The Honeymooners," "Cheers"

WORST "Gilligan's Island," "Three's a Crowd," "Three's Company," "Ball Four," "Green Acres"

BOB WISEHART/*Sacramento Bee* (Sacramento, Calif.)

BEST "The Dick Van Dyke Show," "I Love Lucy," "M*A*S*H," "The Mary Tyler Moore Show," "The Honeymooners"

WORST "Gilligan's Island," "My Mother the Car," "Three's Company," "The Hathaways," "The Jeffersons"

Appendix C

For Further Research

Museum of Broadcasting   1 East 53d Street, New York, N.Y. 10022
An extensive and ever-growing collection of classic radio and television programs is the highlight of this invaluable research facility. Write for visitor or membership information.

Reruns: The Magazine of Television History
Thoughtful criticism and extensive background on vintage television shows. Subscription information: Richard K. Tharp, Publisher, P.O. Box 1057, Safford, Ariz. 85548

Star Data Research   263a West 19th Street, Suite 19, New York, N.Y. 10011
Researcher Brenda Scott Royce specializes in digging up TV credits and background on television personalities, both obscure and well known.

The Television Index
A trade newsletter that provides the broadcast industry with complete, in-depth network program listings each week. Subscription information: Jerry Leichter, Editor in chief, 40-29 27th Street, Long Island City, N.Y. 11101

TV Collector: The Bi-monthly for Collectors of Television Material
Reviews, articles, and episode guides to the best of vintage television. Subscription information: Diane L. Albert, Editor, P.O. Box 188, Needham, Mass. 02192

TV Guide
The best single source for background on TV and television programming. Subscription information: Triangle Publications, Box 400, Radnor, Pa. 19088. *TV Guide* also publishes a useful one-volume index to the magazine, along with yearly supplements. Write Triangle Publications for more information on *The TV Guide 25-Year Index: 1953–77*, and the annual supplements.

Appendix D

Who's Who

This short biographical glossary is designed to provide a quick reference to the careers of the writers, directors, producers, and network executives who appear most prominently in this book. The credits listed are by no means complete but are included to suggest some of the more interesting sideroads that these colorful creators embarked on before— or after—they made their most significant contributions to the classic situation comedy.

HARRY ACKERMAN   CBS vice president of programming in the early 1950s. A key figure in the genesis of "I Love Lucy," he was later executive producer of some of TV's longest-running hit sitcoms, including "Bachelor Father," "Hazel," and "Bewitched," among many others.

DESI ARNAZ   Executive producer of "I Love Lucy." At one time the head of Desilu, a major TV program supplier, he retired in the early 1960s, only to return as executive producer of "The Mothers-in-Law" in 1967.

DANNY ARNOLD   Creator, with Theodore Flicker, and producer of "Barney Miller." A former film editor, he was staff writer for Rosemary Clooney and Tennessee Ernie Ford in the 1950s and later served as story editor on "The Real McCoys," produced "Bewitched" and "That Girl," and was executive producer of "My World and Welcome to It."

WILLIAM ASHER   Most prominent director of "I Love Lucy." He would continue as a top sitcom producer/director on "Bewitched" in the 1960s and as a regular director of "Alice" in the late 1970s.

PETER BALDWIN   Director of "The Dick Van Dyke Show." A top TV director, he joined the MTM stable in the early 1970s, where he directed numerous episodes of "The Mary Tyler Moore Show" and "The Bob Newhart Show," among many others.

JERRY BELSON Staff writer, with Garry Marshall, of "The Dick Van Dyke Show." Among many distinguished credits, he created and wrote—with Marshall— TV's "Odd Couple" and directed a handful of classic "Mary Tyler Moore" episodes.

PETER BONERZ Director of "The Bob Newhart Show." He began as an improvisational actor but emerged from "Bob Newhart" as one of the most sought-after directors in the field.

JAMES L. BROOKS Co-creator of "The Mary Tyler Moore Show" and "Taxi." One of the central forces in the comedy renaissance of the 1970s, the prolific writer was one of the creators of "Rhoda," "Lou Grant," "Room 222," and one of the few sitcom writers to successfully branch out into feature films, though he occasionally continues to devote his energies to television, including 1987's "Tracey Ullman Show."

ALLAN BURNS Co-creator of "The Mary Tyler Moore Show." A prominent TV comedy writer in the 1960s, he began—with partner Chris Hayward—as a scripter for Jay Ward's "Bullwinkle Show" and was one of the founding writers at MTM, where he also created "Rhoda," "Lou Grant," and "The Duck Factory," among others.

JAMES BURROWS Co-creator of "Cheers." The son of playwright Abe Burrows, the one-time Broadway stage manager was one of the brightest young directors at MTM in the mid-seventies before he was tapped as full-time director of "Taxi" in 1978.

BOB CARROLL AND MADELYN PUGH MARTIN DAVIS Co-creators and writers of "I Love Lucy." In addition to their credits as executive producers on "Alice" and "Private Benjamin" in recent years, the team that practically invented the TV sitcom also created "The Tom Ewell Show," "The Lucy Show," and "The Mothers-in-Law."

GLEN CHARLES AND LES CHARLES Co-creators of "Cheers." With their impeccable credentials as writers for "M*A*S*H," "The Mary Tyler Moore Show," and "The Bob Newhart Show," the brothers were a perfect choice to serve as producers and head writers for the first three seasons of "Taxi."

MARC DANIELS The original director of "I Love Lucy" left the series in 1952 to direct "I Married Joan" and was still active when he signed on as staff director of "Alice" in the late 1970s.

STAN DANIELS Producer and writer of "The Mary Tyler Moore Show." A prolific writer who also co-created—with Ed. Weinberger—a long line of TV comedies in the 1970s, including "Doc," "Phyllis," "The Betty White Show," as well as "Taxi" and "The Associates," among others.

DAVID DAVIS Creator, with Lorenzo Music, of "The Bob Newhart Show," and co-creator of "Taxi." He began his career as a youthful director of "Dobie Gillis," later moved into production on "He and She," and teamed up with Lorenzo Music to write and produce early episodes of "The Mary Tyler Moore Show."

MADELYN PUGH MARTIN DAVIS (see Bob Carroll)

SAM DENOFF AND BILL PERSKY Prominent writers on "The Dick Van Dyke

Show." Among their many other writing and production credits, the team went on to create "That Girl," "Good Morning World," and "Lotsa Luck."

THEODORE FLICKER   Creator, with Danny Arnold, of "Barney Miller." He moved from improvisational theater into television comedy in the 1960s, where he earned writing or directing credits on "The Dick Van Dyke Show," "The Andy Griffith Show," and "I Dream of Jeannie," among many others.

JIM FRITZELL AND EVERETT GREENBAUM   Writers for "M*A*S*H." The veteran writers had contributed scripts to a long line of first-rate comedies, including "Mr. Peepers" in the early 1950s and "The Andy Griffith Show" a decade later.

LARRY GELBART   With Gene Reynolds, developed "M*A*S*H" for television. Among his many other credits, he created "United States" for TV, authored *Sly Fox* for Broadway, and wrote *Tootsie* for the big screen.

EVERETT GREENBAUM   (see Jim Fritzell)

CHRIS HAYWARD   Prolific writer for "Barney Miller." Created—with one-time partner Alan Burns—a string of sixties comedies, including "My Mother the Car" and "The Munsters," before teaming with Danny Arnold on "Barney Miller" and "Joe Bash."

DAVID ISAACS AND KEN LEVINE   Executive story editors on "M*A*S*H." The team also served as writers and co-producers of "Cheers" before they created Mary Tyler Moore's underrated comeback series, "Mary," in 1985.

BARRY KEMP   Frequent contributor to "Taxi." He later created MTM's "Newhart."

MORT LACHMAN   Executive producer for "All in the Family." A longtime writer for Bob Hope and producer of numerous TV spectaculars, the veteran writer also produced "Archie Bunker's Place" and "One Day at a Time" for Norman Lear, among many others.

NORMAN LEAR   Creator of "All in the Family." The producer responsible for more ground-breaking comedy series than any other creator in television, including "Mary Hartman, Mary Hartman," "Maude," and "All That Glitters," and many others.

SHELDON LEONARD   Executive producer of "The Dick Van Dyke Show." A major figure in the evolution of quality TV comedy, he produced or created a large and distinguished family of sitcoms for Danny Thomas Productions in the 1950s and 1960s, including "Make Room for Daddy," "The Andy Griffith Show," and "The Real McCoys," among others.

KEN LEVINE   (see David Isaacs)

DAVID LLOYD   Story editor and writer for "The Mary Tyler Moore Show." He also contributed many inspired stories to "The Bob Newhart Show," "Taxi," and "Cheers" and was creator of ABC's "Mr. Sunshine" and cable TV's "Brothers."

GARRY MARSHALL Staff writer, with Jerry Belson, of "The Dick Van Dyke Show." He later created TV's "Odd Couple" and "Happy Days," which became the cornerstone in his formidable comic dynasty of the late 1970s.

BURT METCALFE Executive producer of "M*A*S*H." A former actor and studio casting agent, he later directed and produced numerous episodes of the series and created—with Larry Gelbart—"AfterM*A*S*H."

LORENZO MUSIC Creator, with David Davis, of "The Bob Newhart Show." A former folk singer, he was a staff writer of "The Smothers Brothers Comedy Hour" before he teamed up with David Davis to write many of the best early "Mary Tyler Moore" scripts, which led to the team's assignment to develop and produce "Rhoda."

DON NICHOLL, MICHAEL ROSS, AND BERNIE WEST Producers of "All in the Family." After contributing many of the best scripts during that show's early years, the team later developed "Three's Company" for ABC.

JESS OPPENHEIMER Co-creator and producer of "I Love Lucy." He returned to weekly TV in 1969, when he created "The Debbie Reynolds Show," a series that bore a distinct resemblance to his earlier classic.

JERRY PARIS Director of "The Dick Van Dyke Show." The former actor would eventually be reunited with "Dick Van Dyke" writer Garry Marshall as a regular director of "The Odd Couple" and staff director on "Happy Days."

TOM PATCHETT AND JAY TARSES Influential writers/producers of "The Bob Newhart Show." They went on to create MTM's "The Tony Randall Show" before they hit their stride with the underrated classic "Buffalo Bill" in the early 1980s. Patchett was later a co-creator of "Alf" for NBC.

BILL PERSKY (see Sam Denoff)

NOAM PITLIK Director of "Barney Miller." After a successful acting career that included a regular part on "The Bob Newhart Show," he directed many later episodes of "Taxi" before signing on as staff director of "Mr. Belvedere."

ALAN RAFKIN Director of "The Bob Newhart Show." A respected director with hundreds of sitcom episodes to his credit, including a handful of "Dick Van Dyke" shows and a long stint as director of Norman Lear's "One Day at a Time."

CARL REINER Creator of "The Dick Van Dyke Show." After that series, the writer-director embarked on a very successful career as an actor and director in feature films, though he did return to television as creator of "The New Dick Van Dyke Show" in the early 1970s and as executive producer and star of "Good Heavens" in 1976.

GENE REYNOLDS Producer of "M*A*S*H." The former child actor was an NBC casting director in the 1950s and later directed series as varied as "Peter Gunn," "The Andy Griffith Show," "My Three Sons," and "Hogan's Heroes" before he established his reputation as a top-flight producer on shows like "Room 222" and "Lou Grant."

JOHN RICH Director of "The Dick Van Dyke Show" and producer/director of "All in the Family." A top producer and director whose credits list "Our Miss

Brooks," "Gunsmoke," "My World and Welcome to It," "On the Rocks," "Mr. Sunshine," and "MacGyver," among many others.

MICHAEL ROSS   (see Don Nicholl)

JAY SANDRICH   Director of "The Mary Tyler Moore Show" and "The Bob Newhart Show." After an apprenticeship as assistant director on "I Love Lucy" and "The Dick Van Dyke Show," he directed an astounding array of distinguished series, including most episodes of "He and She," "Soap," and "The Cosby Show," all in addition to his highly influential work at MTM in the early 1970s.

BOB SCHILLER AND BOB WEISKOPF   Prolific contributors to "I Love Lucy" and "All in the Family." Their numerous other TV credits include everything from "Pete and Gladys" to classic episodes of Norman Lear's "Maude."

TONY SHEEHAN   Producer of "Barney Miller." One of the most prolific contributors to that long-running series, he later signed on as executive producer of "Mr. Belvedere."

FRED SILVERMAN   The only broadcast executive to head the entertainment divisions of all three networks. Throughout the 1970s, he was an instrumental figure in the genesis of "M*A*S*H," "Rhoda," "Maude," "Taxi," "Cheers," and "United States," among many others.

LEONARD STERN   Writer, with Sydney Zelinka, of "The Honeymooners." He later scripted "The Phil Silvers Show," produced "Get Smart," and created "He and She," a little-seen but highly influential series of the late 1960s.

JAY TARSES   (see Tom Patchett)

ALAN WAGNER   Vice president of CBS Development from 1967 to 1973. As the executive in charge of new program development, he nurtured "The Bob Newhart Show," "All in the Family," "The Mary Tyler Moore Show," and "M*A*S*H," among others.

REINHOLD WEEGE   Producer and writer of "Barney Miller." He later created and produced NBC's "Night Court."

ED. WEINBERGER   Writer and producer of "The Mary Tyler Moore Show." A prolific writer who was also involved in the creation of "Taxi," 1969's "The Bill Cosby Show," as well as the comedian's later hit, "The Cosby Show," "Doc," "Phyllis," "The Betty White Show," and "Amen," among others.

BOB WEISKOPF   (see Bob Schiller)

BERNIE WEST   (see Don Nicholl)

ROBERT WOOD   President of CBS from 1969 through 1976. The executive changed the face of modern television comedy when he ordered "All in the Family" and "The Mary Tyler Moore Show" added to the network's schedule in the early 1970s.

MICHAEL ZINBERG   Executive producer of "The Bob Newhart Show." He also wrote or directed various episodes of that series, "The Mary Tyler Moore Show," and "Taxi," among others.

Bibliography

General

Bedell, Sally. *Up the Tube: Prime Time TV in the Silverman Years*. New York: Viking, 1981.

Brooks, Tim, and Earle Marsh. *The Complete Directory to Prime Time TV Network Shows: 1946–Present*. New York: Ballantine, 1979.

Brown, Les. *Les Brown's Encyclopedia of Television*. New York: Zoetrope, 1982.

———. *Television: The Business Behind the Box*. New York: Harvest Books/Harcourt Brace Jovanovich, 1971.

Christensen, Mark, and Cameron Stauth. *The Sweeps: Behind the Scenes in Network TV*. New York: Morrow, 1984.

Eisner, Joel, and David Krinsky. *Television Comedy Series: An Episode Guide to 153 TV Sitcoms in Syndication*. Jefferson, N.C.: McFarland, 1984.

Gitlin, Todd. *Inside Prime Time*. New York: Pantheon, 1985.

Halliwell, Leslie. *Halliwell's Film Guide*. New York: Scribner's, 1982.

———, with Philip Purser. *Halliwell's Television Companion*. 2d ed. London: Granada, 1982.

Javna, John. *Cult TV: A Viewer's Guide to the Shows America Can't Live Without*. New York: St. Martin's, 1985.

Katz, Ephraim. *The Film Encyclopedia*. New York: Perigee/Putnam, 1982.

McNeil, Alex. *Total Television: A Comprehensive Guide to Programming from 1948 to the Present*. 2d ed. New York: Viking/Penguin, 1984.

Mitz, Rick. *The Great TV Sitcom Book*. New York: Perigee/Putnam, 1983.

Newcomb, Horace, and Robert S. Alley. *The Producer's Medium: Conversations with Creators of American TV*. New York: Oxford University Press, 1983.

Scheuer, Stephen H. *Who's Who in Television and Cable*. New York: Facts on File, 1983.

Steinberg, Cobbett. *TV Facts: Revised and Updated*. New York: Facts on File, 1983.

Terrace, Vincent. *Encyclopedia of Television Series, Pilots and Specials*. New York: Zoetrope, 1985.

519

Chapter-by-Chapter and Research Sources

Classic Sitcoms contains the most complete guide ever published to ten of America's favorite television comedies. To ensure accuracy, and to keep the information consistent from show to show, the credits that appear in these episode listings were copied—whenever possible—directly from the on-screen credits broadcast at the beginning and end of each of the nearly fifteen hundred episodes listed.

The original network airdates were gathered from weekly listings in *TV Guide* and *The Television Index* and compared with original production company records where these were available. The names that appear in the cast listings—prominent guest stars as well as obscure bit players—were drawn from all of the above sources and compiled with input from one or more of the individuals whose expertise on the various programs in this book is acknowledged elsewhere.

Of course, despite every effort to check and double-check the information gathered between these covers, the author is painfully aware that errors and inconsistencies are inevitable in a work of this scope. Sharp-eyed readers who spot obvious mistakes are invited to write the author in care of the publisher with corrections, so that such inconsistencies can be weeded out of future editions.

Of the hundreds of books and magazine articles consulted during the preparation of this book, the following were particularly useful in providing quotes and invaluable background material.

"I LOVE LUCY"

Andrews, Bart. *The "I Love Lucy" Book.* Garden City, N.Y.: Dolphin/Doubleday, 1985.

Arnaz, Desi. *A Book.* New York: Morrow, 1976.

"Dialogue With Lucille Ball," American Film Institute, *Dialogue on Film.*

McGrath, Douglas. "I Love Lucy: The Collector's Edition." Program notes, CBS Video Library, 1986.

MacKenzie, Alex C., Jr. "A Descriptive Analysis of the Factors That Influenced the Creation of Selected Television Programs, 1946–76." Ph.D. thesis, available from University Microfilms International, Ann Arbor, Mich.

O'Flaherty, Terrence. "TV Will Never Be Quite the Same Again." *TV Guide*, July 6, 1974.

Whitney, Dwight. "We Wrote the Baby Into the Story. We Had To." *TV Guide*, March 31, 1973.

"THE HONEYMOONERS"

Crescenti, Peter, and Bob Columbe. *The Official Honeymooners Treasury: To the Moon and Back With Ralph, Norton, Alice and Trixie.* New York: Perigee Books/Putnam, 1985.

McCrohan, Donna. "The Honeymooners Classic 39." *Reruns Magazine*, no. 22, Spring 1986.

———. *The Honeymooners Companion: The Kramdens and the Nortons Revisited.* New York: Workman, 1978.

———, and Peter Crescenti. *The Honeymooners Lost Episodes.* New York: Workman, 1986.

Shanley, J. P. "Electronicam Said to Cut Costs." *The New York Times*, September 4, 1955.

Stump, Al. "It Was Chaos. Crazy!" *TV Guide*, January 24, 1976.

Zehme, Bill. "Jackie Gleason: The Playboy Interview." *Playboy*, August 1986.

"THE DICK VAN DYKE SHOW"

Gehman, Richard. "Laura Petrie Is Mary Tyler Moore. Or Is She?" *TV Guide*, May 23, 1964.

Lewis, Jerry D. "Carl Reiner: Laughs for Stage, Screen, and Dick Van Dyke." *TV Guide*, January 4, 1964.

Novelli, Rebecca. "Great Shows: The Dick Van Dyke Show." *Emmy Magazine*, Summer 1979.

Raddatz, Leslie. "They've Got No Kick Coming." *TV Guide*, March 27, 1965.

———. "You Don't Give a Desk a Name Because It Has No Moving Parts." *TV Guide*, February 26, 1966.

Rich, John. Interview with the author, October 1986.

Symposium with Morey Amsterdam, Sheldon Leonard, Rose Marie, Carl Reiner, and John Rich. Academy of Television Arts and Sciences, Hollywood, Calif., November 1986.

Tharp, Richard. "The Dick Van Dyke Show." *Reruns Magazine*, no. 14, July 1982, and no. 17, July 1983.

Weissman, Ginny, and Coyne Steven Sanders. *The Dick Van Dyke Show: Anatomy of a Classic.* New York: St. Martin's, 1983.

"What's a Dick Van Dyke?" *TV Guide*, December 9, 1961. Uncredited.

"Who Is That Cutie Playing His Wife?" *TV Guide*, June 2, 1962. Uncredited.

"THE MARY TYLER MOORE SHOW"

Barber, Rowland. "We Are All Pussycats Here." *TV Guide*, February 8, 1975.

Davidson, Bill. "There Was Mary Tyler Moore . . ." *TV Guide*, May 19, 1973.

Ephron, Nora. "A Fond Farewell to the Funniest Show on Television." *Esquire*, February 1977.

Newcomb, Horace, and Robert S. Alley. *The Producer's Medium*. New York: Oxford University Press, 1983.

Pattison, Jim. "The Mary Tyler Moore Show." *Movie Collector's World*, November 30, 1984.

Torgerson, Ellen. "Mary Marrying Lou, Sue Ann Carried Off by King Kong, Ted Baxter as Cronkite's Assistant . . ." *TV Guide*, March 18, 1977.

Weingarten, Paul. "The Kitten That Roared." *Chicago Tribune Magazine*, December 1, 1985.

Whitney, Dwight. "Mary, It Needs One Beat of Wistfulness." *TV Guide*, February 26, 1972.

———. "You've Come a Long Way, Baby." *TV Guide*, September 19, 1970.

"ALL IN THE FAMILY"

Adler, Richard P. *All in the Family: A Critical Appraisal*. New York: Praeger, 1979.

Barber, Rowland. "Bellowing, Half-Baked, Fire-Breathing Bigotry." *TV Guide*, May 29, 1971.

Beck, Marilyn. "Archie Wants Out, But . . ." Syndicated column, November 4, 1977.

Davidson, Bill. "Trouble in Paradise (Part One)," *TV Guide*, April 6, 1974.

———. "The Uprising in Lear's Kingdom (Part Two)," *TV Guide*, April 13, 1974.

"Dialogue on Film: Norman Lear." *American Film Magazine*, June 1977.

Kaufman, Dave. "Archie a Lovable Bigot, Says Lear." *Daily Variety*, August 3, 1971.

Lear, Norman. Interview with the author, December 1986.

MacKenzie, Alex C., Jr. "A Descriptive Analysis of the Factors That Influenced the Creation of Selected Television Programs, 1946–76." Ph.D. thesis, available from University Microfilms International, Ann Arbor, Mich.

O'Connor, Carrol. "I Regret Nothing Except My Own Anger." *TV Guide*, September 22, 1979.

Rich, John. Interview with the author, October 1986.

Turan, Kenneth. "Archie and Edith and Meathead and Gloria: A Family Journal." *TV Guide*, September 3, 1983.

Whitney, Dwight. "An American Institution Rolls On." *TV Guide*, January 6, 1979.

"M*A*S*H"

Alda, Alan. "My Favorite Episodes." *TV Guide*, February 12, 1983.

Berges, Marshall. "Home Q & A: Pat & Larry Gelbart." *Los Angeles Times Magazine*, July 16, 1978.

Corliss, Richard, with Denise Worrell. "M*A*S*H, You Were a Smash." *Time*, February 28, 1983.

Darrach, Brad, with Suzanne Adelson. "M*A*S*H, Goodbye, Farewell and Amen . . ." *People*, March 7, 1983.

Davidson, Bill. "CLASH." *TV Guide*, January 24, 1976.

———. "Vintage Year for Wayne." *TV Guide*, November 2, 1974.

Deeb, Gary. "Crash Course for M*A*S*H?" Syndicated column, January 5, 1982.

Gelbart, Larry. "Its Creator Says Hail and Farewell to M*A*S*H." *The New York Times*, February 27, 1983.

———. "A Mash Note to CBS' M*A*S*H." Los Angeles *Times*, November 3, 1972.

Johnston, David. "The Interplay's the Thing." *TV Guide*, January 5, 1980.

Kalter, Suzy. *The Complete Book of M*A*S*H*. New York: Abrams, 1984.

Metcalfe, Burt. Interview with the author, August 1986.

Raddatz, Leslie. "Cocktail Hour Starts at 4:30." *TV Guide*, August 24, 1974.

Reiss, David S. *M*A*S*H: The Exclusive, Inside Story of TV's Most Popular Show*. Indianapolis: Bobbs-Merrill, 1983.

Walters, Harry F., with Janet Huck. "Farewell to the M*A*S*H Gang." *Newsweek*, February 28, 1983.

"THE BOB NEWHART SHOW"

Berges, Marshall. "Home Q & A: The Bob Newharts." *Los Angeles Times Magazine*, September 14, 1975.

Davidson, Bill. "The Suzanne Pleshette Show." *TV Guide*, December 16, 1972.

Farr, Lynne. Interview with the author, December 1986.

Feuer, Jane, Paul Kerr, and Tise Vahimagi. *MTM Quality Television*. London: BFI Books/The British Film Institute, 1984.

Lochte, Dick. "Friendship by Appointment Only." *TV Guide*, May 11, 1974.

Music, Lorenzo. Interview with the author, November 1986.

Stabiner, Karen. "For Bob Newhart, Affection Is Still the Essence of Successful Comedy." *The New York Times*, December 26, 1982.

Wagner, Alan. Interview with the author, November 1986.

Whitney, Dwight. "Still Button-Down, But No Longer Buttoned Up." *TV Guide*, January 20, 1973.

Witbeck, Charles. "Bob Newhart's New Success." Los Angeles *Herald-Examiner*, December 30, 1972.

Zinberg, Michael. Interview with the author, November 1986.

"BARNEY MILLER"

Arnold, Danny. Interview with the author, November 1986.

Bedell, Sally. *Up the Tube*. New York: Viking, 1981.

Burke, Tom. "As Japanese as Nathan Detroit." *TV Guide*, July 16, 1977.

DuBrow, Rick. "Danny Arnold Is Back on the Beat." Los Angeles *Herald-Examiner*, November 12, 1985.

Dungan, Frank. Interview with the author, November 1986.

Hano, Arnold. "The Only Actor Ever Named After a Gas Tank." *TV Guide*, July 19, 1975.

Rich, John. Interview with the author, October 1986.

Russell, Dick. "Barney Miller's Secret Weapon." *TV Guide*, July 7, 1979.

———. "The World's Gonna Catch Up With Steve Landesberg." *TV Guide*, November 26, 1977.

Sheehan, Tony. Interview with the author, November 1986.
Stein, Jeff. Interview with the author, November 1986.
Whitney, Dwight. "The Man Is an Actor." *TV Guide*, February 7, 1976.

"TAXI"

Boyer, Peter. "NBC: A Night of Triumph." Los Angeles *Times*, September 26, 1983.
Burke, Tom. " 'Taxi' Puts Him in the Driver's Seat." *TV Guide*, April 28, 1979.
Charles, Glen, and Les Charles. Interview with the author, October 1986.
Clark, Kenneth R. " 'Taxi' Picks Up Kane; Vice Versa?" *UPI*, December 3, 1982.
Hicks, Jack. "He Loves to Get Hate Mail." *TV Guide*, June 6, 1981.
Shaw, Ellen Torgerson. "When Latka Says 'Bisha ga ba ba'—She Knows What to Do." *TV Guide*, April 30, 1983.
Weinberger, Ed. Interview with the author, December 1986.
Weingarten, Paul. "The Kitten That Roared." *Chicago Tribune Magazine*, December 1, 1985.
Zinberg, Michael. Interview with the author, November 1986.

"CHEERS"

Charles, Glen, and Les Charles. Interview with the author, October 1986.
Christensen, Mark, and Cameron Stauth. *The Sweeps: Behind the Scenes in Network TV*. New York: Morrow, 1984.
Gregory, Fred. "Every Day Is a Shelley Long Improvisation." *TV Guide*, March 26, 1986.
Keister, Edwin, Jr. "Expect Some Tears With Your 'Cheers.' " *TV Guide*, October 9, 1982.
Kerr, Peter. "NBC Comedy 'Cheers' Turns Into a Success." *The New York Times*, November 29, 1983.
Stauth, Cameron. " 'Cheers,' the Hit That Almost Missed." *Esquire*, February 1984.

Episode Guide Index

About the Author

A former film and TV critic, author Vince Waldron developed a unique appreciation for comedy during his days as an improvisational writer and performer with Paul Sills's Story Theater and at Chicago's famed satirical showcase, The Second City. He currently lives and writes in Los Angeles.